Infosys® Press

In an initiative to promote authorship across the globe, Infosys Press and CRC Press have entered into a collaboration to develop titles on leading edge topics in IT.

Infosys Press seeks to develop and publish a series of pragmatic books on software engineering and information technologies, both current and emerging. Leveraging Infosys' extensive global experience helping clients to implement those technologies successfully, each book contains critical lessons learned and shows how to apply them in a real-world, enterprise setting. This open-ended and broad-ranging series aims to brings readers practical insight, specific guidance, and unique, informative examples not readily available elsewhere.

PUBLISHED IN THE SERIES

.NET 4 for Enterprise Architects and Developers
Sudhanshu Hate and Suchi Paharia

Process-Centric Architecture for Enterprise Software Systems
Parameswaran Seshan

Process-Driven SOA: Patterns for Aligning Business and IT
Carsten Hentrich and Uwe Zdun

Web-Based and Traditional Outsourcing
Vivek Sharma and Varun Sharma

IN PREPARATION FOR THE SERIES

Scrum Software Development
Jagdish Bhandarkar and J. Srinivas

Software Vulnerabilities Exposed
Sanjay Rawat, Ashutosh Saxena, and Ponnapalli K. B. Hari Gopal

Process-Driven SOA

Patterns *for* Aligning Business *and* IT

Carsten Hentrich
Uwe Zdun

CRC Press
Taylor & Francis Group
Boca Raton London New York

Infosys® Press

CRC Press is an imprint of the
Taylor & Francis Group, an **informa** business
AN AUERBACH BOOK

CRC Press
Taylor & Francis Group
6000 Broken Sound Parkway NW, Suite 300
Boca Raton, FL 33487-2742

© 2012 by Taylor & Francis Group, LLC
CRC Press is an imprint of Taylor & Francis Group, an Informa business

No claim to original U.S. Government works

Printed in the United States of America on acid-free paper
Version Date: 20111007

International Standard Book Number: 978-1-4398-8929-9 (Hardback)

Library of Congress Cataloging-in-Publication Data

Hentrich, Carsten.
    Process-driven SOA: patterns for aligning business and IT / Carsten Hentrich, Uwe Zdun.
        p. cm. -- (Infosys press)
    Includes bibliographical references and index.
    ISBN 978-1-4398-8929-9 (hardback)
    1. Service-oriented architecture (Computer science) I. Zdun, Uwe. II. Title.

TK5105.5828.H46 2012
658.4'038--dc23   2011029099

Visit the Taylor & Francis Web site at
http://www.taylorandfrancis.com

and the CRC Press Web site at
http://www.crcpress.com

Contents

Preface

The business environment is in a constant state of flux. Increasing connectedness due to the Internet and globalization is narrowing the gap between cause and effect, leading to rapid feedback loops. Inability to analyze and adapt to these feedback loops makes an organization irrelevant, leading to stagnation and decay. In such a fast-paced environment, agility is of strategic importance to enterprises as they need to continuously optimize their operations and accelerate innovation. This is the only way they can remain relevant and competitive and grow profitably. An approach that is "business process driven and services enabled" provides a great foundation for such continuous change. While business processes are key drivers of value in any organization, services provide a foundation on which business processes can be reconfigured to handle the changes in the business environment. Today, service-oriented architecture (SOA) is being used for achieving strategic objectives across multiple industries, across geographies.

For consumer-facing enterprises, the Internet and mobility are driving significant change. More than 75% of the world is connected using mobile devices, and more than 25% use the Internet. This interconnectivity is leading to accelerated flow of information, and demands for personalization are rapidly increasing. This requires enterprises to partner and integrate with others to continuously deliver new products, services, and experiences. Such integration can quickly lead to complex interdependencies in supply chain and associated systems. These can make future changes difficult, time consuming, and slowly unviable—making the enterprise less amenable to change. A service-oriented approach is important for development of integrated but loosely coupled systems whose components can evolve independently.

In addition, with increasing competition it is becoming paramount to provide unified and integrated experiences through multiple channels—Web, mobile, TV, callcenter, and so on. A services-based approach has become the standard approach for such initiatives.

The rise of emerging economies is opening new growth opportunities for large enterprises. However, these markets require lightweight processes and systems that can scale and evolve rapidly. Enterprises that have built systems using SOA principles are able to rapidly evolve an existing system to serve these newer engines of growth.

Enterprises in asset-heavy industries and logistics are leveraging sensor networks, intelligent decision support systems, and cloud to increase information visibility and improve operational decision making. Intelligent and cloud-based sensor networks create new opportunities owing to the integration of the physical and the virtual worlds. Advanced analytics based on real-time events and sentiments enable new forms of remote services with improved business models for consumer engagement. Also, many experts are propagating new revenue enhancement and cost reduction opportunities leveraging the cloud. Interestingly, for all those key driving forces an architectural foundation that aligns business and information technology (IT) and one that enables flexibility would be a key element. Systems built on SOA principles are more amenable to supporting these requirements.

These developments logically influence a trend within companies toward building smarter organizations. Organizations need to learn, adapt, collaborate, and simplify their internal structures to cope with the pace of these developments. A recent analysis of 75 companies across 12 industries globally found that the companies with a lower level of complexity grew revenues 1.7 times faster than their peers on average. Complexity holds four times the predictive power for revenue growth than company size. Inevitably, successful companies will need to reengineer their platforms and renovate them on a sustained basis. As a result, architecture initiatives are targeting simplification, standardization, modularization, and harmonization. The pressure on flexibility is getting so strong that it is no longer possible not to invest in these architectural innovations to stay competitive. Systems built on SOA principles are more amenable to supporting these requirements.

The SOA has been around for a while; however, interpretations of designing and implementing SOA are manifold. In this book an approach is presented that has actually evolved as a set of successful architectural patterns researched and discovered since 2002. It appears that the key architectural concepts that evolved as successful principles over the years remain independent of actual technologies being used and have proven to be timeless. This book elaborates SOA principles that are foundational for creating an adaptive integrated system—allowing tomorrow's enterprises to continuously evolve processes and systems as the business requirements change.

The patterns presented in this book form timeless and proven solutions to these challenges of business-IT alignment, continuous business optimization, and accelerated innovation. The authors proclaim an approach for architectural flexibility based on SOA that is a mandatory building block in many of the business initiatives aimed at transformation, optimization, and innovation.

From a business transformation perspective, the trends mentioned require an approach that focuses on six key dimensions: ensure adoption and accountability, optimize (simplify) processes, visualize information, orchestrate (global) capabilities, strengthen strategic partnerships, and maximize return on assets. To measure the business value of those transformational initiatives, one has to map value levers to operational levers, map those to processes, and map processes to change enablers. Operational levers form operational business goals that are directly related to processes. It becomes clear that at the architectural core of those transformation initiatives there must be an approach that is business process driven and that relates process design to business goals. That way, it is aligning business and IT. The patterns in this book follow exactly this principle.

From an innovation perspective, we can summarize five key trends in information management: knowledge-driven systems that make use of advanced analytics, distributed (cloud and grid) computing, digital convergence, sensor networks, and mobility. SOA itself is a basis for all these trends by virtue of the need for modular and flexible access to IT fulfilled by SOA.

From the business optimization perspective, an approach focused on measuring, managing, and optimizing business processes is needed. That means an architectural approach is required that makes use of business process management as a discipline. The content of this book also serves this purpose well.

From the trends discussed, it is clear that organizations need an architectural foundation that enables continuous optimization, accelerated innovation, and rapid transformation. That is exactly what this book provides. It provides the architectural basis in the form of proven patterns that have passed the test of time and are rightly positioned to form the stable core of future-ready enterprise architecture.

Subu Goparaju
Head of Infosys Labs

Acknowledgments

It is our pleasure to thank the many people who supported us in creating this book, as either our collaborators or colleagues, by sharing their knowledge with us or by reviewing and commenting on our work.

We wish to thank Andreas Grunewald, who has worked on the implementation of the pattern language walkthrough example presented in Chapter 4. We thank Till Köllmann, who is the coauthor of the paper, "Synchronization Patterns for Process-Driven and Service-Oriented Architectures." Some reworked patterns from this paper are included in this book. There are a number of coauthors of research papers related to the content of this book: Wil van der Aalst, Paris Avgeriou, Schahram Dustdar, and Vlatka Hlupic. Thanks to the IBM Software Group, especially Lucie Schellberg, for supporting this work. We would also like to thank Infosys for its strong support.

Special thanks for reviewing the material in this book go to Paris Avgeriou, Gregor Hohpe, and Till Schümmer, who all provided in-depth reviews for some of the contents.

In addition, we presented parts of the contents of this book at various European Conference on Pattern Languages of Programs (EuroPLoP) and Conference on Pattern Languages of Programs (PLoP) pattern conferences. Many thanks go to all participants of the EuroPLoP and PLoP workshops who commented on our work. Special thanks go to our EuroPLoP shepherds who provided detailed feedback on our EuroPLoP and PLoP papers: Andy Longshaw, Wolfgang Keller, Eduardo B. Fernandez, and Stephan Lukosch.

About the Authors

Carsten Hentrich is chief technologist at Infosys Germany with a focus on innovative solutions for the German market in the area of remote services, business platforms, e-commerce, and cloud computing. He was director of the IT (Information Technology) Architecture and Enterprise Content Management (ECM) competency groups for Financial Services at CSC Germany. Carsten has a strong background as an IT architect and gathered practical experience in SOA (service-oriented architecture), Business Process Management (BPM), and Event-Driven Architecture (EDA) from his prior career at CSC, IBM, and EDS and has been working in advisory roles for clients from different industries. He has published technical articles in renowned journals such as those of the Association for Computing Machinery (ACM) and the Institute of Electrical and Electronics Engineers (IEEE) and speaks at international conferences. Apart from technical topics, Carsten has a passion for innovative leadership and management approaches, which he has demonstrated in successful pioneering implementations, as a speaker at the Academy of Management, and in a publication in the *Harvard Business Review*. He holds a PhD in business information management from Westminster Business School in London, an MSc (Dist) in software engineering from Oxford University, and a BSc (Hons) in computer science from the University of Applied Sciences in Wiesbaden, Germany.

Uwe Zdun is full professor of software architecture at the Faculty of Computer Science, University of Vienna. Before that, he worked as an assistant professor at the Vienna University of Technology and the Vienna University of Economics. He received his doctoral degree from the University of Essen in 2002. His research focuses on architectural decision, software patterns, modeling of complex software systems, service-oriented systems, event-driven architecture, domain-specific languages, and model-driven development. Uwe has published more than 120 articles in journals, workshops, and conferences and is coauthor of the books *Remoting Patterns—Foundations of Enterprise, Internet, and Realtime Distributed Object Middleware* (Wiley) and *Software-Architektur* (Elsevier/Spektrum). He has participated in research and development projects such as INDENICA, COMPAS, S-CUBE, TPMHP, Infinica, SCG, and Sembiz. He is European editor of the journal *Transactions on Pattern Languages of Programming* (TPLoP), published by Springer, and associate editor-in-chief for design and architecture for the *IEEE Software* magazine.

1

Introduction

What This Book Is About

This book is about a special kind of service-oriented architecture (SOA): *process-driven SOA*. To start and to set the scope of this book, let us consider an initial, rather technical, definition of SOA in general: SOA is an architectural concept in which all functions, or services, are defined using a description language and have invokable, platform-independent interfaces that are called to perform business processes [CHT03, Bar03]. Each service is the endpoint of a connection, which can be used to access the service. Communication among services can involve simple invocations and data passing or complex activities of two or more services.

This view of SOA, even though it is rooted in well-known concepts and technologies, such as middleware concepts and systems, is limited to technical aspects. In our experience, one of the key issues in engineering SOAs is the integration of organizational and software model building to provide a conceptual foundation for designing *business-driven SOAs*. In this view, at the core of SOA is a business-oriented approach to architecture, but SOA, as it is described in the first paragraph, seems rather to focus on technical issues. A foundation for an integrated engineering approach seems yet to be missing. Still, many fundamental issues arise due to the separation of business-oriented and technical viewpoints. One solution that has been proposed to solve these problems is process-driven SOAs, that is, SOAs that are based on business processes and utilize process technologies such as business process engines. Our perspective of business-information technology (IT) alignment refers to this context. In this book, we focus on this special kind of SOA and describe time-proven solutions for process-driven SOAs in pattern form.

Please note that many other flavors of SOAs have been proposed, such as SOA concepts focusing on the middleware or Web service aspects, component architectures, enterprise architectures, governance, or even embedded systems or mobile systems. In this book, we only touch on them, if they are linked to process-driven SOAs, but no further.

So, what is a process-driven SOA, and what are the major challenges we address in this book?

Since 2002, workflow technology [LR00] has evolved as an important technological approach for business process management (BPM) [Pri03]. Today, a process engine takes the role of a process controller within the enterprise architecture. The goal of the process engine is to coordinate and distribute tasks in a heterogeneous system environment. In recent years, this approach has been strongly adopted in the SOA area to support *service orchestration*. An important driver for this trend is that IT strategies have changed and demand more support from IT technologies, such as SOA and workflow technology, to flexibly *change and adapt business processes*.

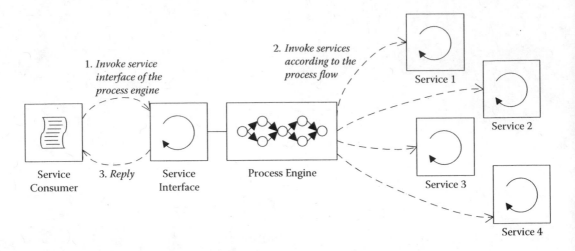

FIGURE 1.1
Basic architecture of a process-driven SOA.

In an SOA, which results from the combination of service-based middleware and process engines, services are invoked to perform business processes. We call this kind of architecture a *process-driven SOA*. In it, the services describe the operations that can be performed in the system. The process flow orchestrates the services via different activities of the process. The operations executed by activities in a process flow thus correspond to service invocations. The process flow is executed by the process engine.

This basic architecture of a process-driven SOA is illustrated in Figure 1.1. A service consumer invokes the service interface of the process engine. Then, the process engine executes the process flow. Some of the activities in the process flow invoke services. Hence, these services are orchestrated according to the process flow. Finally, when the process flow terminates, the process engine replies to the service consumer.

Because—in principle—the service interface of a process engine and the interface of any other service cannot be distinguished, arbitrarily complex architectures can be composed this way. For example, in the example diagram in Figure 1.1, any of the services invoked by the process engine could itself hide another process engine. This process would then be invoked as a subprocess of the invoking process.

A process is a behavioral model expressed in a process modeling language, such as the Business Process Modeling Notation (BPMN), event-driven process chains (EPCs), the Business Process Execution Language (BPEL), or the jBPM Process Definition Language (jPDL), to name but a few existing process modeling languages. Some process models, such as those described in BPEL, are executable and can be instantiated and managed by a process engine. On a process engine, multiple process instances of one or more processes are typically running in parallel. Processes usually work on business data stored in business objects.

Please note that not all processes are executable. For example, processes modeled in languages such as BPMN or EPC are usually not directly executable. Instead, they model the processes from a business perspective only. To make them executable on a process engine, they must be translated into an executable process language such as BPEL or jPDL. This usually means, among other things, adding technical details to the process models.

This book focuses on an overall and integral architectural perspective for process-driven SOA systems. That is, from the perspective taken in this book, it is actually not enough to concentrate on the process engine itself but to view it as an integral part within a larger software architecture.

Process-driven SOAs are introduced into an organization for various reasons. Some exemplary strategic goals for introducing process-driven SOAs are

- flexible business process control,
- integration of legacy systems functionality within business processes,
- automatic invocation of services,
- connectivity to various interfaces,
- scalability,
- automated measurement and monitoring of business processes,
- processes as reusable components,
- business-to-business (B2B) integration, and
- business process automation.

To achieve these strategic goals, architectures must be designed accordingly, balancing both technological and business-oriented forces. To balance these forces, this book introduces time-proven practices presented using the concept of *software patterns* as guidelines for the software design. These software patterns cover the whole design space of designing a process-driven SOA and guide you step by step to a complete architecture and software design, covering the various aspects discussed.

In this context, it is important to note that designing a nontrivial process-driven SOA involves many difficult design and architectural decisions. Examples are as follows:

- Different kinds of processes exist, long-running, business-oriented and short-running, technical processes. How to best integrate them, and how to map them to execution platforms? How to best design the processes to achieve the business goals and fulfill the technical requirements?

- An SOA has many different stakeholders, such as business analysts, management, software designers, architects, and developers, as well as many different types of models these stakeholders need or want to work with. How to present each of them with the best view on the models they need for their work?

- A realistic process-driven SOA contains many systems that need to be integrated, such as various process engines, services, and back-end systems, running on heterogeneous technologies and platforms. How to perform integration in a way that is maintainable and scalable?

- Often, business processes and services within an organization and within different cooperating organizations need to interact with each other and with other external events. How to synchronize all these processes, services, and events?

- Business processes and services need to work with data. How to best integrate the data of the organization into the process-driven SOA?

This book introduces a pattern language that deals with issues such as process modeling, execution, integration, synchronization, and so on. Its main goal is to help solution architects, as well as process and service designers, to master the challenges in designing a stable and evolvable process-driven SOA. In this sense, the book aims to bring together the business and IT worlds.

Target Audience

This book is primarily written for *SOA solution architects* and *SOA designers* as it primarily provides in-depth guidelines on how to cope with various architectural and design decisions that you encounter when designing and implementing a process-driven SOA system. The decisions are described in the form of software patterns that provide a practical guideline to address the key problems in this field using time-proven solutions.

Another primary audience is *SOA developers* who need to realize the service architectures and designs described in this book. For them, the book primarily provides detailed descriptions of the solution for the pattern. That is, considerations of the solution, detailed examples, and case studies illustrating the patterns are provided.

Another primary audience is the *business stakeholders* involved in process-driven SOA projects, such as SOA business analysts or SOA managers, who want to understand the technical solutions applied in a process-driven SOA project. For them, probably mainly the overview parts of the chapters are interesting—not all the technical details.

For all audiences named, the patterns provide a common terminology that can be used for the solutions described in the pattern descriptions throughout their process-driven SOA projects.

A secondary audience is *students* learning about process-driven SOA or *researchers* working on process-driven SOA topics. While this book is no textbook or research-oriented book, it still can be useful for these audiences as a practical introduction to basic and advanced topics in the process-driven SOA field. The material in this book has been used in a number of tutorials and courses on the process-driven SOA topic as educational material. It also has been used in various ways in a number of research projects.

The patterns in this book have emerged from, and are primarily applicable in, the following industries: insurance, banking, media/telecommunication, and automotive/manufacturing. They are validated in this context. Our primary target audience for this reason is people from these industries, although the patterns may also apply to other contexts than those listed. The patterns have not been applied and validated in the embedded systems context.

Software Patterns

This book is based on the concept of *software patterns*. Software patterns provide concrete guidelines for the software design [BHS07b]. They capture reusable design knowledge and expertise that provide proven solutions to recurring software design problems arising in particular contexts and domains [SB03]. Software patterns are a systematic reuse strategy [SB03]: In a pattern, successful software models, designs, or implementations that have already been developed and tested are documented so that they can be applied to similar software problems. Thus, software patterns in the first place help to avoid the costly cycle of rediscovering, reinventing, and revalidating common software artifacts. Patterns provide "timeless" knowledge in the sense that it lasts longer than concrete technologies or implementation concepts [BHS07b, Ale79].

The full power of patterns is only achieved, however, if they are used in the context of each other to form a web of related patterns, more commonly known as a *pattern language*

[Cop96, BHS07a, BHS07b]. A single pattern can only solve a single problem. Patterns in a pattern language, in contrast, build on each other to generate a system [BHS07b]. Hence, a pattern language has a language-wide goal, and it solves the prevalent problems in a particular domain and context [Cop96, BHS07b]. The purpose of the language is to guide the user step by step to reach this goal. A pattern language achieves this by specifically focusing on the pattern relationships in this domain and context. In the domain and context, patterns provide a design vocabulary [BCM+96, BHS07b, GHJV94] that can be used among developers or designers to ease their interaction. In addition, pattern languages also provide the "big picture" of the domain [BHS07b].

Originally, the concept of patterns was invented by Christopher Alexander [Ale77, Ale79], who used the concept of recurring problems and corresponding solutions in the context of towns, buildings, and construction. The basic idea of patterns is that problems arise due to conflicting forces in a given context, and solutions resolve these conflicting forces. For this reason, the pattern approach provides a flexible method for finding appropriate solution concepts, as there is no static and linear process to follow, but rather flexible and context-dependent solutions are created using patterns. Alexander defined a pattern as follows [Ale77]:

> Each pattern is a three-part rule, which expresses a relation between a certain context, a problem, and a solution. As an element in the world, each pattern is a relationship between a certain context, a certain system of forces which occurs repeatedly in that context, and a certain spatial configuration which allows these forces to resolve themselves. As an element of language, a pattern is an instruction, which shows how this spatial configuration can be used, over and over again, to resolve the given system of forces, wherever the context makes it relevant.

The concept of patterns has been successfully applied to software system and architecture design [GHJV94, BMR+96, SSRB00, BCM+96, Cop96, VSW02, HW03, VKZ04, KJ04].

The Appendix provides a detailed overview of patterns related to the patterns presented in this book and provides short thumbnails of each external pattern referenced in this book.

Pattern Form and Pattern Chapter Structure

Several formats for specifying patterns have been proposed that are specialized to the purposes of different types of patterns. In this book, we introduce different types of patterns. For this reason, a pattern format has been chosen that suits all these types. The format consists of seven logical parts: pattern name, context, problem, problem details, solution, solution details, and examples (including some known uses of the patterns).

This core of the pattern descriptions appears in the pattern texts according to this format (presented in more detail in the following discussion). Some other parts of the patterns, such as pattern relationships and bigger case studies, are rather presented in other places in the pattern chapters because they are shown together for a number of related patterns.

When pattern names are referenced in the text, they are written in SMALL CAPS font.

Each pattern chapter starts with a *narrative introduction* to the contents of the chapter. This narrative introduction gives an overview of the patterns described in the chapter and defines the role of each pattern in the pattern language. That is, *related patterns* of the patterns described further in the chapter are mostly described in these narrative introductions. Also, the *common context* of the patterns in a process-driven SOA and in the pattern language is described here. These pattern relationships illustrate how the pattern works in conjunction with other patterns and describe their interplay. In addition, some examples of known uses are given for illustration.

In most chapters, the pattern descriptions follow. Sometimes, between the pattern sections we provide another *narrative* section.

Each pattern has a common appearance in the text (as outlined in the box below). The pattern starts with the *pattern name*. The pattern name has the task to identify the pattern. Pattern names make it possible to use patterns as a common terminology that can be used by architects and designers (i.e., in a software project team or in a community). Then, the sections are outlined and explained in the following box.

PATTERN NAME

The pattern starts with a description of the *context* of the pattern. The context leads to the problem description.

A question summarizes the *problem* of the pattern.

The *detailed problem description* follows. It contains detailed explanations of the addressed problem. Most important, the conflicting *forces* are described in this section. Forces are important factors that influence the design decision for or against the use of a pattern.

A rather short *solution* description follows that outlines the pattern's time-proven solution in one paragraph.

An *illustration* follows to sketch the pattern's solution.

The *detailed description of the solution* follows right after the short solution description. Different figures or models can be used to illustrate the solution. Central to the solution is that it resolves the conflicting forces in the context. Also, some central relationships of a pattern to other patterns are described, but only if they are needed for describing the solution. All other pattern relationships are described in the narrative sections before.

The consequences that result from applying the pattern are also described in this section. There are usually positive and negative consequences. The expected consequences are important as input for the design decision when and how to apply the pattern.

EXAMPLES

Finally, some examples illustrate the pattern. Some examples are artificial but resemble our real-world experiences. Others are taken from known uses of the pattern that are listed as examples of real-world incarnations of the pattern. The known uses illustrate how and where the pattern has been successfully applied in the past.

Some patterns are mainly illustrated using the examples. They have then many, detailed examples. Other patterns are better illustrated by showing how they work together with other patterns. This is often done using *case studies* in which we have found or applied the patterns. Hence, the case studies are another source of examples and known uses of the patterns. They are placed at the end of the pattern chapters.

Structure and Overview of this Book

After this first introductory chapter, this book has three more introductory chapters:

- "Chapter 2—Service-Oriented Architecture: A Business Perspective" introduces SOA from a business viewpoint and provides important motivations for the concepts and patterns presented in this book.

- "Chapter 3—Service-Oriented Architecture: A Technical Perspective" introduces SOA from a more technical viewpoint and provides an architectural framework for SOA. In this sense, it provides the technical background of this book. It introduces the technical SOA perspective using many related patterns for realizing the SOA technologies internally.

- "Chapter 4—Pattern Language Walk-Through: An Example from the Insurance Business" walks you through many of the patterns presented in this book using a larger example from the insurance business. It provides an overview of the pattern language by example.

The main part of this book is the following eight chapters. They propose concepts and methods, especially presented in pattern form, to understand—step by step—how to design a process-driven SOA with a strong focus on the business-IT alignment. In particular, we cover the following topics:

"Chapter 5—Decomposing and Executing Business-Driven and Technical Processes" deals with how to design business processes that consider both the business level and the technical level. The chapter presents the following patterns:

- The DOMAIN-/TECHNICAL-VIEW pattern advises you to split the process models into two views: A *high-level, domain-oriented view* that represents the process in a technology-independent fashion, eliminating all details not needed for the domain task, and a *low-level, technical view* that contains the elements of the domain view and additional technical details. This pattern is useful for refining domain-oriented business processes into executable processes.

- On the one hand, not all business-oriented processes are directly executable; consider for instance the high-level, strategic processes of an organization. On the other hand, not all technical processes need a business-oriented counterpart, as low-level technical details are usually not interesting for business stakeholders. The MACRO-/MICROFLOW pattern provides a guideline on how to design process models in a hierarchical fashion. In the pattern, we refer to long-running, rather business-oriented, processes using the term *macroflow*. We use the term *microflow* to refer to the short-running, rather technical processes. The MACRO-/MICROFLOW pattern advises you to refine macroflows in a strictly hierarchical fashion—starting from high-level, strategic processes to long-running, executable processes. The activities of these executable macroflows can further be refined by microflows.

- The MACROFLOW ENGINE pattern describes how to support macroflows using process or workflow technology.

- The MICROFLOW ENGINE pattern describes how to support a microflow using some engine technology. This is used in more infrequent cases than the MACROFLOW ENGINE. We distinguish MICROFLOWS ENGINES for microflows containing human interactions and MICROFLOWS ENGINES for microflows supporting automatic activities.

"Chapter 6—Integration and Adaptation in Process-Driven SOAs" explains how to incrementally build a flexible and scalable SOA that implements the macroflows and microflows. The chapter presents the following patterns:

- The first concern tackled is the integration of architectural components. We introduce the INTEGRATION ADAPTER pattern for integrating the components of a process-driven SOA. The INTEGRATION ADAPTER pattern is similar to the classical ADAPTER pattern [GHJV94, BHS07a]. However, in contrast to the classical ADAPTER, it translates between the interfaces of two systems connected using asynchronous (or if needed synchronous) connectors and offers a configuration interface, which supports stopping and suspending the adapter.

- To avoid hard-wiring the components and support content-based routing, the CONFIGURABLE DISPATCHER pattern can be used. The CONFIGURABLE DISPATCHER pattern connects client and target systems using a dispatch algorithm that is based on configurable dispatching rules that can be updated at runtime. Hence, it enables us to postpone dispatch decisions until runtime.

- In an SOA, we often apply multiple INTEGRATION ADAPTERS that must be maintained and managed. An INTEGRATION ADAPTER REPOSITORY provides a central repository and maintenance interface for INTEGRATION ADAPTERS that supports management, querying, and deployment of adapters. It hence facilitates reuse of adapters.

- All patterns introduced so far can be used to build a PROCESS INTEGRATION ARCHITECTURE. The PROCESS INTEGRATION ARCHITECTURE pattern is an architectural pattern that defines a specific architectural configuration using the patterns named and other patterns and explains how these patterns can be assembled into a flexible and scalable SOA.

In "Chapter 7—Aligning Business Goals and Service Design," we reiterate on the problems of aligning business goals and service design that have been implicitly introduced in the previous chapters. We explain in more detail the development and design process of how the patterns from the previous chapters can be used to design *business-driven services*.

"Chapter 8—Business Object Integration: How to Deal with the Data?" introduces business objects as an abstraction to deal with the data in a process-driven SOA.

We explain how to integrate business object models into a process-driven SOA, how to synchronize processes on business objects, and how to integrate external systems with heterogeneous data models into the process-driven SOA. The chapter presents the following patterns:

- The most essential pattern for using business objects from services and processes is the BUSINESS OBJECT REFERENCE pattern. It deals with the problem of separating business data from process logic and achieving concurrent access to the data stored in business objects. The pattern advises us only to store references to business objects in the process control data structure.

- Once we decide to use the BUSINESS OBJECT REFERENCE pattern, we must also decide how to store and manage the business objects. One solution is described in the BUSINESS OBJECT POOL pattern; it explains an architectural solution in which a central pool for the business objects is introduced that can be accessed concurrently by multiple processes and services.

- The PRIVATE-PUBLIC BUSINESS OBJECT pattern offers a concept for accessing a business object from within different process activities. The business object is publicly write locked by the first activity that creates a persistent *private image*. Other activities can still read another *public image* but not perform write operations.

- The INTEGRATED BUSINESS OBJECT MODEL pattern explains an architectural solution that allows you to implement a harmonized business object model of two or more external systems to be integrated into the process-driven SOA. The pattern facilitates integration methods such as service-based integration and restructuring for integration.

- The DATA TRANSFORMATION FLOW pattern explains an architectural solution based on a process subflow for data transformation that maps different application-specific business object models to a common business object model. The goal is to enable flexible integration of various external systems.

In "Chapter 9—Process Design: Mapping Domain Views to Technical Views," we introduce a number of process design patterns that describe additional process aspects we frequently must add to a process model when mapping it to a technical view. The chapter presents the following patterns:

- A central pattern in this chapter—because it is frequently used as a foundation for realizing the other patterns—is GENERIC PROCESS CONTROL STRUCTURE. The GENERIC PROCESS CONTROL STRUCTURE advises us to avoid inconsistencies in interdependent process models by designing a common data model for them.

- An exceptional termination of a process can be problematic in an executable process model. The PROCESS INTERRUPT TRANSITION pattern introduces a process interrupt into the process design using a transition condition after the activity or activities that cause the interrupt.

- The ACTIVITY INTERRUPT pattern deals with a similar situation, but here only a single activity of a process is interrupted. This pattern is applicable when an event causes an activity not to be completed (yet) but the process control data can already be updated.

- A special kind of exceptional event is an error in an external system. The PROCESS-BASED ERROR MANAGEMENT pattern describes how to define special attributes for error handling in the process control data structure and let the process design contain error management activities.

- The TIMEOUT HANDLER deals with situations in which an activity executes some application or service or it waits for an external event. If the duration until the application or service replies or until the external event is raised can be long, a timeout event is raised in the activity in case no reply or event arrives in a defined time frame.

- The WAITING ACTIVITY pattern defines an activity type that waits for a predefined duration using an internal timer before it allows the process flow to proceed.

In "Chapter 10—Integrating Events into Process-Driven SOAs," we provide more details on the combination of process-driven SOAs and event-driven architecture (EDA). The chapter provides solutions to capture events that occur in the event space outside the process engine and consider them in the process space of a process instance. The chapter presents the following patterns:

- The basic pattern for linking the process space to the event space is the EVENT-BASED ACTIVITY pattern. It describes how to design activities that actively wait for specific external events to happen. Only if the events happen, the EVENT-BASED ACTIVITY terminates and allows the process instance to proceed.

- The EVENT-BASED PROCESS INSTANCE pattern deals with the problem of how to instantiate a process on the occurrence of a defined external event. The pattern provides an event-based process instantiator component that resides in the event space.

- A special variant of EVENT-BASED PROCESS INSTANCE is the EVENT-BASED PROCESS SPLIT pattern. It describes how to externalize the event-based activity to an external event handler component and split the original business process into several parts at the points where the event-based activity is located. Hence, it offers a solution for the problem of processes that are suspended for a long time because of an EVENT-BASED ACTIVITY waiting for an external event.

- The EVENT DISPATCHER pattern is applied when event sources must be flexibly linked to event listeners. To achieve a decoupling of event sources and listeners, a central EVENT DISPATCHER is used to manage the occurring events.

"Chapter 11—Invoking Services from Processes" addresses the problem that we want to separate the process view of a service invocation and the technical details of that invocation. Each pattern in this chapter addresses specific requirements for the link between process instance and service. The chapter presents the following patterns:

- The SYNCHRONOUS SERVICE ACTIVITY describes how to model a synchronous service invocation in a business process activity.

- The FIRE-AND-FORGET SERVICE ACTIVITY shows how to model a service invocation without any expected output of the service.

- The ASYNCHRONOUS RESULT SERVICE addresses how to model service invocations with asynchronous replies in a business process—with one result.

- The MULTIPLE ASYNCHRONOUS RESULTS SERVICE addresses how to model service invocations with asynchronous replies in a business process—with multiple results.

- The FIRE EVENT ACTIVITY pattern describes how to model activities that fire certain events to be processed by external systems.

- The ASYNCHRONOUS SUBPROCESS SERVICE pattern illustrates how to design a service that only instantiates a subprocess.

- The CONDITION DEADLINE SERVICE pattern addresses how to model time-bound dependencies of business processes on required states of business objects.

In "Chapter 12—Synchronization of Processes Running in Parallel," we address synchronization issues of parallel business processes. In this context, *synchronization* means that execution in terms of the progression through the different activities of a process needs to be synchronized with other business processes running in parallel. The chapter presents the following patterns:

- The REGISTER FOR ACTION pattern describes how to synchronize the execution of functionality of a target system with business processes running in parallel.

- The BUNDLE PROCESS AGENT pattern describes how business objects being generated by different parallel processes can be processed in a consolidated way.

- The PROCESS CONDUCTOR pattern addresses how to enable designers to model dependencies between parallel business processes by flexible orchestration rules.

Finally, "Appendix 1: Related and Referenced Patterns" gives an overview of related pattern material that might be considered for further reading and provides thumbnails of all patterns used in this book.

Guide to the Reader

This book contains a pattern language on process-driven SOA. We designed the book to help the target audiences described. Hence, we assume you are familiar with basics on distributed systems development (in particular Web services systems) and process-driven systems. While you should be able to follow the book with only some architecture, design, and implementation knowledge, if you are not yet familiar with distributed systems development and process-driven systems, we recommend to first look at some tutorials about Web services, process engines, and process modeling languages.

For many people, a hands-on exercise works best to get an initial impression of a technology. For example, you could download a recent free process engine or Web services framework and do the basic tutorials before starting to delve into the topics explained in this book. This hands-on experience will surely make reading this book more valuable for you, as you can more easily follow the advanced concepts described. For example, the NetBeans 6.1 *Developer Guide to BPEL Designer* [Net08] is an easy-to-follow introduction to a free process design tool and engine that invokes services using the BPEL process execution language. Another easily accessible guide to a free process engine is the JBoss jBPM documentation [JBo08]. To learn more about Web services, we recommend familiarization with at least one Web services framework, such as Axis, Axis2, CXF, JBoss WS, .NET Web services, or Sun's Metro Web services, to name a few.

If this book is your first exposure to patterns, you might also benefit from reading a few basic works on patterns first, although this is not necessary to understand the concepts presented in this book. We recommend *Design Patterns* [GHJV94] and Volume 1 of *Pattern-Oriented Software Architecture* [BMR+96] for an impression of some "classical" software patterns. Both books present common pattern concepts and terminology, as well as fundamental patterns in the fields of software design and architecture. If you are familiar with these basic patterns and want to learn more about patterns and their background in software, we recommend *Pattern-Oriented Software Architecture, Volume 5* [BHS07b].

If you are the main target audience, SOA solution architects and designers, we recommend reading or scanning the book at least once from end to end. This way you can extend your own architecture and design vocabulary with the patterns described. An overview on the patterns is given in the previous section and the narrative sections of each pattern chapter. Later, we suggest using the pattern texts as reference material to look up details on the patterns when needed.

If you are an SOA developer and you must just use or realize a few patterns, it is enough to read the sections in which these patterns are located. The narrative sections at the beginning of the chapter give you a good overview of the pattern relationships, and the pattern texts provide you with the details about the patterns. Examples and case studies illustrate the patterns. The overview from this chapter can be used to get a first view of the patterns (or a subset of patterns) and their relations.

If you are a business stakeholder or a general reader who wants to get a high-level overview first, we recommend reading the introductory chapters and then the narrative introductions of each pattern chapter. They should give a fairly good overview of the pattern material presented in this book without delving too deeply into technical details.

For all readers who are not yet familiar with the business perspective on SOA, we recommend reading Chapter 2, which gives a brief overview. Chapter 3 provides our technical perspective on SOA. Hence, we recommend it for all readers who are not familiar with basic SOA design and architecture concepts. For all readers, these two chapters also might be interesting to better understand our view on SOA, but can be skipped by those familiar with basic business or technical aspects of SOAs.

Chapter 4 provides a walk-through of our pattern language for a detailed example. This chapter is advisable for all audiences as an introduction to the patterns and the method described in this book by example.

2

Service-Oriented Architecture: A Business Perspective

Business Agility as a Driving Force

One of the most important issues for businesses these days is the ability to create new structures and processes with minimal effort, that is, to achieve *business agility* [SW03]. There are many reasons why business agility becomes increasingly important:

- Businesses must cope with a rapidly changing business environment that requires changes in days and weeks rather than months and years.
- Businesses must deal with their customers' expectations for more services and less time needed for performing existing services.
- Businesses often try to decrease costs and increase their productivity. This also implies a constant pressure for change.

The demand for software architecture design concepts that follow principles of agility have hence raised much attention in the business community. Today's business world has become dynamic, and change in business and information technology (IT) has become regular practice.

We are facing an extremely dynamic, competitive, and global business environment that has dramatically increased the rate of change in businesses, resulting in mergers and acquisitions, building of alliances and virtual companies, increased time to market, product development, and marketing innovation. Thus, the need for business information system agility is actually born of business pressures in a global market.

The demand for business agility requires software platforms that support dynamic and flexible changes (see, e.g., [CGH+05, DAH05, SW03, SKJ07]). Business process management (BPM) and service-oriented architecture (SOA) are two approaches that consider a high level of agility:

- *BPM* enables the business to design processes, execute them automatically via a process engine, and monitor or control them while they are running. The automation of processes aims at lowering the operational costs, increasing the quality of services delivered to the customer, and increasing the productivity of the business.
- *SOA* allows businesses to design and implement the services orchestrated via the process flow of the business processes. SOA aims to support the business by reducing the costs for custom coding for purposes such as integrating business systems. This should be achieved via reuse of loosely coupled services. Also,

change, maintenance, and integration costs can be decreased. The idea is that this can be achieved because services as atomic entities are easier to change and maintain than monolithic applications. Hence, the difficult integration of monolithic applications can also be eased.

The business goal of merging the two approaches into the *process-driven SOA* approach is to leverage the advantages of both approaches. SOA and BPM used together support the goal of business agility by automating the processes of the business in an easy-to-change, maintain, and integrate fashion.

As a result, SOA and, in particular, process-driven SOA have gained much interest, and businesses are currently planning to undertake broader efforts to build SOA architectures [CGH+05].

The pattern language introduced in this book provides an approach to closing the conceptual gap between model building in business architectures and software architectures, following business process-driven and service-oriented principles. We followed an inductive empirical approach to identify and mine software patterns from real-world SOA systems to understand how organizational and software architectural structures can be integrated and how this integration enables business agility of information systems. Consequently, our definition of *business agility in information systems* is the enablement of information systems to allow quicker organizational changes at lower cost. We understand business agility as a measure of the effort for realizing organizational changes.

Business Process Modeling

A *business process model* is a documentation of a business process using a graphical or textual notation. The business process model is a behavioral model showing how the work in a business is done. That is, a *process* is defined as a specific set of activities that are ordered in time, with a clear beginning and end.

Business process modeling is the act of creating business process models. It is typically performed by business analysts or domain experts. Business process modeling is often performed with goals such as to understand, document, analyze, or improve the business processes of an organization.

At the business level, there are many notations for modeling existing business processes, such as the Business Process Modeling Notation (BPMN), Event-Driven Process Chains (EPCs), UML Activity Diagrams, the Business Process Modeling Language (BPML), and many more. You need to choose the most appropriate notation for your business process modeling goals.

To give you a brief impression of a typical set of elements available in a business process modeling language or notation, an excerpt of the elements available in BPMN is shown in Figure 2.1. As you can see, the first class of BPMN elements is activities. They describe tasks that need to be performed in a business process. Tasks are the basic type of activities. Activities can also be structured and actually hide a subprocess. A second class of BPMN elements is gateways. They are decision points that allow you to split or join the control flow in a business process. Events are externally triggered "things" that can happen to a business process, such as the start or end of a process instance, an external event, an exception, and so on. For both gateways and events, Figure 2.1 only shows an excerpt of the

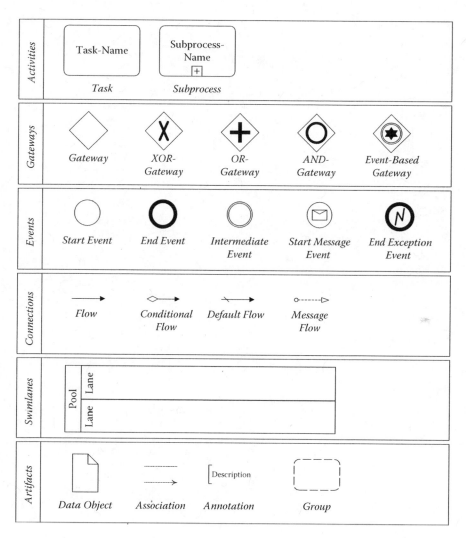

FIGURE 2.1
Excerpt of BPMN elements.

existing symbols. Connections allow you to connect the activities, gateways, and events. They determine the order of the control flow.

Swim lanes can be used to model participants in a business process. A *pool* can be used to model a participant, such as a user, a user role, or a system. A *lane* is a subdivision of a pool that is always applied for the whole pool.

Finally, there are a number of artifacts, such as data objects and their associations, annotations, and groups.

Figure 2.2 shows an example of a composed BPMN diagram on the left-hand side.

In this book, we mainly use the BPMN, EPC, and UML (Activity Diagrams) notations for presenting business process models. We assume that you are familiar with at least one or two of these notations. If you have never seen or used them before, we advise you to read a basic tutorial on some of them first. You can find a multitude of freely available tutorials on the Web, as well as many introductory books.

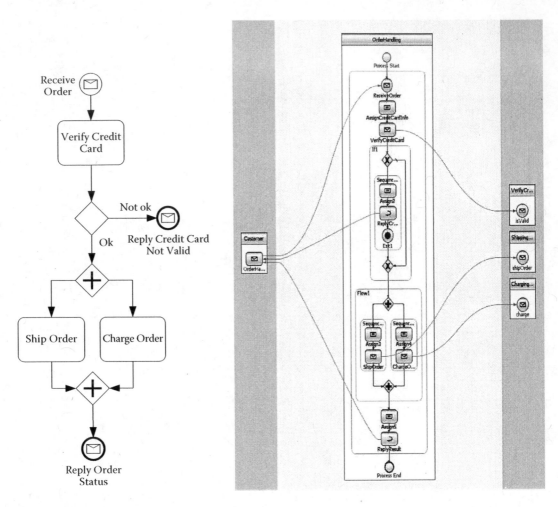

FIGURE 2.2
BPMN business view and BPEL technical view of the same process.

Business Process Modeling versus SOA Modeling

The methodologies and models for designing SOAs are rather in their infancy. One main reason is that SOA methodologies and models so far mainly have focused on technical issues. We can observe that the links of organizational models, such as business processes, roles, and organizational structures, to software models need to be improved to achieve a business-aligned software architecture. This book aims at supporting improved integration of organizational and software architectural model building to provide a conceptual foundation for designing business-driven SOAs. We elaborate in more detail in this book what this integration actually means with the help of empirically mined software patterns.

In reality, business processes (and other models) designed for business purposes and processes (and other models) designed for technical purposes are highly disparate in both structure and content. For example, the two process models shown in Figure 2.2 show the same process, once as a business view in BPMN (left-hand side) and once as a technical view in BPEL (Business Process Execution Language; right-hand side). These models are explained in more detail in Chapter 5. As you can see, the BPEL process model has many more elements; actually, this view even hides many additional details, such as process-variable mappings or service interface descriptions not shown in this process model view. The two models in this example are designed to correspond together. You can imagine how much more disparate these models can become if they are independently designed.

There are numerous reasons for this disparity: The goals why modeling happens are different for business models and technical models. Business models and technical models are usually designed by different people or different teams with a different background and focus. Business purposes for modeling processes other than process automation are, for example, communication among the stakeholders or process simulation. Also, process models are used for documentation (e.g., to document compliance to regulations or standards). These purposes often contradict the needs for technical modeling. For instance, enriching a process model with technical details (e.g., for invoking a service deployed at a host) can make the process model more complex and thus harder to understand and communicate to other stakeholders.

The question arises how to use or adapt the processes modeled for business purposes in a technical SOA context, so that, on the one hand, the business view and technical view can be kept consistent, and on the other hand, both the technical and business purposes of process modeling in an SOA can be supported. We describe patterns addressing this problem in Chapter 5. These patterns describe how to stepwise refine high-level business processes to low-level business processes, which are then translated into technical processes. These technical processes can be further refined using services and technical sub-processes. This method is explained in detail in Chapter 7.

In addition, our pattern language also addresses how to integrate other types of models needed for an SOA. For instance, an SOA requires many architectural components not considered in the business process modeling perspective, such as adapters to external systems, business rule engines, dispatchers, and so on. To integrate the business-oriented view and the technical view also means to consider these additional perspectives. In our pattern language, the processes are used as the main integration point of the two modeling worlds.

Business Process Orientation in Business Information Systems

The latest definitions of the term *business process management* illustrate that workflow technology has become an important conceptual artifact that brings the formerly separate worlds of organizational and technical design into an interdependent context [Pri03]. Conceptually, BPM implies, on a technical level, the usage of technologies that allow business agility. For this reason, BPM has technical consequences and requires corresponding architecture design concepts.

In practice, the design of these platforms is also already strongly demanded by many industries, as the time to react on organizational change requirements is becoming increasingly shorter. The IT of an organization often is a key enabling factor for such organizational changes. Organizationally inflexible technology implies higher efforts in implementing the changes; thus, higher costs are involved than using IT architecture concepts that consider the required kinds of business agility [SW03].

As many organizations are shifting toward process-oriented organizations, IT platforms have to consider the process-oriented approach conceptually. It is expected that process orientation and its effects will become even more important in the future as organizations will build flexible process-driven networks that form virtual companies via process-oriented technology [Cha04, McH95].

We see several streams that have merged into the architectural paradigm of SOA during an evolutionary process since the late 1990s. These streams can be outlined as

- object orientation (OO),
- component orientation,
- distributed object middleware (and service-oriented middleware),
- business process management,
- enterprise application integration (EAI), and
- workflow management.

The result is sociotechnological systems in which organizations, people, and technology are integrated into a big picture using the process-oriented approach as the linking element, providing a flexible platform regarding changes to business processes.

In the past, organizational structure has been the most important instrument for long-term business strategies, but now business strategies have become more flexible because the business requirements and goals are changing much faster. As a result, organizational structures are no longer fixed for several years while a certain business strategy is executed. Rather, strategy making becomes closely linked to execution [NT97]. That means success is determined by the right approach to a strategy process rather than a fixed strategic position. Consequently, strategy is about creating and modifying organizational structures, and it is important to create these new structures quickly and at a low cost [SW03].

An important driver in this context is IT as it is one of the most influential factors for the evolution of businesses today. For this reason, the IT investment can have enabling or disabling effects on business initiatives. Conclusively, the IT investment must prepare an enterprise optimally for the future. In current and future businesses, the degree of achievement concerning effective IT platforms significantly determines the success or failure of a company. The ease of adapting organizational structures is in this view a function of technology. Thus, technology plays a strategic role of enormous importance [SW03].

It should thus be possible to easily change an organization as a holistic system; this may consequently, in some respect, require changing IT easily. Vice versa, approaches for appropriate IT systems must include principles of flexibility at several levels. We have to deal with not only changing program code but also whole architectural components, connections and ways of communication, interactions and processes between people and system components, or even external organizations. Conclusively, business architectures, IT architectures, and the social system of an organization tend to merge in this worldview and become *sociotechnological systems*.

If we take a look at the history of IT systems in business and try to summarize what has been learned in an interdisciplinary context, it is possible to outline a model that represents the idea of a growing and changing sociotechnological organization that views IT and the social system of an organization in interdependence [Hen06].

Extracting Business Processes from Applications

Business process orientation to information systems implies the convergence of business, organizational, and software models and thus aims at providing a framework that allows designing and implementing business, technological, and organizational architecture in interdependence. The notion of a (business) process is the driving and linking concept of all involved aspects.

The key principle in this context is separation of business logic from process logic. Practically, this means that the process logic will be taken out of applications and systems and will be flexibly controlled by a process-driven middleware. These middleware platforms allow for the definition and execution of business processes. A well-established process definition and execution language is, for example, the BPEL standard (explained in more detail in Chapter 3).

The flexibility is achieved by introducing an abstraction layer for process control with such process-driven middleware that allows changing the process flow definition more easily compared to static process implementation within application program code. For instance, consider an SOA in which services can be flexibly composed in a business process flow with the help of such middleware. Figure 2.3 illustrates the decoupling of the process logic by giving an example of a customer entering an order and how this order will be processed within the organization. Decoupling is achieved using a process-driven approach that separates process logic from business logic and extracts the process logic from the application logic.

From a business perspective, the decoupling of the process logic actually represents the most important transformational step that must be taken. Basically, this book deals with the architectural implications of this transformational step and provides patterns as solutions for the recurring issues in this context. On a business architecture level, business processes themselves are understood as components that can be flexibly and easily changed, replaced, and reused on an enterprise-wide basis and even across enterprise boundaries to connect and integrate the processes of different organizations. This is the foundational concept that actually enables business agility.

Process-Aware Information Systems

To summarize, the points made in the previous sections lead to the following conclusion: Evolution of IT systems points to the emergence of a new class of systems that can be identified as *process-aware information systems*. Thus, the notion of process represents a linking element between IT, organizational, and social issues, as business processes are strongly involved in the definition of an organizational structure and its culture on the one hand and its technology on the other hand.

From a business perspective, *process engineering* aims at optimizing the business processes of an organization. It is changes to those business processes that need to be implemented quickly to cope with a dynamic business environment.

Process-aware information systems depict organizational structure more or less directly with technology. For this reason, the corresponding process technology is important for the

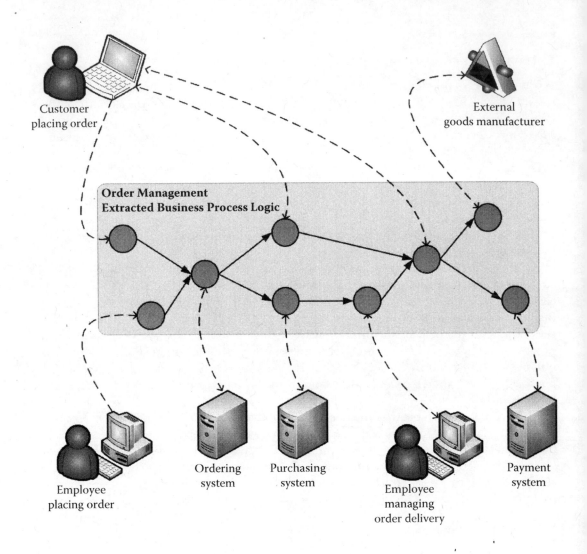

FIGURE 2.3
Decoupling process logic.

future of businesses because this technology conceptually supports the interdependence between IT and organizational structure and provides business agility by technically decoupling business process logic.

In this context, SOA plays an important role. Chapter 3 provides an introduction to SOA from the technical perspective. In particular, the following view of SOA is important for the business perspective: If we leverage the idea of an SOA and introduce the decoupling of process control logic by a service orchestration layer, we will end up with a *process-driven concept for SOA*. In fact, decoupling the process logic implies another level of business agility. Actually, this is the very point at which the perspectives of technical architecture and organizational architecture tend to merge via the process paradigm. For this reason, our pattern language that provides time-proven practices in this context helps to close the gap between the business and the technical perspectives.

The Business Impact of Process-Driven SOA

Process-driven SOA as a strategy to achieve business agility has significant business impact. However, measuring the return on investment (ROI) of SOA endeavors is a complex topic of its own and is largely dependent on the scope and goals of the SOA program. For instance, the questions of road maps, migration strategies, architecture assessments, and governance will all play an important role in capturing the overall business value and impact of a specific SOA program. These questions are related to a specific project situation, and it is for this reason difficult to quantify the impact generically. The systematic approaches and methodologies for addressing these questions also stand as separate issues. As these topics would rather form books of their own, providing concepts, solutions, methods, and including different examples and case studies for measuring and quantifying the impact, we consider it more appropriate for this book only to highlight some of the major points regarding business impact from a qualitative perspective.

Thinking, designing, and implementing processes from a bigger architectural perspective means to get rid of the paradigm of discrete applications that design and use functionality within closed separate application boundaries. That means in the process-driven SOA approach one implements processes rather than separated applications, leveraging functionality on a broader level across the organization. Following this approach at the enterprise level has many qualitative consequences within an organization:

- Business intelligence can be applied on the business process level providing business performance indicators. Differentiating and competitive information becomes available on demand.

- Making the processes *product independent* by standardization and abstraction, and implementing them on an SOA, makes it easier to design and implement new products and thus to reduce time to market. This drives innovation and can be used as a competitive advantage.

- Automation provides space for using human capital in a higher business value space (e.g., customer care). SOA is an enabler for improved business models by reducing administrative tasks. This can be used as a competitive differentiator.

- Processes become easily measurable and can be transparently optimized by applying common quality management systems.

- Consolidation, harmonization, and optimization of the IT landscape can happen in the back end without having an impact on the end users due to the decoupling. Specific optimizations can be made according to their value proposition regarding the business process.

- User interfaces can be harmonized toward process-step-based interfaces. End-user trainings are reduced significantly as all interfaces have the same look and feel.

- Existing integration technologies can be leveraged to save investments and can be combined with more recent technologies, such as products that follow the Service Component Architecture (SCA) standard, for instance.

From an interorganizational perspective, significant qualitative business impact factors can be outlined as well:

- Process-driven SOA provides a strategy for enabling cloud computing services in the domains of PaaS (platform as a service) and SaaS (software as a service).

- Mergers and acquisitions become easier and less cost intense when process-driven SOA strategies are followed as integration can be performed predominantly at the business process level.

- Process-driven SOA provides an enabler for specializing the market toward specific scalable services offered (e.g., a payments provider in a banking industry that offers out-tasking payment transactions or even outsourcing all payment processes). These specializations can be used as a competitive advantage for infiltrating niches for specific services.

- Specialization of services offered by companies and standardization of how process services are technically offered foster the business process outsourcing field and make it easier to compete in a global marketplace. Global virtual organizations can be formed.

3

Service-Oriented Architecture: A Technical Perspective

Introduction

This chapter introduces service-oriented architectures (SOAs) from a technical perspective and provides an architectural framework for SOA. Technically speaking, a *service-oriented architecture* is essentially a collection of services that are able to communicate with each other [Bar03]. But, services in an SOA are not well defined at the moment. Hence, we want to define them using a set of minimal properties we expect from a *service*:

- A service is a distributed object that is accessible via the network.
- A service defines public interfaces, but the exact implementation details are not needed for using the service. That is, using the service with knowledge only about the interface is possible.
- A service is self-contained in the sense that it can be used independently. Of course, a service can internally use other components and services, but the user of the service does not need to be aware of whether the service is atomic or composed.
- A service can be accessed in a platform-independent and protocol-independent way. That is, in principle, the service can be invoked from other platforms than the one it has been developed for or using other communication protocols than the ones it has been developed with.

Although built on similar principles, SOA is not the same as Web services, which indicates a collection of technologies and concepts of their use, such as SOAP (originally Simple Object Access Protocol) and XML (originally Extensible Markup Language; the so-called WS-* land) or HTTP (Hypertext Transfer Protocol) and RESTful (REST = Representational State Transfer) service design. SOA is more than a set of technologies and runs independent of any specific technologies.

SOA is not really a "new" architectural style, but rather it integrates architectural knowledge from other styles, including distributed object middleware frameworks, process-driven architectures, messaging, enterprise application integration (EAI), and many others, in a specific way. The W3C Architecture Group described this specific integration of other styles by the SOA approach when they defined SOA as a special kind of distributed systems architecture with the following properties [W3C04]:

- *Logical view:* The service is an abstracted, logical view of actual programs, databases, business processes, and so on defined in terms of what it does, typically carrying out a business-level operation.

- *Message orientation:* The service is formally defined in terms of the messages exchanged between provider agents and requester agents and not the properties of the agents themselves. The internal structure of an agent, including features such as its implementation language, process structure, and even database structure, are deliberately abstracted away in the SOA: Using the SOA discipline one does not and should not need to know how an agent implementing a service is constructed. A key benefit of this concerns so-called legacy systems. By avoiding any knowledge of the internal structure of an agent, one can incorporate any software component or application that can be "wrapped" in message-handling code that allows it to adhere to the formal service definition.

- *Description orientation:* A service is described by machine-processable metadata. The description supports the public nature of the SOA: Only those details that are exposed to the public and important for the use of the service should be included in the description. The semantics of a service should be documented, either directly or indirectly, by its description.

- *Granularity:* Services tend to use a small number of operations with relatively large and complex messages.

- *Network orientation:* Services tend to be oriented toward use over a network, although this is not an absolute requirement.

- *Platform neutral:* Messages are sent in a platform-neutral, standardized format delivered through the interfaces. XML is the most obvious format that meets this constraint.

In this chapter, we describe the technical aspects of SOA using patterns and pattern languages that have been described previously in the literature.

The Infamous SOA Triangle

In many presentations about SOA, you will encounter the so-called SOA triangle as a rough architectural sketch showing what SOA is all about. On the one hand, this view is flawed in the sense that in reality many of the more important aspects of SOA are omitted. On the other hand, this architecture is not wrong in any sense: It provides a high-level overview of the typical interaction between service clients and providers. So, let us start our tour of SOA by having a pattern-based look at the SOA triangle.

The SOA triangle architecture is quite trivial: A service is offered using a remote interface that employs some kind of well-defined INTERFACE DESCRIPTION [VKZ04] (examples are given in the following). The INTERFACE DESCRIPTION contains all interface details about the service (i.e., the operation signatures and how these operations can be accessed remotely). The service advertises itself at a central service, the lookup service. Applications can therefore look up the advertised services by name or properties to find details of how to interact with the service.

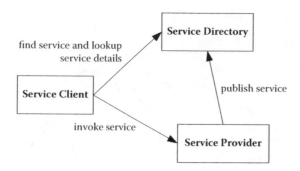

FIGURE 3.1
The SOA triangle.

Figure 3.1 illustrates this basic architecture. A *service provider* offers a service to *service clients*. Of course, often the service is realized fully not only by the service provider implementation, but also by a number of back ends, such as server applications (other SOAs or middleware-based systems such as Common Object Request Broker Architecture (CORBA) or Remote Method Invocation (RMI) systems), Enterprise Resource Planning (ERP) systems, databases, legacy systems, and so forth. Flexible integration of heterogeneous back-end systems is a central goal of an SOA.

Note that the service client is often itself a service provider, leading to the composition of multiple services.

A central role in this architecture is played by the pattern LOOKUP [KJ04, VKZ04]: Services are published in a *service directory*, and clients can look up services. Developers usually assign logical OBJECT IDS [VKZ04] to services to identify them. Because OBJECT IDS are valid only in the context of a specific server application, however, services in different server applications might have the same OBJECT ID. An ABSOLUTE OBJECT REFERENCE [VKZ04] solves this problem by extending OBJECT IDS to include location information, such as host name and port.

The LOOKUP pattern can be used to look up the ABSOLUTE OBJECT REFERENCES of a service. This is done by querying for properties (e.g., provided as key/value pairs) of the service and other details about them, such as the INTERFACE DESCRIPTION of the service, a location where the INTERFACE DESCRIPTION can be retrieved (e.g., downloaded), or other metadata about the service.

From Interface Descriptions to Service Contracts

A explained, the INTERFACE DESCRIPTION pattern plays an important role in SOAs. This pattern addresses in an SOA the problem that the interfaces of service client and service provider need to be aligned, and consequently marshaling and demarshaling need to be aligned to send invocations across the wire. To be able to write meaningful service clients, client developers need to know the interfaces of the services.

The solution is that an INTERFACE DESCRIPTION describes the interface of remote objects. The INTERFACE DESCRIPTION serves as the *contract* between service client and service provider. The SOA middleware can use either code generation or runtime configuration techniques to adhere to that contract.

Example: WSDL Interface Description

In Web service technology (the so-called WS-* land), most INTERFACE DESCRIPTIONS are provided in the Web Services Description Language (WSDL). As an example, let us take a look at a simple WSDL file excerpt describing a *verify credit card service*. At first, a number of namespaces are defined. Next, in the *types* section, an XML Schema file `VerifyCreditCard.xsd` is imported that defines the types used in this WSDL file. Then, a request *message*, receiving an element that is externally defined in an XML schema, is defined, as well as a response *message*, sending an externally defined type. Next, a *port type* is defined that uses the two messages defined previously as input and output messages in an *operation*. The binding section describes how this port type is bound to the SOAP. Finally, the *service* section describes where a service offering a port that implements this binding is deployed.

```xml
<?xml version="1.0" encoding="UTF-8"?>
  <definitions
    ...
    xmlns:soap="http://schemas.xmlsoap.org/wsdl/soap/"
    xmlns:tns="http://orderHandling/"
    xmlns:xsd="http://www.w3.org/2001/XMLSchema"
    xmlns="http://schemas.xmlsoap.org/wsdl/"
    targetNamespace="http://orderHandling/"
    name="VerifyCreditCardService">
    ...
  <types>
    <xsd:schema>
      <xsd:import namespace="http://orderHandling/"
        schemaLocation="VerifyCreditCard.xsd"></xsd:import>
    </xsd:schema>
  </types>
  <message name="isValid">
    <part name="parameters" element="tns:isValid"></part>
  </message>
  <message name="isValidResponse">
    <part name="parameters" element="tns:isValidResponse"></part>
  </message>
  <portType name="VerifyCreditCard">
    <operation name="isValid">
      ...
      <input message="tns:isValid"></input>
      <output message="tns:isValidResponse"></output>
    </operation>
  </portType>
  <binding name="VerifyCreditCardPortBinding"
    type="tns:VerifyCreditCard">
    <soap:binding transport="http://schemas.xmlsoap.org/soap/http"
      style="document"></soap:binding>
    <operation name="isValid">
      ...
      <soap:operation soapAction=""></soap:operation>
      <input>
        <soap:body use="literal"></soap:body>
      </input>
      <output>
        <soap:body use="literal"></soap:body>
      </output>
    </operation>
  </binding>
  <service name="VerifyCreditCardService">
    <port name="VerifyCreditCardPort"
```

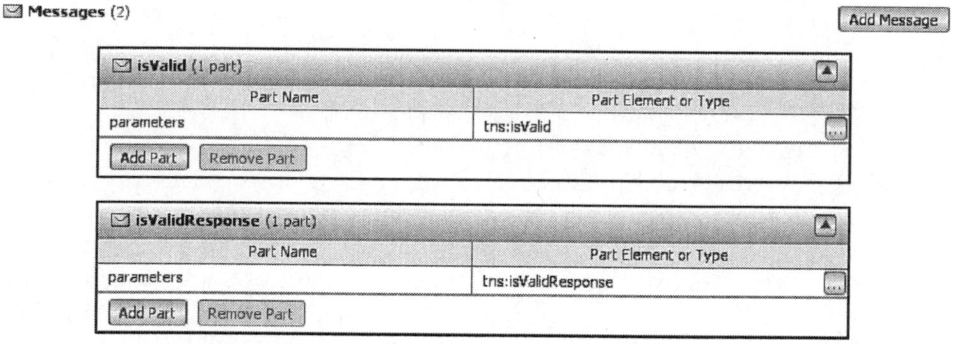

Messages (2)   [Add Message]

isValid (1 part)   [▲]

Part Name	Part Element or Type
parameters	tns:isValid

[Add Part] [Remove Part]

isValidResponse (1 part)   [▲]

Part Name	Part Element or Type
parameters	tns:isValidResponse

[Add Part] [Remove Part]

FIGURE 3.2
WSDL message design with NetBeans.

```
       binding="tns:VerifyCreditCardPortBinding">
       <soap:address location=
       "http://localhost:8080/VerifyCreditCardService/VerifyCreditCard">
       </soap:address>
     </port>
   </service>
</definitions>
```

WSDL specifies everything needed to understand a deployed service. A downside of WSDL is that the various kinds of information mixed in an WSDL file, such as type description, interface description, protocol binding, and service deployment information, are usually defined at different times and possibly by different roles in the development and maintenance teams of a software system. For instance, when we define the interface of a service, we often do not know yet where to deploy it. The service designers are not necessarily the same people as those responsible for deployment. Hence, it often makes sense to generate WSDL code from separate descriptions of these parts or to provide tool support to deal with WSDL files.

For example, Figure 3.2 shows a WSDL message design performed using the NetBeans design tools.

Example: REST INTERFACE DESCRIPTION

WSDL is mainly used in WS-* Web services specifications. An alternative for realizing Web services is Representational State Transfer (REST). In contrast to the WS-* Web services specifications, REST is not a standard. REST is just an architectural style. While REST is not a standard, it does prescribe the use of standards of the Web, such as

- HTTP as a transport protocol;
- URL (uniform resource locator) for identification of resources;
- XML, HTML (Hypertext Markup Language), GIF (graphic interchange format), JPEG (Joint Photographers Expert Group), and so on for resource representations;
- MIME (multipurpose Internet mail extension) types, such as text/xml, text/html, image/gif, image/jpeg, and so on for describing resource types;
- and so on.

In REST, the client transfers from one state to the next by examining and choosing among the alternative URLs in the response document. Just like ordinary Web interactions, REST uses the standard HTTP methods, such as GET, PUT, DELETE, and POST. REST services are generally more resource oriented, than WS-* services. That is, the HTTP methods are used as CREATE/READ/UPDATE/DELETE (CRUD) operations on the resources.

The use of the INTERFACE DESCRIPTION pattern is less obvious for REST than for WSDL-based services. While there are some efforts to define an interface description language for REST services, such as the Web Application Description Language (WADL), many people use either homegrown schemas or a more reflective INTERFACE DESCRIPTION for querying information about the resources. Please note that the INTERFACE DESCRIPTION pattern is not limited to interface description languages and includes those other styles of describing interfaces.

For instance, an HTML representation of a resource might contain a form to inspect the resource and query its interface either in-line or using links. The HTML is returned when a client issues a GET request on the linked INTERFACE DESCRIPTION resource.

Service Contracts

INTERFACE DESCRIPTIONS are a first step toward contracts for services. The concept derives from the design-by-contract concept [Mey97], originally developed for software modules. In essence, service contracts define the interaction between service client and service provider. The reason for using the design-by-contract approach is that a service needs to be specified a step further than simple remote interactions, such as Remote Procedure Call (RPC)-based invocations in a middleware. The elements of a service contract can include the following information about a service:

- communication protocols
- message types, operations, operation parameters, and exceptions
- message formats, encodings, and payload protocols
- pre- and postconditions, sequencing requirements, side effects, and so on
- operational behavior, legal obligations, service-level agreements, and the like
- directory or lookup service

Not all of these contract elements can be expressed easily with today's Web services implementations. Communication channels and messages are usually described with INTERFACE DESCRIPTIONS. The INTERFACE DESCRIPTION of an SOA often needs to be more sophisticated than the INTERFACE DESCRIPTIONS of (OO-)RPC distributed object middleware, however, because it needs to be able to describe a wide variety of message types, formats, encodings, payloads, communication protocols, and so on.

LOOKUP plays an important role in many SOAs because it is used to locate or obtain the INTERFACE DESCRIPTION and ABSOLUTE OBJECT REFERENCE of a service. In addition, some lookup services provide more sophisticated information to describe the service information that is missing in the INTERFACE DESCRIPTION, such as operational behavior, legal obligations, and service-level agreements. In other words, in addition to the lookup of ABSOLUTE OBJECT REFERENCES, the SOA lookup service might offer other elements of the service contract.

The SOA can also be extended with custom directories or repositories allowing for LOOKUP of domain-specific service properties or metadata of services. These might be accompanied by domain-specific schemas or ontologies, such as industry-specific XML schemas like Open Financial Exchange (OFX) [OFX09] or Mortgage Industry Standards

Maintenance Organization (MISMO) [MIS09]. A service contract is usually realized by a mixture of explicit and implicit contract specifications. The elements can be described as explicit service contract specifications—most often provided in electronic form. In principle, all these elements can also be specified only implicitly or nonelectronically.

This would be inconvenient for the technical specification elements because it would be cumbersome, error prone, and costly, if for instance, the ABSOLUTE OBJECT REFERENCES would not be retrieved automatically but instead distributed by hand. Hard-wiring ABSOLUTE OBJECT REFERENCES into a client is also not advisable because this would contradict the principle of loose coupling: A service client should be relatively independent of the location where the service is executed. These technical service contract elements should therefore be specified in some explicit, electronic form following the INTERFACE DESCRIPTION pattern, ideally accessible at runtime—for instance, by using the LOOKUP pattern or providing a download facility for the contract information.

Some other service contract elements, however, are often specified only implicitly or nonelectronically. Examples are the documentation of the services behavior and its implied semantics, business agreements, quality-of-service (QoS) guarantees, legal obligations, and so on. These elements might also be needed in electronic form, when the service client needs to monitor or verify the contract, or when the service provider needs to verify or monitor the quality of the service. For instance, the client or server might observe QoS characteristics of the service (using the QOS OBSERVER pattern [VKZ04], for example) or check that specific business agreements are not violated. In general, monitoring and verification can be implemented using INVOCATION INTERCEPTORS [VKZ04] or OBSERVERS [GHJV94, BHS07a] (these options are explained in more detail in the following).

SOA Layers

Now that we have described the overall architecture of many typical SOAs, let us take a look inside the message-processing architecture of an SOA. An SOA generally has a highly symmetrical architecture on client and server sides, as it can (also) be found in many other modern distributed object middleware systems. In an SOA, the LAYERS [BMR+96, BHS07a] illustrated in Figure 3.3 are typically used for message processing.

The following LAYERS can be identified:

- *Service composition.* The top-level layer of an SOA deals with the composition of services and is optional. At this layer, service orchestration, service coordination, service federation, or business process management (BPM) functionalities are implemented.

- *Client application/service provider.* This layer consists of clients that perform invocations and the actual implementations of the services.

- *Remoting.* This layer implements the middleware functionalities of an SOA (for instance, in the form of a Web services framework). Usually, the details of the client side and the server side are hidden in a BROKER architecture [BMR+96, BHS07a]: A BROKER hides and mediates all communication between the objects or components of a system. The remoting layer itself consists of three layers: invocation, adaptation, and request handling. Beneath the application layer, the patterns CLIENT PROXY [VKZ04], REQUESTOR [VKZ04], and INVOKER [VKZ04] are

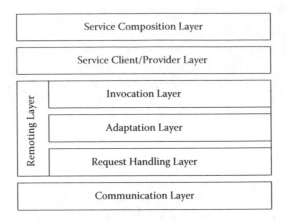

FIGURE 3.3
SOA layers.

     responsible for marshaling/demarshaling and multiplexing/demultiplexing of invocations and replies. The adaptation layer, often implemented using the INVOCATION INTERCEPTOR [VKZ04] pattern, is responsible for adapting invocations and replies in the message flow. The request-handling layer provides a CLIENT REQUEST HANDLER [VKZ04] and SERVER REQUEST HANDLER [VKZ04]. These two patterns are responsible for the basic tasks of establishing connections and message passing between client and server.

- *Communication.* The communication layer is responsible for defining the basic message flow and managing the operating system resources, such as connections, handles, or threads.

In addition to the basic layers that handle the message flow in an SOA, there are a number of orthogonal extension tasks that must be implemented across a number of these layers. Examples of such extensions are management functionalities for services, security of services, and the description of services, for example, in service contracts.

Adaptation in the Remoting Layer

A characteristic property of SOAs is that they are highly adaptable in the remoting layer. The reason for this adaptivity is:

- Possibly, different communication protocols and styles must be supported, even at the same time.
- A number of orthogonal tasks might need to be configured for services, such as management functionalities for services, security of services, monitoring of service contracts, logging, and so on.
- The service might not be implemented by the service object itself but by a back end. A heterogeneous set of back ends should be supported.

    In addition to these requirements, an SOA usually has to be able to be adapted at runtime. Thus, a highly dynamic and flexible architecture is required that supports respective

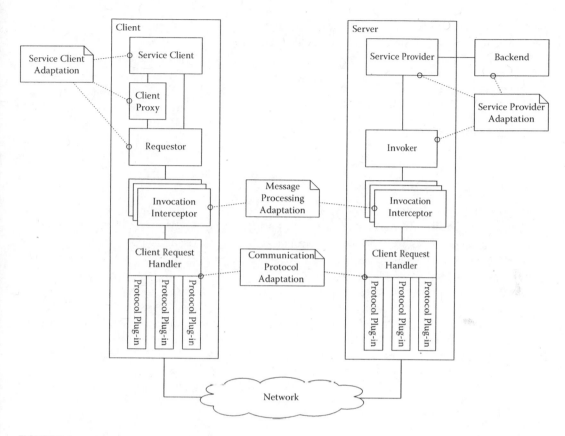

FIGURE 3.4
Adaptation in the remoting layer.

runtime variation points. Figure 3.4 shows the main variation points the remoting layer of an SOA, corresponding to the variation requirements. These are explained in more detail in the remainder of this section.

Communication Protocol Adaptation

As mentioned, on the lowest layer, the communication layer, we require high flexibility regarding the protocols used because usually an SOA allows for a number of communication protocols to be used. These communication protocols might require different styles of communication, such as synchronous RPC, asynchronous RPC, messaging, publish/subscribe, and others.

Variation at the communication layer is usually handled via PROTOCOL PLUG-INS [VKZ04]. PROTOCOL PLUG-INS extend the CLIENT REQUEST HANDLER and SERVER REQUEST HANDLER with support for multiple, exchangeable communication protocols. They provide a common interface to allow them to be configured from the higher layers.

For example, the Web service framework Apache Axis (Version 1) uses, in the default case, HTTP as a communication protocol. But, SOAP also allows for configuring other communication protocols. In Axis PROTOCOL PLUG-INS for HTTP, Java Messaging Service (JMS), SMTP (Simple Mail Transfer Protocol), local Java invocations, and so on are provided. The PROTOCOL PLUG-INS are responsible for implementing specifics of a communication protocol, such as a message queue for JMS-based messaging. The PROTOCOL PLUG-INS can be configured using either an XML-based deployment descriptor or an API. For example, the following code excerpt shows how to configure a JMS transport in Axis using the client APIs:

```
Service service = new Service();
Call call = (Call) service.createCall();
...
call.setTransport(new JMSTransport());
...
```

Message-Processing Adaptation

There is a distinct adaptation layer in the SOA architecture. This adaptation layer is often realized using the INVOCATION INTERCEPTOR pattern. INVOCATION INTERCEPTORS are automatically triggered before and after request and reply messages pass the INVOKER or REQUESTOR. The interceptor intercepts the message at these spots and can add services to the invocation.

Adapting the message processing is necessary to handle various control tasks, like management and logging, or pervasive tasks, like security. These tasks need to be flexibly configurable. In addition, in an SOA, there might be multiple payload formats with different marshaling rules. Thus, there should be some way to handle basic tasks like marshalling flexibly as well. This is often done using custom MARSHALERS [VKZ04] configured as INVOCATION INTERCEPTORS.

Usually, the same INVOCATION INTERCEPTOR architecture can be used on client and server sides. For many tasks, we need to pass additional information between client and server. For instance, for an authentication interceptor on the server side we require additional information to be supplied by the client side: the security credentials (such as user name and password). These can be provided by an INVOCATION INTERCEPTOR on the client side. However, how is this information transported from client to server? This is the task of the pattern INVOCATION CONTEXT [VKZ04]: The INVOCATION CONTEXT bundles contextual information in an extensible data structure that is transferred between client and remote object with every remote invocation.

For example, in Apache Axis the following *LogHandler* is provided as an INVOCATION INTERCEPTOR. It can be hooked into the invocation flow of request or reply messages to log messages. The *MessageContext* is used as an INVOCATION CONTEXT holding the message exchanged, as well as custom data that can be read and written by the INVOCATION INTERCEPTORS.

```
public class LogHandler extends BasicHandler {
  ...
  public void invoke(MessageContext msgContext)
    throws AxisFault {
    ...
    if (msgContext.getPastPivot() == false) {
      start = System.currentTimeMillis();
    } else {
      logMessages(msgContext);
    }
    ...
  }
  ...
}
```

In Apache Axis, the handlers can be configured using XML-based deployment descriptors. For instance, the following code excerpt configures the *LogHandler* together with another handler for a service called *DateService*.

```
<handler
  name="logger"
  type="java:org.apache.axis.handlers.LogHandler"/>
...
<chain name="myChain"/>
  <handler type="logger"/>
  <handler type="authentication"/>
</chain>
...
<service name="DateService" provider="java:RPC">
  ...
  <requestFlow>
    <handler type="myChain"/>
  </requestFlow>
</service>
```

Service Provider Adaptation

The service provider is the remote object realizing the service. Often, the service provider does not realize the service functionality solely, but instead uses one or more back ends. When an SOA is used for integration tasks, it should support multiple back-end types. The goal of providing support for service provider adaptation in an SOA is that only the service interfaces are exposed, and service internals are hidden from the service client. This way, it is possible to provide integration of any kind of back end with one common service provider model.

Service provider adaptation needs to be supported by the remote objects realizing the service, as well as by the INVOKER that is used for invoking them. A common realization of service provider adaptation is to provide one INVOKER type for each back-end type and make INVOKERS flexibly exchangeable (e.g., using deployment descriptors).

Service providers and INVOKERS need to be tightly integrated with the LIFECYCLE MANAGER [VKZ04], which provides a central place for life-cycle management in the SOA. This is because it is important that the INVOKER select the best-suited life-cycle strategy pattern for the service:

- Some services might be implemented as STATIC INSTANCES [VKZ04], which live from application startup to its termination.
- For most systems that access a back end, however, it advisable to use PER-REQUEST INSTANCES [VKZ04], which live only as long as a single invocation.
- When session state needs to be maintained between invocations, CLIENT-DEPENDENT INSTANCES [VKZ04] should be used. The CLIENT-DEPENDENT INSTANCE must implement a session model and a LEASING model [KJ04, VKZ04] compatible with the model of the back end.

The LIFECYCLE MANAGER should also handle resource management tasks, such as POOLING [KJ04, VKZ04] or LAZY ACQUISITION [KJ04, VKZ04].

Service Client Adaptation

Service clients should also be adapted, but the goal of service client adaptation is different from that on the server side; here, independence of service realization and loose coupling are important. As explained, service client adaptation is mainly reached by LOOKUP of services and well-defined INTERFACE DESCRIPTIONS. Other aspects of service client adaptation are the flexible (e.g., on-the-fly) generation of CLIENT PROXIES or the direct use of REQUESTORS to construct invocations on the fly. Finally, the client must be adapted to how the result is sent back (if there is any). Here, usually synchronous blocking, or one of the client invocation asynchrony patterns, described in [VKZ04], is used:

- The FIRE AND FORGET pattern describes best effort delivery semantics for asynchronous operations but does not convey results or acknowledgments.

- The SYNC WITH SERVER pattern describes invocation semantics for sending an acknowledgment back to the client once the operation arrives on the server side, but the pattern does not convey results.

- The POLL OBJECT pattern describes invocation semantics that allow clients to poll (query) for the results of asynchronous invocations, for instance, in certain intervals.

- The RESULT CALLBACK pattern also describes invocation semantics that allow the client to receive results; in contrast to POLL OBJECT, however, it actively notifies the requesting client of asynchronously arriving results rather than waiting for the client to poll for them.

All four patterns can be used when synchronous invocations are insufficient because an invocation should not block. Developers can use FIRE AND FORGET or SYNC WITH SERVER when no result should be sent back to the client. POLL OBJECT is appropriate when a result is required and the client has a sequential programming model, whereas RESULT CALLBACKS require a client with an event-based programming model.

SOA and Business Processes: Integrating Services and Processes

As explained, the top-level layer of many SOA systems is the *service composition layer*. In this section, we view the SOA concept from the perspective of a service composition layer that is process driven. That is, the service composition layer introduces a process engine or workflow engine that invokes the SOA services to realize individual activities in the process (also known as process steps, tasks in the process). The goal of decoupling processes and individual process activities, realized as services, is to introduce a higher level of flexibility into the SOA: Predefined services can flexibly be assembled in a process design tool. The technical processes should reflect and perhaps optimize the business processes of the organization. Thus, the flexible assembly of services in processes enables developers to cope with required changes to the organizational processes while maintaining a stable overall architecture.

In a process-driven SOA, the services describe the operations that can be performed in the system. The process flow orchestrates the services via different *activities*. The operations executed by activities in a process flow thus correspond to service invocations. The

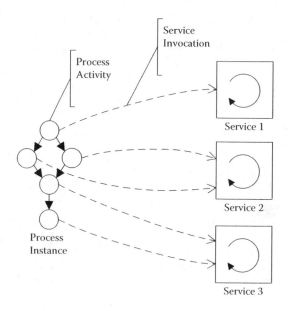

FIGURE 3.5
Service orchestration in a process flow.

process flow is executed by the process engine. This key design is schematically illustrated in Figure 3.5.

In SOAs, different communication protocols and paradigms, such as synchronous RPC, asynchronous RPC, messaging, publish/subscribe, and so on can be used and are supported by SOA technologies, such as Web service frameworks or ENTERPRISE SERVICE BUS (ESB; see separate section on ESB later on in this chapter) implementations. For a process-driven SOA, it can generally be assumed, however, that mainly asynchronous communication protocols and paradigms are used. This is because it cannot generally be assumed that a business process blocks until a service invocation returns. In most cases, in the meantime other activities can be performed by the process. In addition, there are many places in a process-driven SOA where invocations must be queued (e.g., legacy systems that run in batch mode). It is typically not tolerable that central architectural components of the process-driven SOA, such as a central dispatcher, block until an invocation returns. Hence, synchronous service invocations are only used in exceptional cases for which they make sense.

An important aspect when using processes (or workflows) in an SOA is how the two basic concepts, processes and services, relate.

Fundamentally, a process-aware information system can be shaped by five perspectives [JB96, AH02]:

- *control flow* (or process): describes the structure of a process model using the activities from which it is constructed
- *task* (or function): describes a logical unit of work using one or more elementary actions
- *operation* (or application): describes the individual elementary actions from which tasks are composed
- *data* (or information): describes the data elements that are utilized during process execution

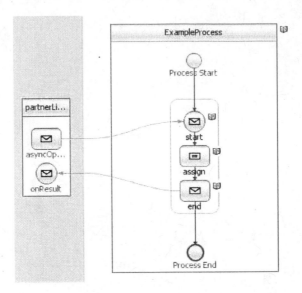

FIGURE 3.6
BPEL process that waits for an incoming service invocation.

- *resource* (or organization): describes the organizational context and structure in which the process executes and how work items can be assigned to resources, ranging from humans to devices

These perspectives can be mapped to the SOA approach in the following way: Services can be understood as a specialization of the general operation perspective; that is, they define the elementary actions from which logical units of work that can be used in the control flow of the process can be constructed. In the perspectives terminology, the logical units of work are called *tasks*. In this book, we use the term *process activities* to denote these tasks.

In conclusion, that means the process control flow orchestrates the services via different process activities, and the operations executed by the activities in a control flow correspond to service invocations.

Usually, in process-driven SOAs the tools and modeling languages define *activity types* that enable you to

- invoke services from the control flow,
- react on service invocations, or
- send replies to services.

For example, in the simple BPEL process shown in Figure 3.6, modeled using the NetBeans BPEL designer, we can see a *start* activity that is modeled using the *Receive* activity type of BPEL that waits for an incoming service invocation. In addition, there is an *end* activity of the *Invoke* activity type of BPEL that invokes an external service. BPEL offers a third activity type for dealing with services (not shown in this example): *Reply*. This activity type can reply to a service invocation.

As far as the data perspective is concerned, it is necessary to distinguish between *process control data* and the *business data* that are transformed via the process flow:

- Control data is introduced solely for the purpose of processing the process. An example of control data is a process variable that is used as the basis for deciding which of two branches of a process should be taken.

- The existence of business data is not dependent on the business process instance. Often, business data is modeled using *business objects*. An example of such a business object could be a customer order that is processed via a process flow. The actual processing of that order is controlled by the control data that depicts the routing rules, for instance.

Each process activity can be interpreted as a certain state of the business object. In an SOA, this means that service orchestration will also have to deal with control data and business objects being transformed and passed from one orchestration step to the next one.

The control flow perspective is managed by a process engine. Generally, today's process engines follow two possible paradigms:

- The traditional paradigm is a *strictly structured* process flow that dictates a strict ordering of activities, as implemented by engines like IBM's WebSphere MQ Workflow or Staffware.

- The *flexibly structured* paradigm is rather innovative and does not dictate a strict ordering of activities; exceptions are rather the rule. An example of that approach is the product FLOWer from Pallas Athena [Pal02].

The Unified Modelling Language (UML) model in Figure 3.7 illustrates the relations of the concepts introduced in this section and especially shows the roles of services in a process-aware system.

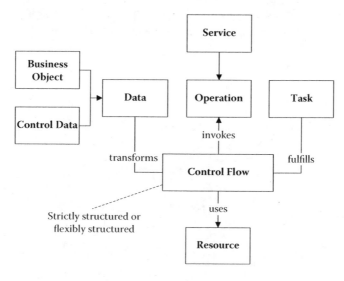

FIGURE 3.7
The role of services in a process-aware system.

Enterprise Service Bus

The ENTERPRISE SERVICE BUS [Erl09] is based on a MESSAGE BUS [HW03] and is an architectural pattern that integrates concepts of SOA, EAI, and workflow management. According to [Erl09], an ESB represents an environment designed to foster sophisticated interconnectivity between services. It establishes an intermediate layer of processing that can help overcome common problems associated with reliability, scalability, and communications disparity.

Within this architectural pattern, various components connect to a service bus via their service interfaces. To connect those components to the bus, service-based INTEGRATION ADAPTERS (see Chapter 6) are necessary. The service bus handles service requests and generally represents a MESSAGE ROUTER [HW03] or BROKER [BMR+96, BHS07a]. Service requests are routed to appropriate components connected to the bus, where services are invoked. As a result, an ESB can act as a CONTENT-BASED ROUTER, MESSAGE FILTER, DYNAMIC ROUTER, AGGREGATOR, or MESSAGE BROKER, to name a few message-routing patterns (see [HW03]).

In addition, message transformation patterns like NORMALIZER, ENVELOPE WRAPPER, or CONTENT ENRICHER (see [HW03]) are applied by the bus to integrate different service interfaces. Often, a REPOSITORY [Eva04] of business objects is connected to the service bus.

In some cases, the service bus and a MICROFLOW ENGINE (see Chapter 5) are implemented by the same component, for example, a message integration middleware such as IBM's WebSphere Business Integration Message Broker or Microsoft BizTalk. That means the service bus itself implements process integration services.

Thus, the service bus is connected to the whole internal service infrastructure, and all services communicate via the bus. Access to those services is classified by different service types. For this reason, it is possible to lookup services by their service type (e.g., process services, information services, interaction services, partner services, etc.). Figure 3.8 sketches the ESB as an architectural pattern. For example, the ESB pattern is implemented by IBM's Business Integration Reference Architecture consisting of products from the WebSphere family. The Service Provider Delivery Environment (SPDE) architecture is an implementation of this reference architecture for the telecommunications industry.

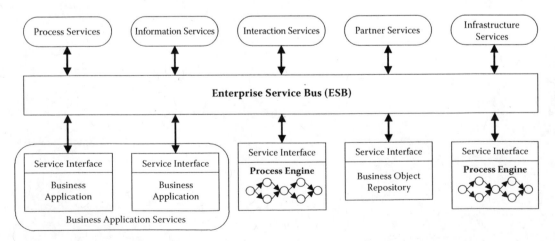

FIGURE 3.8
Enterprise service bus as an architectural pattern.

SOA and Event-Driven Architecture

For many reasons, we often need to observe what happens to the data in an SOA. Examples of such reasons are that we want to monitor the SOA as it runs, we need to analyze log trails for audits, we want to use data traces for business intelligence or business activity monitoring purposes, we want to visualize certain properties of an SOA in a dashboard, and so on. This can be difficult because, in an SOA, data is not (only) stored in a central component but mainly flows between the services (and processes).

Using the message-processing adaptation techniques described it would, for example, be possible to observe the messages that manipulate the data. This can, however, be quite tedious and costly to develop. Often, a better way to observe the SOA (and its data) is to generate *events* from services (and processes). With regard to the data, events are hence used to signal the relevant state changes in the services.

In addition, the services and processes are sometimes interested in the things that happen in other systems or components outside their scope. In the same way that events are used for signaling what happens in the SOA can also be used to signal things that happen in other systems. Then, the services and processes must react to these external events.

An event-driven architecture (EDA) is an architecture that produces, detects, consumes, and reacts to events. At the core of EDA is a PUBLISHER/SUBSCRIBER architecture [BMR+96, BHS07a] in which event subscribers and event publishers are interconnected. When SOA and EDA are combined, services (and processes) are event subscribers and event publishers. The ESB often has the task of routing the event messages from the event publishers to the event subscribers. This core of the EDA architecture is illustrated in Figure 3.9.

An additional problem in this context is that once we collect all the events that happen in an SOA, either using an eventing infrastructure or more primitive means like log files, the amount of information gathered can quickly become huge. The basic events or log entries collected provide only information that is primitive. Hence, tools to help developers pick out specific related events are needed. The events to be observed should be described in terms of the business problem at hand (so-called business events or complex events) rather than relying only on low-level, technical events.

This problem can be addressed using complex event processing (CEP). It allows developers to define patterns or rules for detecting complex events in a series of simple events. Abstractions such as event correlations, event hierarchies, and causal or temporal event relationships can be used to characterize or categorize the events. Actions can be defined if a complex event is detected. CEP can be nicely integrated with long-running business processes as it allows detecting complex events over a long duration.

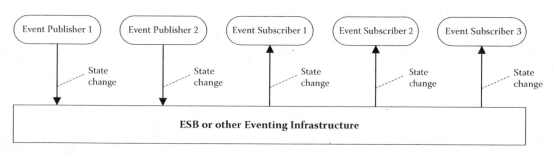

FIGURE 3.9
EDA core architecture.

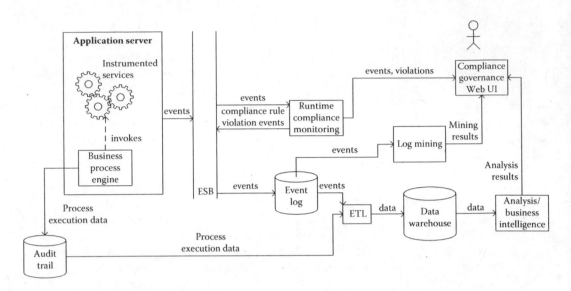

FIGURE 3.10
COMPAS eventing architecture.

In some cases, even prediction from observed events is needed and can be provided via CEP techniques. That is, the observed events should be interpreted and produce a warning prior to an unwanted event such as a failure. For example, CEP can be used to react to potential business risks or opportunities.

As an example of an EDA, in Figure 3.10 you can see the eventing architecture of Compliance-driven Models, Languages, and Architectures for Services (COMPAS) [Com09], a project aiming at providing a generic infrastructure to support compliance to regulations, legislations, business rules, standards, and so on. The system to be observed is a process-driven SOA. The services and processes running in the application servers are instrumented or configured to publish the relevant events at runtime. An ESB is used to connect event publishers and subscribers. In addition, the process engines write process execution data into an audit trail. The compliance events are monitored at runtime (online monitoring) to react on compliance violations that can be detected while the system runs. In the online monitoring component, a CEP engine is used. Violations are shown to the user via a Web user interface (UI). Some compliance violations span longer time frames. Hence, log-mining techniques, as well as ETL (extract, transform, and load) and data-warehousing techniques, are used for offline analysis. The results of these are also analyzed and presented in the Web UI.

4

Pattern Language Walk-Through: An Example from the Insurance Business

Claims Management as a High-Level Business Domain View

In this chapter, we illustrate a running example from the insurance industry in the business area of managing insurance claims. Managing claims is actually one of the core processes in the insurance business. For this reason, improving the effectiveness of handling claims is a field that provides much potential for innovative approaches. By providing this example business scenario, we aim to show how the patterns in this book support the design and implementation of the business architecture and the technical architecture. This example serves as a walk-through of our pattern language covering many patterns presented in this book.

You can read this chapter in two ways:

- You can read it before you read the patterns presented in the following chapters to get an initial overview of what the patterns are about. The example should be intuitive but do not expect to understand all details about all of the patterns being used in the example yet.

- You can read the example (again) after you have completed your study of the pattern chapters. This way you can use this chapter as a "running example" combining patterns from different parts of this book in one comprehensive example.

Many of us have already been in the situation of reporting a claim to an insurance company. For instance, a motor claim is a common example in the case of a car accident. There are also other types of claims. An insurance company usually distinguishes between motor, casualty, and property claims as three substantial types. As far as designing the business processes is concerned, it is important to understand how much those different types of claims actually influence how a claim needs to be treated. Ideally, one would standardize the processes as far as possible, such that only a little distinction is necessary. This would reduce the complexity of the processes. Following the *process-driven SOA* approach, one first needs to design and model the business processes from the high-level domain view, applying the DOMAIN/TECHNICAL VIEW pattern. This pattern advises us to split processes into a technology-independent domain view and a low-level technical view. Hence, a technology-independent domain view of groups of coherent business processes for the claims business would be a suitable first modeling view.

First, a claim is notified, investigated, and negotiated. One might bundle all these business processes into one coherent group to structure the processes, as these are the core processes for handling a claim. During the processing of the claim, some amount of money usually needs to be reserved. As this reservation is often adapted when the knowledge

FIGURE 4.1
Process groups for claims management.

about the claim increases during the investigation, we may understand the processes for claim reserve as a special group as well. Furthermore, we may consider the payment and the closure of a claim as another group as these two things usually happen together. There may be circumstances when a closed claim needs to be reopened, and we may view the processes for claim reopening as another group of processes that may be executed under those special circumstances. To complete the picture of grouping claims processes, we need to consider some other important business scenarios, that is, fraud handling because fraud detection may occur at any time in the overall process, supplier deployment, litigation handling, complaint handling, and claim recovery and claim review. These 10 areas, outlined in Figure 4.1, form our first model of the business architecture in terms of process groups. This model serves as the first step to understand the high-level business domain, according to the DOMAIN/TECHNICAL VIEW pattern. Please note, however, that this is only one possible way of structuring the business domain of managing claims.

To further refine the business domain, we need to identify the business processes within these process groups and model the dependencies between them. Those dependencies describe which process can invoke which other process as a subprocess. To achieve this, a suitable first step is to represent the identified business processes associated to the process groups in a hierarchical view. For instance, for the process group *claims notification, investigation, and negotiation,* we identified the following business processes: claim notification, claim triage and assignment, claim investigation, claim repudiation, and claim negotiation (as shown in Figure 4.2). For the other groups, it can be done analogously. That way, it is possible to provide a model that identifies the business processes of the high-level business domain.

In a second step, the dependencies need to be modeled to understand which process calls other processes as subprocesses. This view of the business domain can be modeled as a simple diagram of the processes being linked to those processes that are called as subprocesses. Using arrows as a directed link, one can show these subprocess invocation relationships. Figure 4.3 shows the dependencies.

Modeling the Claims Management Macroflow Processes

To proceed any further from this first stage of identification of business process groups and business processes, one needs to model the actual business processes. To achieve this following the *process-driven SOA* approach described in this book, we followed the

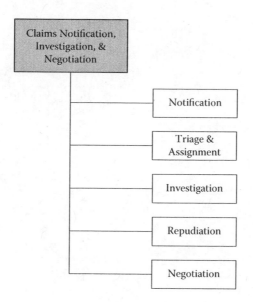

FIGURE 4.2
Identification of processes within a process group.

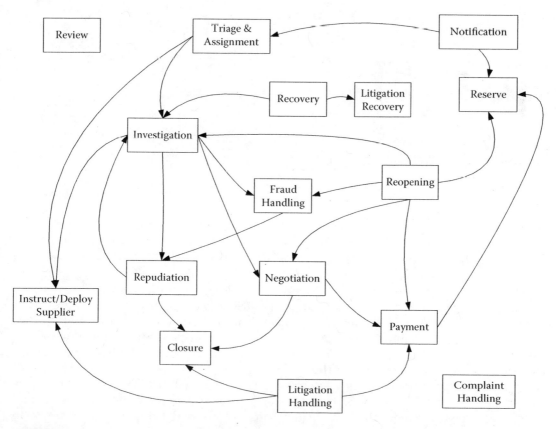

FIGURE 4.3
Claims management process dependencies.

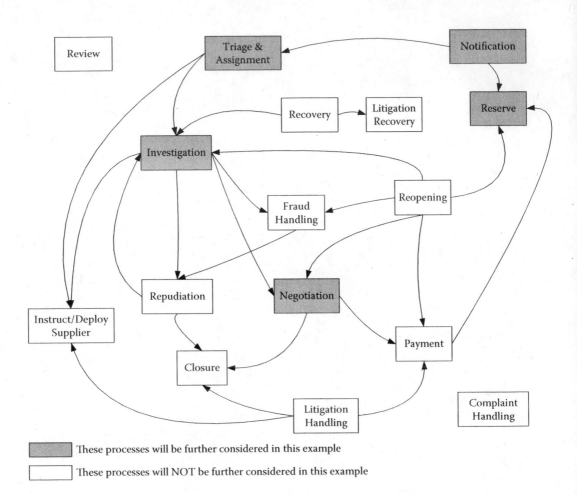

These processes will be further considered in this example

These processes will NOT be further considered in this example

FIGURE 4.4
Selection of processes considered in example.

MACRO-/MICROFLOW pattern. In this pattern, we refer to long-running, rather business-oriented processes using the term *macroflow*. According to the pattern, we start refining the processes from a hierarchical perspective, not considering the short-running, rather technical processes, called *microflows*, in the first modeling steps. For the purpose of this example, we present the macroflow models of a subset of all identified claims management processes. Figure 4.4 highlights which processes are considered further in this example.

To model the processes, we used the modeling tool ARIS from IDS Scheer. The notation we use to present the process models are event-driven process chains (EPCs). EPCs are a standard notation in Architecture of Integrated Information Systems (ARIS). In EPCs, we model processes as logical business functions (process activities) that are connected via events. Events are the output of a business function and may also be trigger events for other functions. The logical connections between events and functions represent the process flow. When modeling the processes, we also show which functions will later require a user interface and which functions will later become automatic services. The actual business events that may trigger a business process are modeled using the prefix *BE* in the event name to point out that these events are trigger events and to distinguish them between the events internal to a process.

Note that we have not considered all real cases of managing claims in the following process models to avoid unnecessary insurance background knowledge. For this reason, the following process models only consider one possible path (the main path if you like) of processing a claim to reduce the complexity and to serve as an effective example. The processes could, however, be extended toward a real claims management scenario starting from this example.

Business Domain View of the Claims Notification Process

The notification process has three functions associated to two different roles (callcenter clerk and claims handler) to model human interaction with the corresponding user interfaces. It also has three functions associated to services, indicating that these functions are automatic and without human interaction. That way, the user interfaces and associated use cases can be identified, and the business services can be identified as well. The model also defines when the claim reserve and the triage-and-assignment process are called as subprocesses. Then, the model represents the macroflow model of the notification process following the MACRO-/MICROFLOW pattern. The notification process is shown in Figure 4.5.

Business Domain View of the Claim Reserve Process

The claim reserve process includes one user interface-related function with a corresponding role (reserve handler) and three identified services. The claim reserve process is shown in Figure 4.6.

Business Domain View of the Triage-and-Assignment Process

The triage-and-assignment process also contains only one user interface-related function and one corresponding role (claims supervisor). It further models two new business services for automatic execution of the associated business functions. The claim investigation process is modeled as an invoked subprocess. The triage-and-assignment EPC model is shown in Figure 4.7.

Business Domain View of the Claim Investigation Process

The claim investigation process consists of only three functions with human interaction. Accordingly, three user interfaces associated to roles are modeled. All three activities are performed by the same role, which is the claims handler role. The claim negotiation process is invoked as a subprocess. The claim investigation process is shown as an EPC model in Figure 4.8.

Business Domain View of the Claim Negotiation Process

The claim negotiation process contains only one new user interface-related function and one corresponding role (claims handler). It further models one new business service for automatic execution of the associated business function. The payment process is modeled as an invoked subprocess. The negotiation EPC model is shown in Figure 4.9.

The EPC process model of the negotiation process contains the function *make offer and communicate*. This function is refined in a more detailed EPC model. This model defines

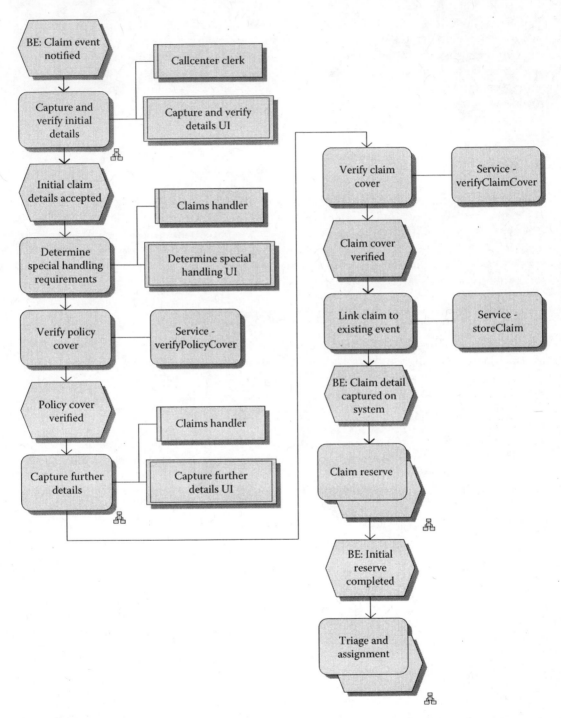

FIGURE 4.5
Notification process.

one new user interface-related function and uses one corresponding role (claims handler). It also uses the user interface *make offer to customer* that has already been identified in

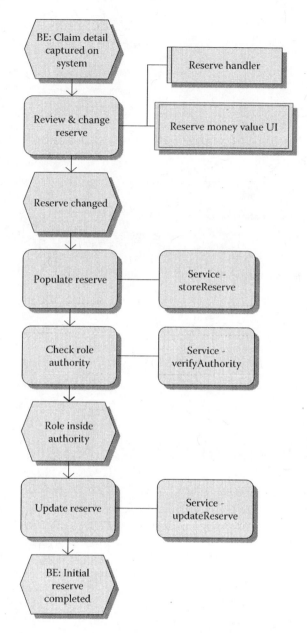

FIGURE 4.6
Claim reserve process.

the superior claim negotiation process. Moreover, it defines two additional services. The model of this process is shown in Figure 4.10.

All other claims processes can be modeled in the same way. The models thus provide a clear view of the number of use cases associated to human interaction and the number of services identified from the processes. Given these modeling results, further refinements are possible following a systematic approach until the final implementation stage is reached. The goal is to provide an effective *process-driven SOA* design and implementation guided by patterns described in this book. Some details of this approach are illustrated in the next sections.

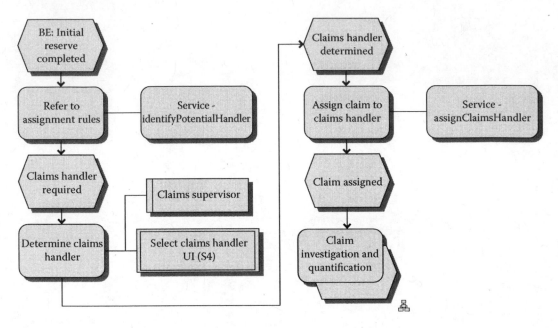

FIGURE 4.7
Triage-and-assignment process.

Modeling Claims Management Use Cases as Microflows

The 10 user interfaces identified in the business process models refer to microflows according to the MACRO-/MICROFLOW pattern. The pattern states that microflows are rather short-running processes that may happen within a use case. In this case, the microflow refers to a page flow and actions done by an actor via the user interface. Those kinds of microflows can be modeled as processes as well, to specify the process within the user interface. We use Unified Modelling Language (UML) activity models to design those microflows. The microflow model of a use case thus represents the refinement of a function identified in the business process. Such a UML microflow is always associated to a use case and the corresponding function (process activity) in an EPC model. Using ARIS as a modeling tool allows us to link the models to navigate from the function of a process to the refined microflow model. As an example, we present the microflow model of the *capture and verify initial details* function from the claim notification process in Figure 4.11. This UML activity model shows different activities with each activity actually associated to a screen (or page) in a page flow. Screen designs can then be created for each activity. The activity model specifies the actual page flow (sometimes also called screen flow). For the other use cases, corresponding models can be created to specify the microflows.

The UML microflow defines four sequential activities, with each activity associated to a screen. From the development process point of view, those screens need to be designed first; later, they will be implemented. The screen design draft for the *capture claimant data* activity in the microflow is shown in Figure 4.12. These kinds of design drafts then serve as specifications for the later implementation.

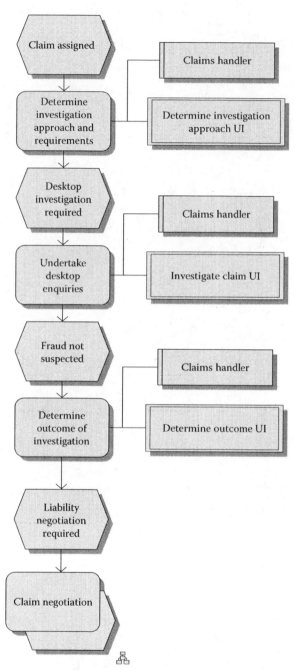

FIGURE 4.8
Claim investigation process.

Claims Data as a Central Resource

As the claims business processes are very much influenced by actual claims as a business object, we need to design the data model for claims as well. The claims data model needs

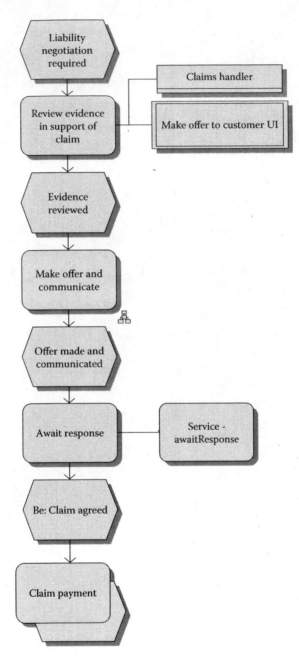

FIGURE 4.9
Claim negotiation process.

to consider at least the most relevant aspects, such as the policy to which the claim refers; the line of business to which the claim refers (i.e., motor, casualty, or property); and the customer associated to the claim. As the claims business processes are also very much influenced by the actual claim, we provide the claim data as a central resource applying the BUSINESS OBJECT POOL pattern. This pattern advises us to centralize the business data in a repository in case business data is relevant to many business processes running in

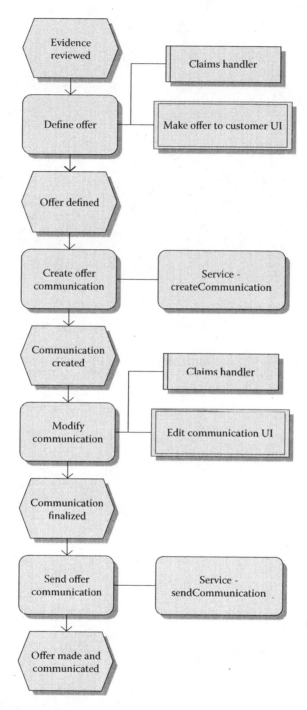

FIGURE 4.10
Make offer and communicate process.

parallel. In our case of claims management, this may happen, for instance, in case of a fraud being detected as a parallel event to a claim already being processed. The business process actually processing the claim needs to be notified of this changed state of

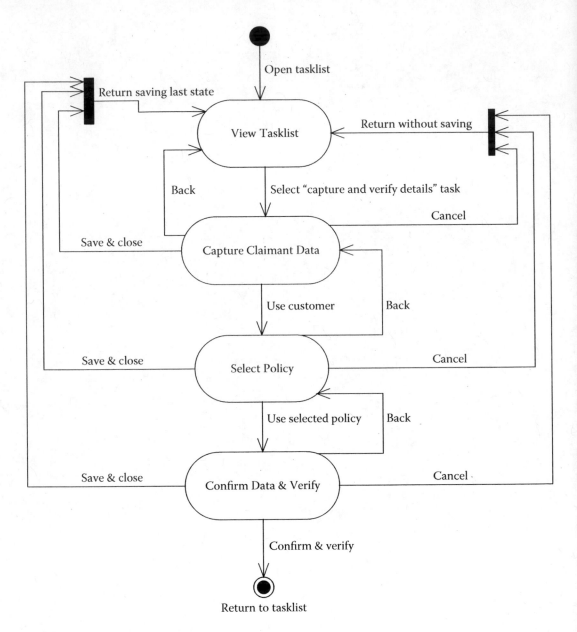

FIGURE 4.11
Capture and verify initial details microflow.

the claim and react properly. In parallel, the actual fraud-handling process needs to be executed on the same claim object. As a result, we need to centralize the claim data. To achieve this, we provide a conceptual data model for claims in a first step. From this conceptual data model, we can refine a physical data model in a second step for implementation on a database management system (DBMS). Figure 4.13 shows the conceptual data model for claims.

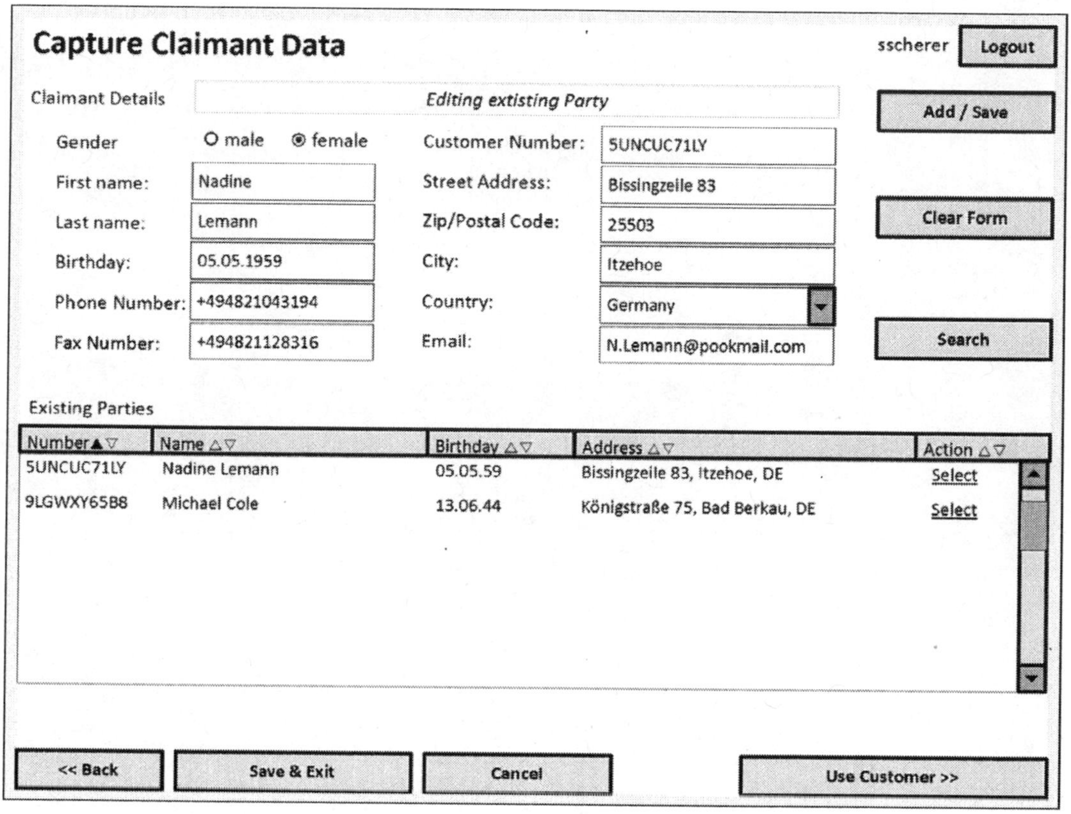

FIGURE 4.12
Screen design draft for the capture claimant data activity.

Technical Architecture for Claims Management

We selected IBM WebSphere Process Server as a MACROFLOW ENGINE to implement the long-running macroflows and a MICROFLOW ENGINE to implement the technical microflows. This platform integrates both types of engines in a single component and is based on BPEL (Business Process Execution Language) as a process execution language. For the macroflow level, it provides extensions to BPEL to allow implementation of human interactions. For the central claims data repository, we use IBM DB/2 to implement the BUSINESS OBJECT POOL. IBM WebSphere ESB (enterprise service bus), another integral component of WebSphere Process Server, is used as the ESB. For implementing the user interfaces, we chose IBM WebSphere Portal. WebSphere Process Server also provides different implementations of INTEGRATION ADAPTERS off the shelf, to connect to different types of systems via standards, such as Web services, IBM WebSphere MQ, or JMS (Java Messaging Service), to name a few adapters. In this example, we use the Web services adapters. Thus, WebSphere Process Server provides an off-the-shelf INTEGRATION ADAPTER REPOSITORY of INTEGRATION ADAPTERS.

The IBM WebSphere Application Server is used as the application server execution environment. For the development environment, we use IBM WebSphere Integration Developer for modeling the technical representations of macroflows and microflows in

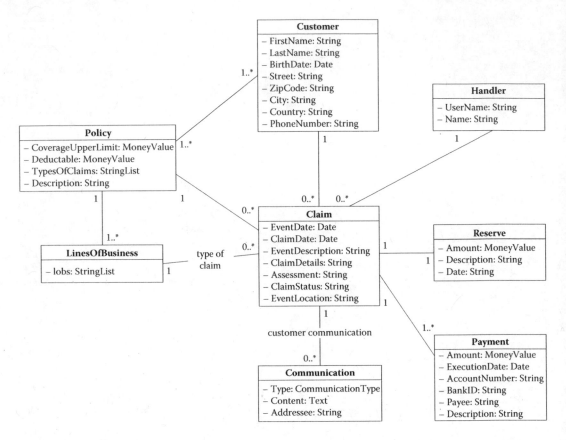

FIGURE 4.13
Conceptual data model for claims.

BPEL. This overall configuration serves as an implementation of the PROCESS INTEGRATION ARCHITECTURE pattern for the purpose of this example. With such an architecture concept, it will be fairly easy to connect other existing systems via service interfaces (e.g., a policy repository or a customer database). For the purpose of this example, we do not consider other possible systems in more detail, as the connection principles remain consistent. Figure 4.14 shows the technical architecture configuration.

Technical Claims Process Modeling and Implementation

The macroflow business processes that have been modeled as EPCs need to be designed in BPEL using WebSphere Integration Developer. As we have already modeled the business processes on the macroflow level, the process structure can be translated without much effort into BPEL.

Only a few adaptations and extensions are necessary (e.g., some error-handling mechanisms). WebSphere Integration Developer provides a visual modeling tool for designing the BPEL processes. The visual models are automatically translated into executable BPEL code (note that WebSphere Process Server implements some extensions to the BPEL

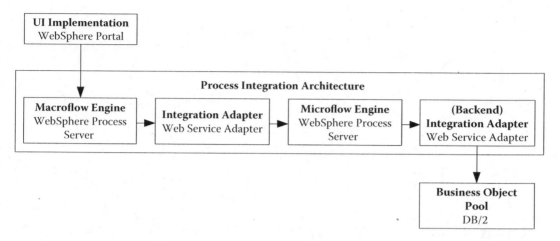

FIGURE 4.14
Technical architecture configuration.

standard). Modeling the claims processes with WebSphere Integration Developer is necessary for the five processes under consideration in this example: notification, reserve, triage-and-assignment, investigation, and negotiation.

As the claims data is centralized in a repository following the BUSINESS OBJECT POOL pattern, the data used in the actual BPEL processes just needs to contain the references to corresponding claim objects in the DB/2 database. Referencing external business objects is actually advised by the BUSINESS OBJECT REFERENCE pattern. The data structure used by the business processes can be kept simple when all the business data is extracted. This way, the processes remain independent of changes to business data.

In our example, the processes do not even have any decision points but just move straight ahead in a simple sequence of activities. For this reason, we follow the solution of the GENERIC PROCESS CONTROL STRUCTURE pattern. This pattern advises to have just one generic data structure used by all BPEL processes to avoid issues when changing the data structures at runtime. The simple data structure we use in this example is shown in Figure 4.15 (modeled in WebSphere Integration Developer). It basically holds the references to an external claims data object in the DB/2 database. Each reference is stored as a key-value pair, where the key identifies the database and the value identifies the object within the database. In this example, it is possible to store a list of such key-value pairs as BUSINESS OBJECT REFERENCES.

These data structures are in WebSphere Integration Developer internally represented as XML Schema definitions (XSDs). The XSD of the *BusinessObjectRef* object is as follows:

```
<xsd:complexType name="BusinessObjectRef">
    <xsd:sequence>
        <xsd:element minOccurs="0" name="key" type="xsd:string"/>
        <xsd:element minOccurs="0" name="value" type="xsd:string"/>
    </xsd:sequence>
</xsd:complexType>
```

The EPCs represent the business domain view, as they model the business domain in a technology-independent manner. The BPEL processes represent the technical domain view of the EPCs as they map the business domain models onto technology. This serves as a specific application of mapping the business domain on the technical domain as stated

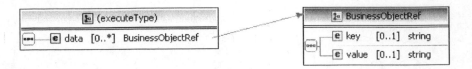

FIGURE 4.15
Implementation of generic claims data.

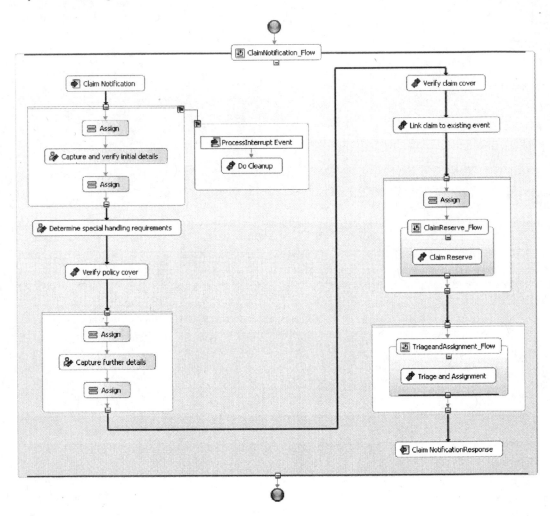

FIGURE 4.16
Claim notification BPEL process.

in the DOMAIN/TECHNICAL VIEW pattern. The technical domain view BPEL models are explained in more detail in the following sections.

Technical Domain View of the Claim Notification Process

The visual model of the BPEL process of the claim notification process is shown in Figure 4.16. The model is much the same as the original EPC model. It is only enriched with a few variable assignment steps and an additional event handler. Those *assign*

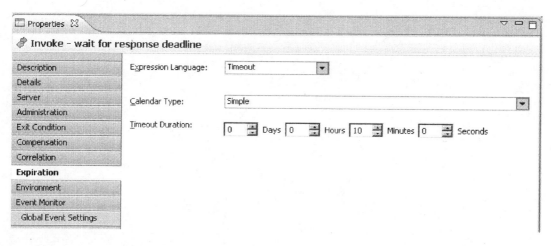

FIGURE 4.17
Implementing timeouts in WebSphere Integration Developer.

steps set variables of the process data. The event handler manages a PROCESS INTERRUPT TRANSITION in case a process interrupt is necessary. In case such an event occurs, a cleanup service is executed, and the process is stopped. A business scenario in which this might occur is the cancellation of a claim. In such a case, it does not make sense to proceed with processing the claim, and the process needs to be stopped. The event-handling mechanism of WebSphere Process Server supports easily modeling of such a PROCESS INTERRUPT TRANSITION via a special event that is being fired. Additional fault handlers might also be added to the BPEL model to handle exceptions of service calls.

The service invoking steps in the process all represent SYNCHRONOUS SERVICE ACTIVITIES. That means these steps invoke services synchronously, and the process waits in the corresponding position until a reply is received from the service. In case special reporting of error information is necessary as return values of the service calls, additional explicit conditional branching is necessary for implementing PROCESS-BASED ERROR MANAGEMENT. This would add up as an additional level of managing errors apart from the normal fault handling that allows retrying the invocation, ignoring the error, or even aborting the process. Those three options then need to be modeled as explicit branching in the process for those service calls to which this applies.

For service calls, it is possible that a timeout occurs. That means a synchronous service invocation does wait to get a reply within a specified time frame. To handle the kinds of timeout, one needs to model a TIMEOUT HANDLER. With WebSphere Integration Developer, handling timeouts can be specified for the service-invoking activities and is shown in Figure 4.17. The tool thus provides built-in functionality to specify TIMEOUT HANDLERS. It becomes quite clear that the BPEL model is enriched with a lot of additional technical information. The transformation from the EPC into the BPEL model is, however, consistent and straightforward.

Technical Domain View of the Claim Reserve Process

The visual model of the BPEL process of the claim reserve process is shown in Figure 4.18. The claim reserve BPEL basically shows the same technical characteristics as the claim notification BPEL, which has already been introduced. There is one aspect that is different from the notification process: The claim reserve process triggers a *fraud handler* in case a

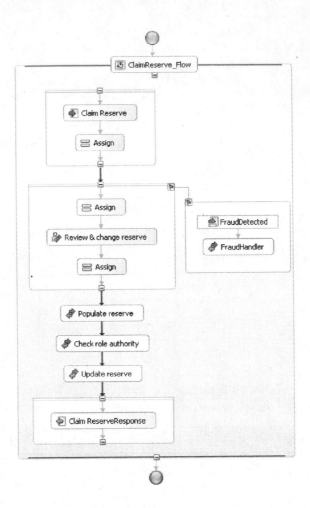

FIGURE 4.18
Claim reserve BPEL process.

fraud might be detected during the *review and change reserve* activity. The fraud handler is a special business process that is being triggered by an event. For this reason, this represents an implementation of the EVENT-BASED PROCESS INSTANCE pattern.

Technical Domain View of the Triage-and-Assignment Process

The visual model of the BPEL process of the *triage-and-assignment* EPC model is shown in Figure 4.19. Apart from the additional steps for assigning values to process data, the BPEL model does not show any additional features compared to the original EPC.

Technical Domain View of the Claim Investigation Process

The visual model of the BPEL process of the *claim investigation* EPC model is shown in Figure 4.20. As the original EPC model of the claim investigation process shows three subsequent functions associated to the same role (claims handler), it has been decided on this technical level to consolidate these three steps from the EPC into a single BPEL activity.

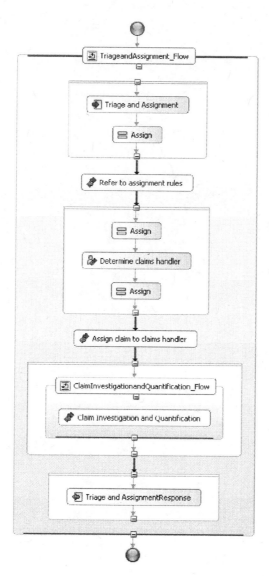

FIGURE 4.19
Triage-and-assignment BPEL process.

Consequently, the user interface of the consolidated BPEL activity needs to capture the identified user interfaces for all three steps from the EPC. These three originally identified user interfaces also need to be consolidated into one user interface component. This consolidation is a technical decision and is hence only presented in the technical domain view. The transformation is also straightforward and consistent, as it is a simple encapsulation in one consolidated step. This can always be considered when subsequent steps associated to the same role occur in the business domain view of a business process. It is, however, a conscious design decision that needs to be made explicitly, as it may be necessary in some cases to keep the steps separate (e.g., for monitoring them explicitly).

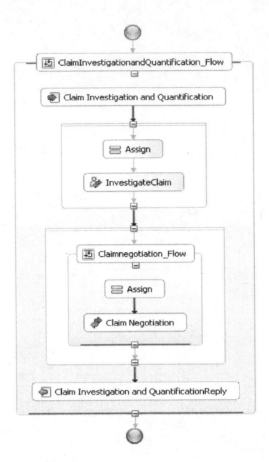

FIGURE 4.20
Claim investigation BPEL process.

Technical Domain View of the Claim Negotiation Process

The visual model of the BPEL process of the claim negotiation EPC model is shown in Figure 4.21. Apart from the additional steps for assigning values to process data, the BPEL model does not show any additional features compared to the original EPC.

The *make offer and communicate* activity is refined as another technical BPEL macroflow. This is also consistent with the EPC model, in which the corresponding function has also been refined by another EPC model. The refined BPEL is the technical representation of this refined EPC model. The visual model of the BPEL process of the *make offer and communicate* process is shown in Figure 4.22.

Technical Design of the Service Interfaces

We are implementing only one generic data structure for all macroflow processes, following the GENERIC PROCESS CONTROL STRUCTURE pattern. For this reason, the service design for the services will be fairly simple. Having only one generic process control structure

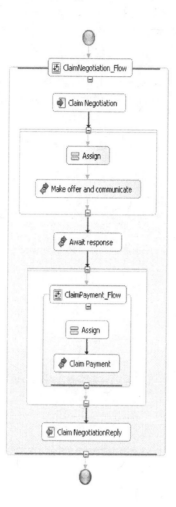

FIGURE 4.21
Claim negotiation BPEL process.

makes the macroflow processes flexible for future changes. The macroflow processes can easily be changed in their structure without any effect on the data structures of the processes and the invoked services. This is possible as all services use the same generic data structure for their parameterization. As a result, the parameter structures of the services are also not likely to change. This reduces time for implementing changes and avoids issues of data mismatch due to inconsistent structural changes to data at runtime (see the GENERIC PROCESS CONTROL STRUCTURE pattern description for more details).

In the EPC models of the claims business process, we have already identified which functions (process activities) will be implemented as automatic services. What needs to be done now is to specify the Web Services Description Language (WSDL) interface descriptions for these services. For all processes, we have identified 11 services that need to be specified in WSDL: *verifyPolicyCover, verifyClaimCover, storeClaim, identifyHandler, assignHandler, storeReserve, verifyAuthority, updateReserve, awaitResponse, createCommunication,* and *sendCommunication*. The services are associated to activities in the BPEL processes. The activities of the processes invoke the services synchronously as described in the SYNCHRONOUS SERVICE ACTIVITY pattern.

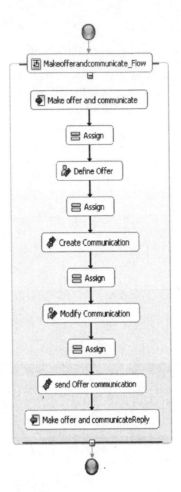

FIGURE 4.22
Make offer and communicate BPEL process.

The BPEL activities associated to user interaction with a corresponding user interface will be implemented via a service invocation as well. We design a dedicated *humanInteraction* service for this purpose. This service also operates with the same generic data structure as used by the BPEL processes and is invoked by the corresponding activity in the BPEL processes as a SYNCHRONOUS SERVICE ACTIVITY. As we use such a generic process control data structure, the parameters of the WSDLs will be the same for all these services. This concept also allows us to easily design new services and connect them to the BPEL processes as the requirements may evolve in the future regarding new services. As an example, we show the WSDL of the *verifyPolicyCover* service. The WSDL shows the generic parameterization representative for all the services.

```
<wsdl:definitions
  name="VerifypolicycoverInterface"
  targetNamespace="http://.../VerifypolicycoverInterface"
  xmlns:tns="http://.../VerifypolicycoverInterface"
  xmlns:wsdl="http://schemas.xmlsoap.org/wsdl/"
  xmlns:xsd="http://www.w3.org/2001/XMLSchema">
```

```
  <wsdl:types>
    <xsd:schema
        targetNamespace="http://.../VerifypolicycoverInterface"
        xmlns:bons0="http://provenSoa_Module/humantasks">
        <xsd:import namespace="http://.../BusinessObjectRef.xsd"/>
        <xsd:element name="data">
        <xsd:complexType>
          <xsd:sequence>
            <xsd:element
                maxOccurs="unbounded"
                minOccurs="0"
                name="input"
                nillable="true"
                type="bons0:BusinessObjectRef"/>
          </xsd:sequence>
        </xsd:complexType>
      </xsd:element>
      <xsd:element name="executeResponse">
        <xsd:complexType>
          <xsd:sequence>
            <xsd:element
                maxOccurs="unbounded"
                minOccurs="0"
                name="response"
                nillable="true"
                type="bons0:BusinessObjectRef"/>
          </xsd:sequence>
        </xsd:complexType>
      </xsd:element>
    </xsd:schema>
  </wsdl:types>
  <wsdl:message name="execute">
    <wsdl:part element="tns:execute" name="execute"/>
  </wsdl:message>
  <wsdl:message name="response">
  <wsdl:part
        element="tns:executeResponse"
        name="executeResponse"/>
  </wsdl:message>
  <wsdl:portType name="Verifypolicycover">
    <wsdl:documentation>
        Generated by WebSphere Business Modeler V6.2
    </wsdl:documentation>
    <wsdl:operation name="execute">
            <wsdl:input
                message="tns:execute"
                name="executeRequest"/>
            <wsdl:output
                message="tns:response"
                name="executeResponse"/>
    </wsdl:operation>
  </wsdl:portType>
</wsdl:definitions>
```

FIGURE 4.23
Create communication BPEL microflow.

FIGURE 4.24
Await response BPEL microflow.

Technical Design of Automatic Microflows and Service Components

There are two BPEL processes that have been refined as microflows. This refinement has been made due to the application of three additional patterns. To describe the application of these patterns, we first need to illustrate the microflows. The first process that contains a microflow is the make offer and communicate process. Within this process, there is a *create communication* SYNCHRONOUS SERVICE ACTIVITY. This activity has been refined as a microflow. The model of the microflow is presented in Figure 4.23.

The second process is the claim negotiation process, which actually contains the make offer and communicate process as a submacroflow. The claim negotiation process includes an *awaitResponse* SYNCHRONOUS SERVICE ACTIVITY. This activity has also been refined as a microflow. The model of the microflow is presented in Figure 4.24.

The purpose of these two microflows is to coordinate the communication regarding the offer to the claimant, which is done, for instance, via a letter or an e-mail. This coordination includes the corresponding receipt of a response from the claimant regarding the offer. The first microflow deals with the creation of the communication and the second microflow with the expected response. The reason why this has been designed this way actually results from the business requirements.

The idea is to consolidate all communication to the same claimant, for example, if there are claims being processed for the same claimant in parallel. This may happen relatively often for business customers. One can imagine a set of buildings being damaged by fire involving several claims that refer to the same claimant (company). To optimize the communication with the claimant, the idea is to gather all communication for the same claimant first and then to send all gathered communication to the claimant in one go. That means, for instance, in case of a letter, for which a claimant has placed five claims, the claimant should receive only one letter and not five. This would decrease postal costs and increase customer satisfaction. The insurance company gains great benefit, especially for larger business customers, when costs are saved and customer satisfaction is improved. The mechanisms can also be used for other types of communication not associated to claims (e.g., information about new insurance products). This would be another element of reusability that provides additional benefit. To achieve this consolidation of the communication and to decouple it from the business processes, two patterns have been applied: REGISTER FOR ACTION and BUNDLE PROCESS AGENT.

The REGISTER FOR ACTION pattern enables the flexible execution of some kind of action on a target system considering dependencies to business processes running in parallel. The flexibility is achieved by offering registration and deregistration services that can be invoked by those parallel-running business processes. The action on the target system is delayed until all registered processes have deregistered. In our example, this applies to claims processes registering for sending some communication to a certain claimant. The actual sending of the communication is delayed until all registered processes have deregistered. For this reason, the first microflow shows a *register* activity and the second microflow *deRegister* activity, invoking the corresponding services.

The actual sending of the communication is done by the send offer communication SYNCHRONOUS SERVICE ACTIVITY of the make offer and communicate BPEL process. This activity invokes a service that sends the communication (object). There may be many processes in parallel invoking this service to send communication (objects) containing offers for claims to the same claimant. This communication needs to be bundled in some way. The actual bundling (e.g., gathering the communication sent by the different processes and generating a consolidated offer letter) is a complex task that needs to be considered by a special service component. Possibly, this complex task needs to be addressed by a dedicated BPEL process that describes how the communication is packaged and sent.

To achieve this, we design a BUNDLE PROCESS AGENT service component that gathers all the communication objects and processes the communication in a consolidated way by executing a BPEL process that defines the steps how to actually package and send the communication. The bundle process will be executed when all processes being registered for the same claimant have deregistered. This is flexibly possible by applying the REGISTER FOR ACTION and BUNDLE PROCESS AGENT patterns in combination.

The wait for response deadline SYNCHRONOUS SERVICE ACTIVITY of the second microflow implements a third pattern, which is a CONDITION DEADLINE SERVICE. The deadline for receiving a response may be set by the claims handler, for instance, in relation to certain circumstances of the claim or the policy. For this reason, this deadline will be associated to the claim object in the database. The CONDITION DEADLINE SERVICE terminates when the response is received within the deadline or when the deadline expires.

Note that both microflows only contain automatic services without human interaction and are for this reason classified as microflows. This example serves to point out that the idea of microflows being *rather* short-running flows is not to be taken literally in all contexts; for example, in this example the deadline may be days or even weeks ahead. In this

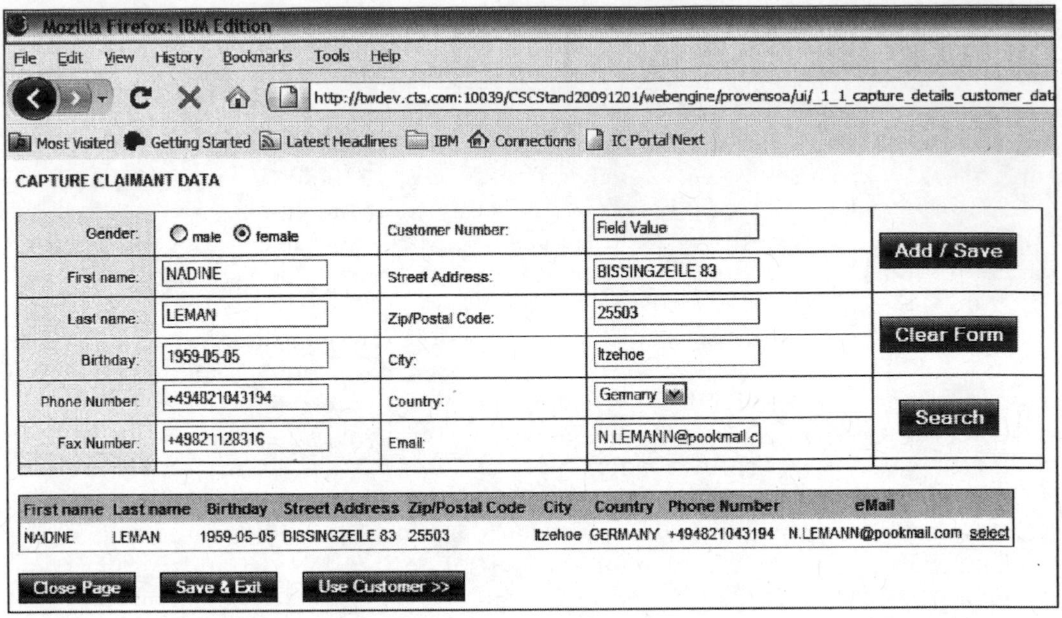

FIGURE 4.25
Screen for capturing claimant data.

case, the important aspect is that the services cannot be separated and need to be executed as one automatic transaction without human interaction. For this reason, they rather classify as microflows.

User Interface Implementation

In the claims business processes, we identified 10 user interfaces that need to be implemented. Those 10 user interfaces can be named *capture and verify details, determine special handling, capture further details, reserve money, determine investigation approach, investigate claim, determine outcome, select claims handler, make offer to customer,* and *edit communication.* The user interfaces are implemented with WebSphere Portal. As an example, we illustrate the WebSphere Portal implementation of the *capture and verify details* user interface from the claim notification process. The user interface contains three major screens for capturing the claimant data, selection of a policy, and confirmation of the data. Figure 4.25 shows the initial screen for capturing claimant data.

When the claimant data is captured, the interface navigates to the next screen to select a policy for the claimant. As one claimant may have several policies, the right policy needs to be selected. Figure 4.26 shows the dialogue to select the policy.

When the policy is selected, the final step in this user interface is the validation and confirmation of the data. The process activity (i.e., the use case microflow) ends with this screen. The data confirmation screen is presented in Figure 4.27.

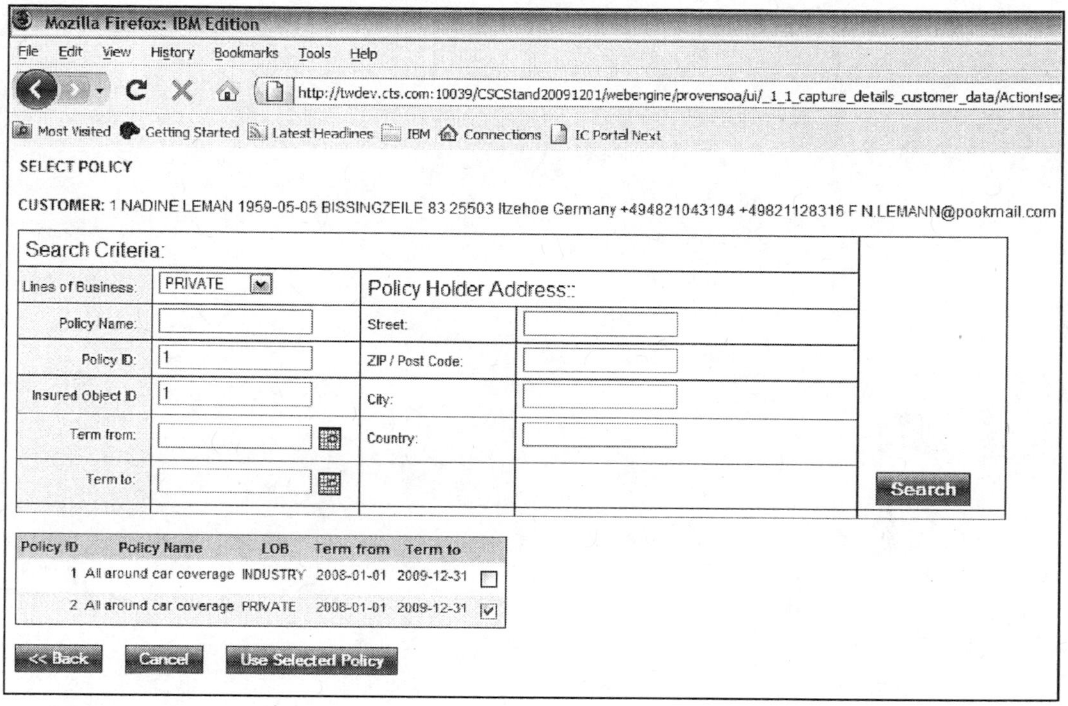

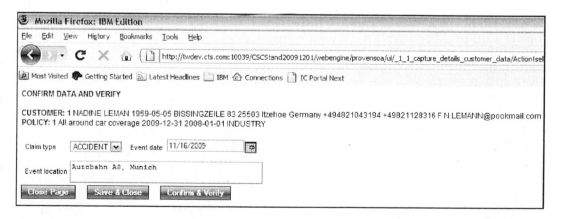

FIGURE 4.26
Select policy screen.

FIGURE 4.27
Confirm data and verify screen.

5

Decomposing and Executing Business-Driven and Technical Processes

Introduction

In many business domains, there is a need to model the processes of the business. A process model defines the behavior of its process instances. The process model is the type of the process instances. That is, process instances are instantiations of the same kind of behavior. Process models are usually expressed in a process modeling language or notation. There are more high-level business-oriented or domain-oriented languages and notations, such as BPMN (Business Process Modeling Notation), EPC (event-driven process chain), Adonis process flows, Unified Modelling Language (UML) activity diagrams, and so on. These focus on expressing the behavior of a business or a domain. In addition, there are technical process modeling or workflow languages that define how a process behavior can be executed on a process or workflow engine. Examples are BPEL (Business Process Execution Language), jPDL (jBPM Process Definition Language), the Windows Workflow Foundation, and XML Process Definition Language (XPDL).* In both cases, the process modeling languages define which elements can be used in the process models.

Consider the following process model example in BPMN. Figure 5.1 shows a simple order-handling process in which first an order is received, then the credit card is verified, and only if it is valid, the process proceeds. Otherwise, the customer is informed of the invalid credit card. Next, in parallel, the order shipment and charging for the order happens. Finally, the order status is reported to the customer.

This process model can describe different things with regard to an organization, depending on the purpose of the business process modeling, such as the following:

- The process model describes how order handling should be performed, as a guideline or documentation of the business. The people involved in the execution of the process instances can deviate from the predefined process if it makes sense. For instance, in some exceptional cases, shipment might be postponed, but once the shipment date is fixed, the order status reply can be sent. This makes sense, for example, in a small business, in which people fulfill the order-handling process and have an overview of the orders they handle.

---

* XPDL actually is not an execution language but a process design format that can be used to store and exchange process diagrams. However, XPDL elements can have attributes that specify execution information. Some process engines, such as Enhydra Shark [Enhydra. Enhydra Shark. http://shark.enhydra.org, 2008], use XPDL directly as their execution language.

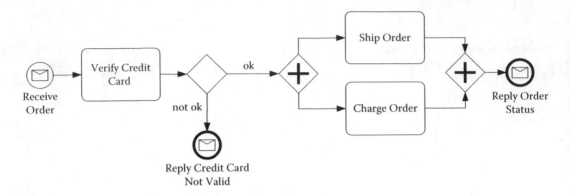

FIGURE 5.1
Simple order-handling process in BPMN. (From C. Hentrich and U. Zdun. A pattern language for process exe-cution and integration design in service-oriented architectures. *Springer LNCS Transactions on Pattern Languages of Programs*, 1, 136–191, 2009.)

- The process model defines how exactly the process instances must behave. An automated process management system ensures that each process instance fol-lows the process model. This makes sense, for instance, in an organization in which a high volume of similar orders with only a few exceptions must be pro-cessed, and the activities in the process are mostly automated. People only handle exceptional cases.

- The process model defines how the process instances should behave in the future. Process modeling is part of a business change initiative, for example, with the goal to improve the business performance. This is also one subgoal of many initiatives intro-ducing service-oriented architectures (SOAs). Such initiatives aim to make the busi-ness processes explicit, optimize them, and then support them through technology.

- The process model has explanatory purposes, such as one of the following: It defines the rationale for what happens in an information system. It links to the requirements of the information technology (IT) system. It defines the data of the process that can be used for reporting purposes. It enables management or other nontechnical stakeholders to analyze and plan the IT system.

Many combinations of these reasons for process modeling are possible, and many other reasons exist. This chapter deals with the situation that you model your business processes and want to implement them using IT support.

The first issue that must be addressed is the semantic difference between a domain-oriented business process like the one depicted previously and an executable process. The BPMN order-handling example is not executable because many technical details are omit-ted. Some examples in the sample process are the following:

- It is unclear how the activities of the process are realized. For instance, the credit card verification could be realized as a service, a subprocess, a piece of program-ming language code, a script, and so on. For a service, for example, we need the endpoint information necessary to access it, such as the host and port where the service is deployed as well as the interface of the service. But, this technical infor-mation is missing in the BPMN example process.

- It is unclear how the data is passed from the incoming message to the process activities. For instance, which credit card information is provided, and how is it used in the process?

- It is unclear how the data is mapped to the interface of a component or service that performs activities, such as credit card verification. How are interface and data differences handled? It is also unclear how the results are mapped into the process, so that the control structures of the process, such as the decision node following the credit card verification in the BPMN example process, can use it.

- It is unclear how exceptions and timeouts are to be handled in this process. For example, what happens if the credit card verification activity never replies or replies with an error message?

All this information can be provided in technical modeling languages, such as BPEL. For instance, a small excerpt follows from a simplistic BPEL process, implementing the BPMN process discussed. In BPEL, the process activities are implemented as services. The example excerpt just shows the code needed to receive the initial message, copy some variables to an input type used in the interface of the *VerifyCreditCard* service, and then invoke that service.

```
<sequence>
 <receive name="ReceiveOrder" createInstance="yes"
    partnerLink="Customer" operation="OrderHandlingOperation"
    xmlns:tns="http://j2ee.netbeans.org/wsdl/OrderHandling"
    portType="tns:OrderHandlingPortType"
    variable="OrderHandlingOperationIn"/>
  <assign name="AssignCreditCardInfo">
    <copy>
      <from>$OrderHandlingOperationIn.
           orderHandlingInputMessage/ns0:creditCardNumber</from>
      <to>$IsValidIn.parameters/number</to>
    </copy>
    <copy>
      <from>$OrderHandlingOperationIn.
           orderHandlingInputMessage/ns0:creditCardHolder</from>
      <to>$IsValidIn.parameters/holder</to>
    </copy>
    <copy>
      <from>$OrderHandlingOperationIn.
           orderHandlingInputMessage/ns0:creditCardSecurityCode</from>
      <to>$IsValidIn.parameters/securityNumber</to>
    </copy>
  </assign>
  <invoke name="VerifyCreditCard" partnerLink="VerifyCreditCard"
    operation="isValid" xmlns:tns="http://orderHandling/"
    portType="tns:VerifyCreditCard" inputVariable="IsValidIn"
    outputVariable="IsValidOut"/>
```

In addition to the BPEL code, we require the WSDL (Web Services Description Language) files that describe the interfaces of the services and the interface of this process and the XML (Extensible Markup Language) Schema definitions of the data types that are passed.

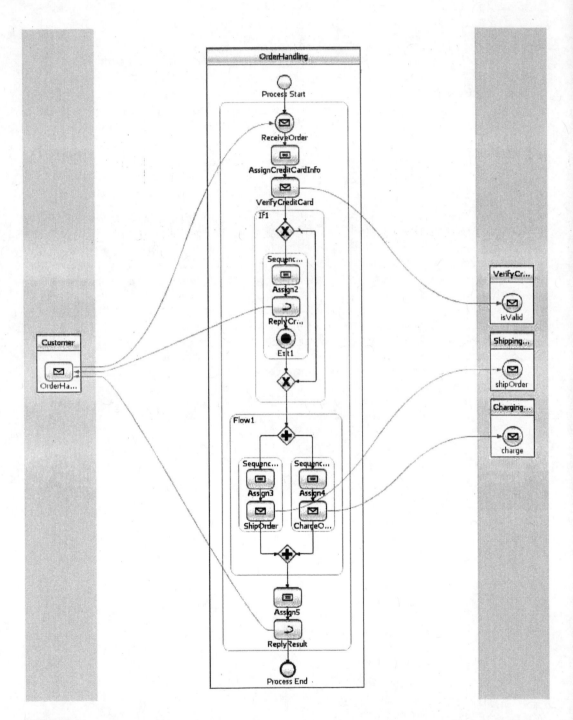

FIGURE 5.2
Simple BPEL process implementation in NetBeans. (From C. Hentrich and U. Zdun. A pattern language for process execution and integration design in service-oriented architectures. *Springer LNCS Transactions on Pattern Languages of Programs*, 1, 136–191, 2009.)

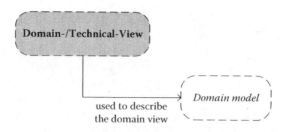

FIGURE 5.3
Pattern relationship domain/technical view.

All these technical specifications are hard to understand and complex even for technical experts. For that reason, many modeling tools exist to create and change them. For example, Figure 5.2 shows a simplistic BPEL process implementation of our order-handling process modeled in the BPEL modeler of the NetBeans IDE. In addition to modeling BPEL graphically, designer tools offer support for designing WSDL interfaces, XML Schema definitions, and data mappings.

If process execution is the main goal of the process modeling, it seems to make sense to model the processes directly in BPEL using such a modeling tool instead of modeling them in BPMN. However, it is rather seldom the case that process execution is the only goal that process modeling is needed for. For example, in most cases when business processes are used, the technical experts are not domain experts themselves and hence need to discuss the processes with the domain experts to incorporate the domain knowledge in the right way. BPEL is usually not a good representation for tasks that involve domain experts because BPEL processes are overloaded with technical details. This is certainly valid for the BPEL code itself. But, it is also the case for what is shown in BPEL modeling tools: While these technical process-modeling tools are a helpful aid for developers, the models they expose are still pretty technical and complex. It is awkward to use them for the discussion with domain experts and usually impossible to let domain experts themselves work with these tools. For the same reasons, they are also not the best solution for technical stakeholders if their work requires only getting a quick overview of the existing processes. The technical process code or the technical process modeling tools should only be used for in-depth technical work.

The DOMAIN/TECHNICAL VIEW pattern solves this problem by splitting the models into two views:

- A high-level, domain-oriented view that represents the process in a technology-independent fashion, omitting all details not needed for the domain tasks
- A low-level, technical view that contains the elements of the domain view and additional technical details

This pattern is applicable not only for process models, but also for all other kinds of models that must be shown in two views. An example is a data model that has a logical data view and a technology-dependent view. Here, the technology-dependent view would model the mapping of the logical view to a database (access) technology. Another example is a class model that represents a high-level DOMAIN MODEL* [Fow02, BHS07a] and

---

* The domain model pattern [Fow02] describes a model of the domain that incorporates both behavior and data.

an implementation model showing how the domain model elements are realized using, for example, a component technology. This pattern relationship is illustrated in Figure 5.3.

So far, we did not distinguish different kinds of processes. However, in a typical SOA in the enterprise field we can observe different kinds of behavior that could be modeled as process flows. For instance, there are strategic, very-high-level business processes that are hard to automate or support through technology. These can be broken down—sometimes in a number of steps—into more specific business processes, such as the order-handling example. The result is long-running business processes, perhaps with human involvement, which can possibly be mapped to a supporting technology. Finally, when implementing these processes, we also observe more processes that are short running and technical. For instance, the verification of the credit card in the example could consist of three steps, each calling an external Web service. Or, the shipping of an order could require a few steps guiding a human operator through a number of graphical user interface (GUI) dialogs for approving the automatically selected inventory items, approving the sending of an invoice, and so on.

The distinction between long-running, business-oriented and short-running, technical processes is an important conceptual distinction that helps us to design process activities at the right level of granularity. In addition, the technical properties of the two kinds of processes are different. For instance, for implementing long-running processes it is typically not appropriate to use ACID transactions. ACID is a term related to database transactions. In the database context, a transaction is a single, logical operation performed on the data. ACID stands for *atomicity, consistency, isolation, and durability*—a set of properties that guarantee that database transactions are processed reliably. Database transactions are either performed completely or not performed at all. If they are not performed, they are "rolled back." This is feasible because database transactions are rather short running. Business transactions, as represented by a business process, in contrast are rather long running. In long-running transactions, it is infeasible to lock resources for the duration of the whole process, which might well be days, weeks, or months. Hence, long-running transactions do not support the ACID properties. Instead of rollbacks, they can only use compensation actions to handle failures. ACID transactions can be used inside of long-running transactions for smaller, short-running tasks. For example, it might be perfectly feasible for more short-running processes of only a few service invocations to lock some resources in a database.

Consider a simple example for short-running and long-running transactions: an application that transfers funds from one account to another. Both accounts can be locked for this transaction to ensure the ACID properties. This is feasible because the whole transaction only takes a few milliseconds. In contrast, an application that requires a human approval after transferring funds is of a long-running nature and should not lock the account resources until the human operator acts. Instead, the transfer should be handled using an ACID transaction, and the following approval should be handled in a long-running transaction with a compensation action that is triggered if the approval is not given. In this compensation action, another ACID transaction that reverses the effects of the first ACID transaction is launched.

The MACRO-/MICROFLOW pattern provides a clear guideline on how to design process models following these observations. In the pattern, we refer to the long-running processes using the term *macroflow*. We use the term *microflow* to refer to the short-running, technical processes. The pattern advises us to refine macroflows in a strictly hierarchical fashion—starting from high-level, strategic processes to long-running, executable processes. The activities of these executable macroflows can further be refined by microflows.

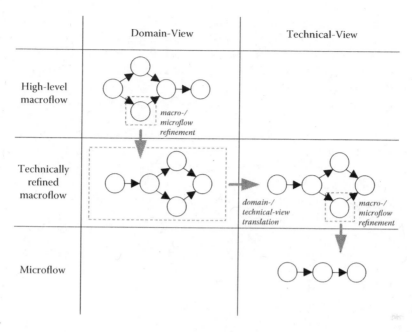

FIGURE 5.4
Exemplification of refining domain view macroflows into technical view microflows.

Microflow activities can be refined by other microflows. That is, an activity of a higher-level process model is refined by a lower-level process model in the form of a subprocess.

The MACRO-/MICROFLOW pattern is closely related to the DOMAIN-/TECHNICAL VIEW pattern (see Figure 5.4): The highest-level macroflows usually only have domain views. The lowest-level microflows often only have a technical view. But, the models in between—in particular the executable macroflows as in the example—have both views as they are relevant to both technical and nontechnical stakeholders.

Figure 5.4 exemplifies the refinement process. It considers two levels of macroflows and one level of microflow. The high-level macroflows are used only by domain experts. Hence, they are only needed in the domain view. Activities of these high-level macroflows are realized by lower-level macroflows. These are at a technically refined level; hence, they can be translated into technical views following the DOMAIN/TECHNICAL VIEW pattern. Finally, some activities of these macroflows are implemented using microflows. These microflows only exist in a technical view, as they are only considered by the technical experts.

The MACRO-/MICROFLOW pattern advises to use a suitable technology for realizing macroflows and microflows. Of course, it is possible to implement both macroflows and microflows using ordinary programming language code. But, often we can provide better support. For instance, macroflows often should be supported with process persistence, model-based change and redeployment, process management and monitoring, and so on. The MACROFLOW ENGINE pattern describes how to support a macroflow using process or workflow technology. An example MACROFLOW ENGINE that could be used in the example is a BPEL process engine.

For microflows, supporting technology is more seldom used. However, if rapid process change or reuse of existing functionality is needed, MICROFLOW ENGINES can be useful. We distinguish MICROFLOW ENGINES for microflows containing human interactions, such as pageflow engines, and MICROFLOW ENGINES for microflows supporting automatic activities, such as message brokers.

In any case, macroflows and microflows can be implemented using either an engine or ordinary services implementations that orchestrate the flows without technology support. For implementing microflows, this is actually a common implementation option. Macroflows are less often implemented without technology support because they require the implementation of functions for management and persistence of long-running flows as explained, which is more work. In general, if no engine technology is used, it is advisable to follow the SERVICE ABSTRACTION LAYER pattern [Vog01] that explains how to architecturally group the services together and avoid scattering their code in one or more components that also realize other tasks. Both MACROFLOW ENGINES and MICROFLOW ENGINES can be seen as a SERVICE ABSTRACTION LAYER for the services they provide, but they go further by providing technology support for implementing the flows.

Figure 5.5 illustrates the relationships of the MACRO-/MICROFLOW pattern to the other patterns introduced in this chapter.

DOMAIN/TECHNICAL VIEW

Various stakeholders participate in the development, evolution, and use of an SOA. Typical technical stakeholders are the developers, designers, architects, testers, and system administrators. Typical nontechnical stakeholders are the domain experts of the domain for which the SOA is created, the management, and the customers.

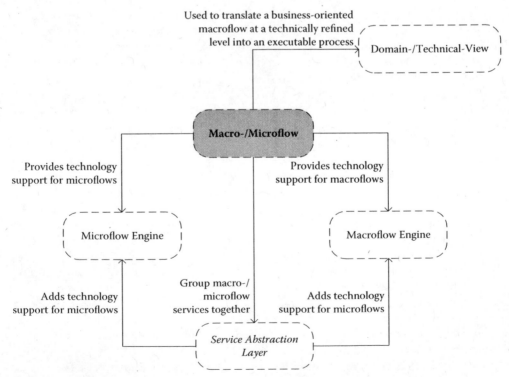

FIGURE 5.5
Pattern relationships of macro-/microflow.

How should executable models be designed if both technical and nontechnical stake-holders need to participate in model creation and evolution?

Designing one model for a number of distinct stakeholders is challenging because the different stakeholders require different information for their work with the model, as well as different levels of detail and abstraction. A typical—often problematic—case in this context is that a model depicts a concern from the domain for which the SOA is created. So, the model is, on the one hand, important for the communication with and among the domain experts, but on the other hand, in an SOA many such models should be automatically processed and executed.

Executable model means that a model is interpreted by an execution engine, or the model representation is compiled and then executed on an execution engine. Here are some examples of executable models:

- A BPEL business process model that is executed on a BPEL engine.
- A role-based access control model that is interpreted by an access control enforcement component.
- A UML or EMF* model that is transformed by the generator of a model-driven software development solution into executable code. In this case, the model is interpreted at the design of the SOA, but at runtime of the generator.

To be executable, a model must contain all technical information needed for execution. The original intent of modeling is often different, however: to serve as a means of communication among stakeholders and for system understanding. The information needed for execution is usually targeted only at one type of stakeholders: the technical developers. This in turn makes the models hard to understand for the domain experts and, in general, hard to use for tasks that require getting an overview of the design. The reason is that the executable models are simply overloaded with too many technical details.

Just consider business processes as one example of SOA models. Domain experts usually design with tools that use diagrams such as or similar to diagrams in BPMN, EPC, Adonis process flows, UML activity diagrams, and so on. The diagrams usually contain only the information relevant for the business. Often, such models are hard to automate because they miss important technical information, such as how data is passed or transformed or where a service to be invoked is located and with which interface it is accessed. Technical process modeling languages such as BPEL, jPDL, Windows Workflow Foundation, or XPDL, in contrast, contain all this information. This makes them not only useful for technical execution but also complex and hard to understand for domain-oriented tasks.

Provide each model required both for domain-oriented tasks, such as getting an overview of the design, and technical tasks, such as execution of the model, in two views: a domain view and a technical view. All elements from the domain view are either imported or mapped into the technical view. The technical view contains additional elements that enrich the domain model elements with the technical details necessary for execution and other technical tasks (see Figure 5.6).

---

* Eclipse Modeling Framework; see [Ecl09].

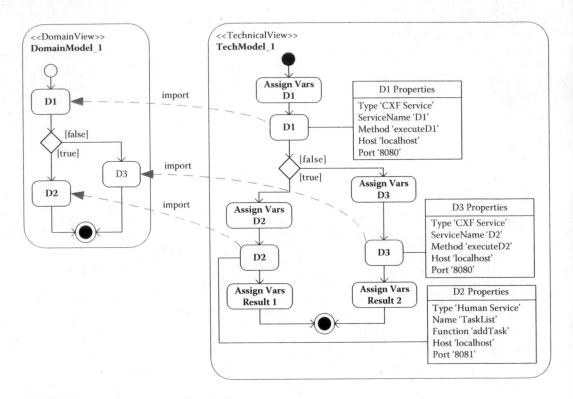

FIGURE 5.6
Mapping a domain view to a technical view. (From C. Hentrich and U. Zdun. A pattern language for process execution and integration design in service-oriented architectures. *Springer LNCS Transactions on Pattern Languages of Programs*, 1, 136–191, 2009.)

To realize the DOMAIN/TECHNICAL VIEW pattern, the elements from the domain view must be imported or mapped into the technical view. This can be done in various ways. Basically, the differences between these variants of the pattern are the mechanisms used for the import and the mapping and the degree of automation.

- The simplest variant of the pattern is to perform a manual translation to map the domain model elements into the technical view. First, for each domain model element, the most appropriate modeling construct for representing the domain model element in the technical view is chosen, and then the translation is performed. Next, the technical model is enriched with all information needed for technical tasks, such as execution and deployment. This variant of the pattern has the benefit of flexibility: Any modeling languages can be mapped in any suitable way. As a creative design step is needed for the mapping, no formal link or mapping between the modeling languages is required, but the translation can happen on a case-by-case basis. This variant incurs the drawback that—for each change— manual effort is required for performing the translation, and consistency between the models must be ensured manually.

- Sometimes, translation tools between a modeling language for domain models and a modeling language for technical models exist, such as a BPMN-to-BPEL mapping tool. In the mapping process, somehow the additional technical information must be added. For instance, it can be given to the translation tool using an additional configuration file. Using this additional information and the domain view model, the translation tool generates a technical view corresponding to the domain view. This variant of the pattern can potentially reduce the manual mapping effort and ensure consistency automatically. It can even be realized for two distinct modeling languages. However, not always does an automatic mapping provide the best mapping. Especially for two languages with highly different semantics, the automatic mapping can cause problems. For instance, technical models can become hard to understand and debug if they are automatically generated from a domain model with different semantics.

- If both models, technical view and domain view, are described based on a common metamodel, ordinary model extension mechanisms, such as package import, can be used. Extensions in the technical view are then simply added using ordinary extension mechanisms for model elements, such as inheritance or delegation. This variant makes it easy to maintain consistency between the view models. Modeling tools can, for instance, allow designers to start modeling in the domain view and enrich it with technical details in property views. As an alternative, you can generate the domain view from the technical view model. In this case, you just strip the technical information provided in the technical view.

If the domain view is not generated from the technical view, for all the imported domain model elements, all changes should be performed in the domain view. They should then be propagated to the technical view. This means the following for the three variants of the pattern:

- If manual translation is used, translating the changes made to the domain models is required. Change propagation is a main drawback of this variant: If changes are made to one model and they are forgotten to be propagated or incorrectly propagated, the models are becoming inconsistent.

- If an automatic translation tool is used, the tool must be rerun, and it regenerates the domain elements in the technical view. An alternative is a round-trip translation: Changes to the technical view can be translated back into the domain view. Round-trip translation is often not advisable, as tools tend to generate hard-to-read source code, and creating a well-working round-trip tool set is a substantial amount of work.

- If integration based on a common metamodel and package imports are used, changes to the domain model are automatically reflected in the technical view. Hence, no efforts for change propagation are required in most cases. Only if changes cause incompatibilities in dependent models must the models be adapted accordingly.

Example: Manual BPMN-to-BPEL Translation

We have seen a simple example of a manual BPMN-to-BPEL translation in the introduction of this chapter.

Example: View-Based Modeling Framework

The View-Based Modeling Framework (VbMF) [TZD07] is a model-driven infrastructure for process-driven SOAs. It uses the model-driven approach to compose business processes, services, and other models that are relevant in an SOA. VbMF abstracts each concern in its own view model. Each VbMF view model is a (semi)formalized representation of a particular SOA concern. The view model specifies the entities and relationships that can appear in a view.

In particular, there is a core view model from which each other view model is derived. The main task of the core view model is to provide integration points for the various view models defined as part of VbMF, as well as extension points for enabling the extension with views for other concerns.

The view models derived from the core are *domain views*. Example domain views are collaboration, information, orchestration, long-running transactions, data, and compliance metadata. In addition to these central concerns, many other concerns can be defined. Each of these view models is extending either the core model or one of the other view models. These view models contain no technology-specific information but only information understandable to the domain expert.

In addition, VbMF defines a second level of extensional view models, derived from these domain view models: the *technical views*. For specific technologies realizing the domain views, such as BPEL, WSDL, BPEL4People, WS-HumanTask, Hibernate, Java services, HTML (Hypertext Markup Language), or PDF (portable document format), VbMF provides technical view models, which add details to the general view models that are required to depict the specifics of these technologies. Figure 5.7 provides an overview of the VbMF view models and their relationships.

The integration of view elements is done using modeling abstractions, such as inheritance and associations, as well as matching algorithms, such as name-based matching. Integration is performed in the transformation templates of the *openArchitectureWare* code generator.

The separation of view abstraction levels helps enhance the adaptability of the process-driven SOA models to business changes. For instance, the business experts analyze and modify the domain views to deal with change requirements at the level of the business. The technical experts work with technical views to define necessary configurations so that the generated code can be deployed into the corresponding runtime (i.e., the process engines and Web service frameworks). This view-based separation into two view layers, domain views and technical views, also helps to better support the various stakeholders of the SOA: Each stakeholder views only the information necessary for the stakeholder-specific work. Hence, the view-based approach supports involving domain experts in the design of SOAs.

Example: BPMN-to-BPEL Transformation Tools

The BPMN2BPEL tool [Bpm08] is an Eclipse plug-in for transforming BPMN processes, modeled in Eclipse, to BPEL. Like many other such tools, the tool can only translate the information that is present in BPMN, which might mean that technical details are not considered and semantic differences between BPEL and BPMN are not translated in the best way.

It has been discussed [Dik08] how to transform a BPMN model from the Oracle Business Process Analysis Suite to an executable BPEL process. The article also discussed the semantic differences between BPMN and BPEL. If processes are not translatable using the tool, the article advised changing the BPMN process by removing arbitrary cycles that are valid in BPMN but not in BPEL.

Example: Sculptor

Sculptor [For08] is a cartridge for openArchitectureWare, a model-driven software development infrastructure. Sculptor enables developers to focus on the business domain view, which is designed in a textual, domain-specific language using concepts from Eric Evans's book *Domain-Driven Design* [Eva04], such as service, module, entity,

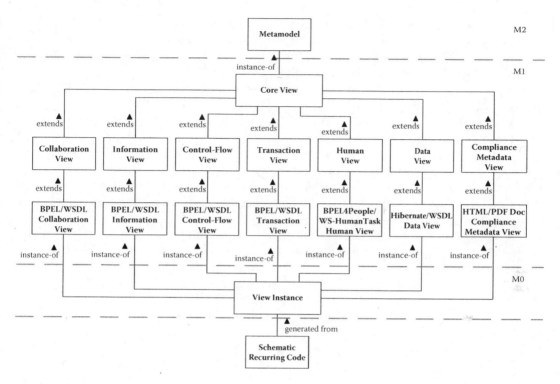

FIGURE 5.7

Overview of the VbMF view models. (From C. Hentrich and U. Zdun. A pattern language for process execution and integration design in service-oriented architectures. *Springer LNCS Transactions on Pattern Languages of Programs*, 1, 136–191, 2009.)

value object, repository, and so on. The code generator is used to generate Java code for well-known frameworks, such as the Spring Framework, Spring Web Flow, JSF, Hibernate, and Java EE. The technical view is added using configurations and manually written code.

MACRO-/MICROFLOW

If your system is or should be described using process models, it makes sense to think about automating the processes using process technology. Usually, if an organization decides to use business processes to depict their business, high-level and mostly business-oriented models are created.

How can conceptual or business-oriented process models be implemented or realized?

One important aspect to consider when implementing or realizing business processes is the nature of the processes to be executed. For instance, many typical business processes are long-running flows, involving human tasks. Such a business process can run for many hours, days, or even weeks before it is finished. In such cases, the process technology must support persisting the process instances, as the process states should not get lost if a machine crashes. The process instance should not occupy memory and other system resources when it is not active. It should be possible to monitor and manage the process instance at runtime. Also, the processes should be interruptible via a process management interface. Such functionalities are supported by process or workflow engines. Process engines usually express processes in a process execution language, such as BPEL, jPDL, Windows Workflow Foundation, or XPDL.

In contrast to the long-running kind of flows, short-running flows need to be considered. These often have a more technical nature and rather transactional or session-based semantics. One example is a process in which a number of steps are needed to perform a booking on a set of back-end systems. Another example is guiding a human user through a pageflow of a few Web pages. In these examples, process instance persistence is not really needed, and typical process execution languages make it rather awkward to express these flows. Hence, it makes sense to realize them using special-purpose modeling languages and technology. For instance, a message flow model and message broker technology or a pageflow model and pageflow engine technology could be used to realize the two examples.

Please note that the named technologies are just examples: The distinction of short-running and long-running flows is first a conceptual distinction. Any suitable technology can be chosen. For instance, it is also possible to implement both short-running and long-running flows using ordinary programming language code (e.g., Java source code or code written in a scripting language)—may be provided as a service. However, as in both cases some features, such as process persistence, wait states, concurrency handling, and so on, are needed repeatedly, reusing existing technologies often makes sense.

Finally, in some cases, it turns out that automating the process is not useful or feasible. Then, an entirely manual process fulfilled by people and using no automation whatsoever can be chosen as a realization of a process as well. Another example is high-level processes, such as strategic business processes of an organization, which would need concretization before they could be implemented using technology at all.

Unfortunately, in practice often long-running and short-running flows, as well as technical and nontechnical concerns, are intermixed. Often, concerns with different semantics are modeled in one model. This practice frequently causes confusion as business analysts do not understand the level of technical detail, and technical modelers do not have the expertise to understand the business issues fully. Thus, these models tend to fail their primary purpose: to communicate and understand the processes and the overall system design.

In addition, models are sometimes mapped to the wrong technology. For instance, a short-running transactional flow should not be realized using a process engine for long-running flows, and vice versa, as the different technologies exhibit significantly different technical characteristics.

Structure a process model into two kinds of processes: macroflows and microflows. Strictly separate the macroflow from the microflow and use the microflow only for refinements of the macroflow activities. The macroflows represent the long-running, interruptible process flows, which depict the business-oriented process perspective. The microflows represent the short-running, transactional flows, which depict the IT-oriented process perspective (see Figure 5.8).

The MACRO-/MICROFLOW pattern provides a conceptual solution in which two kinds of flows are distinguished:

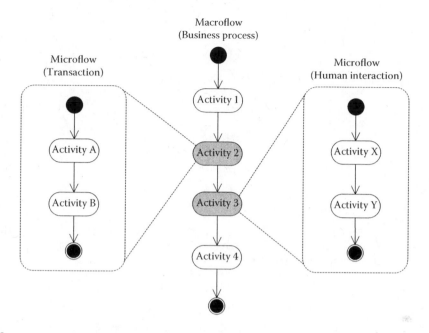

FIGURE 5.8
Structuring macroflow and microflow. (From C. Hentrich and U. Zdun. A pattern language for process execution and integration design in service-oriented architectures. *Springer LNCS Transactions on Pattern Languages of Programs*, 1, 136–191, 2009.)

- *Macroflows* represent the business-oriented, long-running processes.
- *Microflows* represent the IT-oriented, short-running processes.

The MACRO-/MICROFLOW pattern interprets a microflow as a refinement of a macroflow activity. That is, a microflow represents a subprocess that runs within a macroflow activity. This separation of macroflow and microflow has the benefit that modeling can be performed in several steps of refinement. First, the higher-level macroflow business process can be designed, considering that business process activities will be further refined by microflows. Vice versa, if certain microflows already exist, the business process can be modeled accordingly, so that these IT processes fit in as business process activities at the macroflow level. However, this also incurs the drawback that the conceptual separation of the MACRO-/MICROFLOW pattern must be understood and followed by modelers, which requires additional discipline.

The refinement concepts of the MACRO-/MICROFLOW often require adjusting IT processes and business processes according to the concerns of both domains—business and IT—to bring them together. The modeling effort is higher than in usual business modeling as more aspects need to be taken into consideration, and at all refinement levels, activities must be designed at the right level of granularity.

A microflow model can be linked to one or many macroflow activities. The consequence is that the types of relationships between macroflow and microflow are well defined. Microflows and macroflows both have a defined input and output, that is, a well-defined functional interface. However, the functional interfaces between IT processes and business processes must be understood and considered by all stakeholder-manipulating process models.

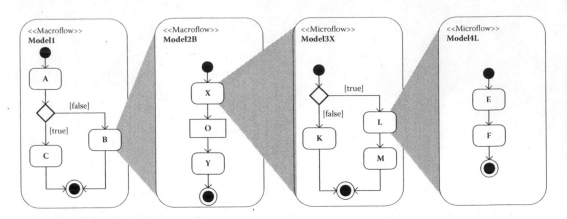

FIGURE 5.9

Example of macroflow and microflow refinement. (From C. Hentrich and U. Zdun. A pattern language for process execution and integration design in service-oriented architectures. *Springer LNCS Transactions on Pattern Languages of Programs*, 1, 136–191, 2009.)

Multiple levels of both macroflows and microflows can be modeled. That is, high-level macroflows can be refined by lower-level macroflows. The same is possible for microflows. The refinement is strictly hierarchical: An activity in the high-level process is always refined by a low-level subprocess, realizing the activity. A microflow is never refined by a macroflow. Figure 5.9 shows an example of two levels of macroflow refinement and two levels of microflow refinement.

The microflow can be directly invoked as a subprocess that runs automatically, or it can represent an activity flow that includes human interaction. As a result, two types of links between a macroflow activity and a microflow exist:

- *Link to a microflow for an automatic activity (transaction):* A short-running, transactional IT process defines a detailed process model of an automatic activity in a higher-level business process. It represents an executed business function or transaction at the business process level.

- *Link to a microflow for human interaction:* If an activity of a business process is associated to a user interface (UI), the IT process is a definition of the coherent process flow that depicts the human interaction. This process flow is initiated if a human user executes the business process activity.

The microflow level and the macroflow level distinguish conceptual process levels. Ideally, both levels should be supported by suitable technology. An example for a macroflow technology is a process execution engine, such as a BPEL engine. An exemplary microflow technology for automatic activities is a message broker that provides a message flow modeling language. For short-running human interactions, technologies such as pageflow engines can be used.

Both types of microflows are often hard-coded using ordinary code written in a programming language. Sometimes, an embedded scripting language is used to support flexible microflow definition within another language, such as Java or C#. If this implementation option is chosen, a best practice is to provide the microflows as independent deployment units (e.g., one service per microflow), so that they can be flexibly changed and redeployed. Microflow implementations should be architecturally grouped together (e.g., in a SERVICE ABSTRACTION LAYER [Vog01]) and not scattered across the code of one or more components, which also realize other tasks.

In the ideal case, the modeling languages, techniques, and tools should support the conceptual separation of macroflows and microflows, as well as the definition of links between macroflow activities and microflows using the two types of links described.

This pattern is strongly related to the DOMAIN/TECHNICAL VIEW pattern because, typically, at the point at which the macroflows are mapped to technologies, we need both views. That is, the macroflows require in any case a domain view (e.g., modeled in BPMN, EPC, or Abstract BPEL), as macroflows need to be discussed with domain experts from the business. At the point at which macroflows are mapped to technologies, we also need a technical view of the macroflow (e.g., modeled in BPEL, jPDL, Windows Workflow Foundation, or XPDL). The same duality can be observed for microflows. Here, in any case, a technical view is needed, as all microflows are executable. Sometimes, an additional domain view is needed, for instance, if microflow models should be designed together with domain experts. Just consider a pageflow model: A domain view would just graphically show the pageflow, and a technical model adds the technology-dependent details.

A common solution for combining the MACRO-/MICROFLOW and DOMAIN/TECHNICAL VIEW patterns is as follows:

1. High-level macroflows that depict strategic business processes and that are not implemented are designed only using a domain view (this step is optional).
2. The high-level macroflows are refined by lower-level macroflows that are implemented and offer a domain view as well as a technical view.
3. The macroflows invoke microflows that only have a technical view.

Example: UML Model of Macroflow and Microflow

Figure 5.10 shows an exemplary UML model for explicitly supporting the MACRO-/MICROFLOW pattern. The model shows different kinds of macroflows and microflows and the relationships between them. The MACRO-/MICROFLOW pattern generally provides a conceptual basis for the development of such models, which could, for instance, serve as a foundation for model-driven software development.

Examples: Macro-/Microflow Support in Process Engines

- In IBM's WebSphere technology [Ibm08], the MACRO-/MICROFLOW pattern is reflected by different technologies and methodologies being used to design and implement process-aware information systems. Different kinds of technologies and techniques for both types of flows are offered. On the macroflow level, workflow technologies are used that support integration of people and automated functions on the business process level. An example is IBM's WebSphere Process Choreographer, which is a workflow-modeling component. The microflow level is rather represented by transactional message flow technologies that are often used in service-oriented approaches. Examples are the WebSphere Business Integration Message Broker and the WebSphere InterChange Server. At the macroflow level, a service is invoked that is designed and implemented in detail by a microflow that performs data

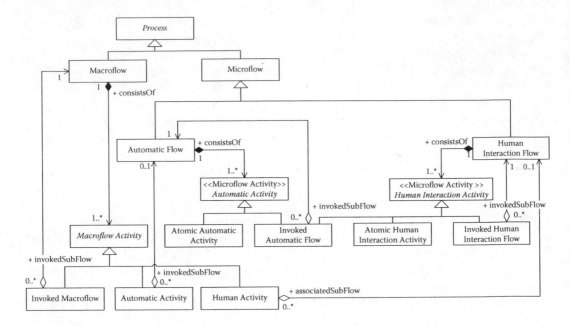

FIGURE 5.10
Exemplary UML for supporting the macro-/microflow pattern. (From C. Hentrich and U. Zdun. A pattern language for process execution and integration design in service-oriented architectures. *Springer LNCS Transactions on Pattern Languages of Programs*, 1, 136–191, 2009.)

transformation and routing to a back-end application. Moreover, aggregated services are often implemented at the microflow level using these kinds of message flow technologies.

- GFT's BPM Suite GFT Inspire [Gft07] provides a modeler component that uses UML activity diagrams as a notation for modeling the macroflow. Microflows can be modeled in various ways. First, there are so-called step activities, which allow the technical modeler to model a number of sequential step actions that refine the business activity. In the step actions, the details of the connection to other systems can be specified in a special purpose dialog. This concept is especially used to invoke other GFT products, such as the document archive system or a form-based input. Alternatively, the microflow can be implemented in Java snippets, which can be deployed to the server—together with the business process. Finally, services can be invoked that can integrate external microflow technologies, such as message brokers.
- JBoss's jBPM engine [JBo08] follows a slightly different model as the core component is a Java library and hence can be used in any Java environment. The jBPM library can also be packaged and exposed as a stateless session Enterprise Java Beans (EJB). JBoss offers a graph-based designer for the macroflow process languages and works with its own proprietary language, jPDL. A BPEL extension is also offered. The microflow is implemented through actions that are associated with events of the nodes and transitions in the process graph. The actions are hidden from the graphical representation, so that macroflow designers do not have to deal with them. The actions invoke Java code, which implements the microflow. The microflows need not be defined directly in Java but can also be executed on external microflow technology, such as a message broker or a pageflow engine.

Example: Novell exteNd Director

Novell's exteNd Director [Nov08] is a framework for rapid Web site development. It provides a pageflow engine implementing microflows for human interaction. A workflow engine realizes long-running macroflows. A pageflow activity in the workflows is used to trigger pageflows. This design follows the MACRO-/MICROFLOW pattern.

MACROFLOW ENGINE

You have decided to model parts of your system using macroflows to represent long-running business processes, for instance, following the MACRO-/MICROFLOW pattern. The simplest way to implement and execute your macroflow process models is to translate them manually into programming language code. But, as many tasks and issues in a macroflow implementation recur, it would be useful to have some more support for macroflows.

How can macroflow execution be supported by technology?

One of the main reasons to model macroflows is to enable organizations to cope with business changes. The reasoning behind this idea is that if you model your processes explicitly, you understand the implementation of your business better and can more quickly react to changes in the business. Changes in the business are reflected by changes in the corresponding macroflows. Today, many IT systems support business processes, and the required changes often involve significant changes in IT systems, with high costs and long development times. In a dynamic business environment, these costs and long development times are often not acceptable, as conditions might have already changed when old requirements are implemented.

One of the major reasons for this problem is that business process logic is scattered in the program code. The required changes thus imply to change program code in various systems. The result is a fragmentation (or structural gap) of business processes and IT systems that support them.

Often, many different skills are required to achieve this as the systems are implemented on varying platforms with different technology, programming paradigms, and languages. The heterogeneity of systems and concepts leads also to problems for domain experts, who have to roughly understand the adaptations of the changed systems. Frequently, the desired business process, as it was originally designed, cannot be realized due to limitations of existing systems or because of the high efforts required to implement the changes.

The complexity generated by this heterogeneity and the interdependencies between the systems let projects fail even before they have started as the involved risks and costs may be higher than the estimated benefit of the business process change. Thus, incremental evolution cannot be achieved. As a result, IT has gained the reputation of just being a cost driver but not a business enabler. In many cases, this problem causes a situation in which no significant and innovative changes are made, and solving prevalent problems is postponed as long as possible.

Hand coding business processes without technology support also means that recurring functionality required for executing macroflows, such as process persistence, wait states, process management, or concurrency handling, needs to be realized as well. That is, effort is required to develop and maintain these functionalities.

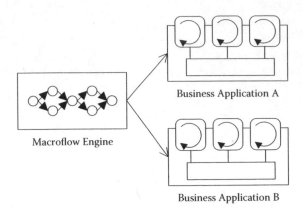

Macroflow Engine

Business Application A

Business Application B

FIGURE 5.11
A macroflow engine. (From C. Hentrich and U. Zdun. A pattern language for process execution and integration design in service-oriented architectures. *Springer LNCS Transactions on Pattern Languages of Programs,* 1, 136–191, 2009.)

Use a dedicated macroflow engine that supports executing long-running business processes (macroflows) described in a business process modeling language. Integrate business functions as services (or modules) that are invoked by the macroflow activities. Changes of macroflows are supported by changing the macroflow models and deploying the new versions to the engine at runtime (see Figure 5.11).

The main participant of the pattern of the MACROFLOW ENGINE is the engine component that allows developers to describe the business process logic by changing the business process definitions. Using a MACROFLOW ENGINE in an architecture means to decouple the business process logic from the IT systems. However, effort is needed to introduce an architecture based on a MACROFLOW ENGINE. The pattern has the best effects if applied as a long-term approach to architecture design and application development. Short-term goals may not justify the efforts involved.

Macroflow definitions are defined using a process modeling language. The engine executes the models, written in that modeling language. Changes occur by modifying the macroflow models and deploying the changed versions on the engine. Using this architecture, business process definitions can be flexibly changed, and the corresponding processes in IT systems can be adapted more easily than in macroflow implementations, scattered throughout the program code.

Please note that some MACROFLOW ENGINES provide a programmatic interface to define business processes. This form of process definition is often more appealing to developers than graphical models. Even though no modeling language is used, this variant still offers the benefits of the MACROFLOW ENGINE pattern: The business process is defined in one place, the MACROFLOW ENGINE's functions can be reused, and the business process can be managed.

The models executed by a MACROFLOW ENGINE represent a technical view of a macroflow, as described in the DOMAIN/TECHNICAL VIEW pattern, and are usually expressed in business process execution languages, such as BPEL, XPDL, Windows Workflow Foundation, or jPDL. In many cases, a domain view of the models is defined as well, for instance, in high-level process modeling languages, such as BPMN or EPC.

Applications are understood as modules that offer business functions (e.g., as services). If the MACRO-/MICROFLOW pattern is applied, of course, a service can internally realize a microflow implementation. The MACROFLOW ENGINE does not see these internal details, however, but only the service-based interface. The business functions are orchestrated by the business process logic described in the modeling language of the MACROFLOW ENGINE. Business functions are either completely automatic or semiautomatic, representing a human interacting with a system.

Business functions are represented in the macroflow as macroflow activities. They are one of a number of different activity types, supported by the engine. Other example activity types are control flow logic activities, data transformation activities, and exception-handling activities. The MACROFLOW ENGINE concentrates on orchestration issues of macroflow activities but not on the implementation of these activities. The actual implementation of macroflow activities is delegated to functionality of other systems with which the engine communicates.

The MACROFLOW ENGINE offers an Application Programming Interface (API) to access the functionality of the engine (i.e., processing of automatic and semiautomatic tasks). It further offers functions for long-running macroflow execution, such as process persistence, wait states, and concurrency handling. It also offers an interface for managing and monitoring the processes and process instances at runtime.

Various concepts exist for orchestration of macroflow activities in a MACROFLOW ENGINE. Two common examples are

- Strictly structured process flow, such as in terms of directed graphs with conditional paths (the most common variant in commercially used products and tools)
- Flexibly structured flow of activities (e.g., by defined pre- and postconditions of macroflow activities)

If business processes have already been realized in existing systems, developers must first extract the implemented business process logic from the systems and model them in the modeling language of the MACROFLOW ENGINE. Hence, in such cases, introducing the MACROFLOW ENGINE pattern has the drawback that efforts must be invested to extract the business process logic from existing systems implementations and to modify the architecture.

Example: UML Model of a MACROFLOW ENGINE

Figure 5.12 shows a simple UML model of a MACROFLOW ENGINE design that could be used as a starting point if one would realize a MACROFLOW ENGINE from scratch. The *macroflow engine* supports a simple management interface for *macroflows*. These have a number of *macroflow activities*. A *macroflow activity* is assigned to a *resource*; a *resource* can be some virtual actor, like an IT system acting in a certain role or a human actor who interacts with an IT system. As far as a human actor is concerned, constraints may be applied to make the macroflow activity only accessible to a defined set of users (e.g., by roles and rights that a user must have to be able to process a macroflow activity). The *macroflow activities* always invoke a *business function*, whether the *business function* is executed with support of a human being or whether it is completely automatic. Control data, such as process variables, is transformed during the execution of *macroflow activities*.

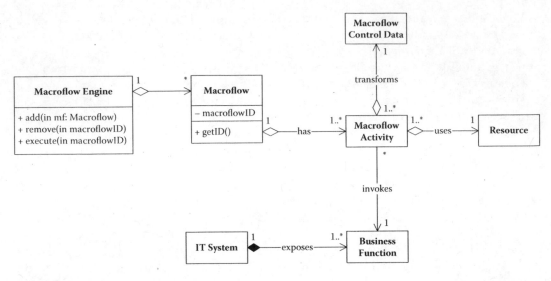

FIGURE 5.12
Example UML model of a macroflow engine. (From C. Hentrich and U. Zdun. A pattern language for process execution and integration design in service-oriented architectures. *Springer LNCS Transactions on Pattern Languages of Programs*, 1, 136–191, 2009.)

Examples: Macroflow Engine Products

- IBM's WebSphere Process Choreographer is the workflow-modeling component of WebSphere Studio Application Developer Studio, Integration Edition, which provides a MACROFLOW ENGINE. The workflow model is specified in BPEL.
- In the latest WebSphere product suite edition, the two products WebSphere Process Choreographer and WebSphere InterChange Server have been integrated into one product, called WebSphere Process Server. Consequently, this new version offers both a MACROFLOW ENGINE and a MICROFLOW ENGINE.
- GFT's BPM Suite Inspire [Gft07] provides a designer for macroflows that is based on UML activity diagrams. The business processes can be deployed to an application server that implements the MACROFLOW ENGINE for running the business processes. The engine also offers an administrator interface for monitoring and management of the processes.
- JBoss's jBPM [JBo08] is an open-source MACROFLOW ENGINE for graph-based business process models that can be expressed either in jPDL or BPEL as modeling languages. jBPM offers a Web-based monitoring and management tool.
- ActiveBPEL [Act07] is an open-source BPEL engine that acts as a MACROFLOW ENGINE for business processes modeled in BPEL.
- Novell's exteNd Director [Nov08] is a framework for rapid Web site development. It provides a workflow engine realizing long-running macroflow.

MICROFLOW ENGINE

You have realized that the business functions (services) that are orchestrated by macroflows in your system can be understood as short-running, technical processes. Following the MACRO-/MICROFLOW pattern, you introduce microflow models for representing these processes. In many cases, the "conceptual" notion of microflows is useful and sufficient, and microflows are implemented without supporting technology, for instance, using ordinary programming language code or scripts written in a scripting language.

You can further support microflows in hard-coded solutions: A best practice for realizing hard-coded microflows is to place them in their own coding units that can be independently deployed (e.g., each microflow is implemented as its own service in a distinct microflow SERVICE ABSTRACTION LAYER [Vog01]). Support of embedded scripting or dynamic languages for defining microflows can even further support the flexibility of microflow definition and deployment. For many cases, this solution is absolutely good enough. In some cases, however, you would like to get more support for microflow execution.

How can microflow execution be supported by technology?

It takes considerable time and effort to realize and change processes if the technical microflow details are hand-coded in programming language code. Consider implementing a microflow for human interaction. If you realize a hand-coded implementation using a UI technology, you could write a thin client Web UI or a fat client GUI, hand code certain microflows for human interactions in a layer on top of the UI, and provide a service-based interface to that microflow layer, so that the hand-coded microflow implementations can be accessed from macroflows. Consider performing simple changes to such a design, such as adding or deleting an activity in the microflow. Every change requires programming efforts. In a dynamic environment, in which process changes are regular practice, this might not be acceptable.

The design described in this example incurs another drawback: It requires discipline from the developers. Developers must place every microflow in the SERVICE ABSTRACTION LAYER for microflows. If developers do not strictly follow such design guidelines, the consequence is that microflow code is scattered through one or many components; hence, changes are even more difficult and costly to implement.

For these reasons, in highly dynamic business environments, a similar level of support for changing and redeploying microflows as provided for the macroflow models in a MACROFLOW ENGINE might be needed.

Even though rapid changes and avoiding scattered microflow implementation are the main reasons for requiring a better support for microflows, some other requirements for technology support exist, such as the following:

- In integrated tool suites, to provide a uniform user experience, tool vendors would like to provide tooling that is similar to the macroflow tooling, including a modeling language for microflows.

- Even though microflows are short-running processes, in some cases it might be necessary to monitor and manage the microflows. Providing monitoring and management for hand-coded microflows usually requires a substantial amount of work.

- Microflows also require recurring functionalities, such as realizing transaction semantics, accessing databases, or handling pageflows. Hence, reusing existing components providing these functionalities is useful.

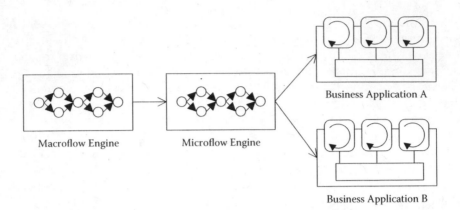

FIGURE 5.13
A microflow engine. (From C. Hentrich and U. Zdun. A pattern language for process execution and integration design in service-oriented architectures. *Springer LNCS Transactions on Pattern Languages of Programs*, 1, 136–191, 2009.)

Apply the business process paradigm directly to microflow design and implementation by using a microflow engine that is able to execute the microflow models. The microflow engine provides recurring tasks of the microflows as elements of the microflow modeling language. It supports change through changing microflow models and redeployment to the engine. All microflows of a kind are handled by the same microflow engine (Figure 5.13).

If a MICROFLOW ENGINE is used, the microflow processes are defined in a microflow modeling language. Processes can be flexibly changed through microflow deployment. The microflow logic is architecturally decoupled from the business applications and centrally handled in one place. The MICROFLOW ENGINE concentrates on orchestration issues of microflow activities but not on implementation of these activities. The actual implementation of microflow activities is delegated to functionality of integrated systems the engine communicates with or to human users.

There are two main kinds of MICROFLOW ENGINES, corresponding to the two kinds of microflows:

- MICROFLOW ENGINE *for automatic activities:* These engines support full-automatic and transaction-safe integration processes. Hence, they offer functions for short-running transactional microflow execution. As integration processes usually must access other technologies or applications, many MICROFLOW ENGINES for automatic activities also support technology and application adapters, such as Open Database Connectivity (ODBC), Java Database Connectivity (JDBC), XML, Web service, SAP, or Siebel.

- MICROFLOW ENGINE *for human interactions:* These engines support pageflow handling functionalities. A pageflow defines the control flow for a set of UI pages. The pages usually display information and contain controls for user interaction. Many pageflow engines focus on form-based input.

The microflow modeling language is a technical modeling language. In many cases, only a technical view of these models is exposed, but some tools also expose a high-level view of the integration processes. If this is the case, the DOMAIN/TECHNICAL VIEW pattern is realized by the microflow models. The goal could, for instance, be to enable designers and architects to gain a quick overview of the microflows. That is, here the domain view depicts a technical domain: either the integration behavior of the systems or the human interactions. Hence, the domain experts are software designers and architects in this case.

Defining executable microflow models using a modeling language does not mean a MICROFLOW ENGINE must be used. An alternative, for instance, is to generate microflow execution code in a programming language using a model-driven code generator. Use of a MICROFLOW ENGINE should be carefully considered as it has some disadvantages as well. Usually, it is not possible to define a custom microflow modeling language for existing engines, and many existing languages are much more complex than needed for very simple microflow orchestrations. This means additional effort as developers, designers, and architects must learn the microflow modeling language. The MICROFLOW ENGINE is an additional technology that must be maintained. The additional engine component adds complexity to the system architecture.

The MICROFLOW ENGINE has the advantage that the models are accessible at runtime (e.g., for reflection on the models) and can be manipulated by redeployment. Management and monitoring of running processes is possible—through either an API or a management and monitoring tool. A tool suite similar to the macroflow tools can be provided. Recurring functionalities can be supported by the MICROFLOW ENGINE and reused for all microflows.

Example: UML Model of a MICROFLOW ENGINE

Figure 5.14 shows a simple UML model of a MICROFLOW ENGINE design that could be used as a starting point if one would realize a MICROFLOW ENGINE from scratch. The basic feature of this MICROFLOW ENGINE design is execution of defined microflow integration process logic by orchestrating *microflow activities*. Analogous to the similar MACROFLOW ENGINE example presented, each activity transforms CONTROL DATA that is used to control the orchestrations of microflow activities and invokes a FUNCTION of an IT SYSTEM. The main difference from the previous example is that here the functions are services exposed by IT systems, not business-related functions. The invocations are performed automatically and in a transaction-safe way.

Example: Java Page Flow Architecture

The previous example mainly illustrates a schematic design of a MICROFLOW ENGINE for automatic activities. A similar design could also be used as a core for a MICROFLOW ENGINE for human interactions. But also, we must define how to integrate the MICROFLOW ENGINE component into the UI architecture. Many UIs follow the MODEL-VIEW-CONTROLLER (MVC) pattern [BMR+96, BHS07a]. We want to illustrate one example design for the Java Page Flow Architecture that provides an implementation of a MICROFLOW ENGINE for human interactions. A Java Page Flow consists of two main components: controllers and forms. Controllers mainly contain a control flow, defined by so-called actions and forwards. The forms associated to the actions and forwards are mainly JSP pages.

Figure 5.15 is an example from [MK08] that shows a mapping of the Java Page Flow Architecture to MVC, as implemented in the Apache Beehive project. The main engine component, executing the microflows, is used as the MVC controller. JSP and the NetUI tag libraries are used to display the information in the view. Any model layer can be used; it is not determined by the pageflow engine. In this example architecture, the controls technology from the Apache Beehive project is used as a model layer technology.

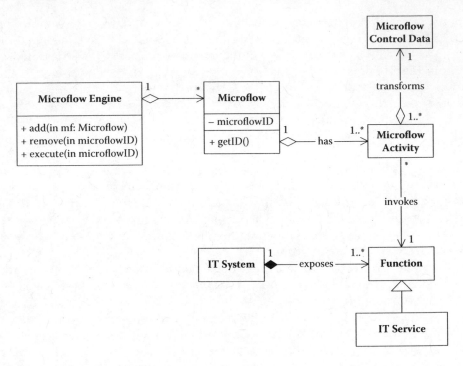

FIGURE 5.14
Example of a UML model of a microflow engine. (From C. Hentrich and U. Zdun. A pattern language for process execution and integration design in service-oriented architectures. *Springer LNCS Transactions on Pattern Languages of Programs,* 1, 136–191, 2009.)

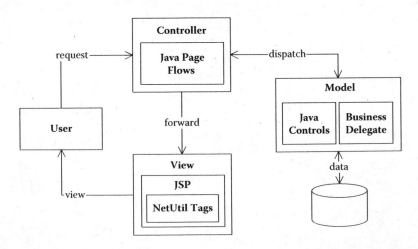

FIGURE 5.15
Mapping of Java Page Flow Architecture to MVC. (From C. Hentrich and U. Zdun. A pattern language for process execution and integration design in service-oriented architectures. *Springer LNCS Transactions on Pattern Languages of Programs,* 1, 136–191, 2009.)

Examples: MICROFLOW ENGINE Products

- The WebSphere Business Integration Message Broker [Ibm08] and the WebSphere InterChange Server [Ibm08] both realize MICROFLOW ENGINES. Both middleware products can also be used in conjunction. The WebSphere Business Integration Message Broker is used for simpler functions, such as adapter-based integration or dispatching. The product offers support for off-the-shelf adapters, message routing, and transformation. WebSphere InterChange Server offers transaction safe integration process execution. Process definition is done via a GUI, and the product also offers a very large set of INTEGRATION ADAPTERS for most common technologies and applications.

- The Integration Server of webMethods (now integrated in the Fabric BPM suite) [Web07] provides a MICROFLOW ENGINE that supports various data transfer and Web services standards, including JSP, XML, Extensible Stylesheet Language Transformation (XSLT), SOAP (Simple Object Access Protocol), and WSDL. It offers a graphical modeler for microflows that models the microflow in a number of sequential steps (including loop steps and branching), as well as a data-mapping modeler.

- iWay's Universal Adapter Suite [iWa07a] provides an Adapter Manager [iWay07b] for its intelligent, plug-and-play adapters. The Adapter Manager is a component that runs either alone or in an EJB container and executes adapter flows. The basic adapter flow is that it transforms an application-specific request of a client into iWay's proprietary XML format, invokes an agent that might invoke an adapter or perform other tasks, and transforms the XML-based response into the application-specific response format. The Adapter Manager provides a graphical modeling tool for assembling the adapters, the Adapter Designer. It allows developers to specify special-purpose microflows for a number of adapter-specific tasks, such as various transformations, routing through so-called agents, encryption/decryption, decisions, and so on. Multiple agents, transformations, and decisions can be combined in one flow. The Adapter Manager hence provides a special-purpose MICROFLOW ENGINE focusing on adapter assembly.

- The Java Page Flow Architecture, explained previously, is a technology defining MICROFLOW ENGINES for human interactions. Apache Beehive is a project that implements the Java Page Flow Architecture using Java metadata annotations. The implementation is based on Struts, a widely used MVC framework. BEA WebLogic Workshop is another implementation of the Java Page Flow Architecture; it provides a declarative pageflow language.

- Novell's exteNd Director [Nov08] is a framework for rapid Web site development. It provides a pageflow engine that orchestrates pageflows consisting of XForm pages.

Case Study: Business Transformation of Telecom Order Management

In a large telecommunications company, our patterns were used in a business transformation project in the domain of order management. The main goal of this project was the transformation of the management of various kinds of orders representing a large number of use cases. A technical platform was required to provide flexibility in changing the business processes, especially as far as the introduction of new products (services) from the telecommunications provider is concerned. Another major goal was the increased process automation and increased speed of order fulfillment. Thus, a redesign of the overall order management business processes was necessary. To achieve these goals, a new architectural concept was needed not only to integrate existing IT infrastructure but also to support conceptually the idea of organizational agility.

As a result of the demand of an architectural paradigm that supports organizational agility while integrating the existing IT systems and infrastructure, and thus saving investments, a process-driven SOA approach was chosen. The main general architectural pattern was the ENTERPRISE SERVICE BUS (see Chapter 3). This pattern unifies the access to applications and back ends using services and service adapters and by using message-oriented, event-driven communication between these services to enable flexible integration. The integration of the process-driven approach with SOA was solved by applying the PROCESS INTEGRATION ARCHITECTURE pattern (see Chapter 6).

The technology used for implementing the service bus was IBM WebSphere Message Broker with WebSphere MQ as the main messaging platform. Consequently, this message broker was also used to implement the microflow level.

As far as the macroflow level is concerned, two technologies were used as MACROFLOW ENGINES that serve two different purposes:

- WebSphere MQ Workflow was used to depict the main business processes for managing all orders.

- The business processes related to technical activation issues were implemented with OMS Metasolv (now acquired by Oracle). This product is well established in the telecommunications industry and includes some off-the-shelf features that make it suitable for this specific domain. This mainly covers very technical parts of the fulfillment process (e.g., technically activating a new ISDN/DSL [Integrated Services Digital Network/digital subscriber line] account).

To provide flexibility for the business logic concerning the configuration of rules for products and services, the Selectica business rules engine was used as a Business Rules Management system (BRMS). Various existing IT systems necessary for processing the orders were integrated via the service bus (e.g., an existing customer management system). An architectural overview is given in Figure 5.16.

At the time the project commenced, the customer had already modeled business processes, with Visio representing the purely business-related view without considering the architectural concept. Thus, these processes did not follow the concepts of service orientation and did not consider aspects of flexibility and configurability of the process architecture. A gap analysis pointed out many major issues with these business processes, which resulted in the decision that the processes could not be implemented as part of this architecture as they failed the major design guideline to provide flexibility. The major issues detected in this gap analysis are the following:

- *Inconsistent process hierarchy:* The business process structures in terms of a deterministic behavior of calling subprocesses were not modeled appropriately.

- *Missing structure concerning detailed modeling:* The processes varied widely in considering business and technical details. These two concerns were not separated and modeled accurately in encapsulated processes.

- *Inconsistent interfaces when calling subprocesses:* The business data passed between processes and the generated and captured events from the processes did not match.

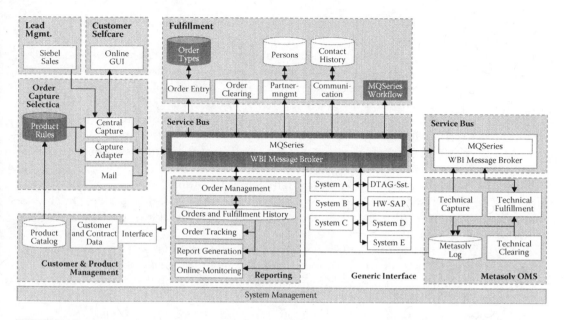

FIGURE 5.16

Architectural overview of the case. (From U. Zdun, C. Hentrich, and S. Dustdar. Modeling process-driven and service-oriented architectures using patterns and pattern primitives. *ACM Transactions on the Web (TWEB)*, 1(3), 14:1–14:44, 2007.)

- *Error-prone flow logic:* Many processes have been designed as huge constructs, with only a subset of all possible events and cases considered.

- *No synchronization with business object model:* The processes did not consider an underlying business object model, such that it was not clear which objects were processed in these processes and whether the structures of the processes matched a business object model.

- *No synchronization issues considered:* Many processes run in parallel, and events may be generated from parallel processes that influence the behavior of a running process (e.g., the cancellation of a currently processed order). These events were not considered in the models.

- *Redundancy:* Many processes showed redundant structures, which contradicts the concept of using encapsulation to reduce effort and increase flexibility.

All these issues pointed out that the business processes did not match the customer's intended business goals. A sound metamodel was required to resolve these issues and to provide a process model that suited the SOA approach and the business goals.

This is a pretty typical situation: High-level business processes designed solely by domain stakeholders usually do not fulfill the requirements of processes that must be concretized to a level that the DOMAIN/TECHNICAL VIEW pattern can be applied. In rare cases, only a specialization of the high-level domain views to lower-level domain views, which can be mapped to technical views, is needed. But, often processes designed with only the domain view in mind lack important issues (like the ones summarized) that make those models unsuitable for mapping to executable models. Hence, in most cases, a redesign of the high-level domain views is needed first, which leads to low-level domain views that can indeed be mapped to technical views. As a consequence, the high-level models must also be revised to contain activities that represent the new lower-level macroflows in their activities as subprocesses.

In addition to the DOMAIN/TECHNICAL VIEW pattern, we followed the MACRO-/MICROFLOW pattern. We developed detailed process models within a component-oriented process architecture concept. Our models show the macroflows and microflows as UML2 activity models. We used the pattern primitive extensions described in [ZHD07] to denote macroflows and microflows. These UML stereotype-based extensions are relatively intuitive. Also, the microflows in GUIs were modeled that way. The primitives thus allowed us to precisely specify and integrate the knowledge gained from the patterns in the models following a consistent modeling style.

Figure 5.17 shows the high-level process architecture for order management. The process architecture is represented as a set of process components that stand as independent but interacting units. The order management process itself and its high-level components are modeled as a macroflow.

The macroflow models presented have been used as domain views when applying the DOMAIN/TECHNICAL VIEW pattern. For instance, the technical view of the *order management* process shown in Figure 5.17 was then implemented as a generic workflow with WebSphere MQ Workflow.

Each process component was then refined into more fine-grained components, which are still macroflows. They are modeled via the *macroflow* and *macroflowSteps* (used for modeling sequential submacroflows) stereotypes down to the final processes that represent elementary business activities. Figure 5.18 shows the more fine-grained models of the *communication, finalization,* and *order entry* process components. We indicate the activity from the order management process that is refined by the macroflow process models using the *refinedNodes* tag value.

Complex business services used in these elementary business activities have been modeled using microflows. They are modeled via the *microflow* and *microflowSteps* (used for modeling sequential submicroflows) stereotypes. The orchestration of more fine-grained services was designed as UML2 activity diagrams that primarily use the *process control data-driven invocation* primitive (this describes an invocation based on the process control data). The technical flows make use of IT services and combine them to satisfy the requirements of the business services. The following example from the case study shows a business service to validate an order. Different quality attributes of the order are checked via a set of fine-grained services that are executed in a sequence. Figure 5.19 presents a *basic order-checking* service modeled as a microflow.

At the lowest level of microflow decomposition, we provide many details about the kinds of invocation, the used invocation data, and the correlation of invocations. This allowed for a detailed specification at this level. Figure 5.20 shows the detailed model of the *check customer financial status* business service.

This check customer financial status service consists of an asynchronous request for the financial status of a customer. The actual financial status information is captured in a second service call that operates with the request ID provided by the first call. That means, although the detailed technical services operate asynchronously, the business service check customer financial status simulates synchronous behavior by encapsulating the asynchronous request and reply. In this case, the request is actually satisfied by an external organization (i.e., the request and reply services are services of an external business partner).

Prior to starting process modeling activities, a business object model underlying the business processes was designed to represent the structure of orders. As a result, the redesigned business processes related not only to the mentioned process architecture

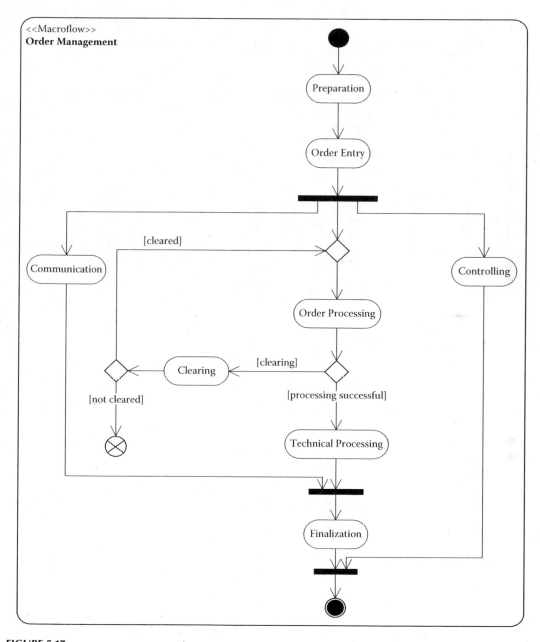

FIGURE 5.17
Order management process architecture. (From U. Zdun, C. Hentrich, and S. Dustdar. Modeling process-driven and service-oriented architectures using patterns and pattern primitives. *ACM Transactions on the Web (TWEB)*, 1(3), 14:1–14:44, 2007.)

concept but also to a specified business object model. Following that approach, it could clearly be modeled which objects were the subject of activities in processes and which attributes needed to be passed to services. A few iterations were necessary to balance the requirements from the services with the business objects model, such that all parameters demanded by the services were available in the business objects. More details about modeling business object models can be found in Chapter 8.

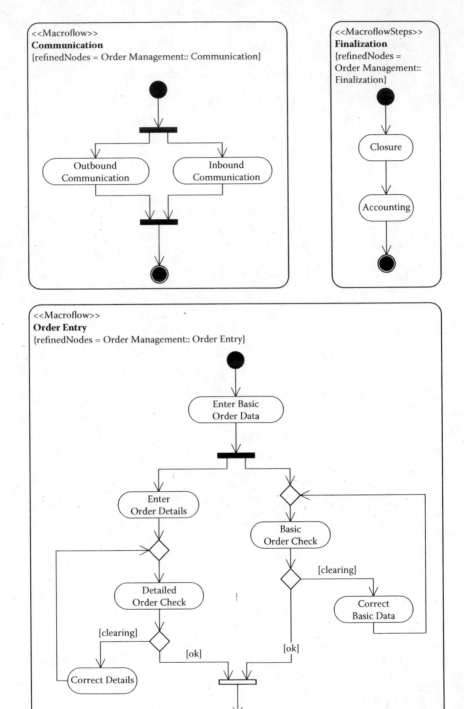

FIGURE 5.18
Models of refined processes. (From U. Zdun, C. Hentrich, and S. Dustdar. Modeling process-driven and service-oriented architectures using patterns and pattern primitives. *ACM Transactions on the Web (TWEB)*, 1(3), 14:1–14:44, 2007.)

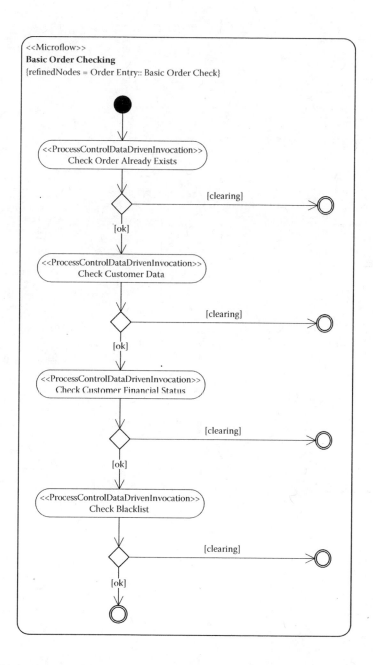

FIGURE 5.19
Basic order-checking service modeled as microflow. (From U. Zdun, C. Hentrich, and S. Dustdar. Modeling process-driven and service-oriented architectures using patterns and pattern primitives. *ACM Transactions on the Web (TWEB)*, 1(3), 14:1–14:44, 2007.)

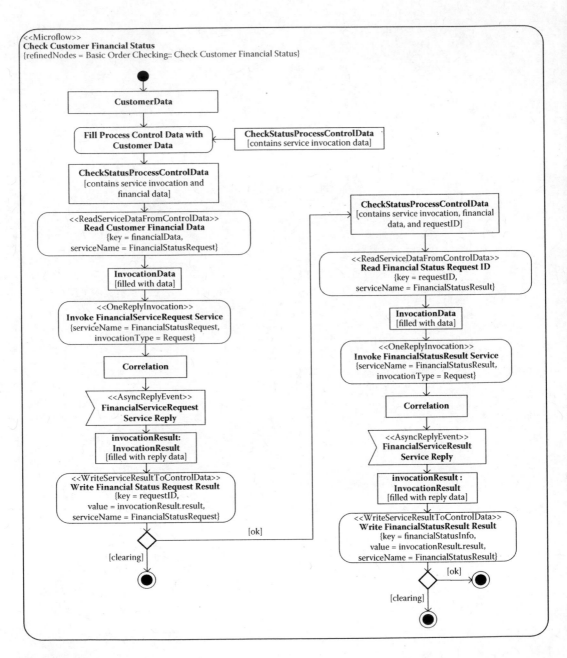

FIGURE 5.20

Microflow model of the check customer financial status service. (From U. Zdun, C. Hentrich, and S. Dustdar. Modeling process-driven and service-oriented architectures using patterns and pattern primitives. *ACM Transactions on the Web (TWEB)*, 1(3), 14:1–14:44, 2007.)

6

Integration and Adaptation in Process-Driven SOAs

Introduction

In Chapter 5, we mainly discussed how to realize various types of executable process flows, macroflows, and microflows and how to connect them to services that realize functions in the processes. In a real-world service-oriented architecture (SOA), usually not all services are implemented by the SOA developers, but in most cases a number of existing (legacy) systems, such as custom business applications, databases, and off-the-shelf business applications (such as SAP or Siebel), must be integrated.

Consider a typical starting point: Your organization uses two primary business applications. The first step to build an SOA orchestrating functions provided by those legacy applications is to provide them with a service-oriented interface. This is usually an incremental and nontrivial task (see Chapter 7). But, let us assume we are able to find suitable business services to access these applications. To support orchestration through executable business processes, we design high-level macroflows representing the business processes of the organization—from the business perspective. Following the MACRO-/MICROFLOW and DOMAIN/TECHNICAL VIEW patterns, the high-level macroflows are refined step by step into executable macroflows. Next, we realize the executable macroflows in a macroflow engine and use the macroflow activities to invoke the services exposed by the business applications. The result is an architecture as shown in Figure 6.1.

Unfortunately, often the interfaces provided by the legacy business applications are not identical to what is expected in the business processes. The business application services expose the—often rather technical—interfaces of the legacy business applications. The macroflow processes, in contrast, require interfaces that correspond to the business activities in the processes. Changing the macroflows to use the technical interfaces does not make sense because we want to keep the macroflows understandable for business stakeholders. In addition, hard-wiring process activities to the volatile interfaces of back ends is not good because for each change in the back end the process designs would have to be changed.

For these reasons, it makes sense to introduce INTEGRATION ADAPTERS for process integration, exposing the interfaces that the macroflows require (as shown in Figure 6.2). The INTEGRATION ADAPTER pattern is similar to the classical ADAPTER pattern [GHJV94, BHS07a]. However, in contrast to the classical ADAPTER, it translates between the interfaces of two systems connected using asynchronous (or, if needed, synchronous) connectors. In case of asynchronous communication, requests and responses are related by applying the CORRELATION IDENTIFIER pattern [HW03]. To make the INTEGRATION ADAPTER maintainable at runtime, the COMPONENT CONFIGURATOR pattern [SSRB00] is applied. That is, the adapter offers a configuration interface, which supports stopping and suspending the adapter.

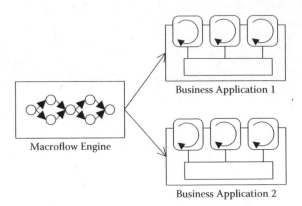

FIGURE 6.1
Macroflow engine invoking services exposed by business applications. (From C. Hentrich and U. Zdun. A pattern language for process execution and integration design in service-oriented architectures. *Springer LNCS Transactions on Pattern Languages of Programs*, 1, 136–191, 2009.)

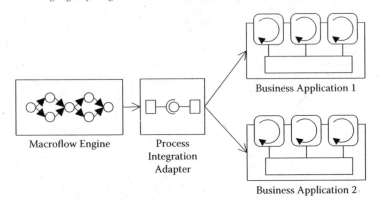

FIGURE 6.2
Integration adapter connecting a macroflow engine with business applications. (From C. Hentrich and U. Zdun. A pattern language for process execution and integration design in service-oriented architectures. *Springer LNCS Transactions on Pattern Languages of Programs*, 1, 136–191, 2009.)

The pattern also enables maintenance of both the connected target system and the adapter by being suspendable and stoppable. Macroflow engine technology often provides such INTEGRATION ADAPTERS for connecting the processes to back-end services. These adapters perform interface adaptations and data transformations, as well as data-mapping tools to design the transformations.

In many cases, the abstraction of business application services through an adapter is not enough. Still, the macroflows contain technical issues that go beyond simple adaptations and data transformations and rather deal with orchestration tasks. As explained in the MACRO-/MICROFLOW pattern, these technical flows should not be realized in a MACROFLOW ENGINE but be strictly distinguished from the macroflows—and realized as microflows. For such a small-scale architecture, it is usually enough to provide a few hard-coded services in a distinct microflow tier, as shown in Figure 6.3.

In this architecture, the business applications are hardwired in the service implementations. That means if the applications need to be stopped for maintenance, the whole SOA must be stopped. If the application service interfaces need to be changed, all dependent

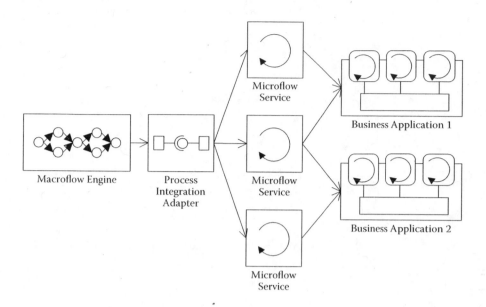

FIGURE 6.3
Macroflow engine invoking hard-coded microflow services. (From C. Hentrich and U. Zdun. A pattern language for process execution and integration design in service-oriented architectures. *Springer LNCS Transactions on Pattern Languages of Programs*, 1, 136–191, 2009.)

services must also be changed. This is okay for small SOAs with limited maintenance and availability requirements. But, consider requiring the SOA to continue to run while new versions of the business applications are deployed. This can be resolved by applying the INTEGRATION ADAPTER pattern again: We provide INTEGRATION ADAPTERS for the business applications as illustrated in Figure 6.4.

The pattern relationships of the integration adapter pattern introduced so far are summarized in Figure 6.5.

Now, consider running this SOA for a while and our organization merges with another organization. That means the information system of that other organization needs to access our SOA. If the other organization uses explicit business processes as well, it is likely that it runs its own MACROFLOW ENGINE. We can perform the integration of the two systems by providing that other MACROFLOW ENGINE with a process integration adapter that integrates the microflow services of our SOA with the business activity interfaces required by the macroflows of the other organization. The resulting architecture is sketched in Figure 6.6.

The macroflow tier is currently hardwired to the technical tiers. If dynamic content-based routing to microflows and back ends is needed or load balancing to multiple servers hosting the services should be provided, the introduction of a CONFIGURABLE DISPATCHER (as shown in Figure 6.7) between macroflow tiers and technical tiers can be beneficial to provide more configurability and flexibility. The CONFIGURABLE DISPATCHER pattern connects client and target systems using a dispatch algorithm that is based on configurable dispatching rules that can be updated at runtime. Hence, it enables us to postpone dispatch decisions until runtime.

Over time, we might realize that increased microflows are needed, and increased recurring tasks are performed in the microflows. In addition, it might make sense to make the microflow orchestrations more configurable. Hence, as a last step, we replace the microflow service tier by two MICROFLOW ENGINES: a pageflow engine to realize the human

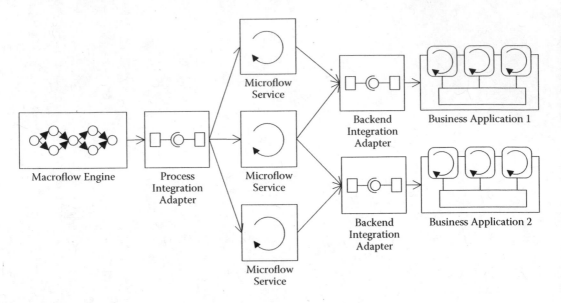

FIGURE 6.4
Macroflow engine invoking microflow services using back-end integration adapters. (From C. Hentrich and U. Zdun. A pattern language for process execution and integration design in service-oriented architectures. *Springer LNCS Transactions on Pattern Languages of Programs*, 1, 136–191, 2009.)

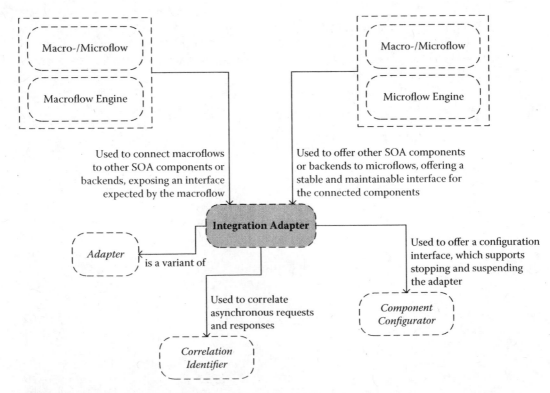

FIGURE 6.5
Integration adapter pattern relationships.

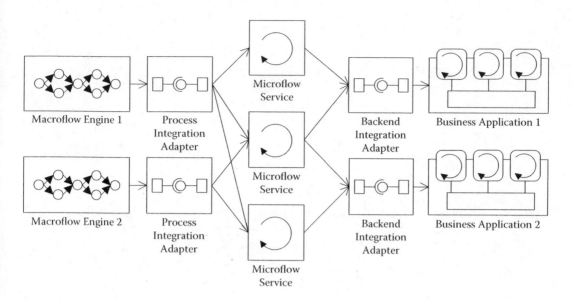

FIGURE 6.6
Mutliple macroflow engines invoking microflow services. (From C. Hentrich and U. Zdun. A pattern language for process execution and integration design in service-oriented architectures. *Springer LNCS Transactions on Pattern Languages of Programs,* 1, 136–191, 2009.)

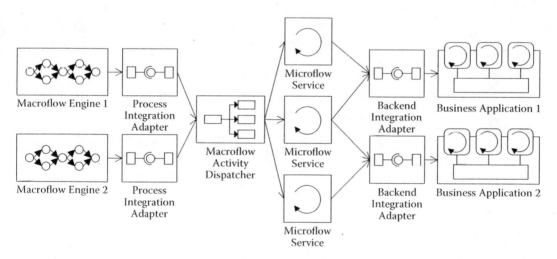

FIGURE 6.7
Using a macroflow activity dispatcher. (From C. Hentrich and U. Zdun. A pattern language for process execution and integration design in service-oriented architectures. *Springer LNCS Transactions on Pattern Languages of Programs,* 1, 136–191, 2009.)

interaction microflows and a message broker to realize the automated microflows. This is illustrated in Figure 6.8.

In our SOA, we have applied multiple INTEGRATION ADAPTERS that must be maintained and managed. Consider further the organization develops other SOAs for other business units that use similar technologies and must operate on similar back ends. Then, it makes sense to introduce an INTEGRATION ADAPTER REPOSITORY for the back-end adapters. The INTEGRATION ADAPTER REPOSITORY pattern provides a central repository and maintenance

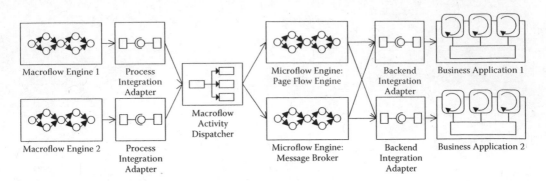

FIGURE 6.8

Adding microflow engines to the architecture. (From C. Hentrich and U. Zdun. A pattern language for process execution and integration design in service-oriented architectures. *Springer LNCS Transactions on Pattern Languages of Programs*, 1, 136–191, 2009.)

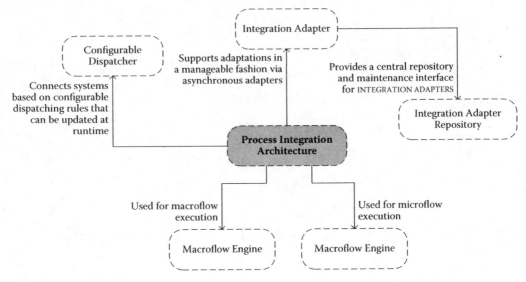

FIGURE 6.9

Process integration architecture pattern relationships.

interface for INTEGRATION ADAPTERS that support management, querying, and deployment of adapters. It hence facilitates reuse of adapters.

The sketched, incrementally built architecture in this example follows the PROCESS INTEGRATION ARCHITECTURE pattern. This pattern defines a specific configuration using a number of other patterns. It explains a specific architectural configuration of how the other patterns can be assembled to a flexible and scalable SOA.

One of the primary advantages of following the PROCESS INTEGRATION ARCHITECTURE pattern is that it enables architects to build up an SOA incrementally—just as in this example walk-through. A process-driven SOA initiative is usually a large-scale project in which multiple new technologies must be learned and integrated. Hence, step-by-step introduction of extensions, following an approach that is known to scale well to larger SOAs, is highly useful.

The PROCESS INTEGRATION ARCHITECTURE pattern defines the architecture built using a number of other patterns. This is illustrated in Figure 6.9.

INTEGRATION ADAPTER

In an SOA, various systems need to be connected to other systems. For instance, in a process-driven SOA, among others, the MACROFLOW ENGINES, MICROFLOW ENGINES, business services, and back-end systems must be connected. The systems in a process-driven SOA are heterogeneous systems, consisting of diverse technologies running on different platforms and communicating over various protocols. When different systems are interconnected and the individual systems evolve over time, the system internals and sometimes even the public interfaces of these systems change.

How can heterogeneous systems in an SOA be connected and the impacts of system and system interface changes be kept in acceptable limits?

Connecting two systems in an SOA means that a client system must be aligned with a target system that captures the requests, takes over the task of execution, and generates a response. For instance, if a MACROFLOW ENGINE or MICROFLOW ENGINE is the client, it acts as an orchestrator of process activities. Some of these activities are tasks that need to be executed by some other system. But, in many cases, the target systems are different from what is expected in the process engine. For instance, different technology, different synchronization mechanisms, or different protocols are used. In addition, in case of asynchronous communication, we must provide a way to connect heterogeneous technologies in such a way that the client can correlate the response to the original request.

One important consideration, when connecting systems in an SOA, is the change impact. Changes should not affect the client of a system, if possible. For instance, changes to integrated systems should not have effects on the processes that run in process engines.

In many change scenarios, downtimes of the whole SOA for maintenance are not tolerable. That is, changing a system should not mean that the other systems of the SOA must be stopped, but they should be able to continue to work, as if the changed system would still be functioning. Apart from this issue, internal system changes can be tolerated in an SOA as long as the public interfaces exposed as services do not change.

However, many changes include interface change. Often, the public interface of a system changes with each new release of the system. In this context of ongoing change and maintenance, the costs and efforts of changes should be kept at a minimum level. The impact of changes and the related testing efforts must also be kept within acceptable limits.

If your organization is in control of the system that must be changed, sometimes it is possible to circumvent these problems by avoiding changes that influence other systems. However, in an SOA usually many systems provided by external vendors or open-source projects are used. Examples are back-end systems, such as databases, SAP, or Siebel, as well as SOA components, such as MACROFLOW ENGINES or MICROFLOW ENGINES. Changes cannot be avoided for these systems. Migration to a new release is often forced as old releases are not supported anymore, or the new functionality is simply required by the business.

Apart from migration to a new version, the problem also occurs if a system shall be replaced by a completely different system. In such cases, the technology and functional interfaces of the new system are often highly different, causing a significant change impact.

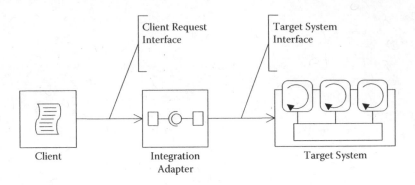

FIGURE 6.10

An integration adapter. (From C. Hentrich and U. Zdun. A pattern language for process execution and integration design in service-oriented architectures. *Springer LNCS Transactions on Pattern Languages of Programs*, 1, 136–191, 2009.)

If two systems must be connected in an SOA and keeping the change impacts in acceptable limits is a goal for this connection, provide an INTEGRATION ADAPTER for the system interconnection. The adapter contains two connectors: one for the client system's import interface and one for the target system's export interface. Use the adapter to translate between the connected systems. The adaptation covers, for instance, different interfaces, protocols, technologies, and synchronization mechanisms. Use CORRELATION IDENTIFIERS to relate asynchronous requests and responses. Make the adapter configurable by using asynchronous communication protocols and following the COMPONENT CONFIGURATOR pattern, so that the adapter can be modified at runtime without having an impact on the systems sending requests to the adapter (see Figure 6.10).

The core of the solution of the INTEGRATION ADAPTER pattern is the same as in the classical, object-oriented ADAPTER pattern [GHJV94, BHS07a]: An adapter connects the interfaces of a client and a target and translates between the two interfaces. For instance, if the client is a process engine, it acts as a sender in terms of sending out requests for activity execution, which are received by the adapter and transformed into a request understood by the target system. The INTEGRATION ADAPTER pattern adds to the solution of the ADAPTER pattern by supporting integration at the architectural level of connecting distributed and heterogeneous systems.

In the ADAPTER pattern, invocations are mainly synchronous, object-oriented message calls in the local scope. An INTEGRATION ADAPTER must first consider distributed requests and responses, which can be sent either synchronously or asynchronously. Receiving a request or response can work via push or pull mechanisms. The request contains an identifier for the function to be executed and input parameters. The INTEGRATION ADAPTER transforms the request into a format that can be understood by the target system's interface and technology. The request will be forwarded to the target system after the transformation is performed. After the adapter has received a response of the target system, the response is transformed back into the format and technology used by the interface of the client.

To make the INTEGRATION ADAPTER maintainable at runtime, the COMPONENT CONFIGURATOR pattern [SSRB00] should be applied. That is, the adapter offers a configuration interface that supports stopping and suspending the adapter. The adapter is stopped when new versions of the adapter must be deployed. The adapter is suspended when new versions of the target system are deployed or the adapter is configured at runtime. Later, after maintenance activities are finished, the adapter can resume its work and process all requests that have arrived in the meantime. The INTEGRATION ADAPTER can also offer a finalization function such that it finishes all ongoing activities properly and then terminates itself.

To realize an adapter with a COMPONENT CONFIGURATOR interface, the adapter must be loosely coupled to other systems, which is achieved by using connectors to client and target systems, as well as asynchronous communication protocols. As requests must be accepted at any time, no matter whether an adapter is at work or temporarily suspended, an asynchronous connector should be used to receive the requests and to send the responses. That is, the connector must be decoupled from the adapter to continue to accept requests if the adapter is not active.

Basically, asynchronous communication is only required on the client side, that is, for systems that access the adapter. The target system does not necessarily need to be connected asynchronously. For instance, a connected system might only offer a synchronous interface, or the system is a database that is connected via synchronous Structured Query Language (SQL). That also means the connector may accept requests and queue them until they are processed by the adapter.

In case of asynchronous communication, requests and responses are related by applying the CORRELATION IDENTIFIER pattern [HW03]. That is, the client sends a CORRELATION IDENTIFIER with the request. The adapter is responsible for putting the same CORRELATION IDENTIFIER into the respective response, so that the client can relate the response to its original request. For instance, if the client is a process engine, the CORRELATION IDENTIFIER identifies the activity instance that has sent the request.

If supported by the target system, the CORRELATION IDENTIFIER will also be used on the target system side to relate the response of the target system back to the original request. Consequently, the target system will have to send the CORRELATION IDENTIFIER back in its own response so that the adapter can recapture it. The response will also contain the result of the execution. If CORRELATION IDENTIFIERS cannot be used with the target system, for instance, because it is a legacy system that you cannot change, the INTEGRATION ADAPTER must implement its own mechanism to align requests and results.

The transformations performed by the adapter are often hard-coded in the adapter implementation. In some cases, they need to be configurable. To achieve this, the adapter can implement transformation rules for mapping a request including all its data to the interface and request format of the target system. Transformation rules can also be used for the response transformations. Data-mapping tools can be provided to model such transformation rules.

An INTEGRATION ADAPTER is useful for flexible integration of business applications from external vendors. It also becomes more popular to provide interconnectivity by supporting generic adapters for common standards, such as XML (Extensible Markup Language) and Web Services. That is the reason why many vendors deliver such adapters off the shelf and provide open access to their Application Programming Interface (APIs). As standard adapters can be provided for most common standards or products, solutions following the INTEGRATION ADAPTER pattern are usually reusable.

One drawback of INTEGRATION ADAPTERS is that potentially many adapters need to be managed if many systems exist where adapters for different purposes, systems, or technologies are required. Hence, maintenance and deployment of adapters might become problematic and must be done in a controlled way. The INTEGRATION ADAPTER REPOSITORY offers a way to manage adapters in a centralized and controlled way.

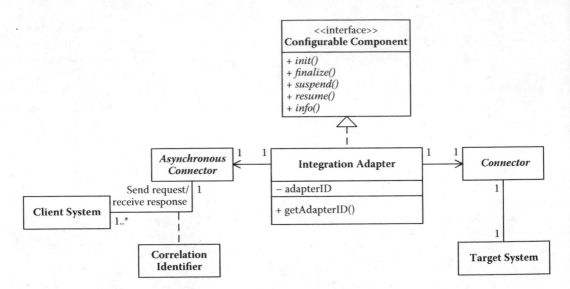

FIGURE 6.11
UML example of an integration adapter solution. (From C. Hentrich and U. Zdun. A pattern language for process execution and integration design in service-oriented architectures. *Springer LNCS Transactions on Pattern Languages of Programs,* 1, 136–191, 2009.)

If an adapter is suspended for a long time or if the amount of requests sent to a suspended adapter is high, then the request queue may contain many requests that take a long time to be processed or the requests may even have timed out. The workload of requests and the amount of requests that an adapter can process must be in balance. Middleware is required to queue the requests.

Example: Simple Example Model of an Integration Adapter in UML

Figure 6.11 shows an exemplary model for the internal design of an INTEGRATION ADAPTER solution in the Unified Modelling Language (UML). This adapter design receives asynchronous requests from a client system and translates them into synchronous requests for a target system. While waiting for the response, the adapter stores the CORRELATION IDENTIFIER sent by the client and adds it to the respective response message that is sent back to the client. The INTEGRATION ADAPTER offers an API for adapter configuration:

- The adapter can be initialized with *init()*.
- The adapter can be stopped with *finalize()*.
- The connected target system can be maintained. Then, the adapter must be suspended using the *suspend()* operation, and after the maintenance it can *resume()*.
- The adaptation status can be queried with *info()*.

Example: Process Integration Adapter Design in UML

Let us consider now a slightly more complex example of an INTEGRATION ADAPTER: an adapter that connects a process engine (i.e., a MACROFLOW ENGINE or MICROFLOW ENGINE) to a target system. Using INTEGRATION ADAPTERS for process integration has the benefit of a clear model for the communication between a process engine and the connected target systems.

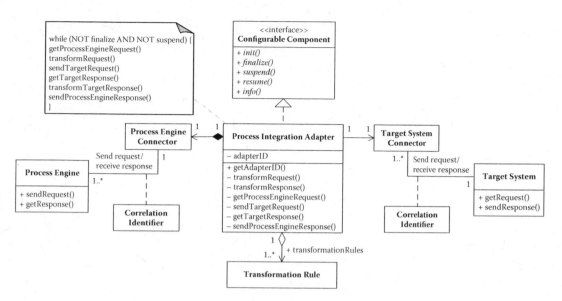

FIGURE 6.12
UML example of a process integration adapter. (From C. Hentrich and U. Zdun. A pattern language for process execution and integration design in service-oriented architectures. *Springer LNCS Transactions on Pattern Languages of Programs,* 1, 136–191, 2009.)

In this example, both connectors are asynchronous. The adapter must translate between the two CORRELATION IDENTIFIERS. The adapter uses the same interface for configuration as in the previous example. It follows a predefined protocol of a few operations to perform the adaptation.

Both request and response messages are transformed using transformation rules. Many process engines offer data-mapping tools for graphical design of the transformation rules. Figure 6.12 illustrates the structure of this process integration adapter design in UML.

The process integration adapter has a straightforward adaptation behavior, as shown in the sequence diagram in Figure 6.13.

Examples: INTEGRATION ADAPTER Suites

- WebSphere InterChange Server [Ibm08] offers a very large set of INTEGRATION ADAPTERS for most common technologies and applications. Users can extend the set of adapters with self-defined adapters.
- The transport providers of the Mule ESB (enterprise service bus) [Mul07] provide INTEGRATION ADAPTERS for transport protocols, repositories, messaging systems, services, and other technologies in the form of their connectors. A connector provides an implementation for connecting to an external system. The connector sends requests to an external receiver and manages listeners to receive responses from the external system. There are predefined connectors for HTTP (Hypertext Transfer Protocol), POP3/SMTP (Post Office Protocol 3/Simple Message Transfer Protocol), IMAP (Internet Message Access Protocol), Apache Axis Web Services, Java Database Connectivity (JDBC), JMS (Java Messaging Service), Remote Method Invocation (RMI), and many other technologies. Components can implement a common component lifecycle with the following life-cycle interfaces: *initializable, startable, callable, stoppable,* and *disposable.* The predefined connectors implement only the disposable and initializable interfaces.

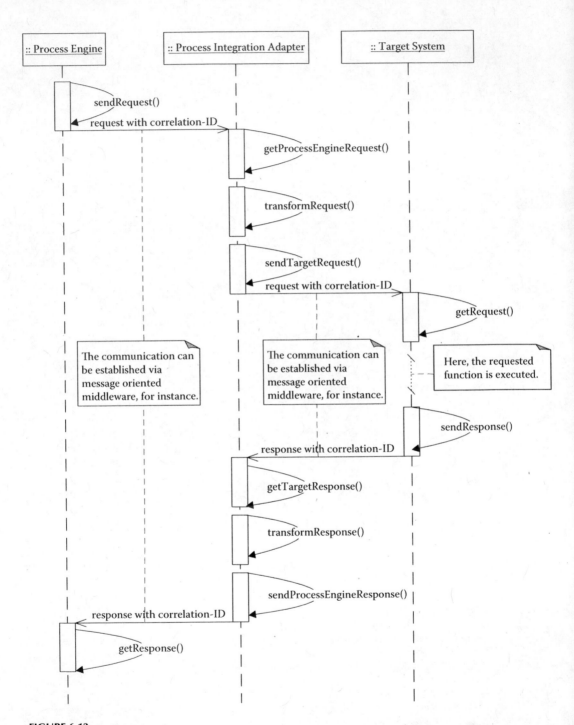

FIGURE 6.13
Adaptation behavior of a process integration adapter. (From C. Hentrich and U. Zdun. A pattern language for process execution and integration design in service-oriented architectures. *Springer LNCS Transactions on Pattern Languages of Programs,* 1, 136–191, 2009.)

- iWay's Universal Adapter Suite [iWa07a] provides so-called intelligent, plug-and-play adapters for over 250 information sources and broad connectivity to multiple computing platforms and transport protocols. It provides a repository of adapters, a special-purpose MICROFLOW ENGINE for assembling adapters called the Adapter Manager, a graphical modeling tool for adapter assembly, and integration with the MACROFLOW ENGINES and EAI (enterprise application integration) frameworks of most big vendors.
- WebSphere MQ Workflow [Ibm08] offers a technical concept called a user-defined program execution server (UPES), which implements this pattern for process integration. The UPES concept is a mechanism for invoking services via XML-based message adapters. The basis of the UPES concept is the MQ Workflow XML messaging interface. The UPES concept is all about communicating with external services via asynchronous XML messages. Consequently, the UPES mechanism invokes a service that a process activity requires, receives the result after the service execution has been completed, and further relates the asynchronously incoming result back to the process activity instance that originally requested execution of the service (as there may be hundreds or thousands of instances of the same process activity).
- CSC offers within their e4 reference meta-architecture the concept of INTEGRATION ADAPTERS for process integration. For an insurance customer in the United Kingdom, the e4 adapter concept has been used to integrate FileNet P8 Business Process Manager with an ENTERPRISE SERVICE BUS based on the WebSphere Business Integration Message broker.
- Within the Service Component Architecture (SCA) concept of IBM's WebSphere Integration Developer various INTEGRATION ADAPTERS are offered off the shelf (e.g., for WebSphere MQ, Web services, or JMS).

INTEGRATION ADAPTER REPOSITORY

Various systems shall be connected via INTEGRATION ADAPTERS. That means a large number of adapters is used or can potentially be used in an SOA.

How can a large number of INTEGRATION ADAPTERS be maintained and managed?

INTEGRATION ADAPTERS are important to connect systems that have incompatible interfaces and to minimize the change impact when multiple systems are integrated. But, with each system integrated into an SOA, the number of adapters to be maintained grows. In addition, when the adapters evolve, new adapter versions need to be supported as well, meaning that multiple versions of each adapter actually need to be maintained and managed.

The organization running the SOA does not always also provide the adapters. Especially for standard software, vendors offer INTEGRATION ADAPTERS. The result is often a large set of reusable standard adapters. Reusable adapter sets can also be built inside an organization, for instance, if the organization builds multiple SOAs and wants to reuse the adapters from previous projects. To facilitate reuse of adapters, it should be possible to search and query for an adapter or an adapter version in such a larger adapter set.

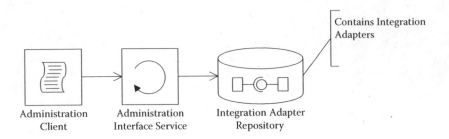

FIGURE 6.14

An integration adapter repository. (From C. Hentrich and U. Zdun. A pattern language for process execution and integration design in service-oriented architectures. *Springer LNCS Transactions on Pattern Languages of Programs*, 1, 136–191, 2009.)

Managing multiple INTEGRATION ADAPTERS also introduces a deployment issue: Usually, connected systems should not be stopped for deploying a new adapter or adapter versions. Instead, it should get "seamlessly" deployed at runtime. That means tools should support seamless deployment.

The problem of INTEGRATION ADAPTER maintenance and management especially occurs in larger architectural contexts, for which different systems have to communicate and larger sets of adapters exist. The problem does not have such a great impact within the boundaries of one closed component or application as the whole component or application needs to be redeployed if changes are made.

Use a central repository to manage the INTEGRATION ADAPTERS as components. The INTEGRATION ADAPTER REPOSITORY provides functions for storing, retrieving, and querying of adapters, as well as adapter versioning. It also provides functions for automatic deployment or supports automatic deployment tools. The automatic deployment functions use the COMPONENT CONFIGURATOR interface of the INTEGRATION ADAPTERS to suspend or stop adapters for maintenance. The functions of the repository are offered via a central administration interface (see Figure 6.14).

The INTEGRATION ADAPTERS are stored in a central repository that offers operations to add, retrieve, and remove adapters in multiple versions. Optionally, the repository can provide functions to search for adapters and adapter versions by given attributes.

In the simplest case, the INTEGRATION ADAPTER REPOSITORY just identifies the adapter by an *adapter ID* (e.g., the name) and version. More sophisticated variants of the INTEGRATION ADAPTER REPOSITORY pattern support metadata about the adapters as well.

An INTEGRATION ADAPTER REPOSITORY can be used to support adapter deployment. In the simplest form, it fulfills tasks for external deployment tools, such as delivering the right adapter in the right version. But, it can also provide the deployment functions itself.

The automatic deployment functions use the COMPONENT CONFIGURATOR interface of the INTEGRATION ADAPTERS. That is, maintenance or deployment tasks are supported because each single adapter can be stopped and restarted, new adapters or adapter versions can be deployed, and old adapters can be removed via a centralized administration interface.

It is important that requests sent to adapters are processed asynchronously (see INTEGRATION ADAPTER pattern) to bridge maintenance times when the adapters are modified. The requests are queued while the adapter is suspended. The pending requests be processed when the adapter restarts work after maintenance or after an adapter is replaced by a new adapter. The deployment functions must trigger this behavior of the adapters.

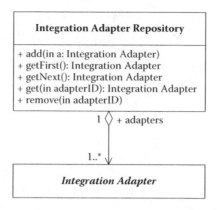

FIGURE 6.15
UML example of an integration adapter repository. (From C. Hentrich and U. Zdun. A pattern language for process execution and integration design in service-oriented architectures. *Springer LNCS Transactions on Pattern Languages of Programs*, 1, 136–191, 2009.)

The INTEGRATION ADAPTER REPOSITORY pattern addresses the flexible management of adapters at runtime. Following the pattern, changes to adapters can be deployed rather quickly and easily.

However, the pattern requires changing the adapters because a configuration interface is necessary for maintaining the adapters. As all adapters must implement the interface needed by the repository, putting third-party adapters with a different interface into the repository is not trivial. In some cases, it is impossible to add the required configuration functions to the third-party adapter; in other cases, writing a wrapper for the third-party adapter's interface is required.

Example: Simple INTEGRATION ADAPTER REPOSITORY Design in UML

Figure 6.15 shows the simplest INTEGRATION ADAPTER REPOSITORY design possible. In this design the INTEGRATION ADAPTERS are just managed and retrieved using the adapter ID. This design can easily be extended with more sophisticated search-and-query options. For instance, we could add metadata about the adapters. Using simple versioning, we could further improve the repository design.

Currently, the provided administration interface only supports deployment by delivering the adapter using *get()*. More sophisticated deployment functionality could be added that can stop a running adapter, deploy a new adapter, and initialize an adapter.

Examples: Repositories of INTEGRATION ADAPTERS Suites

- WebSphere InterChange Server [Ibm08] offers an INTEGRATION ADAPTER REPOSITORY in which a predefined large set of INTEGRATION ADAPTERS is provided. Self-defined adapters can also be added.
- The connectors of transport providers of the Mule ESB [Mul07] are, like all other components in Mule, managed by either the Mule container or an external container such as Pico or Spring. The container manages the life cycle of the connectors using the component life-cycle interfaces, which the components can optionally implement. Thus, the container acts as an INTEGRATION ADAPTER REPOSITORY for the connectors.
- iWay's Universal Adapter Suite [iWa07a] provides a repository of adapters in the Adapter Manager [iWa07b]. The graphical modeler of iWay, the Adapter

Designer, is used to define document flows for adapters. The Adapter Designer can be used to maintain and publish flows stored in any Adapter Manager repository. The adapters in the repository can be deployed to the Adapter Manager, which is a MICROFLOW ENGINE used for executing the Adapter flows.

CONFIGURABLE DISPATCHER

In an SOA, multiple systems need to be integrated. You cannot always decide at design time or deployment time which service or system must execute a request.

At runtime, how is it decided which service or system has to execute a request?

There are numerous issues that require a decision about request execution at runtime. Some examples are as follows:

- As system architectures usually change over time, it is necessary to add, replace, or change systems in the back end for executing process activities. In many process-driven systems, this must be possible at runtime. That is, it must be dynamically decided at runtime which component has to execute a request (e.g., sent by a macroflow activity). If the architecture does not consider these dynamics, then modifications to the back-end structures will be difficult to implement at runtime.

- Scalability can be achieved through load balancing, meaning that multiple services on different machines are provided for serving the same type of requests. Depending on the load, it must be dynamically decided using a load-balancing scheme or algorithm in which service is invoked.

- Sometimes, for realizing the same functionality, multiple systems are present in an organization. For instance, if two or more organizations have merged and the information systems have not yet been integrated, then it is necessary to decide based on the content of a request to which system the request must be routed. For instance, if multiple order-handling systems are present, orders can be routed based on the product IDs/categories.

- If some functionality is replicated, for instance to support a hot standby server, requests must be sent to all replicas.

All these issues actually point to well-known issues in distributed architectures and can be conceptually classified as dimensions of transparency [Emm00]: access transparency, location transparency, migration transparency, replication transparency, concurrency transparency, scalability transparency, performance transparency, and failure transparency. The core problem is thus how to consider those dimensions of transparency appropriately.

One important aspect of handling dynamic request execution decisions properly is that the rules for these decisions can also change at runtime. For instance, consider changing the system architecture, adding more servers for load balancing, requiring different content-based routing rules, or adding additional replicas. In all these cases, the rules for routing the requests change.

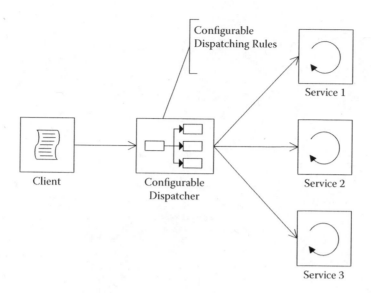

FIGURE 6.16

A configurable dispatcher. (From C. Hentrich and U. Zdun. A pattern language for process execution and integration design in service-oriented architectures. *Springer LNCS Transactions on Pattern Languages of Programs*, 1, 136–191, 2009.)

Use a CONFIGURABLE DISPATCHER that picks up the incoming requests and dynamically decides on the basis of configurable dispatching rules where and when the request should be executed. After making the decision, the CONFIGURABLE DISPATCHER forwards the requests to the corresponding target system, which handles the request execution. New or updated dispatching rules can be deployed at runtime (see Figure 6.16).

The dispatcher decides based on dispatching rules. The term *rule* is not strictly defined, however. Any directive that can decide—based on an incoming request—how to handle the request can be used. For instance, the rules can be implemented as event-condition-action rules, and a rule engine can be used to interpret the rules. Another implementation variant is to embed a scripting language interpreter and execute scripts that perform the decision.

In any case, the rules must be triggered on dispatching events (mainly incoming requests). They must be able to evaluate conditions. That is, the rule engine or interpreter must be able to access the relevant information needed for evaluating the conditions. For instance, if content-based routing should be supported, the content of the request must be accessible in the rule implementation. If round-robin load balancing should be implemented, the accessible target systems as well as a state of the round-robin protocol need to be accessed. Finally, functionality to realize the decision is needed, such as a command that tells the dispatcher to which target system it should dispatch the request.

The CONFIGURABLE DISPATCHER pattern supports the flexible dispatch of requests based on configurable rules. These dispatching rules can be changed at runtime. Dynamic scripting languages or rule engines enable developers to update dispatching rules on the fly. If this is not possible (e.g., because the rules are hard-coded in the dispatcher's implementation code), the dispatcher can apply the COMPONENT CONFIGURATOR pattern [SSRB00] to suspend dispatching while the rules are updated. In any case, the dispatcher should provide a dynamic rule maintenance interface.

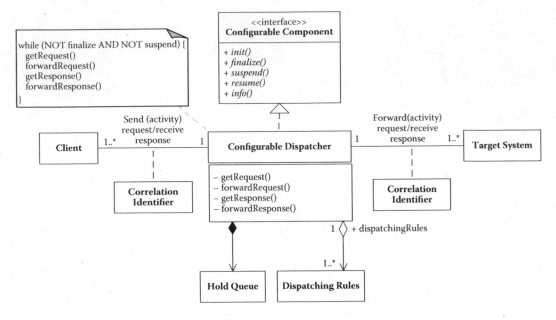

FIGURE 6.17
UML example of a configurable dispatcher. (From C. Hentrich and U. Zdun. A pattern language for process execution and integration design in service-oriented architectures. *Springer LNCS Transactions on Pattern Languages of Programs*, 1, 136–191, 2009.)

The dispatcher also has the task to pick up the request result from the component and send it back to the adapter. It is optionally possible to apply dispatching rules for the results as well. If asynchronous communication is used, a CORRELATION IDENTIFIER [HW03] is used to correlate the requests and responses.

The CONFIGURABLE DISPATCHER pattern can be used to make the workload in an SOA manageable by scaling the architecture in terms of adding instances of services or systems to execute the requests. However, a central component like a CONFIGURABLE DISPATCHER is a single point of failure. It might be a bottleneck and hence have a negative influence on the performance of the whole system.

Example: Simple Asynchronous CONFIGURABLE DISPATCHER Design in UML

Figure 6.17 shows an exemplary model for an asynchronous CONFIGURABLE DISPATCHER. The dispatching rules are simply stored in aggregated objects. The dispatcher design uses a CONFIGURABLE COMPONENT interface to suspend the dispatcher while the dispatch rules are updated. The dispatcher follows a simple linear algorithm to forward requests and responses (of course, this algorithm can also be parallelized). The CORRELATION IDENTIFIER pattern is used to correlate asynchronous requests and responses.

Examples: CONFIGURABLE DISPATCHERS in Workflow and ESB Products

- Using IBM's WebSphere Business Integration Message Broker [Ibm08], a CONFIGURABLE DISPATCHER can be implemented with a message flow definition that represents the dispatching logic. The dispatching rules are stored in a database and are accessed via a database access node in the flow.

- The Service Container of the Mule ESB [Mul07] offers support for content-based and rule-based routing. Inbound and outbound message events, as well as responses, can be routed according to declarative rules that can be dynamically specified. A number of predefined routers are available (based on the patterns in [HW03]). Predefined (or user-defined) filters, like a payload-type filter or an XPath filter, can be used to express the rules that control how routers behave.
- Apache ServiceMix [Apa07] is an open-source ESB and SOA tool kit. It uses the rule language Drools to provide rule-based routing inside the ESB. The architecture is rather simple: A Drools component is exposed at some service, interface, or operation endpoint in ServiceMix, and it will be fired when the endpoint is invoked. The rule base is then in complete control over message dispatching.

PROCESS INTEGRATION ARCHITECTURE

Process technology is used and the basic design follows the MACRO-/MICROFLOW pattern. Process technology is used at the macroflow level, and back-end systems need to be integrated in the process flow. The connection between the macroflow level and the back-end systems needs to be flexible so that different process technologies can (re)use the connection to the back-end systems. The architecture must be able to cope with increased workload conditions (i.e., it must be scalable). Finally, the architecture must be changeable and maintainable to be able to cope with both changes in the processes and changes in the back ends. All those challenges cannot be mastered without a clear concept for the whole SOA.

How is a process-driven SOA assembled in a way that is flexible, scalable, changeable, and maintainable?

To properly consider the qualities of the attributes flexibility, scalability, changeability, and maintainability, a number of issues must be addressed. First, there are technology specifics of the process technology being used at the macroflow level. In principle, implementations of macroflow activities represent reusable functions that are not restricted to one specific process technology but can rather be used with different types and implementations of process engines. If the process technology is tightly coupled to implementations of activities, changes in the process technology may potentially have a larger impact on the corresponding activity implementations, which means a loss of flexibility.

Activities at the macroflow level are usually refined as microflows following the MACRO-/MICROFLOW pattern. Thus, one has to consider where and how these microflows are executed. Aspects of scalability must be considered to cope with increasing workload. As requests for activity execution are permanently initiated and business will usually go on day and night, we also have to deal with the following question: What further mechanisms are necessary to maintain the whole architecture at runtime?

Changes to the microflow and macroflow should be easy and of low effort. Actual back-end system functionality will be invoked at the microflow level, and it is obviously an issue how this can be achieved, as those back-end systems are in principle independent and are subject to individual changes themselves. The impact of these changes must be kept within acceptable limits in a way that those changes can be managed.

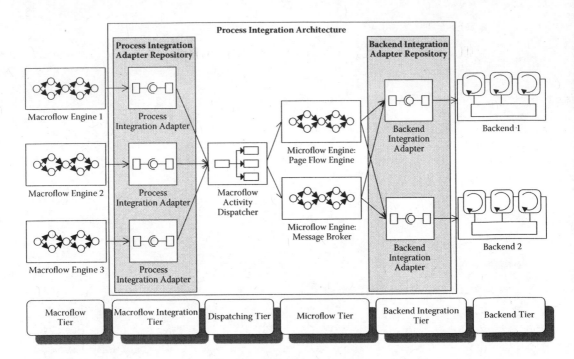

FIGURE 6.18
A process integration architecture. (From C. Hentrich and U. Zdun. A pattern language for process execution and integration design in service-oriented architectures. *Springer LNCS Transactions on Pattern Languages of Programs*, 1, 136–191, 2009.)

Provide a multitier PROCESS INTEGRATION ARCHITECTURE to connect macroflows and the back-end systems that need to be used in those macroflows. The macroflows run in dedicated MACROFLOW ENGINES that are connected to the SOA via INTEGRATION ADAPTERS for the connected services. Microflows are realized in a distinct microflow tier, and they either run in dedicated MICROFLOW ENGINES or are implemented as microflow services. The back-end systems are also connected to the SOA using INTEGRATION ADAPTERS. To cope with multiple back ends, multiple microflow engines are used. CONFIGURABLE DISPATCHERS are used for routing, replication, and load balancing (see Figure 6.18).

The PROCESS INTEGRATION ARCHITECTURE pattern assumes service-based communication. That is, the systems connected in PROCESS INTEGRATION ARCHITECTURE are exposed using service-oriented interfaces and use services provided by other systems in the PROCESS INTEGRATION ARCHITECTURE to fulfill their tasks. In many cases, asynchronous communication is used to facilitate loose coupling. Then, usually CORRELATION IDENTIFIERS are used to correlate the requests and results. Sometimes, it makes sense also to use synchronous communication, for instance, because blocking on results is actually required or a back end in batch mode can only work with synchronous invocations.

The PROCESS INTEGRATION ARCHITECTURE provides a flexible and scalable approach to service-oriented and process-driven architectural design. The main architectural task of a PROCESS INTEGRATION ARCHITECTURE is to connect the macroflows, representing the executable business processes, to the back-end systems and services providing the functions needed to implement these processes. In a naïve approach to architectural design, we would simply invoke the services (of the back-end systems) from the macroflow activities running in the MACROFLOW ENGINE. But, this only works well for small examples and very small-scale architectures. The benefit of the PROCESS INTEGRATION ARCHITECTURE is that we can start from this very simple architecture and enhance it step by step as new requirements emerge. The possible enhancements are described by the other patterns of this pattern language.

The PROCESS INTEGRATION ARCHITECTURE introduces multiple tiers:

- The *macroflow tier* hosts the implementations of the executable macroflows. Usually, MACROFLOW ENGINES are used to execute the macroflows.

- The *macroflow integration tier* is a common extension to the macroflow tier. It introduces one INTEGRATION ADAPTER for the processes per MACROFLOW ENGINE. This adapter integrates the process activities with the technical functions provided by the SOA. That is, it connects the business-oriented perspective of the business activities in the macroflows to the technical perspective of the services and microflows.

- The *dispatching tier* is an optional tier that can be added to the PROCESS INTEGRATION ARCHITECTURE if content-based routing, load balancing, replication, or other dispatching tasks are needed for connecting the macroflow requests to the microflow or service execution.

- The *microflow tier* is a common tier if the PROCESS INTEGRATION ARCHITECTURE design follows the MACRO-/MICROFLOW pattern. This makes sense if short-running, technical orchestrations of services are needed. In the simplest version, a number of hard coded services can be provided for microflow execution. A more sophisticated realization introduces MICROFLOW ENGINES.

- The *back-end integration tier* is an optional tier used to provide back ends with an interface that is needed by the SOA. As this tier uses INTEGRATION ADAPTERS to enable independent maintenance of back-end systems, it is highly recommended to introduce this tier for SOAs that need to continue operating while connected systems are maintained.

- The *back-end tier* contains the systems that are connected to the SOA and performs the functions required to execute the business processes. Typical back-end systems are off-the-shelf business applications (such as SAP or Siebel), custom business applications, databases, services, and so on. The back-end systems are usually connected to the SOA via service-based interfaces that expose the API of the back-end system without great modifications. For providing a specific interface to the SOA, INTEGRATION ADAPTERS in the back-end integration tier should be used.

The PROCESS INTEGRATION ARCHITECTURE pattern provides a systematic way to scale up a process-driven SOA. It can be applied for a single MACROFLOW ENGINE, and multiple engines can be added later. Similarly, only a few services or business applications can be initially provided, and later more services or business applications can be added. In both cases, the INTEGRATION ADAPTER pattern provides a clear guideline on how to perform the connection in a maintainable fashion. The INTEGRATION ADAPTER REPOSITORY pattern should be used if a larger number of adapters must be maintained.

The various systems connected in the PROCESS INTEGRATION ARCHITECTURE are treated as exchangeable black boxes. The business applications, macroflows, and microflows can be maintained as independent systems as long as the service interfaces do not change. Load balancing and prioritized or rule-based processing of requests can be supported, for instance, via the CONFIGURABLE DISPATCHER. Many existing off-the-shelf engines can be used in a PROCESS INTEGRATION ARCHITECTURE, which might reduce the necessary in-house development effort.

The PROCESS INTEGRATION ARCHITECTURE pattern has the drawback that greater design effort might be necessary compared to simpler alternatives because of the multitier model with corresponding loosely coupled interfaces. To buy (and customize) different off-the-shelf engines or systems can be costly, just like in-house development of these engines or systems. Hence, for small, simple process-driven SOAs, consider starting with a single process engine and follow the MACRO-/MICROFLOW pattern only conceptually. A more sophisticated PROCESS INTEGRATION ARCHITECTURE can then still be introduced later, when requirements for higher flexibility, scalability, changeability, and maintainability arise.

In various parts of the PROCESS INTEGRATION ARCHITECTURE pattern, business objects (or business data) must be accessed. The business objects relevant to microflows and macroflows essentially form a CANONICAL DATA MODEL [HW03] for storing process-relevant business data. The BUSINESS OBJECT REFERENCE pattern (see Chapter 8) is used to keep the references to the business objects in the process flows (macroflows and microflows) and services.

Example: Step-by-Step Design of a PROCESS INTEGRATION ARCHITECTURE

A schematic example for a step-by-step design of a PROCESS INTEGRATION ARCHITECTURE was given in the introduction of this chapter.

Examples: Known Uses of PROCESS INTEGRATION ARCHITECTURES

- In a supply chain management solution for a big automotive customer in Germany, the PROCESS INTEGRATION ARCHITECTURE pattern was applied. WebSphere MQ Workflow was used as the MACROFLOW ENGINE. The integration adapters, the dispatching layer, and the microflow execution level were implemented in Java. The application services were implemented using MQ messaging technology. In this realization of the pattern, a Java architecture was implemented to represent the CONFIGURABLE DISPATCHER, a MICROFLOW ENGINE, and the INTEGRATION ADAPTERS. No off-the-shelf middleware was used.

- For a telecommunications customer in Germany, the PROCESS INTEGRATION ARCHITECTURE pattern was used in a larger-scale variant. The MICROFLOW ENGINE was implemented by an ENTERPRISE SERVICE BUS based on WebSphere Business Integration Message Broker. WebSphere MQ Workflow has been used as the process engine at the macroflow layer. The off-the-shelf MQ Workflow adapters provided by the message broker served as the process integration adapters. The architecture was laid out initially to support different instances of MQ Workflow engines to cope with a growing workload using a dispatcher represented as a routing flow that routes the messages received by the adapter to another message broker instance. New message broker instances were created according to the growing workload.

- A simple variant of the pattern is implemented in IBM's WebSphere Integration Developer, which includes WebSphere Process Server, a process engine that represents both the micro- and macroflow levels. It further offers an architectural concept, the SCA to wire up services, including the corresponding adapters.

Case Study: Java Implementation of Process-Based Business Services Integration

In the following, we present a case study in which the patterns from this chapter (and Chapter 5) were implemented in the context of a Java back-end framework for process-based services integration. The framework was designed and implemented in the context of a supply chain management solution in the automotive industry. The subject of this framework is the execution of automatic activities that integrate services. The framework consists of four elements that will be implemented in this example as architectural components:

- *Job generator engine:* Transforms messages sent by process engines (MQ Workflow UPES messages in this case) into an enterprise-wide standard job definition format. The job generator decouples the process engines (in this case, MQ Workflow) from actual activity implementations. This component implements the INTEGRATION ADAPTER pattern. WebSphere MQ Workflow implements the MACROFLOW ENGINE pattern.

- *Job dispatcher engine:* Is responsible for prioritized distribution of generated jobs to different distributed components that are responsible for executing the jobs. Moreover, the dispatcher is responsible for sending the job results delivered from those components back to the job generator engine. This component implements the CONFIGURABLE DISPATCHER pattern.

- *Activity execution engine:* Is responsible for executing generated jobs that represent activity implementations related to business services integration. This component implements a MICROFLOW ENGINE and execution services for the microflows.

- *Business service interface repository:* Offers standardized interfaces to integrated business services. This component implements the INTEGRATION ADAPTER REPOSITORY and the INTEGRATION ADAPTER patterns.

Figure 6.19 illustrates the architecture of the process-based business services integration solution.

The integration mechanism for the MQ Workflow is the UPES concept. UPES is a WebSphere concept and the acronym stands for *user-defined program execution servers.* The Java UPES is offered as a Web application. Via Java UPES, processes can invoke methods of Java objects. All four architectural components realize the UPES implementation in the context of MQ workflow. Via the UPES concept, the business services integration solution can easily be integrated in a PROCESS INTEGRATION ARCHITECTURE. This kind of integration using the UPES has been used in many projects, such as this specific supply chain management project from a large automotive company, where the actual framework was

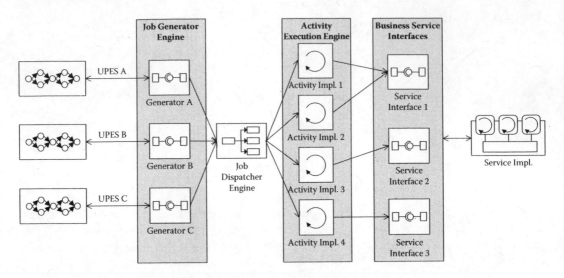

FIGURE 6.19
Architecture of a process-based business services solution.

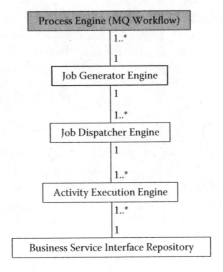

FIGURE 6.20
Component relationships of the process-based integration case.

developed. Other projects in the banking industry that make extensive use of MQ messaging have applied the UPES integration as well because it is consistent with existing well-established MQ messaging integration platforms already available in many larger banks.

The components are connected via asynchronous messaging mechanisms. However, as far as business services invocation and integration are concerned, the architecture considers both synchronous and asynchronous business services. For the architecture to be scalable and flexible, there are one-to-many relationships between all five components (the four service integration components plus MQ Workflow). This is shown in Figure 6.20.

The UPES mechanism provides an implementation of the CORRELATION IDENTIFIER pattern [HW03]. The *activity implementation correlation ID* is an element of all exchanged UPES

XML messages that is used to correlate a return message to an activity instance. Moreover, the CORRELATION IDENTIFIER is used to connect all architectural components, that is, the job generator engine, the job dispatcher engine, the activity execution engine, and the business service interface repository (only in case of asynchronous business services) as the tokens will be passed from one component to the next one and will also be returned until they arrive again at the process engine.

A UPES is basically just a message queue definition from the point of view of MQ Workflow. An activity instance will send a request message to that message queue, and the message can thus be processed by an external component. The return message will be sent by that external component to a defined input queue. MQ Workflow takes the messages out of that input queue and relates the return message back to an activity instance using the activity implementation correlation ID. That is, the CORRELATION IDENTIFIER and the process flow can carry on to the next activity, as defined by the process model.

The job generator engine is the back-end interface to the MQ Workflow process engine and thus implements the INTEGRATION ADAPTER pattern. The task of the job generator engine is to decouple the message format of the process engine from a standardized message format used for job definitions. Thus, an incoming request in a UPES queue will be transformed into a standardized job definition message format and will be forwarded to a job dispatcher engine, representing a CONFIGURABLE DISPATCHER, which is responsible for further processing the jobs. For this reason, the job generator engine decouples the product-specific process integration logic from job-based integration logic. The job generator engine contains a set of job generators, being based on an MQ Workflow INTEGRATION ADAPTER, which listen to input queues (UPES). The job generators are responsible for taking the messages out of the queues, transforming them into the job definition format, completing the message with some additional information, and forwarding the jobs to the dispatcher.

Thus, parallel processing of messages in different queues is possible. If a job has been processed, the result will be reported back to the job generator by the job dispatcher engine in a corresponding job result queue. The job generator will transform the job result into a return message for the process engine and will put the message in the input queue of the process engine. Eventually, each job generator listens to two queues and writes to two other queues. The UML model in Figure 6.21 illustrates the structure of the job generator engine.

Basically, the job generator engine is a repository of job generators. Once a job generator is started by calling its *init()* method, it will start to listen to queues and thus to process the incoming messages. The forward and backward transformation of messages will be implemented by a *concrete job generator* in the methods *requestToJob()* (forward transformation into the job definition format) and *jobResultToReply()* (backward transformation from job definition format to the UPES XML format). Most of the development projects that have used this architectural framework implementation within the overall program have used XML definitions and corresponding messages for the job definition format. The following sequence diagrams illustrate the forward (see Figure 6.22) and backward (see Figure 6.23) transformation of messages.

The *get()* operation, the message transformation, and the *put()* operation must be understood as one transaction. As far as this aspect is concerned, WebSphere MQ can be used as the transaction coordinator. Thus, transaction security is ensured via WebSphere MQ.

To dispatch and finally execute a job, the job definition must at least contain two additional pieces of information (compared to the original request from the process engine) that must be added by the job generator:

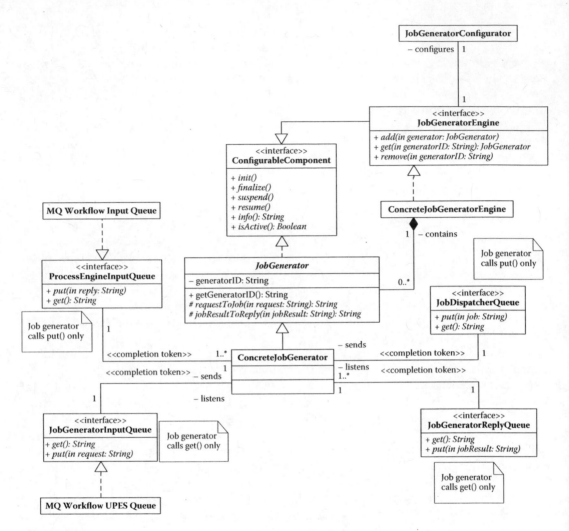

FIGURE 6.21
Structure of the job generator engine.

- the activity execution engine that is responsible for processing the job and
- the activity implementation that actually executes the job within the activity execution engine.

The job generator will add this information to the job definition by putting the input queue name of the corresponding activity execution engine and the identifier of the activity implementation into the job definition message. The job dispatcher engine represents a CONFIGURABLE DISPATCHER and will thus simply read the jobs from the input queue and forward them to the activity execution engine that is defined in the job. In addition, the dispatcher will add the name of its reply queue to the job definition before forwarding the message.

If an activity execution engine has finished execution of a job, it will send a job result message back to the dispatcher. The reply queue of the dispatcher has previously been

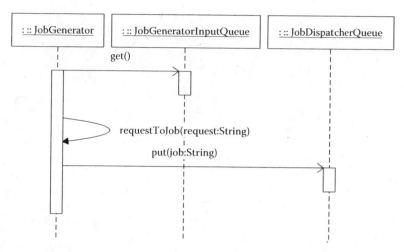

FIGURE 6.22
Forward transformation of messages.

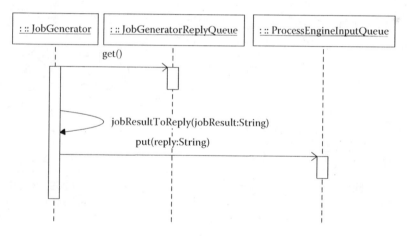

FIGURE 6.23
Backward transformation of messages.

dynamically added to the job definition by the dispatcher. The dispatcher will take that response message and forward the reply to the job generator defined in the job definition.

The UML diagram in Figure 6.24 illustrates the job dispatcher engine design.

Sequence diagrams illustrate how the job dispatcher engine distributes the jobs to different activity execution engines (see Figure 6.25) and how the job results are redispatched to the job generator engine (see Figure 6.26). Obviously, the basic functionality is principally similar to the job generator engine. Analogous to the job generator engine, the interdependent *get()* and *put()* operations are implemented as transactions.

The activity execution engine implements a MICROFLOW ENGINE and is responsible for executing and managing activity implementations (i.e., business logic that is related to automatic activities in business process models). Thus, a concrete activity implementation that actually represents an execution service for microflows will call business services and will set the process control data as specified by the process logic (the referenced process activity), depending on the results of the service calls. The results of the called business

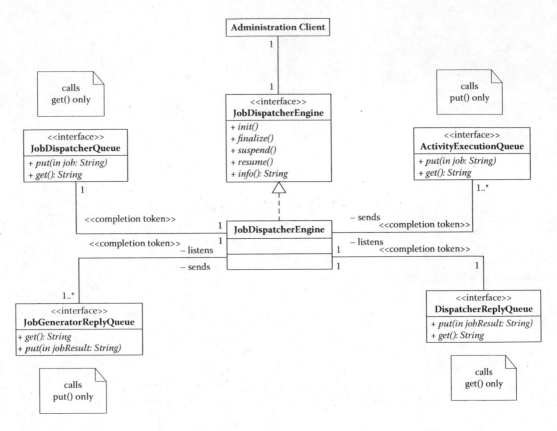

FIGURE 6.24
Structure of the job dispatcher engine.

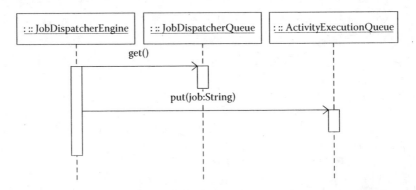

FIGURE 6.25
Dispatching of jobs.

services will be reported back to the process instance via the process control data that will be sent in the job result. This reporting procedure of the job result goes backward via the job dispatcher engine, to the job generator engine, and finally to the process engine (MQ Workflow). Thus, job results move backward on the same path that they used to arrive at an activity execution engine but they move back in reverse order.

An activity execution engine has an input queue where the jobs are delivered to be executed by the engine. The engine then retrieves the activity implementation that is

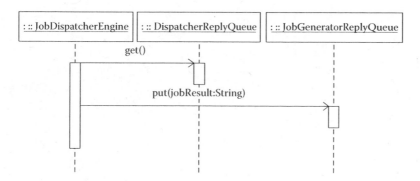

FIGURE 6.26
Redispatching jobs back to the dispatcher.

associated to the job from a repository (the job definition contains the identifier of the activity implementation). Once an activity implementation is retrieved from the repository, the input data that is also included in the job definition will be passed to the activity implementation. Ultimately, the activity implementation will be executed, and its execution will be controlled. If an activity implementation has finished execution of a job, the job result that is delivered as output by an activity implementation will be put in the reply queue of the corresponding dispatcher engine (the queue identifier is also included in the job definition). Conclusively, many activity implementations will be executed in parallel by the activity execution engine. For this reason, an activity implementation is executable as a thread in the activity execution engine.

A concrete activity implementation will invoke certain business services. It might be necessary to access business objects associated to the process instance to do this as those objects may provide the necessary data for invoking a service (e.g., customer details like name, address, account numbers, etc.). As an activity implementation has received the process control data as input, it will have access to references of the corresponding business objects of the process instance.

The implementations of interfaces to business services will be kept in repositories to decouple them from the activity execution engine. A concrete activity implementation will thus get access to the required business service interfaces via access to a business service interface repository.

Figure 6.27 shows the activity execution engine design.

A concrete *ActivityExecutionEngine* will get the jobs from the *ActivityExecutionQueue* by calling its *get()* method. As mentioned, the job definition contains the *ActivityImplementation* identifier for executing the job. Therefore, the engine will retrieve the appropriate *ActivityImplementation* from the *ActivityImplementationRepository* by calling the *get()* method of the repository and by passing the ID of the *ActivityImplementation* as a parameter of the method call. As illustrated in the diagram, this *get()* method will search for the *ActivityImplementation* object and will return a clone of the object in the repository. By using this technique, it is easily possible to execute several instances of the same *ActivityImplementation* and to configure objects in the repository in parallel.

The *ActivityExecutionEngine* will generate the arguments for executing the *ActivityImplementation* from the job definition by calling its *createArguments()* method. Thereafter, the engine will call the *getReplyInfo()* method to determine whether the *ActivityImplementation* will receive asynchronous results from business services. The string delivered by *getReplyInfo()* provides information concerning how many asynchronous

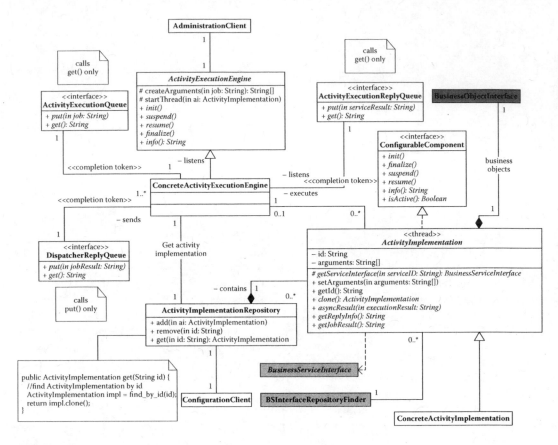

FIGURE 6.27
Structure of the activity execution engine.

results are expected as an *ActivityImplementation* may invoke several asynchronous service calls.

To set the input data for the *ActivityImplementation,* the method *setArguments()* will be called with the previously generated arguments. Finally, the *ActivityExecutionEngine* will start the ActivityImplementation as a thread within the engine by calling its *startThread()* method. Asynchronous replies from business service interfaces will be collected by the engine from the *ActivityExecutionReplyQueue.* The sequence diagram in Figure 6.28 illustrates the process of initializing and starting an *ActivityImplementation.*

After an *ActivityImplementation* has been initialized and started, the subsequent flow of method calls depends on whether there are asynchronous replies from business services. Ultimately, the engine will collect the job result from the thread by calling the *getJobResult()* method after the thread has finished. The sequence diagram in Figure 6.29 illustrates the message flow.

If there are asynchronous replies from business services, the *ActivityExecutionEngine* will be responsible for collecting those results and informing the corresponding *Activity-Implementation* thread that a service result has arrived. The *ActivityImplementation* is responsible for incorporating that service result in the overall job result. The relationship between an *ActivityImplementation* instance and an asynchronous reply from a business service is achieved by the CORRELATION IDENTIFER (called *completion token* here), which will be part of the reply message of the service. Those reply messages are delivered in

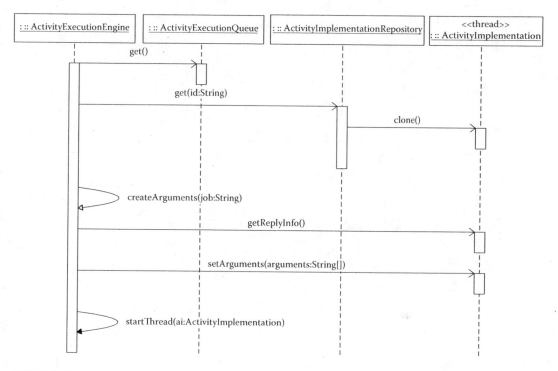

FIGURE 6.28
Initializing and starting an activity implementation.

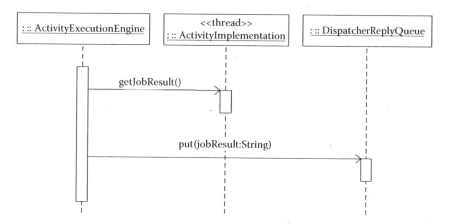

FIGURE 6.29
Message flow for getting the job result.

the *ActivityExecutionReplyQueue*. In case of asynchronous replies, the *ActivityExecution-Engine* must consequently manage these relationships and inform the appropriate thread about an incoming result. Figure 6.30 illustrates the design for managing asynchronous responses.

Apart from the relationships between completion tokens and *ActivityImplementation* instances, the engine has to remember how many asynchronous responses are expected. This information has been obtained from the *getReplyInfo()* method of the *Activity-Implementation* instance. Conclusively, it is possible to manage those incoming responses

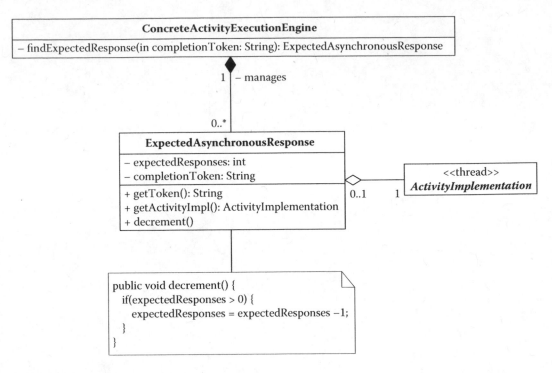

FIGURE 6.30
Design for managing asynchronous responses.

by keeping the relationships of the completion token, the number of expected responses, and the corresponding *ActivityImplementation* instances in a list. An *ActivityImplementation* can eventually be informed about a service result by calling its *asyncResult()* method. Finally, the *decrement()* method must be called to register the service result as accepted. The sequence diagram in Figure 6.31 illustrates the flow of method calls.

The necessary initialization of an *ActivityImplementation* (i.e., retrieving the required business service integration interfaces from the business service interface repository and creating a *BusinessObjectInterface* object) is implemented in the *init()* method of the *ActivityImplementation*. The business service interface repository will be accessed via a repository finder.

The business services interface repository component is an INTEGRATION ADAPTER REPOSITORY of standardized interface implementations realizing INTEGRATION ADAPTERS to various synchronous and asynchronous business services. The repository will be accessed via a repository finder as the location of the repository might change.

In principle, a business service interface represents an INTEGRATION ADAPTER to a business service and just declares a standardized *invoke()* method for a service. A concrete implementation of this interface will actually integrate the business service. If the service is asynchronous, the reply will be sent to a defined reply queue, which will be read by the corresponding activity execution engine. The name of the reply queue can be passed as a parameter of the *invoke()* method. If a business service interface shall be retrieved from the repository, the repository will return a clone of the interface.

The UML diagram in Figure 6.32 shows the business service interface repository design.

The class *BSInterfaceRepositoryFinder* implements a repository finder. Furthermore, the abstract class *BusinessServiceInterface* declares the standard interface for business services

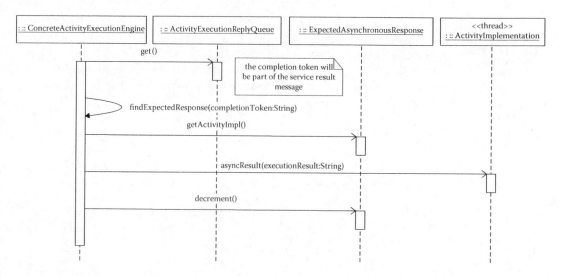

FIGURE 6.31
Message flow for asynchronous responses.

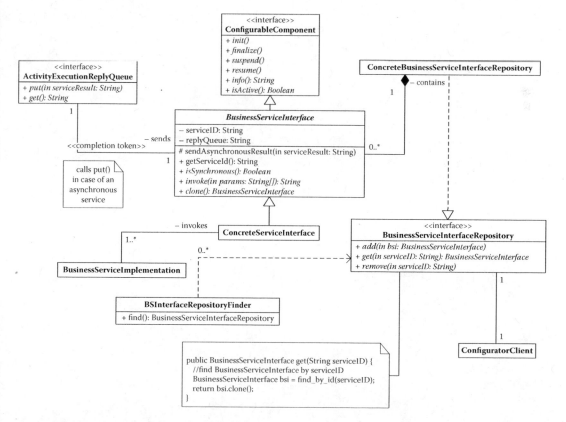

FIGURE 6.32
Business service interface repository design.

including the *invoke()* method. If the service interface is synchronous, then the *invoke()* method will deliver the service result. If the service interface is asynchronous, the concrete implementation of the business service interface will put the service result in the *ActivityExecutionReplyQueue*. To achieve this, the concrete interface implementation generates an internal thread to capture the asynchronous service result and forward it to the *ActivityExecutionReplyQueue*.

7

Aligning Business Goals and Service Design

Problems of Aligning Business Goals and Service Design

If you compare the technical perspective of a service-oriented architecture (SOA) and the business perspective, as discussed in Chapters 2 and 3, or technical and nontechnical views of a business process, as discussed in Chapter 5, you might come to the conclusion that these two worlds—even though sophisticated process and workflow technology exists—are hard to integrate. Indeed this is the case. In fact, this whole book is an attempt to bridge the gap between the business and technology views in SOAs.

The business is mainly driven by (often very high-level) business goals. One main task of the SOA is hence that the business goals are properly mapped to services (or processes as a special kind of services that orchestrate other services). This is difficult because, on the one hand, business goals must be broken down into requirements for services. On the other hand, we must also consider existing applications, technical resources, and off-the-shelf vendor products when designing the services. We need a clear decision on which services must be designed and implemented considering the constant evolution of services.

In the SOA context, it is rather difficult to decide which services are actually required to satisfy the business goals. Actually, it is even worse as the problem starts with the prior step: It is necessary to break down high-level strategic business goals into more fine-grained goals that must then be transformed into requirements for the services. For this reason, the problem, on one hand, is to decide on a decomposition of business goals and provide a rationale for this structure.

On the other hand, we are usually dealing with an existing IT infrastructure, and it is necessary to offer available application functionality as services. These applications imply limitations on the functionality as an application will deliver only a certain set of functions that can be offered as services. The existing functionality must also be related to the strategic business goals to have a basis for the decision on which existing functionality is ready to use. That means a priori it is not obvious whether this existing functionality is sufficient to support the business goals or whether additional functionality must be developed within single applications. It must be decided which functionality of which application must be extended and whether this is possible at all with an acceptable effort.

Please note that similar situations arise for the data of existing applications (see also the discussion in Chapter 8). The existing data might also be different from the data expected by some business goals, and often it is hard to reengineer existing applications to offer exactly the data needed to realize a new business goal.

As far as off-the-shelf vendor products are concerned, these issues consequently influence evaluation of vendor products and the decision regarding which product best suits the requirements (i.e., the selection of right products within the information technology

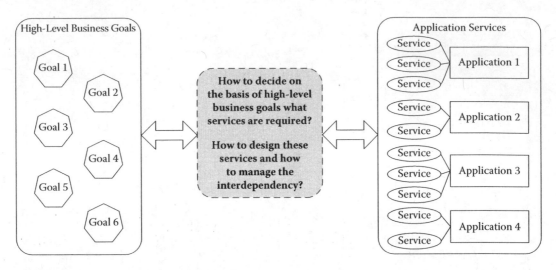

FIGURE 7.1
Major problems aligning business goals and service design.

[IT] strategy context). The best strategic decision might be to replace some of the existing applications, migrate to new versions, or leave some of the existing systems in their current state of functionality.

This major problem of aligning the business goals and service design, addressed in one way or the other by many of the patterns presented in this book, is illustrated in Figure 7.1.

The decision process to decide on the requirements of services that need to be defined is a nontrivial process that has to consider evolutionary aspects of the business. An engineering approach is required to define and break down business goals and map them to requirements of services. The approach should further allow for planning the definition and design of these services. It should also consider the evolution of the business as the business goals might change over time.

Even though we have not yet discussed our patterns in terms of an engineering process, we have already hinted at this process in the narrative sections and case studies of Chapters 5 and 6. Actually, these patterns define an approach to incrementally design service from high-level macroflows down to low-level services using both technical and domain views. Also, a clear guidance for mapping the process and service design to architectural components is given.

In the next section, we outline this general engineering approach for designing *business-driven services* based on the patterns from Chapters 5 and 6. We generally recommend applying this incremental and highly iterative approach when applying our pattern language for designing SOAs. The patterns in the rest of the book rather focus on detailed issues in the context of this general approach to engineering process-driven SOAs.

Designing Business-Driven Services

Our approach to design *business-driven services* (i.e., services that reflect both the business and technology requirements) is to design services using a convergent top-down and bottom-up engineering approach, in which high-level business goals are mapped to to-be macroflow business process models that fulfill these high-level business goals and more fine-grained business goals are mapped to activities within these processes. Those macro-flow business process activities are further refined by engineered microflows that merge bottom-up and top-down engineered application services.

This approach has already been exemplified in a number of examples and case studies in Chapters 4 to 6. Here, we want to reiterate on it explicitly.

The high-level business goals defined by strategic management can be mapped to to-be models of business processes. Following the MACRO-/MICROFLOW pattern as a conceptual foundation to structure business processes, it is possible to design the to-be macroflow business processes that represent these high-level business goals.

These high-level macroflows usually only have domain views because they are used only by domain experts. Hence, they are only needed in a domain view. Activities of these high-level macroflows are realized by lower-level macroflows. These are defined at a technically refined level. At this state, they can be translated into technical views following the DOMAIN/TECHNICAL VIEW pattern.

After the technical refinement of macroflows, it is possible to derive integration services for the macroflows, for instance, following the INTEGRATION ADAPTER pattern. These activities of the macroflows are implemented using microflows. Following the DOMAIN/TECHNICAL VIEW pattern, these microflows usually only exist in a technical view as they are only used by the technical experts. The design of these microflows is done by mapping existing application functions to services as follows:

- Existing services are modified, or new services that are missing are designed to fulfill the requirements of the macroflow integration services, or

- Existing services are orchestrated in microflow models to realize a composed service that fulfills the requirements.

The result is a set of *business-driven services* that are invoked and orchestrated in micro-flows that fulfill the requirements of the macroflow integration services.

It might turn out that the implementation of the to-be macroflow business processes implies unacceptable effort or exceeds the limits of the project budget or time frame. A typical reason is that too many difficult modifications to existing services are necessary. Also, too much effort might be required for implementing new *business-driven services*. In such cases, it might be necessary to adapt the to-be macroflows and thus the high-level business goals to stay within acceptable limits of the project budget and time frame. Then, a migration plan needs to be developed to achieve the original business goals and evolve the originally desired to-be macroflow business processes via several stages or projects.

That means one should possibly plan for a few iterations until all interdependent elements of the various models match: the high-level business goals, the to-be macroflow business process models, the macroflow integration services, the microflows, and the business-driven services. As far as architecture management is concerned, procedures and tools are useful to manage these dependencies and the changes being initiated.

A business-driven service in a microflow might be a composed service, where the business-driven service invokes a set of more fine-grained services (which possibly invoke even more fine-grained services). This decompositional structure should be considered as rather static and not subject to regular changes. If the orchestration of the more fine-grained services needs to be configurable, the orchestration will usually be modeled as a submicroflow. Configurability is thus the design criterion to decide whether to have a static decomposition or a configurable decomposition via submicroflows.

An execution service for a microflow can be offered, possibly following the INTEGRATION ADAPTER pattern again. Figure 7.2 summarizes this interdependent and convergent top-down and bottom-up driven approach for identifying and designing business-driven services.

Applying this incremental engineering approach together with our pattern language has a number of benefits. A main advantage is that business-driven services link services of business applications to high-level business goals. Identification and design of services is guided by a traceable convergent engineering approach—the pattern implies a methodology to design the services. Decisions on configurability of services are already included in the very early phase of service identification. Limitations of project budget and timeline are considered when creating a service model by considering the efforts to realize the services. Existing application functionality is considered to be offered as services and can be related to business processes.

However, the incremental engineering approach also has the drawback that it requires several iterations that need to be planned to match the macroflow and microflow process models with the service model.

Example: Revisiting the Pattern Language Walk-Through Example

To illustrate the approach of designing business-driven services, we reflect on the pattern language walk-through example, as described in Chapter 4. This pattern language walk-through example from the insurance business actually demonstrates the business-driven services design approach. The high-level business goals for redesigning the claims management business processes from Chapter 4 are as follows:

- *Goal 1:* Standardization of business processes to provide a common quality standard in the organization and across different country locations.
- *Goal 2:* Increase efficiency by industrializing the claims management processes and by automating as much as possible; use human potential freed from automation for improved customer relationship management to achieve increased customer satisfaction.
- *Goal 3:* Provide technical and organizational flexibility to easily and quickly improve the handling of claims and to quickly react to changed market conditions.
- *Goal 4:* Provide transparency to business processes, simplify the business processes, and enable systematic monitoring during execution with business measures to indicate opportunities for improvement.

Goals 1 and 4 first need to be addressed within the actual design of the claims business processes. In the example from Chapter 4, these goals are reflected in the processes by standardizing as much as possible for all types of claims (i.e., motor, property, and casualty claims). The processes are independent from these types of claims as the process flows modeled as event-driven process chains (EPCs) do not show conditional logic that is dependent on these types of claims. This also introduces an element of simplification that refers to goal 4.

Goal 2 is systematically addressed by identifying in the processes which functions can be automated. Those functions are modeled as services in the EPCs. Harmonizing the user interfaces by hiding the heterogeneity of back-end systems also reflects the standardization request of goal 1. Goal 3 is first simply addressed by actually modeling the claims processes. The models provide transparency of how claims are handled and

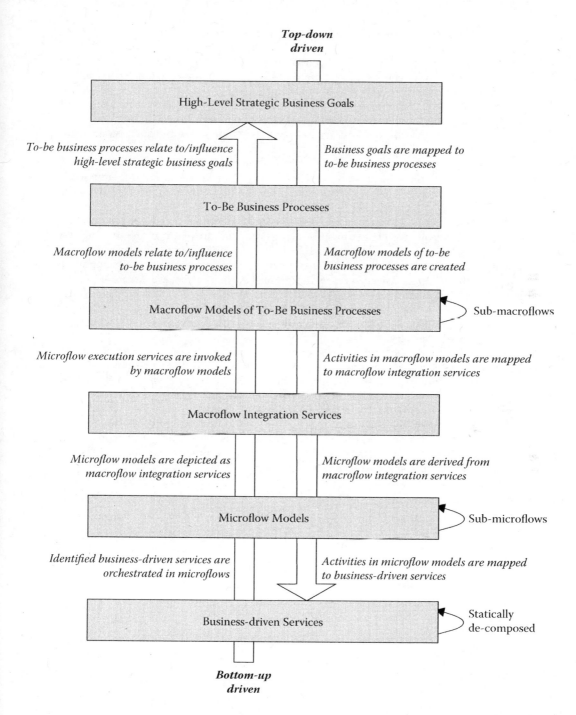

FIGURE 7.2
Convergent top-down and bottom-up approach for business-driven service design.

thus provide the foundation for improving them. The transformation from the business domain view to the technical domain is performed by a direct mapping of these processes onto a process middleware (i.e., WebSphere Process Server). Hence, the views can be kept fairly consistent, which reduces the efforts in the development life cycle. Using a process middleware enables easy monitoring of the processes during execution, as requested by goal 4.

The transparency of modeled business processes allows reengineering them to improve their effectiveness and efficiency from the pure organizational perspective. Reengineering the processes has been done in this case to reach the goals of simplification and automation. The automation of the processes frees human potential from a lot of work that has been done manually before and that can be automated in the future. This saves a lot of time for the employees, which can be invested in improved customer care (goal 2). It will also be possible to handle more customer requests with the same personnel. For instance, in case of an aggressive acquisition on the market to increase the customer base, the increased workload could be handled with a stable amount of employees.

In summary, all the business goals have been addressed by the design of the to-be processes.

The relevant to-be business processes have been identified by decomposing them into process groups for claims management. From the process groups, the relevant claims management business processes have been identified and modeled as macroflow processes in EPC notation. All these modeling activities so far refer to the top three stages of the business-driven services design approach. The services identified in the EPCs have been designed as Web services in the context of modeling the EPCs as BPEL (Business Process Execution Language) flows with WebSphere Integration Developer. This service design stage reflects the macroflow integration services stage, according to the business-driven services design approach.

Some of the identified services in the example from Chapter 4 needed to be refined as microflows. The services that have been refined as microflows are the *createCommunication* service and the *awaitResponse* service. For those two services, microflow models have been designed that invoke low-level services from the business-driven services stage. In general, these service invocations may also refer to services that already exist in the service portfolio. For this reason, the design of the microflows is dependent on the design of those low-level services, which reflect the convergent bottom-up design approach at this stage. Indeed, for the macroflow integration services stage, existing services from the portfolio, which refer to this level of integration, need to be considered as well. In this example, however, all services needed to be newly designed.

8

Business Object Integration: How to Deal with the Data?

Introduction

Business Object Models

Business processes typically need to operate on some business data. In this book, we interpret the data models of external systems as well as the data models defined in the service-oriented architecture (SOA) from an object-oriented (OO) perspective. That is, the data models are represented using business objects, and all business objects, their attributes, and their relationships are defined in a *business object model*.

Please note that the process-oriented and service-oriented perspectives advocate a more behavioral, stateless view of the system than objects. However, they usually perform operations on data. This data can be represented in many different ways. We assume the use of an OO model for the access to data in a process-driven SOA—to follow the business object concept. This is a proven practice, especially for larger process-driven SOAs.

In fact, *data* seems to be a forgotten child in SOA approaches. One could ask why we propose an approach considering OO while also being service oriented. Do these approaches not contradict each other? We are convinced that they do not as services need to deal with data structures to describe and define the input and output parameters of the services. These parameters are usually not simple data types but rather represent complex structures that can be interpreted as objects. In our opinion, SOA and OO approaches are, for this reason, complementary approaches.

We apply OO concepts to tackle the issues related to the "data" perspective in SOA that is rather a functional than a data-driven approach. OO offers suitable concepts for describing data structures that fit very well to current programming languages and technology used in conjunction with SOA, such as Java/Java Platform, Enterprise Edition (JEE) or C#/.NET. OO languages are still leading edge in these recent technology approaches related to SOA. As a result, we propose an OO approach for tackling the data-related issues in SOAs. The patterns in this chapter thus contribute to solving data issues in SOA.

Figure 8.1 is a simple example of a business object model for storing customer contact information. The model just allows us to specify customers and addresses, as well as a relationship between them: A customer can have multiple addresses in different time frames.

Modeling of business object models has been addressed in various disciplines, such as data modeling, modeling for software analysis, and domain-driven design. Hence, you find different names for business object models in the literature, such as data model, analysis model, or domain model. In this book, we only consider the use of such models

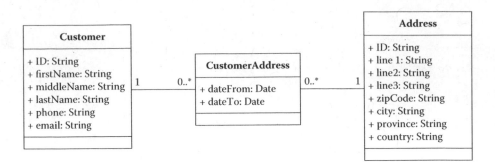

FIGURE 8.1
Example of a business object model for storing customer contact information.

in service-oriented and process-driven systems but do not explain how to design them. Some excellent pattern books on this topic are *Domain-Driven Design* by Eric Evans [Eva04], *Analysis Patterns* by Martin Fowler [Fow96], and *Data Model Patterns* by David Hay [Hay95]. Please refer to these and other sources for more details on how to design the business object model.

Another related issue—also not covered in this book—is how to map the OO business object model to database technology and its predominate relational data model. Much has been written on this topic. For more details, we would like to recommend the *Patterns for Object/Relational Mapping and Access Layers* by Wolfgang Keller [Kel09] and Martin Fowler's *Patterns of Enterprise Application Architecture* [Fow02].

The most essential pattern for using business objects from services and processes, presented in this chapter, is the BUSINESS OBJECT REFERENCE pattern. It deals with the problem of separating business data from process logic and achieving concurrent access (possibly from multiple processes and services) to that data stored in business objects. The pattern advises to only store references to business objects in the process control data structure.

Consider the business object model example given. At any point in time, a customer instance can be accessed by many different business processes, as well as many different instances of the same business process. Hence, it makes no sense to make the customer data part of the control structure of the process. Instead, it should be stored in an external container, so that different business processes or services can use it concurrently.

Once we decide to use the BUSINESS OBJECT REFERENCE pattern, we must also decide how to store and manage the business objects. One solution is described in the BUSINESS OBJECT POOL pattern; it explains an architectural solution in which a central pool for the business objects supports processes that have logical interdependencies. The processes can hence interact with each other without comprising their technical independence.

Figure 8.2 illustrates how BUSINESS OBJECT REFERENCES and a BUSINESS OBJECT POOL are utilized in a process-driven SOA. Various MACROFLOW ENGINES and MICROFLOW ENGINES read and write business objects by reference. The access happens concurrently from the activities of the process instances running in the engines. The BUSINESS OBJECT POOL interface is responsible for handling the concurrency. For instance, it can implement queuing or transactions.

Not all data in a process-driven SOA is necessarily stored in a dedicated BUSINESS OBJECT POOL. Another option is that the business objects are hosted in external systems. This option is explained in the next section. Figure 8.3 shows how the patterns relate.

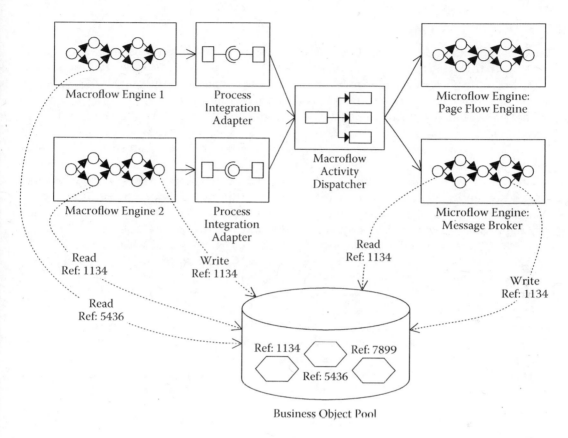

FIGURE 8.2
Business object references and a business object pool in a process-driven SOA.

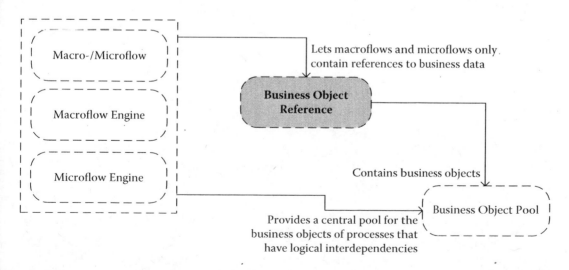

FIGURE 8.3
Business object reference pattern relationships.

Synchronization on Business Objects

Business objects often serve as a central resource for many process instances that run in parallel. In this context, issues may occur when different process instances try to access the same business object. Consider, for example, a write operation to the same business object should be performed by two different process instances.

The PRIVATE-PUBLIC BUSINESS OBJECT pattern offers a concept for accessing a business object from within different activities. The business object is publicly write-locked by the first activity that creates a persistent *private image*. Other activities can still read another *public image* but not perform write operations.

The ACTIVITY INTERRUPT pattern (see Chapter 9) describes activities that allow interrupting and resuming work done on business objects within the activity. Thus, this pattern is used in conjunction with PRIVATE-PUBLIC BUSINESS OBJECTS: The PRIVATE-PUBLIC BUSINESS OBJECTS enable users to store intermediate states and lock the private image until the interrupted business transaction has been completed.

The BUSINESS OBJECT REFERENCE pattern takes the separation of business data and process engine into account. BUSINESS OBJECT REFERENCES can point to PRIVATE-PUBLIC BUSINESS OBJECTS. Often, BUSINESS OBJECT REFERENCES point to business objects in a BUSINESS OBJECT POOL. To support controlled modifications of the central business objects in the pool, the PRIVATE-PUBLIC BUSINESS OBJECT pattern can be applied.

In summary, the PRIVATE-PUBLIC BUSINESS OBJECT pattern introduces a way to handle business objects referenced by and modified in activities, especially in the context of the ACTIVITY INTERRUPT pattern. The change of a state of a PRIVATE-PUBLIC BUSINESS OBJECT can also represent an event that is fired and processed by an EVENT DISPATCHER (see Chapter 10).

The pattern relationships of the PRIVATE-PUBLIC BUSINESS OBJECT pattern are illustrated in Figure 8.4.

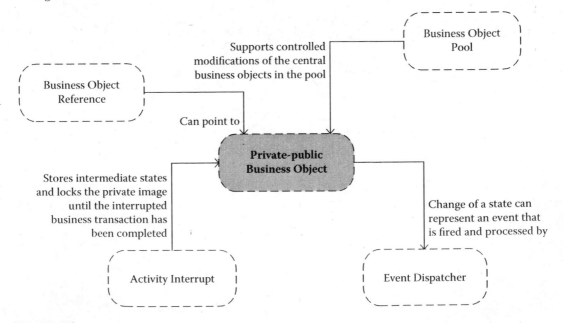

FIGURE 8.4
Private-public business object pattern relationships.

Integrating External Systems

An important goal for using services is often to integrate heterogeneous systems in a flexible manner so that organizations can quickly react to changes in the business. One important aspect in this respect is that usually the services are used for integrating a number of *external systems.* With this term, we refer to systems that need to be integrated into the service-oriented system. External systems include systems of the organization or systems of other organizations. When integrating systems via a process-driven and service-oriented approach, application-specific business object models need to be consolidated somehow and integrated via the process flow.

Typically, many of the external systems are "legacy systems," such as mainframe applications. But, there are many other kinds of external systems, such as standard systems like SAP or other third-party systems. One of the key ideas in recent SOA definitions is to save the investment that has been made in existing information technology (IT) infrastructure and applications and provide flexible means for integrating them. This, however, is difficult as most of these external systems have been independently developed, or at least there is a certain level of independence in their historical evolution. For this reason, external systems often implement *heterogeneous data models.*

Heterogeneous models of the data are not necessarily a problem because this is where *stateless services* can help. Our recommendation is first to consider service-based wrapping for integration: Services are used to expose interfaces to the external system, and an activity type for invoking services is used to invoke these service interfaces from the process instances. In this chapter, we first explain this kind of integration in the section "Service-Based Integration of External Systems."

To assume that service-based integration alone is sufficient to integrate all kinds of external systems, however, is not enough. Sometimes, the data in the external systems that the business processes access and manipulate must be considered. In the section "Data Integration Issues in SOAs," we explain typical data integration issues that make service-based integration insufficient.

In the section "Restructuring the External System for Service-Based Integration," we explain how to deal with situations in which the business object model of an external system does not meet the requirements of the processes. Essentially, we recommend assessing whether it makes sense to apply small restructurings to the external system so that service-based integration is possible after the restructuring.

These two solutions, service-based integration of external systems and restructuring the external system for service-based integration, explain basic alternatives for refactoring a single business object model into a "harmonized" model for a process-oriented architecture. However, in larger systems, it is necessary to consider multiple refactorings of business object models and their interdependencies from the perspective of the whole process-driven SOA. In many situations, this cannot be explained in terms of a single refactoring process but must be addressed at the architectural level. We present two architectural patterns that can be applied in this context:

- The INTEGRATED BUSINESS OBJECT MODEL explains an overall architectural solution that allows you to implement a harmonized business object model. The two refactoring solutions service-based integration of external systems and restructuring the external system for service-based integration are applied in the context of building an INTEGRATED BUSINESS OBJECT MODEL when it is appropriate.

- DATA TRANSFORMATION FLOW explains an architectural solution based on a process subflow for data transformation that maps different application-specific business object models to a common business object model. The goal is to enable flexible integration of various external systems.

BUSINESS OBJECT REFERENCE

Business data—usually represented using business objects—needs to be accessed from processes. If business data would be part of the process control data structure, it is not possible to access the same business data from different process instances (at the same time) as the process control data is exclusively accessible by the corresponding process instances to which the control data belongs. In addition, putting the business data into the process control data structure would violate the principle of separation of concerns.

How are flexible changes and concurrent access from multiple processes and services to business objects supported?

The concept of separation of concerns (i.e., separation of business logic from process logic in the worldview of a process-driven architecture) implies that business objects are managed outside the process engine and will for this reason not be modeled in the process control data structure.

Static binding of business objects to process instances is simply not sufficient in this case. Long-running processes require flexibility concerning structural changes to business objects because business requirements may change over time. As data structures will be bound to a process instance at instantiation time, structural changes to the business objects will not be possible if the business objects are directly modeled in the process control data structure. Moreover, binding the business objects to the process instance would imply structural changes to the process control data structure whenever the business objects change, which should be avoided (see also the GENERIC PROCESS CONTROL STRUCTURE pattern).

Apart from that, static modeling of business objects in the process control data would mean that each process instance works with separate objects, which is actually not the case. Rather, there may be several process instances reading and modifying the same business objects concurrently.

These issues must be solved not only for processes that access business objects but also for ordinary services accessing the business objects.

Store only references to business objects in the process control data structure or in a service implementation and keep the actual business objects in an external container. Via these references, access to business objects in the container can then be established whenever necessary (see Figure 8.5).

The technical representation of the business process (or service) will consider only references to external business objects but not the actual business objects themselves. Those

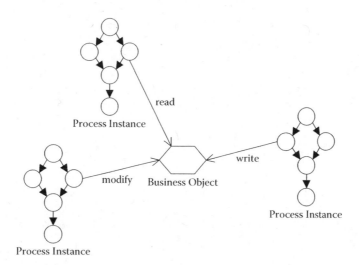

FIGURE 8.5
Business object reference.

business objects will be stored in a separate container outside the process engine or service implementation.

Business objects can be stored in any kind of container. The container can, for instance, be a BUSINESS OBJECT POOL or an external system, such as an application server or mainframe hosting the business objects.

As a result, different process instances or services can modify the same business objects concurrently, and they can react to state changes of the business objects. For example, if a process instance wants to access a business object that has been deleted by a concurrent process instance, it gets a "reference invalid" exception. This can happen, for instance, if an order has been cancelled.

This pattern mainly supports the flexible management and maintenance of business objects in an SOA. It supports the controlled concurrent access to business objects from different process instances and allows making changes to business objects without affecting the process control data as only references are stored in the process control data. Business object data will only be loaded from the container when required during process execution in the application.

As a consequence, on the one hand, the performance increases in the process engine because no large amount of business data is carried for process execution. On the other hand, there is also a trade-off concerning performance because the business object must be retrieved from the container in every activity.

The process control data structure must keep the references to those external business objects and must contain attributes to store these references. This solution implies higher development effort compared to modeling the business data in the process control data structure.

Application of this pattern principally influences the design of a process control data structure as attributes are required to store references to external business objects. If the GENERIC PROCESS CONTROL STRUCTURE pattern is applied, then generic attributes to store references to business objects must be defined in the process control data structure.

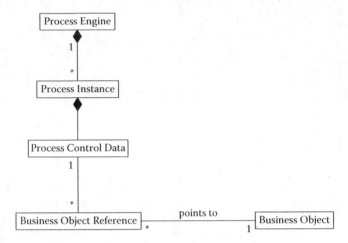

FIGURE 8.6
Example of a business object reference design in UML.

Example: Schematic UML Design of Business Object References

Figure 8.6 illustrates schematically in the Unified Modelling Language (UML) how the BUSINESS OBJECT REFERENCE is used in the process engine and the control data structure of its instances. All BUSINESS OBJECT REFERENCES point to business objects, usually stored in an external container.

Example: Business Object References in a Generic Process Control Structure

In a number of projects, the BUSINESS OBJECT REFERENCE pattern has been implemented using reusable attributes in a GENERIC PROCESS CONTROL STRUCTURE that reference business objects in a database. The chosen DBMS (database management system) in these projects has been DB/2 or Oracle. All projects have used Java as the programming platform to access the business objects from applications. The *metadataID* of each BUSINESS OBJECT REFERENCE identifies the type of business object, which basically points to a concrete database where the object is contained. The *objectID* attribute of a business object reference points to an entity in that database.

Via access classes in a Java framework implementation, a business object can be dynamically determined by a given reference (*metadataID* and *objectID*). The framework implementation searches for the *objectID* in the database identified by the *metadataID* and generates a Java access object that allows reading and writing attributes of the business object. In addition, check-out and check-in operations are provided to enable concurrent access to business objects from various applications.

BUSINESS OBJECT POOL

Business processes are often interdependent in their flow logic. That is, a running process may have effects on other processes being executed in parallel. Technically, each process has its own data space that carries the control data for executing a business process and is thus independent of other processes.

How are the logical data interdependencies between processes implemented while retaining the technical data independence of the processes?

Business processes in execution have their own data space (i.e., the data spaces of business processes running in parallel are disjoint). Actually, this is necessary to provide a business process instance with full control over the execution of the instance—from a technical point of view. Logically, however, business processes are interdependent. That means processes often depend on the results of other processes—or even on events being generated by other processes. For instance, consider a business process handling an order: During this process, the customer decides to cancel the order. This is an event being generated outside the control of the actual order fulfillment process, but the order fulfillment should react accordingly to this event, that is, by stopping the fulfillment or rolling back certain things that have already been done.

The other way around, one might consider a point in the order fulfillment process that is a point of no return. That means at some point in the fulfillment process, the order cannot be cancelled anymore. Consequently, the order fulfillment process generates the respective status of the order. If the customer wants to cancel the order, the order cancellation process needs to consider this point of no return, for instance, by informing the customer that the order can no longer be cancelled.

It is necessary and useful that the data spaces of each process instance are disjoint—to keep the process instances as separate and autonomous entities. But, this makes it hard to depict the data-related interdependencies of the processes. In any case, the behavior of the process must be deterministic. The process logic has to consider all possible events that may occur and depict those events by some decision logic and the corresponding paths of execution.

Keep the business objects in a central pool that can be accessed in parallel by all processes of the process domain. Attributing changes to objects in the pool can then be used as triggers to corresponding behavior in interrelated business processes. The processes can access the central pool during their execution and react on those attribute values (see Figure 8.7).

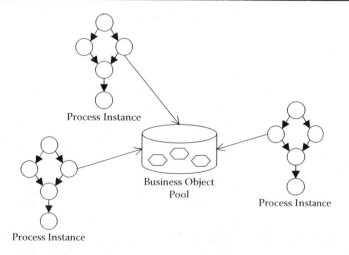

FIGURE 8.7
Business object pool.

Treating the business objects as central resources and allowing access to those central-ized business objects enables, in principle, parallel processes to read and write the data of the business objects. One process might write certain attributes of a business object (e.g., a change in the status of the object). Another parallel process might then read the status information and react to the attribute values correspondingly. Often, the pool of business objects is realized as a central REPOSITORY [Eva04].

Process instances can use their disjoint data spaces to store information that is only rel-evant for the process instance but of no interest for other process instances, such as data to implement the decision points in control flow logic. This data is generally of no relevance to other processes but only the instance itself. Information that has central relevance will be stored in a central business object kept in the BUSINESS OBJECT POOL.

Concurrency issues may occur if several process instances have write access on the same business object, for instance. Traditional locking mechanisms can be used to solve some of these issues. Accessing the business objects takes some additional computational time, and if large amounts of data need to be read, caching mechanisms might be suitable.

The access to business objects in the BUSINESS OBJECT POOL from the data space of a pro-cess instance can be realized via BUSINESS OBJECT REFERENCES that point to objects in a central REPOSITORY [Eva04]. The REPOSITORY is often necessary for revision and reporting purposes to store the business objects manipulated in business processes for historical reasons. To allow for controlled modifications of central business objects, the PRIVATE-PUBLIC BUSINESS OBJECT pattern can be used. This pattern offers a solution to the problem of hiding modifications to business objects as long as the process activities that manipulate the objects are not yet finished. The BUSINESS OBJECT POOL may be a representation of an INTEGRATED BUSINESS OBJECT MODEL.

By accessing the BUSINESS OBJECT POOL and observing attribute values of those objects, a process instance may react in its control logic on an attribute value. The attribute value might have been set by another process running in parallel. Hence, the pattern allows the process logic and its data spaces to be defined independently from other process, but still logical interdependencies can be depicted.

However, the process model must exactly define on what events it is able to react, and the business objects must be accessed via process activities. Sometimes, representing process interdependencies only by using central business objects is not enough. Then, usually new services or processes must be defined to realize the (more complex) interdependent behavior.

Example: Schematic UML Structure of a BUSINESS OBJECT POOL

The main part of Figure 8.8 has been shown before for illustrating the schematic struc-ture of a BUSINESS OBJECT REFERENCE. The BUSINESS OBJECT POOL pattern has almost the same schematic structure; it only adds a *BusinessObjectPool* class that contains the busi-ness objects to which the BUSINESS OBJECT REFERENCE points. Implementation-wise the *BusinessObjectPool* can be realized using database technology, as a view on a legacy system, using an application or component server that hosts the business objects, or on top of any other container technology.

Example: SAP Webflow

In SAP Webflow [FBP03], the Business Object Repository provides definitions of the busi-ness object-type components and their implementation. If an object type is defined in the Business Object Repository, it can be used by workflows. A Business Object Repository Browser enables workflow designers to navigate the Business Object Repository.

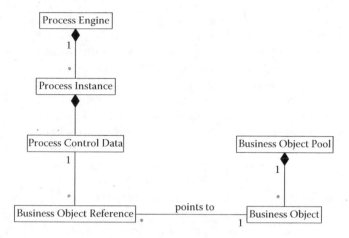

FIGURE 8.8
UML example of a business object pool.

The business objects corresponding to the types can be

- business object types reflected in the data model
- organizational types such as company code or sales organization
- technical object types such as text, note, work item, or archived document

That means the actual business objects are contained in various SAP components. The Business Object Repository provides a unified, OO view on this BUSINESS OBJECT POOL.

PRIVATE-PUBLIC BUSINESS OBJECT

Business processes are concurrently accessing business objects. When business processes access business objects in parallel, concurrency issues occur.

How can business processes access shared business objects in a controlled way to avoid concurrent updates and to limit the visibility of uncommitted changes?

Business objects representing the business data of a company or system are usually accessed from within defined business process activities. Such objects are typically managed and persistently stored in central data stores or business applications (e.g., a BUSINESS OBJECT POOL). Activities that process business objects during their execution may access these with a BUSINESS OBJECT REFERENCE that is uniquely identifying a business object.

If such activities are executed in parallel, conflicts will arise due to parallel write accesses. Also, the read accesses to a business object can be problematic if the business object also is currently processed by another activity. Parallel read accesses can result in a problem because business object modifications made in the context of one activity will be visible immediately to other system activities when the corresponding business object transaction is committed. If a business activity involves user interactions, for example, a referenced business object may be modified subsequently by multiple user-invoked transactions that are actually representing only intermediate states of a business object.

The modifications and thus intermediary states are immediately accessible by parallel activities if the changes are committed after each interaction. This behavior is usually not wanted because only the final state shall be visible and not the intermediary states. A microflow may also offer a user to undo modifications, for example. If a parallel activity reads the processed business object, it may operate on a temporary and thus invalid business object state.

The problem of parallel read access to a business object is especially present in the context of ACTIVITY INTERRUPTS (see Chapter 9). An ACTIVITY INTERRUPT interrupts the current activity and restarts it. Considering business object modifications in this scenario, it is rather obvious that it is necessary to save the current work done on business objects so information is not lost and to be able to reestablish the context when resuming the activity at a later time.

When the user interrupts some work, modified business objects may not always be in a consistent state. Consider an activity that involves entering a large amount of data, such as a detailed customer feedback form. When the user processing the activity wants to interrupt this work, the data entered so far shall not get lost but shall not be publicly visible either because not all data of the feedback form has been entered yet. Thus, it may be necessary that interruptible activities allow saving inconsistent states of associated business objects. These states shall not be publicly visible (that is, not become available in the system) until all data is consistent and the activity is finished. The read access to the business object shall be limited to the state it had before the changes were made.

Furthermore, parallel changes to a business object shall be prohibited. If an activity processes a business object and another activity performs parallel changes, the object will enter an inconsistent state.

In the context of the ACTIVITY INTERRUPT pattern, if an object has been modified before an ACTIVITY INTERRUPT happens, the corresponding user expects to resume at the same point (i.e., the activity's context has to remain consistent). Therefore, a business object modified within this interruptible activity shall be locked by the activity to prohibit parallel changes. In other words, write access shall be limited to the processing activity to guarantee a deterministic behavior of the business transaction spanned by the activity.

These fundamental problems are related to existing mechanisms in the area of transactional systems, like, for example, database transactions and locking features that prevent parallel updates by write locks and ensure limited data visibility during a running transaction. Yet, these technical solutions to data visibility and write control do not provide a solution within the context of more complex business scenarios as we can observe them in process-driven systems.

Introduce PRIVATE-PUBLIC BUSINESS OBJECTS that expose two separate images of the data contained in a business object: a private and a public image. A PRIVATE-PUBLIC BUSINESS OBJECT allows making changes on its "private" image prior to publishing the changes to its "public" state and enforces a write-lock for other activities as long as a private image exists (see Figure 8.9).

The concept of separation of business logic from process logic implies that the modification of business data is done on business objects that are managed outside the process engine. Even if business objects are stored via a DBMS, updates to a business object from within a business activity will often be performed in more than one single database transaction (i.e., a short-running transaction). That means processing of a business activity can

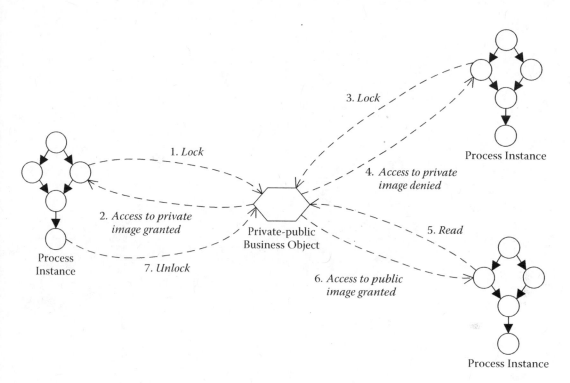

FIGURE 8.9
A private-public business object.

involve several user interactions. Each user interaction typically spans a database transaction in this scenario. The activity itself, though, spans a business transaction (i.e., a long-running transaction) that shall not be committed until the activity is finished.

A PRIVATE-PUBLIC BUSINESS OBJECT has a public and a private image. Both images contain the same business object attributes. The private image is created during a business transaction and reflects the state of the object, which is only visible from within this transaction (i.e., the processing activity). The public image of the object reflects its state, which is always publicly visible. When the activity commits the first modifications of a PRIVATE-PUBLIC BUSINESS OBJECT, a private image is created that exposes the data of the business object, including the changes. Any read access to the business object from within another business activity returns the public image of the object, which does not contain these modifications. Any parallel write access will be prohibited if a private image exists.

Read access to the business object issued from the activity, which initially performed the changes, will return the private image and thus reflects all modifications made in that business transaction so far. When the activity is finished, it explicitly publishes these modifications. The changes stored in the private image are merged into the public image and will then be accessible to all system activities.

To be able to differentiate between the activities that access the object, a unique activity or business transaction identifier (ID) has to be introduced. The identifier has to be compared with the owning transaction ID during each read and write request. Thus, the business transaction that created the private image is stored in that image.

Figure 8.10 shows the possible transitions between private and public states of PRIVATE-PUBLIC BUSINESS OBJECTS. The object is in a private state if a private image of the object exists and in a public state if it has no private image. A PRIVATE-PUBLIC BUSINESS OBJECT is

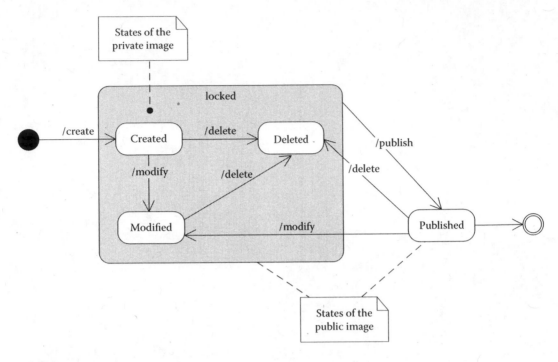

FIGURE 8.10
State transitions of a private-public business object. (From C. Hentrich. Synchronization patterns for process-driven and service-oriented architectures. *Springer LNCS Transactions on Pattern Languages of Programs,* 103–135, 2009.)

either in one of the private states (*created, modified,* or *deleted*) or it is in public (*published*) state. The figure also shows the state *locked.* This is the state of the public image once a private image exists.

The differentiation between the private states *created, modified,* and *deleted* allows us to apply the appropriate merge operation when publishing the changes. When the object is initially created, no public image exists. The publish operation will invoke the public image to be created. If the object is deleted before the first publish operation is called, then no public image has to be created. Once a public image exists, the business object can either enter the states *private-modified* or *private-deleted.* If a private image exists or the business object is not in the *published* state, its public image is write-locked.

The pattern can be implemented in several ways depending on the technology used to store business objects in the system and the way services access these objects. When using a relational database to store business objects, the concept of a PRIVATE-PUBLIC BUSINESS OBJECT can be realized by introducing two database schemas, one for the private images and one for the public images of the business objects.

Ideally, activity implementations (services) do not have to deal with the different images themselves but simply perform operations on the business object. The special persistence mechanism required for PRIVATE-PUBLIC BUSINESS OBJECTS is handled by the persistence layer of an application that encapsulates the required write and read logic.

Using the PRIVATE-PUBLIC BUSINESS OBJECT pattern, business objects may be write-locked for a long time, which may block execution of parallel processes. As a consequence, this aspect enforces a clear and integrated design of business processes and business objects. The PRIVATE-PUBLIC BUSINESS OBJECT pattern allows users of a process management system

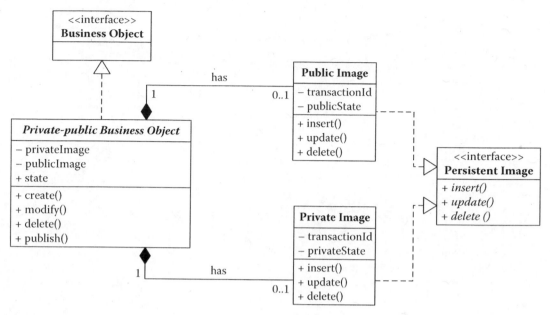

FIGURE 8.11
UML-based design example for a private-public business object. (From C. Hentrich. Synchronization patterns for process-driven and service-oriented architectures. *Springer LNCS Transactions on Pattern Languages of Programs,* 103–135, 2009.)

using the ACTIVITY INTERRUPT pattern (see Chapter 9) to save modifications of business objects made within the activity in inconsistent states prior to finishing the activity.

The PRIVATE-PUBLIC BUSINESS OBJECT pattern introduces significant additional logic and implementation effort. For example, the realization of the pattern requires implementing a custom persistence framework for such business objects or extension of existing frameworks. For this reason, one needs to be clear whether access synchronization to business objects is a must-have requirement to avoid unnecessary development effort.

Example: UML-Based Design of PRIVATE-PUBLIC BUSINESS OBJECTS

Figure 8.11 shows an example design of a PRIVATE-PUBLIC BUSINESS OBJECT as a realization of a generic business object interface. It offers a common interface to the public and private images. The images are both realizations of the *persistent image* interface, and they both link to the business transaction via the *transactionId* attribute.

Example: Parallel Access to a Business Object

Figure 8.12 gives an example of parallel access to a PRIVATE-PUBLIC BUSINESS OBJECT that is modified during the execution of a business process activity represented as a microflow. The first modification of the object within the activity (*process instance A*) creates a private image reflecting the changes and enforces a write-lock on the public image of the object. Parallel activities can still read the public state of the object but are not eligible to perform any changes (*process instance B*). The public image remains in the state "locked" during the processing and interruption of the activity. The activity may modify the private image of the object until the user finishes the activity. When finishing the activity, the private image is merged into the public image and deleted afterward. The write-lock is freed, and the object is in the state "published" again.

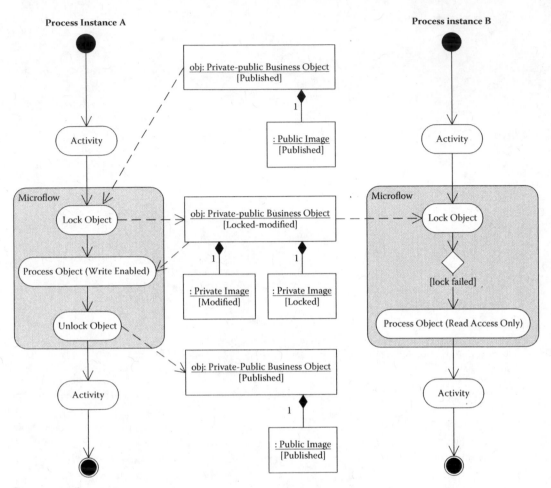

FIGURE 8.12
Example of parallel access to a private-public business object. (From C. Hentrich. Synchronization patterns for process-driven and service-oriented architectures. *Springer LNCS Transactions on Pattern Languages of Programs,* 103–135, 2009.)

Example: Persistence Logic for PRIVATE-PUBLIC BUSINESS OBJECTS

Figure 8.13 gives an example of the persistence logic for PRIVATE-PUBLIC BUSINESS OBJECTS using a relational database. To keep information about the transaction locking of a business object, the column *TransactionId* is contained in each table of the public and private schema. The states of the private and public images are stored in the *PrivateState* and *PublicState* columns.

In the example, a customer object is being updated and another object is being deleted during a long-running transaction (e.g., via an ACTIVITY INTERRUPT). The changes performed during this activity are logged in a transaction log table. This is needed to keep track of the operations to be executed when the long-running transaction is committed (i.e., the business objects are published).

The following code fragment gives a high-level example of an implementation of the publish method of the PRIVATE-PUBLIC BUSINESS OBJECT. Depending on the state, a database row in the public schema will be inserted, updated, or deleted for an existing private image. The database operations (e.g., executed via Java Databse Connectivity (JDBC)) are supposed to be encapsulated within the implementation of the *PublicImage* class.

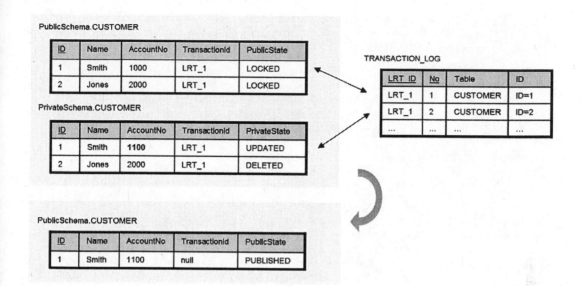

FIGURE 8.13
Persistence logic using a relational database. (From C. Hentrich. Synchronization patterns for process-driven and service-oriented architectures. *Springer LNCS Transactions on Pattern Languages of Programs,* 103–135, 2009.)

```
public abstract class PrivatePublicBusinessObject
      implements BusinessObject {
   private PersistentImage privateImage;
   private PersistentImage publicImage;
   private int state;

   public synchronized void publish() {
      if (state==STATE_CREATED) {
         publicImage = new PublicImage();
         // Copy all attributes of private to
         // public image
         copyAttributes(privateImage, publicImage);
         // Set the state and insert the row
         publicImage.setState(STATE_PUBLISHED);
         publicImage.setTransactionId(null);
         publicImage.insert();
         // Delete private image
         privateImage.delete();
      } else if (state==STATE_MODIFIED) {
         // Merge all changes of private to
         // public image
         mergeAttributes(privateImage, publicImage);
         // Set the state and update the row
         publicImage.setState(STATE_PUBLISHED);
         publicImage.setTransactionId(null);
         publicImage.update();
         // Delete private image
         privateImage.delete();
      } else if (state==STATE_DELETED) {
         // Persistently delete public and
         // private images
         publicImage.delete();
         privateImage.delete();
      }
   }
   ...
}
```

Simple data access becomes more complex in this scenario. Imagine all customer objects visible in the context of a specific long-running transaction are to be retrieved by a simple query like the following:

```
SELECT NAME FROM CUSTOMERS WHERE ((NAME LIKE 'AB%'))
```

This query has to be changed to retrieve all public images except for the ones currently processed in this long-running transaction (identified by *<current_LRT_ID>*) and perform a union with the private images that are in this transaction but are not marked as deleted:

```
SELECT NAME FROM PublicSchema.CUSTOMERS
WHERE (NAME LIKE 'AB%') AND TransactionId <> <current_LRT_ID>
OR TransactionId is null
UNION
SELECT NAME FROM PrivateSchema.CUSTOMERS
WHERE (NAME LIKE 'AB%') AND TransactionId = <current_LRT_ID>
AND PrivateState <> <deleted>
```

This query retrieves the correct data depending on the current scope (within a long-running transaction or not). It should be encapsulated in an adequate way (e.g., by offering special database union views).

Examples: Uses of Private-Public Business Objects in Various Applications

- In a supply chain management solution in the automotive industry, the pattern has been implemented in a programming framework to control the access to central business objects.
- In the insurance industry, the pattern has been implemented in a claims management solution to control concurrent access to claims as business objects during parallel-running business processes that handle the claim.
- In the context of enterprise content management solutions, the pattern has been used in projects in insurance and banking to control the access to central documents using IBM FileNet.

Service-Based Integration of External Systems

In an SOA, the most important pattern of integration is to offer services [Eva04] that provide the integration of an external system. A service is an operation offered as an interface, without encapsulating state. Service interfaces solve the basic problem of how to represent loosely coupled interfaces. However, loose coupling is hard to achieve if the external system design forces us to hard-code dependencies to stateful interfaces or communication protocol details in the process models or integration code.

For a connection to the process-oriented layer, we must meet the requirements of the process-oriented SOA, but most often the external system does not fulfill them a priori. We do not want to hard-code them in the process models, which should be kept flexible, changeable, and understandable to the domain expert. Typically, a central requirement of a process-driven SOA is that the services can be used to integrate any kind of system in the same way and allow process designers to flexibly assemble processes from the services offered by the external systems. The services should hide all details of the communication with the external system from the process designer.

Consider, for instance, integrating a mainframe that only supports batch processing. From the perspective of the process designer, this system should be integrated in the same way as a Web service that was specifically written for this task. However, different service developers use different approaches to design SERVICES and integrate them into process models. This means that the desired information hiding is hard to achieve, and process designers must cope with these differences.

An in-house guideline for SERVICES development can solve this problem only partially. For instance, if services are used that are not developed in house (e.g., services offered by an external standard system like SAP), guidelines on their design cannot be imposed.

To solve this problem, we must adapt both the external system and the process model:

1. For each entity in the external systems that needs to be exposed to the process-driven architecture, define one or more stateless SERVICES on top of the existing interfaces of the external system.

2. Define or use a special SERVICE activity type in the process engine that wraps invocations to external services. This way, SERVICE invocations are represented as atomic activities in the process flow. The SERVICE activity type can be used in business processes to flexibly assemble services because all details of the communication with the external system are hidden in the wrapper activity. Instantiate and use the SERVICE activity type in process models whenever an external system needs to be invoked.

The main task of the SERVICE is to translate a service-based invocation into the interface of the external system and translate the responses back into a service-based reply. Hence, the relevant interfaces of external systems are integrated into the SOA using SERVICES, exposing a view on the external systems that reflects the requirements of the process-driven SOA. Figure 8.14 illustrates the service-based integration of external system functions in process activities.

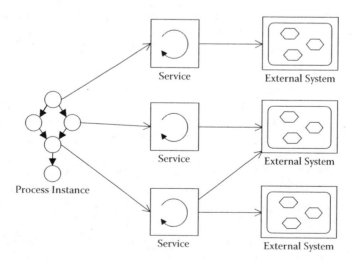

FIGURE 8.14
Service-based integration of external system functions in process activities.

The goal of decoupling processes and individual process activities, realized as SERVICES, is to introduce a higher level of flexibility into the SOA: Predefined services can be flexibly assembled in a process design tool. The technical processes should reflect and perhaps optimize the business processes of the organization. Thus, the flexible assembly of services in processes enables developers to cope with required changes to the organizational processes while maintaining a stable overall architecture.

If a service exists or can be built that equals the required meaning of a process activity, an activity can be mapped to exactly one service. However, in reality this is not always possible. For instance, an activity in a process might need to wrap a whole set of application services because each service only fulfills a part of the overall functionality requested by the more coarse-grained process activity.

The main driving factor for the integration of services and process activities should always be that the process activity type needs to be understandable in the context of the process models. A one-to-one integration between service and activity is easy to build and maintain. Hence, it should be chosen if possible, but only if its meaning fits well into the context of the process model. There are also other driving factors for the integration of services and process activities that need to be considered, such as reusability of services in different activity types or design for foreseeable future changes.

Often, more than one application needs to be wrapped to fulfill the goal of the activity. Consequently, designing and implementing the integration of the activity with application services is not trivial and introduces a whole new set of problems. These problems are addressed in more detail by the PROCESS INTEGRATION ARCHITECTURE pattern, which provides an architectural concept for achieving this integration. In particular, an INTEGRATION ADAPTER for the process can be provided to depict the functionality requested by a process activity as one service, which is composed of more fine-grained services. These patterns thus allow designers to solve issues that arise when the services cannot be directly designed and implemented according to the requirements of process activities and directly invoked via the process flow.

Ideally, the application services can be designed according to the requirements of a process activity. However, requirements might change; thus, processes might also change. For this reason, it is often better to provide the services in terms of self-contained functions of an application that are based on the entities of the application. That is, the services are designed according to the specific business object model applied by an application. The consequence is that processes and application services are more loosely coupled and thus more flexible. There is the trade-off, however, that larger integration effort and greater complexity for implementing the integration is required.

In this respect, the MACRO-/MICROFLOW pattern can be used to conceptually decouple the fine-grained application SERVICES that are required within the integration context from long-running processes. Following the MACRO-/MICROFLOW pattern, the fine-grained application SERVICES are orchestrated in a microflow (i.e., a more fine-grained technical integration process). The PROCESS INTEGRATION ARCHITECTURE pattern provides flexible means for implementing both the one-to-one and the one-to-many relationship between process activities and application services.

The relationships of the patterns that can be used for service-based integration are shown in Figure 8.15.

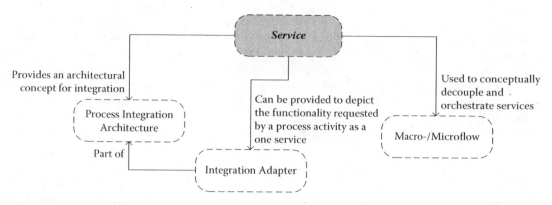

FIGURE 8.15
Service-based integration: pattern relationships.

Data Integration Issues in SOAs

In the context of business processes, usually all business objects, their attributes, and their relationships are defined in a *business object model* (as explained previously). Within its scope, the business object model usually defines unified semantics. In many cases, the scope of a business object model is one external system or the BUSINESS OBJECT POOL of the SOA.

Semantic integration is usually hard to achieve between various business object models. Often, even seemingly simple abstractions, such as a customer object, are hard to unify for all systems of a number of organizations that need to interact. In many cases, this is not even possible for the systems of a single organization. Here, the services that interconnect these systems must support the *business model integration*.

When various business object models need to be integrated in an SOA, often a purely SERVICE-based integration is infeasible or impossible because of data integration issues. Examples are

- incompatible data definitions,
- inconsistent data across the enterprise,
- data redundancy,
- data incompleteness,
- data availability issues,
- data ownership issues, or
- update anomalies.

All these problems can only be addressed at a broader scope than a single service. In practice, often massive hand-coding efforts are used to resolve these issues, which require a lot of time and are often hard to maintain in the long run. Instead of using such "ad hoc solutions," it is advisable to follow a more systematic approach—in terms of both the refactoring processes and the architectural solutions.

As a real-world example, consider an automobile rental company that has grown in the last years, has merged with two other companies, and now consists of three independently working territorial branches. Each branch represents a company being acquired over the years to serve a territorial market. Transparent business processes shall now be implemented, following an SOA approach that allows renting cars via the Internet, independent of the territorial assignment. The data models in the various branches are different as each branch uses independently grown systems. Moreover, customer data is redundant in these systems: They use inconsistent automobile identification mechanisms, there is inconsistent formatting of data, and there are incorrect or incomplete values in the data fields. If common business processes shall be implemented for these branches, these data issues must be resolved first.

Certainly, the cost for resolving these issues needs to be balanced with the business case associated with improving the business processes. However, in this chapter we assume that this business case has been made and concentrate on the solutions of resolving these problems. The discussion concerning the business case should be made separately and prior to starting an engagement or project in this direction. For this reason, we do not consider these aspects any further.

Let us consider the example in more detail. Consider the rental car company uses the two classes shown in Figure 8.16 in their business object model to represent customer contact data—the same information as also presented in our previous example.

Consider one of the external systems uses the business object model presented at the beginning of this chapter. The two business object models have a number of data integration issues:

- In the car rental model, the classes are named differently from the first example.
- In the car rental model, there is no association class, but only two direct associations.
- A rental car customer cannot have o..* addresses, but only two addresses: one home and one company address.
- The notion of historic addresses (*fromDate* and *toDate*) from the first example are not supported by the car rental model.
- The notion of company and home address does not exist in the previous model. Also, the field *sendInvoiceToHomeAddress* is missing in the first model.
- Some fields are differently named or have other types.
- In the car rental model, the e-mail and phone data are associated to an address, whereas before they were associated to the customer.

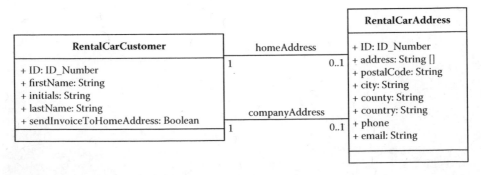

FIGURE 8.16
Business object model example for a rental car company.

If we want to integrate the two business object models, let us say using a query service that queries for customers and addresses across the two systems, resolving the data integration issues is not trivial in all cases. Of course, the different names are easy to resolve. But for the different types used for identification, we already require an ID mapping between *String*-based IDs and *ID_Number*-based IDs. If the notion of company and home address should be present in the query service, it is unclear what should be returned if objects of the first model are queried. Also mapping the potential *n* addresses and the historic addresses to the car rental model is not easily possible. Finally, in the car rental model, a customer can have multiple phone numbers and e-mail addresses. It is unclear which one should be delivered when querying for one using the design of the first example model.

All these issues can, for instance, be resolved using conventions or by raising exceptions when something cannot be delivered. But, this a design choice: Is a convention or raising exceptions really enough? Or, do we require a better integration? If so, we basically have three choices that are not mutually exclusive and usually include the service-based integration of external systems describe previously:

- Try restructuring the external system for service-based integration as explained in the next section. This solution is usually much work as it means to change the two or more existing systems, but if it succeeds it might deliver a conceptually clean solution.

- Often, restructuring the external system for service-based integration is hardly possible because of the efforts involved or because the two systems need the different kinds of information for reasons implied by the business domain. It is hard or impossible to find agreement on a common business object model. In such cases, it might still be possible to design an INTEGRATED BUSINESS OBJECT MODEL only for the process-driven SOA that utilizes the information in the two systems.

- We can use data transformations to change the data in the business object models in a way that suits the SOA. We can, for example, use a special kind of microflow for data transformation, as described in the DATA TRANSFORMATION FLOW pattern. Such transformations are needed for simple service-based integration of external systems as well as for transforming to an INTEGRATED BUSINESS OBJECT MODEL.

The resulting relationships of the patterns are shown in Figure 8.17.

Restructuring the External System for Service-Based Integration

When integrating systems into a process-driven architecture, the first choice should be to follow service-based integration of external systems, as described previously. This, however, might fail because the external system is a legacy system that is not structured in a suitable way to allow for offering its business object model via SERVICES.

One possible reason is the data integration issues introduced in the previous section. If these data integration issues occur, it might be necessary to think about a better solution than performing individual mappings within wrapper SERVICES (maybe repeatedly).

In addition to data-mapping problems, it might be possible that an external system does not offer appropriate interfaces to access the relevant data at all via a pure wrapper

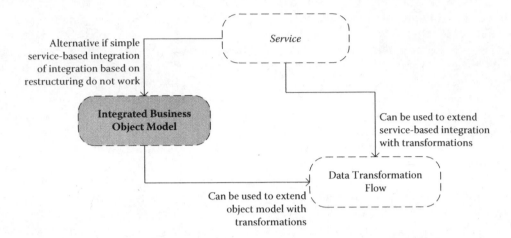

FIGURE 8.17
Integrated business object model pattern relationships.

SERVICE. Sometimes, the data is accessible but not in a suitable way. Consider, for instance, a legacy system that offers only a batch interface. It might be possible that the performance of this interface is not good enough for an integration task. Or, the data model and the interfaces require repetitive invocations via the wrapper SERVICE, which downgrades the performance of the overall system. Or, a legacy system does not offer session abstractions that can be used for aligning interdependent stateless service invocations; hence, the performance of interdependent invocations is weak. In other words, often the external system was designed without having the requirements of integration in an SOA in mind and thus cannot fulfill the requirements of the SOA.

Such issues can arise even when the developers only need to integrate two interfaces. Consider a simple point-to-point integration between two systems is needed. In this simple case, the interfaces between the two integrated systems need to be mapped to exchange data. This is only possible in simple wrapper SERVICES if the mapping of (data) types can be completely performed within the service implementation.

In a larger SOA with a dedicated service orchestration layer, things become even more complicated. This is because the different business object models of the involved external systems need to be consolidated somehow to achieve a flexible orchestration within the process flow.

To avoid these problems, sometimes restructuring the external system is an option:

1. Assess whether a restructuring is possible according to the following criteria: The system evolution should be as nonintrusive and minimal as possible. It should not break existing client code. Substantial portions of the system should remain unchanged. If the assessment is positive, restructure the application-specific business model of an integrated external system by evolving the system to meet the new requirements introduced by the process-oriented architecture.

2. Next, offer service interfaces so that the business process can access the evolved external system using service-based integration of external systems as described previously.

Before applying a restructuring of an application-specific business model, it is necessary to consider that it may not be possible at all or with acceptable effort to restructure the business object models of legacy applications such that they work consistently together. The requirements of the business processes need to be considered by a business object model designer so that the business object model is suitable for representing the domain architecture of the business processes. Also, it is necessary to consider changing requirements (e.g., in case another legacy application needs to be integrated in a process flow). It is important to consider whether a restructuring can be done with minimal changes so that existing assets are preserved and existing client code is not broken. That is, existing external interfaces should remain compatible.

A restructuring should only be performed if all these considerations lead to the conclusion that it is possible to restructure the application-specific business object model of an external system. In addition, if the restructuring is possible with acceptable effort, it should be considered before considering integration following an INTEGRATED BUSINESS OBJECT MODEL or using a DATA TRANSFORMATION FLOW. This is because most often it is easier to make local changes to the data of a system in the system itself than to evolve the data in an external mapping component (which is part of the business process).

INTEGRATED BUSINESS OBJECT MODEL

External systems (i.e., systems that have so far not been part of the process-driven SOA) should be integrated into a process-driven SOA. In many cases, the external systems are legacy systems. Simply integrating the external system using SERVICES fails because of data integration issues. Restructuring the business object model of each of the external systems proves to be difficult, infeasible, or even impossible because the external systems cannot or should not be changed or adapted. Local, independent changes in the application-specific business object models are often not enough to resolve data integration issues, such as incompatible data definitions, inconsistent data across the enterprise, data redundancy, and update anomalies.

> How can data integration issues in business object models be resolved if service-based integration and business object model restructuring are not feasible?

Data integration issues, such as incompatible data definitions, inconsistent data across the enterprise, data redundancy, and update anomalies, can occur when integrating data or interfaces of two or more systems into a process-driven architecture. These issues often cannot be resolved in a suitable way using only wrapper SERVICES. Usually, in such cases one should try to restructure the business object models first. But, consider a legacy system in which the source code is not available. Or, no experts for the languages or platforms used by a legacy system are working for the company anymore. Perhaps a significant investment is needed to make changes to the legacy system, and the extra costs should be avoided. Such situations are highly unwanted, but nonetheless they occur.

Let us consider the other case: restructuring each business object model of the systems to be integrated is possible and feasible. Still situations occur in which restructuring is not applicable if a "global" perspective is needed for data integration. Consider, for instance, two or more application-specific business object models need to be integrated in a process flow. Sometimes, data integration issues cannot be (effectively) solved by only changing the local applications. For instance, if one data model depicts an address as a custom data

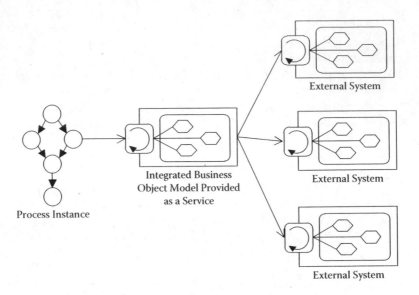

FIGURE 8.18
An integrated business object model.

record and the other one as a string, we need to write conversion code between the two incompatible data types at the "global" level. That is, we create a "global" view based on the combination of the information in the different application-specific business object models.

Design an INTEGRATED BUSINESS OBJECT MODEL that consolidates the structures of the involved business object models. Map the relevant parts of the application-specific business object models into the INTEGRATED BUSINESS OBJECT MODEL and perform the data integration tasks at the global level. The INTEGRATED BUSINESS OBJECT MODEL depicts the requirements of the related business processes; that is, it provides a process-related, global view of the application-specific business object models (see Figure 8.18).

The parts of the application-specific business object models that are subject to exposed services are mapped into the INTEGRATED BUSINESS OBJECT MODEL. The exposed services are usually integrated into the process flow using wrapper SERVICES that are invoked by activities in the process flow.

The INTEGRATED BUSINESS OBJECT MODEL design has to consider all requirements of the process domain in terms of the services that the processes need to expose. The model must be consistent with all integrated applications and with the service requirements of the processes.

Flexible aspects of the INTEGRATED BUSINESS OBJECT MODEL should be described by metadata mechanisms. An abstraction from concrete structures to more abstract structures, defined by metadata, helps to manage an INTEGRATED BUSINESS OBJECT MODEL centrally. For instance, flexible data structures within business objects can be defined via XML (Extensible Markup Language). Which areas are subject to change is detected by an analysis of application-specific business object models and design issues detected in the business process requirements.

The INTEGRATED BUSINESS OBJECT MODEL pattern introduces an architecture that allows developers to start with the "standard" solution of an SOA, to use the SERVICES pattern, and to wrap it with an activity in the process flow. This should always be the first choice because this solution is simple and offers loose coupling. When this fails, it should be checked whether restructuring the business object models of the external systems makes sense. Finally, an INTEGRATED BUSINESS OBJECT MODEL can be introduced either in addition to those other measures or as an alternative.

Unanticipated changes to the INTEGRATED BUSINESS OBJECT MODEL might occur during the evolution and lead to some restructuring. In fact, taking the right level of design abstraction with metadata that anticipates future changes while providing enough concrete structures is still rather an art than a science.

The DATA TRANSFORMATION FLOW pattern provides an approach for designing and implementing the necessary mapping from application-specific business object models to the INTEGRATED BUSINESS OBJECT MODEL.

When the model is implemented, the actual business objects will be stored in a central BUSINESS OBJECT POOL.

The CANONICAL DATA MODEL [HW03] pattern describes a similar approach to designing a data model that is independent from specific applications. The INTEGRATED BUSINESS OBJECT MODEL pattern can be viewed as a specialization of it within a process-driven SOA context. SERVICES are used to access the external system from a SOA.

Example: Simple Example Structure of an INTEGRATED BUSINESS OBJECT MODEL

Figure 8.19 illustrates how an INTEGRATED BUSINESS OBJECT MODEL is designed. The INTEGRATED BUSINESS OBJECT MODEL integrates all involved application-specific business object models, and the business processes are defined on top this model. The INTEGRATED BUSINESS OBJECT MODEL—if designed using appropriate metadata mechanisms—is open for integrating additional external business object models.

Example: Integrating Customer Contact Data Models

We need to integrate the two customer contact data models we have introduced in this chapter. The goal of the integration is to provide a unique query service interface for the process-driven SOA. We are not able to access the external systems; hence, restructuring the external system for service-based integration is not an option.

The INTEGRATED BUSINESS OBJECT MODEL should be designed with the information needed by the process-driven SOA in mind. That is, first you should elicit which information is needed from the two application-specific business object models.

In our case, we can describe the requirements for the query API of the query service. All information that can be queried should also be part of the INTEGRATED BUSINESS OBJECT MODEL.

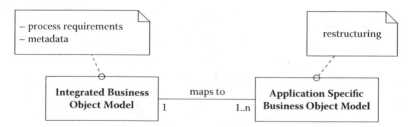

FIGURE 8.19
Example structure of an integrated business object model.

- It should be possible to obtain any customer using some unique ID.
- It should be possible to obtain a list of customers by first name, last name, phone number, and e-mail address.
- It should be possible to obtain any address using some unique ID.
- It should be possible to obtain a list of addresses by a string content contained in the address, the zip code, the city, the province, or the country.
- It should be possible to obtain all addresses of a customer.
- It should be possible to obtain the address of a customer.

Figure 8.20 shows a design of a query service that fulfills these requirements using a simple interface. The two classes *IBOMCustomer* and *IBOMAddress* represent the INTE-GRATED BUSINESS OBJECT MODEL. The query service uses the two SERVICES for accessing the external systems to obtain the information from the two application-specific business object models.

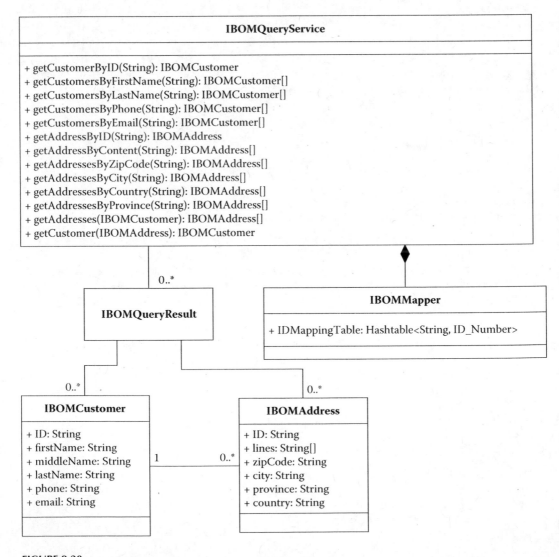

FIGURE 8.20
Query service for customer contact data business object model.

In this step, a number of data transformations and conventions for the mapping are needed. This can, for instance, be done using a DATA TRANSFORMATION FLOW. Some examples of mappings that must be performed to resolve the data integration issues identified before are

- The class *IBOMMAPPER* provides a mapping between *String*-based and *ID_Number*-based IDs using a simple hash-table-based mapping. The STRING-based IDs are used in the INTEGRATED BUSINESS OBJECT MODEL.
- The home e-mail address and phone number from the car rental model are selected for *IBOMCustomer* as the default if the customer has both a home and company e-mail address or phone number.
- Only the current addresses are used. The *dateTo* and *dateFrom* from the first model are ignored. The home and company addresses from the second model are just added as two addresses to the list (i.e., this semantic information is ignored).
- All address content is stored in the *lines* array.
- The fields that are named differently are just mapped without modification.

Example: The Use of an INTEGRATED BUSINESS OBJECT MODEL in Standards and Reference Architectures: The Example of New Generation Operations Systems and Software Shared Information and Data Model

To aim for standardization is one possible reason to define an INTEGRATED BUSINESS OBJECT MODEL. This, of course, is possible in the context of a single organization or a few collaborating organizations, but sometimes if multiple organizations or even a whole industry need to agree on a business object model, standardization efforts in standardization bodies or in the context of reference architectures are pursued. It makes sense to look for a standardized INTEGRATED BUSINESS OBJECT MODEL in your domain first, before you try to define one on your own. To illustrate this scenario, let us have a look at the example of NGOSS: the New Generation Operations Systems and Software [Tmf09]. NGOSS is a standard for making the development and use of operations support systems, mainly in the telecommunications industry, more flexible and easier. It provides reference architecture for the business processes in operations support. One part of NGOSS is the shared information and data (SID) model [Rei07], which provides an INTEGRATED BUSINESS OBJECT MODEL for NGOSS applications.

The SID model is an OO model defined in UML. The goal of SID is to provide a generic language for describing management information for the telecommunications industry. The model specifies eight domains: market/sales, products, customers, services, resources, suppliers/partners, common business, and enterprise. Using the models categorized into these domains, basically the entire business of a telecommunications operator is covered.

DATA TRANSFORMATION FLOW

Systems need to be integrated via a business process-driven and service-oriented approach, and the systems have heterogeneous business object models. For example, a transformation between the business object models of two systems integrated into an SOA is needed. Major goals of an SOA are loose coupling and flexibility. These properties should not be compromised by hard-coding data integration details. In a process-oriented SOA, it is also necessary to map the data integration steps conceptually to the process flow to be able to configure data integration changes easily from process design tools.

How is the data from business object models integrated in a process model in a flexible and changeable way?

In SOAs, the systems have usually been independently developed and have changed over time. As a result, it is usually not trivial to depict the business objects provided as input and output parameters of one system onto the business object model used by the target system. Consequently, some kind of mapping and transformation will be necessary. The structures and the semantics of the business object models must map somehow.

In this context, mapping means that business objects and the attributes of them need to be projected onto business objects and corresponding attributes of the target model. This mapping must be maintainable, and the mapping architecture must be extensible. It should be possible to react on typical change requirements, such as an increased workload, a business object model change, or integration of a new application with minimum effort.

This means especially that no programming effort should be necessary to change (minor) details of the data integration. Somehow, we need to depict and configure data integration between business object models in the process so that it is possible to use process design tools for the mapping process and for rapidly changing the mapping.

Implement the data transformation as a microflow (i.e., running as a process subflow) that uses mapping components that are based on configurable transformation rules to project one business object model onto another. Technology that supports rule-based data transformation is used to change the transformation rules at runtime. Perform the mapping steps as activities of a microflow to make the data transformations configurable from the process design tool (see Figure 8.21).

The mapping logic to project one business object model onto another is encapsulated in a component that performs the transformation. The mapping logic is implemented by configurable mapping rules associated to a component. There may be several of these components in the DATA TRANSFORMATION FLOW. The DATA TRANSFORMATION FLOW pattern leads to an architecture in which the mapping flows are encapsulated in maintainable units that can be flexibly composed.

In a process-driven and SOA, the DATA TRANSFORMATION FLOW should be realized by a MICROFLOW ENGINE, and the mapping components are represented as (reusable) process

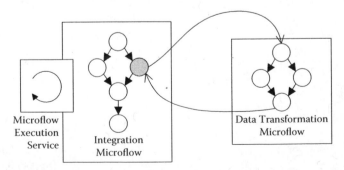

FIGURE 8.21
A data transformation flow.

flows in this engine. The process flows perform the transformation of the business object models. The individual activities in the process flow represent transformation steps.

The invoking process of a DATA TRANSFORMATION FLOW can be either a macroflow or microflow. In many cases, the DATA TRANSFORMATION FLOW is a subflow of a microflow: A service executing a microflow can be invoked by macroflow process activities. All data transformation is done in data transformation subflows. The microflow service thus realizes the composition of the mapping functionality according to the requirements of the integration process.

Appropriate technology is required to implement the mapping flows. For instance, a message broker with transformation functionality can be used to achieve this or another integration middleware. The mapping may cause performance issues if the logic becomes complicated or storage functions are required to keep the transformed objects in databases. Thus, this pattern may only be suitable in larger SOA contexts, where this kind of flexibility is actually required.

The DATA TRANSFORMATION FLOW pattern realizes the transformations from application-specific to synthesized models when the INTEGRATED BUSINESS OBJECT MODEL pattern is applied. When realizing the transformation in a mapping flow, message transformation patterns will be applied (e.g., MESSAGE TRANSLATOR, CONTENT ENRICHER, and CANONICAL DATA MODEL [HW03]). A conceptual mapping microflow represents a mapping component in the spirit of MESSAGING MAPPER [HW03]. The DATA TRANSFORMATION FLOW pattern can be realized as part of an ENTERPRISE SERVICE BUS.

Example: Simple UML Structure of a DATA TRANSFORMATION FLOW

Figure 8.22 illustrates one possible realization in a flow model in the Unified Modelling Language (UML): A MICROFLOW ENGINE exposes an integration microflow as a service that can be invoked by process activities. All data transformation is done in data transformation subflows. The microflow thus realizes the composition of the mapping functionality according to the requirements of the integration process.

Example: Using a Process Designer's Mapping Tool to Realize DATA TRANSFORMATION FLOWS

Many process design tools support mapping tools with which data transformations can be defined. Hence, the process flow can be used to orchestrate a number of such mappings. For instance, we can use the NetBeans BPEL (Business Process Execution

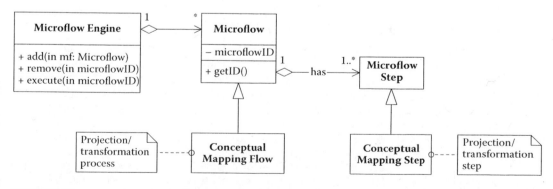

FIGURE 8.22
UML example for a data transformation flow.

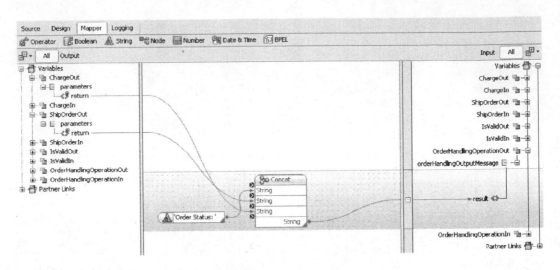

FIGURE 8.23
Example using NetBeans BPEL designer's mapping tool.

Language) designer [Sun09] to define a number of mappings in BPEL assignments. A BPEL process that only performs such data transformations can be used as a microflow in other BPEL processes. The benefit of using BPEL for data transformation is that we can use existing process design tools and use BPEL features such as calling external services for data transformation. The downside of using BPEL for microflows is that it is usually treated by the process engine like a long-running business process, meaning a certain performance overhead. It is advisable to restrict such DATA TRANSFORMATION FLOWS to short-running transactional flows, even though BPEL would support features for long-running processes as well, to keep the data flows understandable and manageable: The DATA TRANSFORMATION FLOW should not contain unrelated tasks.

Figure 8.23 shows an example of a mapping designed in the NetBeans BPEL designer's mapping tool. It concatenates a static string with two string result variables. As a result, another string is produced.

Please note that many implementations of DATA TRANSFORMATION FLOWS do not use a graphical mapping designer as in this example, but the mappings are defined in a program code or a script. Such a hard-coded microflow can then be exposed as a service. This has the advantage of a better performance, but the disadvantage that process modeling tools cannot be used.

Example: Support of DATA TRANSFORMATION FLOWS in DBMSs and Data Warehouses

Many DBMSs support some kind of transformations that can be connected in a flow. In many cases, the flow must be hard coded using programming language code or scripts. That is, tools for orchestration of DATA TRANSFORMATION FLOWS do not always exist.

For example, Microsoft's SQL Server Integration Services [Mic09] offer transformations for aggregating, merging, distributing, and modifying data in data flows. The transformations can also perform lookup operations and generate datasets. Transformations include row and rowset transformations, such as data type conversion, split and join transformations such as merge and lookup, business intelligence transformations such as fuzzy lockup and fuzzy grouping, and transformations for auditing purposes.

TiBCO's Spotfire platform [Tib09] is another example that enables users to visualize and analyze their data. Like many other analytics or data warehouse systems, DATA TRANSFORMATION FLOWS are used in the "loader" component: A data transformation is used when data needs to be transformed before it is loaded into Spotfire. The main goal of using a DATA TRANSFORMATION FLOW is to automate the import process.

Many other data-warehousing tools use data transformations in a similar way in the loader component of their extract, transform, load (ETL) process. Another example is Oracle's Warehouse Builder [Ora09a]. It supports data transformation flows in its loader. Data flow operators, such as aggregator, expression, or filter, are provided to transform data in a mapping. Predefined transformations in the following categories can be used: administration, character, control center, conversion, date, numeric, Online Analytical Processing (OLAP), others, SYS, spatial, streams, and XML. In addition, custom transformation can be created by the user. Custom transformations can use predefined transformations as part of their definition. Also, transformation libraries consisting of a set of reusable transformations can be defined and used.

Case Study: Business Object Integration in a Telecommunications SOA Project

In an SOA project for a telecommunications customer in Germany, the task was to build a larger SOA architecture based on an ENTERPRISE SERVICE BUS. The architecture has been based on IBM WebSphere technology. WebSphere Business Integration Message Broker has been used as the MICROFLOW ENGINE to realize the conceptual mapping flows and the service bus.

The project has focused on restructuring the business model for order management and depicting redesigned business processes on the SOA platform. We have followed the INTEGRATED BUSINESS OBJECT MODEL pattern to form an integrated object model for processing various types of orders. For historical reasons, many different systems have been involved in the ordering and fulfillment of products as new products have been developed over time and quick tool support has been implemented. There has been redundant data in these various systems.

An integrated and business process-oriented approach needs to take into account the overall process perspective of ordering products and integrating the various systems involved in the business processes. Hence, the data models of these systems to be integrated have been mapped to business object models, and the INTEGRATED BUSINESS OBJECT MODEL for the overall business processes has been developed.

To achieve this, the redundancies of data in the systems have been identified by looking for the same conceptual entities in each system. For instance, the customer, or information on related contracts to the customers, could be found in many of these systems. However, the data associated to these conceptual entities have not been the same in all the systems. There was some overlap, and this overlap needed to be identified to define a representation in the INTEGRATED BUSINESS OBJECT MODEL. The second step was thus to identify the overlaps and to depict the commonalities in the INTEGRATED BUSINESS OBJECT MODEL. The common representation had to be chosen in a way that allows integrating the systems by DATA TRANSFORMATION FLOWS. It was thus possible to extract the redundancies and to develop an INTEGRATED BUSINESS OBJECT MODEL for the business processes systematically. The INTEGRATED BUSINESS OBJECT MODEL did not contain redundant data but consolidated the views of the systems involved in the business processes.

This INTEGRATED BUSINESS OBJECT MODEL has been implemented in a separate DB/2 data store, used by the executed business process as a BUSINESS OBJECT POOL. That means the

DB/2 database served as the technology for realizing the BUSINESS OBJECT POOL. The various business processes running in parallel were able to access the business objects concurrently, and the objects were realizing all requirements of the overall business processes. BUSINESS OBJECT REFERENCES are used from the processes to refer to the business objects in the BUSINESS OBJECT POOL.

One critical factor of flexibility regarding the object model was the products being ordered by customers. To reduce the time to market, the processes needed to be designed in a way that products being ordered and processed are easy to change. For this reason, the notion of product has been designed in the INTEGRATED BUSINESS OBJECT MODEL using metadata description mechanisms in XML. The mandatory and optional attributes of a product could be flexibly specified using an XML-based language.

The DATA TRANSFORMATION FLOWS have been implemented using message transformation mechanisms of the WebSphere Business Integration Message Broker. This broker offers functionality for defining reusable message transformation flows that serve as the DATA TRANSFORMATION FLOWS to map object models. The messages are transported via WebSphere MQ.

Service-based integration of external systems has been applied as well. In some cases, it was even possible to directly integrate the application services in the process flow, as both process activity and service, mapped one on one. One example is the integration of a legacy customer application. This application basically is a database containing a customer table and some related tables. In case of a larger business customer, there is a whole hierarchy of subcustomers, for instance, representing different geographical locations. The customer table as an entity has been wrapped by services offering read/write access to the customer repository. In addition, simpler services have been implemented, such as checking whether a customer already exists in the customer repository. This is a simple service that just returned a *Boolean* value. However, no persistent data needed to be stored in a business object in this case as the process logic depicts the corresponding path of execution for the Boolean values, true or false.

As WebSphere MQ Workflow and the integrated application had MQ messaging interfaces, only some simple transformation was necessary in terms of DATA TRANSFORMATION FLOWS. The DATA TRANSFORMATION FLOWS basically performed the mapping of different data structures and types between the customer application and the services.

A concrete example for these data transformations can be found in the context of a service that allows retrieving customer data. The customer repository had information split across many tables, such as the basic customer data like name and address in one table, contract data of the customers in another table, and the customers' account data in a separate table, as a customer may have several accounts. The service represents the retrieval of all these data in a consolidated way as this was the requirement of the corresponding business process activity. For this reason, transformation flows implement the consolidation of the basic customer data, the contract data, and the account data to make them available by a single service. The consolidated data have been put in an XML message representing the output of the service.

Figure 8.24 provides an overview of the INTEGRATED BUSINESS OBJECT MODEL. The model represents the order domain and the product domain and the relations between products and orders. Moreover, the model shows that no specialized classes have been designed for dedicated products.

The special products have been configured in XML; the following example shows the definition of the DSL/ISDN (digital subscriber line/Integrated Services Digital Network) product:

```
<ProductType name="BundleDSLOnline" id="ProductBundleDSLOnline"
             sellable="true">
  <Documentation>
    <ShortDescription>
      This is the product bundle ISDN / DSL and Online
    </ShortDescription>
    <DetailedDescription>
      Detailed description...
    </DetailedDescription>
  </Documentation>
  <ProductRef name="ISDN/DSL" ref="ProductIsdnDSL" />
  <ProductRef name="Online" ref="ProductOnline" />
  <AttributeRef name="Customer class" type="CustomerClass" />
  <AttributeRef name="Installation price" type="Number" />
  <AttributeRef name="Tariff" type="Tariff" />
</ProductType>

<ProductType name="ISDN/DSL" id="ProductIsdnDSL"
             sellable="false" marketingName="-">
  <Documentation>
    <ShortDescription>
      This is the type definition of the product ISDN /
      DSL
    </ShortDescription>
    <DetailedDescription>
      Detailed description...
     </DetailedDescription>
  </Documentation>
  <AttributeRef name="Tariff" type="Tariff" />
  <AttributeRef name="Upstream bandwidth" type="Bandwidth" />
  <AttributeRef name="Downstream bandwith" type="Bandwidth" />
  <AttributeRef name="Damping" type="Damping" />
  <RuleRef name=" UpDownBandwidthConstraint "
           ref-"UpDownBandwidthConstraint" />
</ProductType>

<ProductType name="Online" id="ProductOnline"
             sellable="false" marketingName="Online">
  <Documentation>
    <ShortDescription>
      This is the type definition of the product
      Online
    </ShortDescription>
    <DetailedDescription>
      Detailed description...
    </DetailedDescription>
  </Documentation>
  <AttributeRef name="Tariff" type="Tariff" />
  <AttributeRef name="ImDSLBundle" type="Boolean" />
  <RuleRef name="OnlineTariffBandwidthConstraint"
           ref="OnlineTariffBandwidthConstraint" />
</ProductType>
```

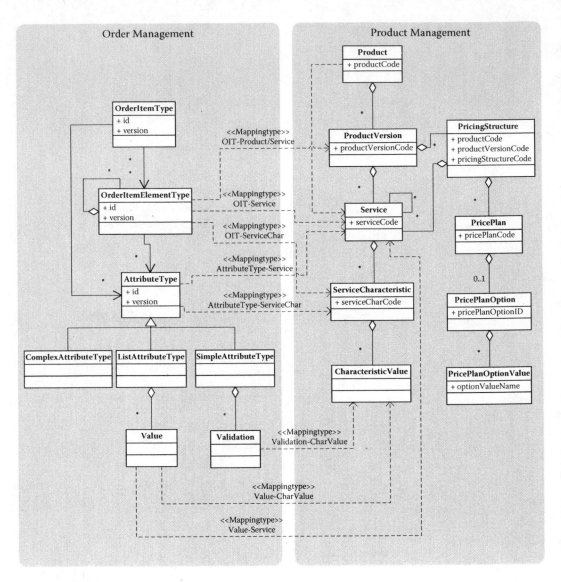

FIGURE 8.24
Integrated business object model of the case study.

The XML product definitions have been stored in terms of a product catalogue. An order only references the products by their product code, as we can see in Figure 8.24: The *Product* class contains the product code as an attribute. The product code is basically an ID of a product to identify it in the product catalogue. The product catalogue and the products may thus be easily changed without modifying the INTEGRATED BUSINESS OBJECT MODEL, whereas the business objects themselves have been stored in a BUSINESS OBJECT POOL implemented using the DB/2 database.

The corresponding user interfaces for data entry and for processing the products could thus be designed generically as the metadata structure could be interpreted and the user interfaces were constructed generically. Implementing a new or improved product was basically an act of configuration, although some amendments and enhancements in the business processes also needed to be designed and implemented in this case. The SOA approach provided an effective means to do that. However, the effort was minimized as the design considered the notion of product to be a variable construct and changes were limited to a minimum. The INTEGRATED BUSINESS OBJECT MODEL thus had to depict the domain of orders considering the requirements of the redesigned business processes and the integrated applications.

Recent technologies directly support the business object integration patterns used in this case study. For instance, IBM WebSphere InterChange Server and WebSphere Process Server conceptually support the design of INTEGRATED BUSINESS OBJECT MODELS. Application-specific object models addressed by application adapters can be mapped via tool support to the INTEGRATED BUSINESS OBJECT MODEL. Of course, the business object integration patterns are not restricted to WebSphere technology. They are also applicable with other platforms that support process-driven and service-oriented approaches, such as Staffware.

This case study is typical for using the business object integration pattern in SOAs. Similar projects have been conducted, for instance, in the banking industry. In finance, we usually deal with old legacy systems, implemented in Cobol, running on large mainframe computers. These systems represent a huge investment that often needs to be protected, not at least because of their reliability and stability. The SOA approach is interesting for the financial industry because most of the processes are rather strongly formalized, and SOA promises an approach for integration and flexibility.

There are other similar projects that we conducted in the automotive industry, especially in supply chain management. In supply chain management, we usually deal with business processes that run across different departments, involving various stakeholders, and even across companies (suppliers). In such supply chain contexts, heterogeneity of the system landscape involved in the business processes is rather the norm than the exception.

The business object integration patterns address common problems arising in SOA projects that are built considering existing and historically grown legacy systems or—more generally speaking—systems being developed independently. Often, these legacy systems represent island solutions for requirements that needed to be implemented quickly and in an evolutionary context. The problems also occur in situations in which no broader IT strategy is defined and systems grow independently. When taking a business process-driven and service-oriented perspective, some data integration issues usually arise, such as data redundancies. This is due to the broader and integrated view taken by the SOA approach. SOA often forces developers to solve these—sometimes long-known—issues in a systematic way. The problems addressed by the business object integration patterns are often inherent and most probably predictable in projects that extend system boundaries and take an enterprise-wide view.

For this reason, SOA offers a systematic approach for tackling data integration issues that are often very well known and existing for years. SOA, as an architectural concept, is not the solution to these well-known integration problems, but it provides a means to approach them systematically and effectively. It is rather the systematic detection and the solutions aligned with business goals represented by the business process-oriented approach that makes the business object integration patterns valuable.

9

Process Design:
Mapping Domain Views to Technical Views

Introduction

In Chapter 5, and more specifically in the DOMAIN/TECHNICAL VIEW pattern, we explained how domain views of business processes differ from technical views. In our examples in Chapter 5, we mainly concentrated on the technical details that need to be added to a process model to make it executable on a process engine. Enriching a process with technical details is surely an important part of the mapping described in the DOMAIN/TECHNICAL VIEW pattern. However, in many cases this is not enough. The *process design* also must be changed during the mapping. In this chapter, we introduce a number of process design patterns that describe additional process aspects that we frequently must add to a process model when mapping it to a technical view.

The patterns described in this chapter deal with the following concerns: integrating process control data, interrupting processes or activities, error management with regard to external systems, and reacting on events coming from other systems. Usually, these concerns are not modeled in domain views of business processes in order to concentrate on the main task of domain-oriented process design: to model the business. For a good technical process design, however, it is often necessary to revise the process design itself if one of these concerns plays a role.

The relationships of the DOMAIN/TECHNICAL VIEW pattern to the patterns presented in this chapter are outlined in Figure 9.1. The patterns are explained in the following text.

A central pattern in this chapter—because it is frequently used as a foundation for realizing the other patterns—is GENERIC PROCESS CONTROL STRUCTURE. Fundamentally, there are two types of data that concern a process model: business data and control data. The BUSINESS OBJECT REFERENCE pattern advises us to keep business data out of the business processes. It is stored in business objects that are only accessed by reference. Given that we follow this pattern in our process design, there is only control data left in the business process. When two or more processes need to be integrated, inconsistencies can arise if the process data structures change.

Consider the following scenario: Process A is instantiated with a certain definition of a data structure. This process contains a subprocess B. That means there will be a certain point in time when process A dynamically instantiates process B as a subprocess. The process model defines how process A transfers the necessary data to process B by mapping rules as process B may have different data structures. This mapping of data is defined by the corresponding implementation of the processes. Thus, there is a data dependency of these processes.

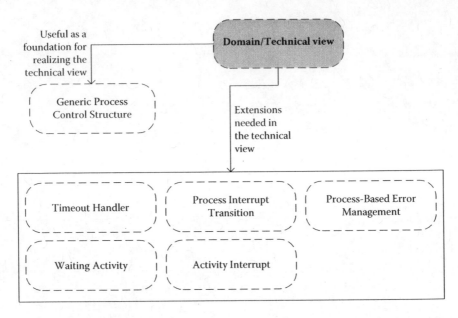

FIGURE 9.1
Domain/technical view pattern relationships.

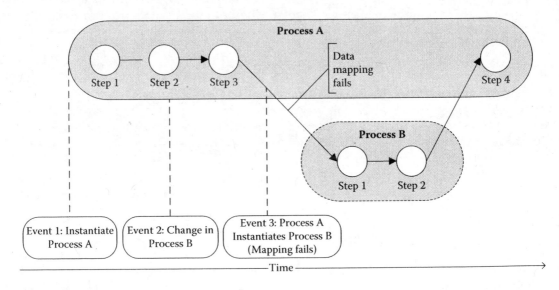

FIGURE 9.2
A generic process control structure.

Consider now there is a running instance of process A, and process A has not yet come to the point at which process B is dynamically instantiated. In Figure 9.2, this situation is indicated by the time frame between event 1 and event 3. Furthermore, we assume that a new requirement has been implemented in a new version of process B. This new version modifies the data structures of process B, for example, by changing the data type of an attribute in the structure, and is deployed after process A has been instantiated. In Figure 9.2, this situation is indicated by event 2. We have to keep in mind that the data-mapping rules for process A instantiating process B have been statically bound at instantiation time of process A. If our running instance of process A now comes to the point at which process B is dynamically instantiated as a sub-process, it will instantiate the new version of process B by applying the old data-mapping rules. The result is data inconsistency. In Figure 9.2, this situation is indicated by event 3.

Even version control does not provide a solution to this problem. For instance, in the example it would be necessary to create a new version of processes A and B to introduce a change in the data structure interface between them. That means the data dependencies between processes must be managed somehow because it is necessary to identify the effect that a potential change to a data structure will have and to find out what processes are affected.

In addition, this change will only take effect with a new instance of process A—all the running instances of processes A and B still have to apply the old version. It may thus take a long time until the change really has an effect, namely, at the point in time when all old instances of process A have terminated, and only new versions of processes A and B are instantiated. The effects that many cascading changes will have over a longer period of time result in many different versions of the same processes running in parallel, and all these different versions must be handled by the applications using them. Usually, this results in unacceptable maintenance efforts and complexity of the system. Versioning might be a solution if the processes are only running over a short period of time (e.g., a few seconds), but in businesses processes that run for several weeks and months, a nearly unmanageable complexity might be generated.

The GENERIC PROCESS CONTROL STRUCTURE advises us to avoid such inconsistencies by designing a common data model for a number of interrelated processes (and the services or systems they access). This data model is relatively stable because (1) control data does not tend to change often in its structure, and (2) we specifically use generic data structures that do not change the structure but only the semantics (i.e., how they are interpreted by the processes and services).

In contrast to the GENERIC PROCESS CONTROL STRUCTURE pattern, all other patterns presented in this chapter deal with situations in which an exceptional event occurs in an external system that has an influence on the process. In all these patterns, the process design is altered to cope with the exceptional situation.

The next two patterns in this chapter, PROCESS INTERRUPT TRANSITION and ACTIVITY INTERRUPT, deal with situations in which a process or an activity in a process must be interrupted. Like the control data integration issues, dealt with by the GENERIC PROCESS CONTROL STRUCTURE pattern, interrupts are something usually not considered during domain-oriented process design.

But, when technical design of a process is done, we must consider situations in which the process is interrupted due to some external event that was not considered in the original domain-oriented process design. Examples of such external events are a customer cancelling an order before the order-handling process has finished or an external system signaling a timeout event to a process instance that is waiting for user input. Often, such exceptional causes of process termination are forgotten in the domain-oriented process design.

From a technical point of view, an exceptional termination of a process can be problematic. For instance, the process might have acquired resources that must be released or performed business data changes that must be rolled back. Often, exceptional termination must be documented. The PROCESS INTERRUPT TRANSITION pattern solves this problem by altering the process design to contain a process interrupt using a transition condition after the activity or activities that cause the interrupt. This activity or these activities must hence be designed to react on signal events that result in process interrupts. Cleanup and

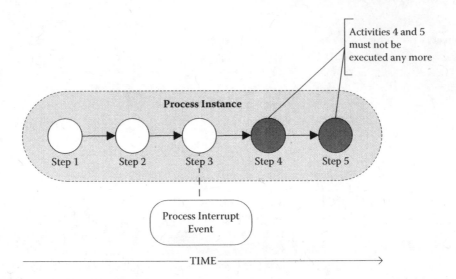

FIGURE 9.3
A process interrupt transition.

documentation are handled in a new exceptional path in the process model. Figure 9.3 illustrates the general solution of the PROCESS INTERRUPT TRANSITION pattern.

The ACTIVITY INTERRUPT pattern deals with a similar situation, but here only a single activity of a process is interrupted. This pattern is applicable when an event causes an activity not to be completed (yet), but the process control data can already be updated. For example, consider a human who pauses his or her work on the activity (e.g., he or she is going for a lunch break) but does not want the changes to become lost.

The ACTIVITY INTERRUPT pattern supports such situations by adding an exit condition to the process design for the activity that might get interrupted. If this exit condition is false, the process engine interrupts the activity, stores the updated control data, and when the process instance is resumed, it restarts the activity with the updated data as input data.

Figure 9.4 illustrates how the process design is altered during the translation from the domain view to the technical view of a business process if step 2 and step 3 can potentially contain an ACTIVITY INTERRUPT.

A special kind of exceptional event is an error in an external system. It is relatively easy to deal with errors in a process itself because the same team or individuals are responsible for the error and the process design. In contrast, errors in external systems connected to the process can be more difficult to handle, for instance, because different teams and individuals, maybe even in different organizations, might be responsible for the external system.

In such situations, it is advisable to apply the PROCESS-BASED ERROR MANAGEMENT pattern. It describes how to define special attributes for error handling in the process control data structure and alter the process design to contain error management activities in the technical process design. The pattern advises us to delegate the responsibility for reporting errors to the integrated external systems. The process instance can react to those errors using the information provided by the integrated external system, such as an error description or who is responsible for the error.

Figure 9.5 illustrates the PROCESS-BASED ERROR MANAGEMENT pattern. A process instance is executed normally, until it reaches step 3. In this activity, an external system is invoked that causes an error and signals an error event to the process instance. The process then

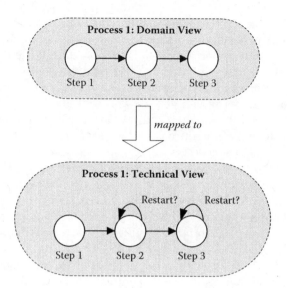

FIGURE 9.4
The domain/technical view mapping for activity interrupts.

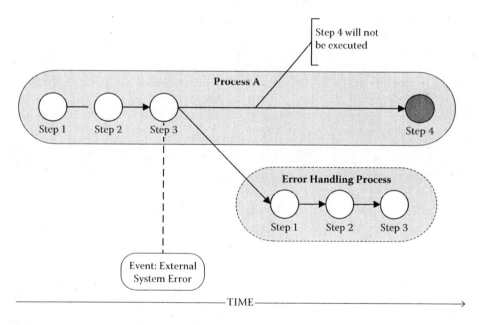

FIGURE 9.5
Process-based error management.

branches into an error-handling subprocess, which receives the error information from the external system as input. Step 4 in the normal execution flow of the process instance is not executed.

It can be seen that the pattern provides for a process-based way of error handling. Branching into a subprocess for error handling is not necessary but is advisable when the error-handling activities can be reused.

The final two patterns presented in this chapter deal with process-internal timing issues. The first of these patterns, TIMEOUT HANDLER, deals with situations in which an activity executes some application or service, or it waits for an external event. If the duration until the application or service replies or until the external event is raised can be long, it makes sense to raise a timeout event in the activity in case no reply or event arrives in a defined time frame. A TIMEOUT HANDLER is a generic and reusable activity type to react on the timeout event. It can be used to retry the activity, abort the process, or ignore the timeout.

The TIMEOUT HANDLER pattern is similar to the PROCESS-BASED ERROR MANAGEMENT pattern. Whereas PROCESS-BASED ERROR MANAGEMENT describes a solution for handling errors that are reported by components integrated in the process flow, a TIMEOUT HANDLER exclusively handles timeout situations. Thus, a TIMEOUT HANDLER can be realized as a special subset of an implementation of the PROCESS-BASED ERROR MANAGEMENT pattern. The EVENT-BASED ACTIVITY pattern (see Chapter 10) introduces activities that listen for events occurring outside the scope of the process instance. Activities of that type will usually be defined with a timeout value and might require the use of a TIMEOUT HANDLER.

The second pattern that deals with process-internal timing issues, presented in this chapter, is the WAITING ACTIVITY pattern. It defines an activity type that waits for a predefined duration using an internal timer before it allows the process flow to proceed.

The EVENT-BASED ACTIVITY pattern (see Chapter 10) describes a general event-aware activity. An activity of that kind terminates on the occurrence of a defined external event. One variation of a WAITING ACTIVITY pattern is to use a special EVENT-BASED ACTIVITY. The event the activity subscribes to is created by a timer. This is only valid, though, if the timer is not known in the scope of the process instance and has to be seen as an external event source.

Figure 9.6 illustrates the relationships of the two timing-related patterns to the EVENT-BASED ACTIVITY pattern.

Application of the patterns BUSINESS OBJECT REFERENCE, PROCESS INTERRUPT TRANSITION, ACTIVITY INTERRUPT, PROCESS-BASED ERROR MANAGEMENT, TIMEOUT HANDLER, WAITING ACTIVITY, and EVENT-BASED PROCESS SPLIT has implications for the design of a GENERIC PROCESS CONTROL STRUCTURE. That is, these patterns imply the definition of generic attributes that depict the concerns of these patterns in a GENERIC PROCESS CONTROL STRUCTURE:

- If the BUSINESS OBJECT REFERENCE pattern is applied, generic attributes to store references to business objects must be defined in the GENERIC PROCESS CONTROL STRUCTURE.

- If the PROCESS INTERRUPT TRANSITION pattern is applied, a generic attribute to handle process interrupt transitions must be defined in the GENERIC PROCESS CONTROL STRUCTURE.

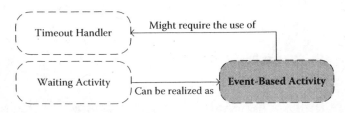

FIGURE 9.6
Event-based activity pattern relationships.

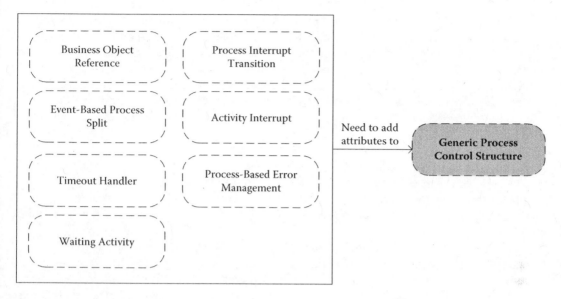

FIGURE 9.7
Generic process control structure pattern relationships.

- If the ACTIVITY INTERRUPT pattern is applied, a generic attribute to handle activity interrupts must be defined in the GENERIC PROCESS CONTROL STRUCTURE.

- If the PROCESS-BASED ERROR MANAGEMENT pattern is applied, generic attributes to handle error messages must be defined in the GENERIC PROCESS CONTROL STRUCTURE.

- If the TIMEOUT HANDLER pattern is applied and retries are supported, generic attributes to define the maximum retries and retry count must be defined in the GENERIC PROCESS CONTROL STRUCTURE.

- If the WAITING ACTIVITY pattern is applied, generic attributes to define waiting time frame must be defined in the GENERIC PROCESS CONTROL STRUCTURE.

- If the EVENT-BASED PROCESS SPLIT pattern (see Chapter 10) is applied, a reusable process identifier attribute must be defined in the GENERIC PROCESS CONTROL STRUCTURE.

Figure 9.7 illustrates these pattern relationships.

GENERIC PROCESS CONTROL STRUCTURE

Processes work with two types of data: the control data for controlling the process flow and the business data transformed via the process flow. If a process invokes a service or another process due to the data dependencies between the invoking process and the invoked service or process, there might be a problem if the process data structure of the invoked process changes: The possibly long-running invoker might not know about the change and instantiate the process assuming an invalid version of the process data structure or invocation interface. This situation can be largely avoided for business data by storing it externally to the process in business objects that are only referenced via BUSINESS OBJECT REFERENCES. But, for the process control data, this situation is hard to avoid.

How can inconsistencies of the process data structures between a long-running process and the process or service it invokes be avoided, even if the process data structures change?

When a process is instantiated, a clone of its process template will be generated, and the clone (i.e., the process instance) will be executed on the process engine. Analogous to object instantiation in Java, for instance, the process definition will be determined at instantiation time. That is, the process instance will execute the model that has been valid at instantiation time.

However, a process instance may run for several months, depending on the business process that it implements. As an example, consider a business process realizing a supply chain. This longevity of processes is rather the general rule than the exception. A big issue in this context is changes to the data structures of processes invoked from these long-running business processes. But also, other long-running invokers, such as applications or services, for which we cannot change the data structures passed to invocations on the fly, face the same problem.

The data structure definitions are statically bound to the process instance at instantiation time, which causes data inconsistencies when the data structures of dynamically instantiated processes or services have been changed in the meantime.

Unfortunately, even version control may not really provide a suitable solution because it is not possible to version the single data structure interfaces without versioning the process models that use them as the data structures are statically bound to the process models. To introduce a new version of a data structure, it is thus necessary to create a new version of all processes using this data structure as an interface when invoking another process.

For a macroflow process and all the macroflow processes, microflow processes, and services it directly or indirectly invokes, define a GENERIC PROCESS CONTROL STRUCTURE. This data structure standardizes the process control data of these communicating processes and services. It is designed in a way that it is only subject to semantic change but not structural change. Attributes in this generic data structure can be used for different purposes and thus with varying (or generic) semantics. The concrete semantics of attributes are defined by providing additional attributes that contain meta-information (see Figure 9.8).

If a generic and reusable process data structure is used for all processes and services invoked by a macroflow, it is actually possible to avoid structural changes on the data structure. This GENERIC PROCESS CONTROL STRUCTURE has to include all concerns of process control needed in the communication of the macroflow and the directly and indirectly invoked processes and services. This means the generic process data structure must be designed to capture the requirements of many concrete process data structures.

The key idea of how to design a GENERIC PROCESS CONTROL STRUCTURE is that a structural change to data is problematic with regard to invocation relationships between processes, but a semantic change is not. Consequently, a structural change must be avoided, but semantic flexibility should be supported.

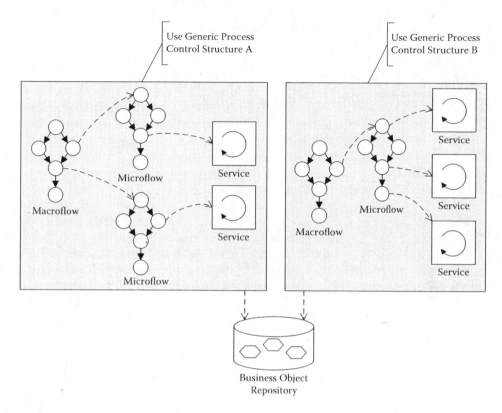

FIGURE 9.8
Using a generic process control structure.

To define such a GENERIC PROCESS CONTROL STRUCTURE, it is necessary to gather the general requirements for controlling a process. If possible, all business data should be kept external to the process in business objects that are only referenced following the BUSINESS OBJECT REFERENCE pattern. Thus, the GENERIC PROCESS CONTROL STRUCTURE designer can exclusively focus on aspects that are necessary for controlling the process flow.

Striving for semantic flexibility usually implies additional development effort because it must be dynamically decided, based on the metainformation, how to interpret the contents of the structure. Thus, complexity is increased at this level. There is also additional effort necessary to handle semantic errors. Semantic errors will usually be detected by inconsistencies between the metainformation and the contents. These error-detecting and error-handling algorithms must be implemented by the application or a general framework. It is recommended to define a format for the metainformation (e.g., an XML [Extensible Markup Language] schema). However, the specification of this data format represents an additional development effort, and the format might also be subject to change. Ensuring type safety also can cause some efforts because type safety must be ensured by programming the consistency check based on a self-defined metamodel.

If the GENERIC PROCESS CONTROL STRUCTURE pattern is applied, some of the most difficult data-mapping problems are implicitly solved because no structural changes that would require complicated mappings will occur. As a consequence, process modeling is much simpler and less error prone because no difficult mapping rules must be applied and understood. Another benefit is that process models can be easily reused because interfaces between these processes are structurally standardized.

Applications have to take care of interpreting the data structures that are flexibly used in a semantic sense. This, of course, is more complex than interpreting simple, custom interfaces.

In principle, to apply the pattern, we need to standardize only the GENERIC PROCESS CONTROL STRUCTURE for one macroflow process and all invocation dependencies it has. But, if we start with high-level macroflows of an enterprise and these macroflows interact with each other, quickly we can reach a situation in which all processes of an enterprise should be supported by one GENERIC PROCESS CONTROL STRUCTURE. There might be quite some design effort necessary to develop such a standardized GENERIC PROCESS CONTROL STRUCTURE that suits all purposes of the enterprise and that captures all necessary metainformation. However, it is actually possible to achieve this goal as long as the principle of separation of concerns is strictly followed with regard to the two types of process data: No application-specific business data should be contained in the process data structures, only process control data. This is important because business data (and its structure) tends to change often, and it is hard to describe business data in a generic fashion for all processes, services, and business applications of an organization. In contrast, process control data changes less often and is rather easy to categorize into generic data structures. Consider a simple example: It is often difficult to agree on a single view of the customer data required for different business applications in a company, but defining a data structure for a string as a transition control or a common BUSINESS OBJECT REFERENCE is usually possible.

Example: Schematic UML Metamodel of a GENERIC PROCESS CONTROL STRUCTURE

Figure 9.9 shows a principle design of a GENERIC PROCESS CONTROL STRUCTURE in the Unified Modelling Language (UML). In this example, a generic data structure is defined, consisting of a number of substructures. Concrete data structures are used for defining application-specific representation of the generic data structure (or its substructures). Only the concrete data structures might be subject to structural change, whereas the generic data structure is designed in a way that the structures stay the same, but only the semantics are changed.

Example: Designing a GENERIC PROCESS CONTROL STRUCTURE Model

The following list of requirements represents an example of how a requirements specification for a GENERIC PROCESS CONTROL STRUCTURE could look. It will further be demonstrated how these requirements can be transformed into a design for a GENERIC PROCESS CONTROL STRUCTURE model. In the example, we demonstrate how this design can be implemented using WebSphere MQ Workflow.

The following specification requirements must be realized:

- Multiple references to external business objects that are subject of the business process are necessary. This requirement results from the BUSINESS OBJECT REFERENCE pattern.
- Staff information must be defined to dynamically assign who/what is the actor of which activity (it could be a person, an organizational unit, a role, etc.).
- It must be possible to set actual process control data to handle conditional transitions between activities.
- A set of flexibly usable filter and sorting attributes is required to define dynamic filter and sorting constraints on user work lists based on different application data.
- Error management is needed (e.g., in case an integrated business service reports an error). This requirement results from the PROCESS-BASED ERROR MANAGEMENT pattern.

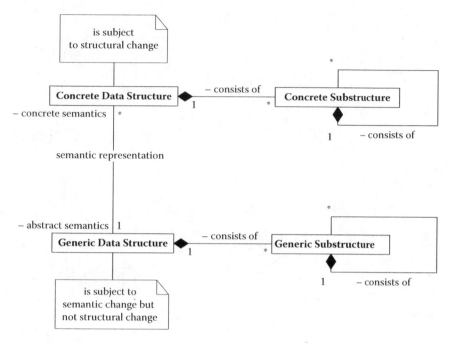

FIGURE 9.9.
UML design example for generic process control structure.

- It must be possible to abort a process if the process must not finish normally due to external circumstances. This requirement results from the PROCESS INTERRUPT TRANSITION pattern.
- A controlled activity interrupt must be possible if the data of an activity is manipulated but the process must not yet continue to the next step. This requirement results from the ACTIVITY INTERRUPT pattern.
- Text messages shall be used as a tool for interpersonal communication between activities.
- An application-specific business process ID is needed to implement relation ships between principally independent subprocesses. This requirement results from the EVENT-BASED PROCESS INSTANCE pattern.
- A set of *multipurpose string objects* is required that can be flexibly used. Sometimes, it is necessary to have some kind of container for application-specific process information. For this reason, it is necessary to have such a container in the data structure. As no complex business data should be transported in the process, string objects are absolutely sufficient.
- It is necessary to store metainformation about the data structure contents to provide some variability on the semantics of the data structure. One could imagine several versions that unambiguously define different semantics of the multipurpose objects, for instance. The metainformation thus indicates how to interpret the contents of the flexible parts of the data structure.
- A set of numeric and string helper attributes is required that temporarily store data for later reuse (e.g., for data-mapping purposes).
- An attribute is required for setting expirations of activities dynamically. Some *process engines* have a feature that an activity may expire if the activity has not been processed in a defined time. This expiration time can be defined statically in the process model or dynamically at runtime. For this reason, an attribute is required to set the expiration time dynamically, if required.

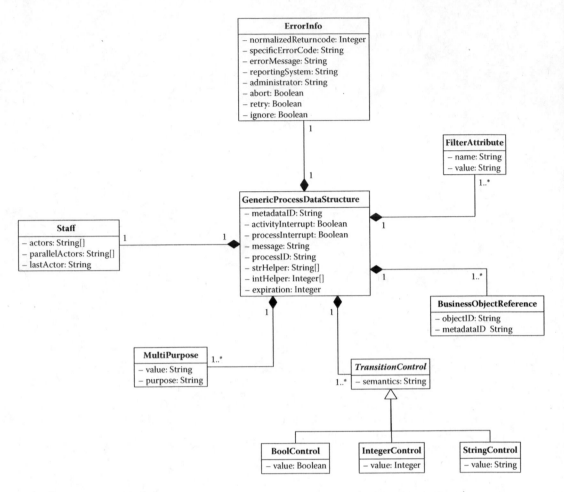

FIGURE 9.10
Detailed UML design example for generic process control structure.

The resulting GENERIC PROCESS CONTROL STRUCTURE that realizes these requirements is shown in Figure 9.10. This structure can then be implemented on the process engine and can be used either in every process of an enterprise or for a defined set of macroflows and dependent processes. As a result, the interfaces between these processes are structurally standardized.

The model in Figure 9.10 illustrates how the semantics of the control data can be variably defined. For instance, the abstract class *TransitionControl* defines the attribute *semantics* to set the semantics of a control object dynamically. Thus, a *BoolControl* object might contain the semantics "credit limit > 50000 Euro." In another process model, the same object might be associated to different semantics. The corresponding Boolean attribute "value" will indicate whether the condition is true or false.

Another example is the attribute *metadataID* from class *GenericProcessDataStructure*. Via this attribute, metainformation about the concrete semantics of the structure can be obtained. For instance, the actual metainformation could be stored in a container outside the process engine as an XML schema, and the *metadataID* just points to that metadata object. In this case, it would be used as an application of the BUSINESS OBJECT REFERENCE pattern. However, the metainformation provides a unique interpretation of the contents of the structure for the applications using it. The other elements of the presented GENERIC PROCESS CONTROL STRUCTURE also follow this principle of semantic abstraction.

This example demonstrates how a GENERIC PROCESS CONTROL STRUCTURE can encode generic semantics and thus define an interface between processes that does not need to change as far as its structure is concerned because it is possible to standardize the necessary general structural aspects for controlling processes by this interface. As a result, interface dependencies between processes are reduced to a minimum level of complexity, and changes to the control structure are manageable as those changes will only reference varying semantic interpretations of certain attributes within a process as a component and will not concern other processes (loose coupling).

Example: Implementing the GENERIC PROCESS CONTROL STRUCTURE Model in WebSphere MQ Workflow

WebSphere MQ Workflow implements a MACROFLOW ENGINE originally designed according to the basic standards of the Workflow Management Coalition (WfMC) [Wfm95]. Fundamentally, it consists of a *Buildtime* component to model the process flows and a *Runtime* component, in which the defined processes are instantiated and executed. Moreover, it offers Application Programming Interfaces (APIs) in several programming languages (e.g., Java and C++). Cross-platform application integration is supported via XML messaging interfaces.

The process models are exported from the Buildtime component in a process definition language format called Flowmark Definition Language (FDL). This process definition language is derived from the Workflow Process Definition Language (WPDL) standard [WfMC99], which has been developed by the WfMC. Exported process definitions can then be imported into the Runtime component. The FDL thus functions as the process definition interchange format between the Buildtime and Runtime components.

The following code is a WebSphere MQ Workflow implementation of the example of the GENERIC PROCESS CONTROL STRUCTURE described in the example of designing a GENERIC PROCESS CONTROL STRUCTURE model. The code is presented in FDL. Multiplicities of the original UML model have been restricted to fixed values as FDL only supports fixed-size arrays. Moreover, FDL does not support the *Boolean* data type. For this reason, Boolean attributes have also been depicted as strings, following a business rule that only string values of "TRUE" and "FALSE" are allowed to represent the Boolean values. Moreover, the type *Integer* is not supported as well, but only the type *Long*. As a result, attributes of type Integer are depicted using Long.

```
STRUCTURE 'ErrorInfo'
  'normalisedReturncode': LONG;
  'errorMessage': STRING
    DESCRIPTION "";
  'reportingSystem': STRING
    DESCRIPTION "";
  'administrator': STRING
    DESCRIPTION "";
  'abort': STRING
    DESCRIPTION "";
  'retry': STRING
    DESCRIPTION "";
  'ignore': STRING
    DESCRIPTION "";
END 'ErrorInfo'

STRUCTURE 'FilterAttribute'
  'name': STRING;
  'val': STRING
    DESCRIPTION "";
END 'FilterAttribute'
```

```
STRUCTURE 'BusinessObjectReference'
  'metadataID': STRING;
  'objectID': STRING;
END 'BusinessObjectReference'

STRUCTURE 'Staff'
  'actors': STRING(20);
  'parallelActors': STRING(30);
  'lastActor': STRING;
END 'Staff'

STRUCTURE 'MultiPurpose'
  'val': STRING;
  'purpose': STRING;
END 'MultiPurpose'

STRUCTURE 'StringControl'
  'semantics': STRING;
  'val': STRING;
END 'StringControl'
STRUCTURE 'IntegerControl'
  'semantics': STRING;
  'val': LONG;
END 'IntegerControl'

STRUCTURE 'BoolControl'
  'semantics': STRING;
  'val': STRING;
END 'BoolControl'

STRUCTURE 'GenericProcessDataStructure'
  'metadataID': STRING
    DESCRIPTION "";
  'activityInterrupt': STRING
    DESCRIPTION "";
  'processInterrupt': STRING
    DESCRIPTION "";
  'message': STRING
    DESCRIPTION "";
  'processID': STRING
    DESCRIPTION "";
  'strHelper': STRING(5)
    DESCRIPTION "";
  'intHelper': LONG(5)
    DESCRIPTION "";
  'expiration': LONG
    DESCRIPTION "";
  'errorInfo': 'ErrorInfo'
    DESCRIPTION "";
  'filterAttributes': 'FilterAttribute'(6)
    DESCRIPTION "";
  'objects': 'BusinessObjectReference'(30)
    DESCRIPTION "";
  'staff': 'Staff'
    DESCRIPTION "";
  'multiPurpose': 'MultiPurpose'(30)
    DESCRIPTION "";
  'boolCtrl': 'BoolControl'(30)
    DESCRIPTION "";
  'strCtrl': 'StringControl'(30)
    DESCRIPTION "";
```

```
'intCtrl': 'IntegerControl'(30)
   DESCRIPTION "";
END 'GenericProcessDataStructure'
```

The data structure has originally been modeled with the Buildtime process modeling tool of WebSphere MQ Workflow. Once defined with Buildtime, the data structure can be associated to any process model defined in Buildtime. Exported process models will then contain the data structure. The contents of the data structure can then be passed from one activity to the next. The next FDL example illustrates how this is done. The sample shows a simple process definition with two activities. The GENERIC PROCESS CONTROL STRUCTURE is associated to the process as input and output data structure as well as to the two activities.

```
PROCESS 'GenericProcessDataStructureSample'(
'GenericProcessDataStructure',
'GenericProcessDataStructure')
  DO NOT PROMPT_AT_PROCESS_START
  PROGRAM_ACTIVITY 'Activity1' (
'GenericProcessDataStructure',
'GenericProcessDataStructure')
    START MANUAL WHEN AT_LEAST_ONE CONNECTOR TRUE
    EXIT AUTOMATIC
    PRIORITY DEFINED_IN INPUT_CONTAINER
    PROGRAM 'Foo'
    SYNCHRONIZATION NESTED
  END 'Activity1'
  PROGRAM_ACTIVITY 'Activity2' (
'GenericProcessDataStructure',
'GenericProcessDataStructure')
    START MANUAL WHEN AT_LEAST_ONE CONNECTOR TRUE
    EXIT AUTOMATIC
    PRIORITY DEFINED_IN INPUT_CONTAINER
    PROGRAM 'Foo'
    SYNCHRONIZATION NESTED
  END 'Activity2'
  CONTROL
    FROM 'Activity1' TO 'Activity2'
  DATA
    FROM 'Activity1' TO 'Activity2'
    MAP '_STRUCT' TO '_STRUCT'
  DATA
    FROM 'Activity2' TO SINK 1
    MAP '_STRUCT' TO '_STRUCT'
  DATA
    FROM SOURCE 1 TO 'Activity1'
    MAP '_STRUCT' TO '_STRUCT'
END 'GenericProcessDataStructureSample'
```

Example: GENERIC PROCESS CONTROL STRUCTURE in Business Process Execution Language with WebSphere Integration Developer

WebSphere Integration Developer supports modeling data structures for Business Process Execution Language (BPEL) processes with a visual modeling tool based on Eclipse. WebSphere Integration Developer is the development environment for WebSphere Process Server, which is the runtime environment. Internally, the data structures are represented as XML Schema Definitions (XSDs) in WebSphere Integration Developer. The visually modeled data structures can also be viewed in their XSD representation within the development tool.

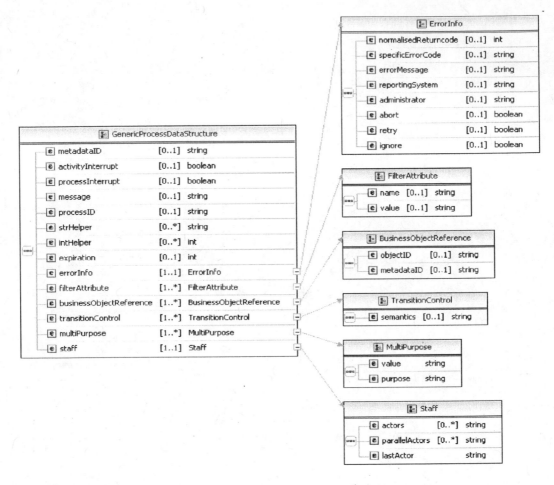

FIGURE 9.11
Generic process control structure in BPEL with WebSphere Integration Developer.

Figure 9.11 shows an implementation of the example of the GENERIC PROCESS CONTROL STRUCTURE described in the example of a GENERIC PROCESS CONTROL STRUCTURE model. The figure shows the visual model of the structure.

The following XSD source code represents the corresponding generated code for the visually modeled data structure:

```xml
<?xml version="1.0" encoding="UTF-8"?>
<xsd:schema targetNamespace="http://provenSoa/data"
     xmlns:xsd="http://www.w3.org/2001/XMLSchema"
     xmlns:Q1="http://provenSoa/data">
     <xsd:complexType name="GenericProcessDataStructure">
          <xsd:sequence>
               <xsd:element minOccurs="0" name="metadataID"
                    type="xsd:string">
               </xsd:element>
               <xsd:element minOccurs="0" name="activityInterrupt"
                    type="xsd:boolean">
               </xsd:element>
               <xsd:element minOccurs="0" name="processInterrupt"
                    type="xsd:boolean">
               </xsd:element>
```

```
                    <xsd:element minOccurs="0" name="message"
                          type="xsd:string">
                    </xsd:element>
                    <xsd:element minOccurs="0" name="processID"
                          type="xsd:string">
                    </xsd:element>
                    <xsd:element minOccurs="0" name="strHelper"
                          type="xsd:string" maxOccurs="unbounded">
                    </xsd:element>
                    <xsd:element
                          minOccurs="0" name="intHelper" type="xsd:int"
                          maxOccurs="unbounded">
                    </xsd:element>
                    <xsd:element minOccurs="0" name="expiration"
                          type="xsd:int">
                    </xsd:element>
                    <xsd:element minOccurs="1" name="errorInfo"
                          type="Q1:ErrorInfo">
                    </xsd:element>
                    <xsd:element minOccurs="1" name="filterAttribute"
                          type="Q1:FilterAttribute" maxOccurs="unbounded">
                    </xsd:element>
                    <xsd:element
                          minOccurs="1" name="businessObjectReference"
                          type="Q1:BusinessObjectReference"
                          maxOccurs="unbounded">
                    </xsd:element>
                    <xsd:element minOccurs="1"
                          name="transitionControl"
                          type="Q1:TransitionControl" maxOccurs="unbounded">
                    </xsd:element>
                    <xsd:element minOccurs="1" name="multiPurpose"
                          type="Q1:MultiPurpose" maxOccurs="unbounded">
                    </xsd:element>
                    <xsd:element name="staff" type="Q1:Staff"
                          minOccurs="1">
                    </xsd:element>
              </xsd:sequence>
      </xsd:complexType>

      <xsd:complexType name="ErrorInfo">
              <xsd:sequence>
                    <xsd:element minOccurs="0" name="normalisedReturncode"
                          type="xsd:int">
                    </xsd:element>
                    <xsd:element minOccurs="0" name="specificErrorCode"
                          type="xsd:string">
                    </xsd:element>
                    <xsd:element minOccurs="0" name="errorMessage"
                          type="xsd:string">
                    </xsd:element>
                    <xsd:element minOccurs="0" name="reportingSystem"
                          type="xsd:string">
                    </xsd:element>
                    <xsd:element minOccurs="0" name="administrator"
                          type="xsd:string">
                    </xsd:element>
                    <xsd:element minOccurs="0" name="abort"
                          type="xsd:boolean">
                    </xsd:element>
                    <xsd:element minOccurs="0" name="retry"
                          type="xsd:boolean">
```

```xml
                </xsd:element>
                <xsd:element minOccurs="0" name="ignore"
                        type="xsd:boolean">
                </xsd:element>
        </xsd:sequence>
</xsd:complexType>

<xsd:complexType name="FilterAttribute">
        <xsd:sequence>
                <xsd:element minOccurs="0"
                        name="name" type="xsd:string">
                </xsd:element>
                <xsd:element minOccurs="0"
                        name="value"
                        type="xsd:string">
                </xsd:element>
        </xsd:sequence>
</xsd:complexType>

<xsd:complexType name="BusinessObjectReference">
        <xsd:sequence>
                <xsd:element minOccurs="0" name="objectID"
                        type="xsd:string">
                </xsd:element>
                <xsd:element minOccurs="0" name="metadataID"
                        type="xsd:string">
                </xsd:element>
        </xsd:sequence>
</xsd:complexType>

<xsd:complexType name="TransitionControl">
        <xsd:sequence>
                <xsd:element minOccurs="0" name="semantics"
                        type="xsd:string">
                </xsd:element>
        </xsd:sequence>
</xsd:complexType>

<xsd:complexType name="BoolControl">
        <xsd:complexContent>
                <xsd:extension base="Q1:TransitionControl">
                        <xsd:sequence>
                                <xsd:element name="value"
                                        type="xsd:boolean">
                                </xsd:element>
                        </xsd:sequence>
                </xsd:extension>
        </xsd:complexContent>
</xsd:complexType>

<xsd:complexType name="IntegerControl">
        <xsd:complexContent>
                <xsd:extension base="Q1:TransitionControl">
                        <xsd:sequence>
                                <xsd:element name="value"
                                        type="xsd:int">
                                </xsd:element>
                        </xsd:sequence>
                </xsd:extension>
        </xsd:complexContent>
</xsd:complexType>
```

```
<xsd:complexType name="StringControl">
    <xsd:complexContent>
        <xsd:extension base="Q1:TransitionControl">
            <xsd:sequence>
                <xsd:element name="value"
                        type="xsd:string">
                </xsd:element>
            </xsd:sequence>
        </xsd:extension>
    </xsd:complexContent>
</xsd:complexType>

<xsd:complexType name="MultiPurpose">
    <xsd:sequence>
        <xsd:element name="value"
                type="xsd:string">
        </xsd:element>
        <xsd:element name="purpose"
                type="xsd:string">
        </xsd:element>
    </xsd:sequence>
</xsd:complexType>

<xsd:complexType name="Staff">
    <xsd:sequence>
        <xsd:element name="actors" type="xsd:string"
                maxOccurs="unbounded" minOccurs="0">
        </xsd:element>
        <xsd:element name="parallelActors" type="xsd:string"
                maxOccurs="unbounded" minOccurs="0">
        </xsd:element>
        <xsd:element name="lastActor"
                type="xsd:string">
        </xsd:element>
    </xsd:sequence>
</xsd:complexType>
</xsd:schema>
```

PROCESS INTERRUPT TRANSITION

If a process is instantiated, it will run according to its flow definition until the defined end is reached (normal process termination). But, sometimes a process instance should react to an external event by aborting the process flow before the process end is reached. Examples of such external events are a customer cancelling an order before the order-handling process has finished or an external system signaling a timeout event to a process instance that is waiting for user input. The allocated resources should be freed.

How can an instantiated process be interrupted and allocated resources be freed in a controlled way if external circumstances (outside the process engine) force the process instance to stop before the normal process end is reached?

A macroflow only captures the flow logic from a business point of view. Once a process instance is created on the MACROFLOW ENGINE, it will run according to the defined flow logic until the defined end. In this context, the problem occurs that it might be necessary to stop a running process instance because external circumstances force the process to stop. For example, a customer could cancel the order that is currently processed by a process instance. A high-level business process model usually does not capture all these possible external circumstances and the necessary reactions to them. However, when providing a technical view for the domain-oriented macroflow, as described in the DOMAIN/TECHNICAL VIEW pattern, technically it is absolutely necessary to stop a superfluous process instance. This is required, for instance, because it does not make sense to process a cancelled order. Of course, the same problem also occurs for microflow implementations.

A process instance may allocate certain resources, such as storing temporary process data in a database or making changes to the state of an external system. For example, the process instance could have entered an order in a central ordering system. Thus, just physically deleting the process instance will not be a sufficient solution because temporarily allocated resources will not be freed, and state changes to external systems will not be rolled back.

It might also be required to document the process interrupt for revision purposes. That is, information must be kept regarding why the process was terminated abnormally, for instance, in the audit trails or process logs.

Model a process interrupt in the process flow design using a transition condition after the activity or activities that cause the interrupt. The process flow design includes a cleanup activity if the interrupt condition is true. If external events cause the process interrupt, they should be received in the activity or activities that cause the process interrupt. That means the activity or activities must be designed to wait for and signal events that result in process interrupts (see Figure 9.12).

The issue addressed by PROCESS INTERRUPT TRANSITION is similar to handling exceptions in a program. The atomic unit in a process is an activity. For this reason, a controlled interrupt of a process can only be achieved between activities (i.e., in a *transition* from one activity to the next). As a result, a controlled process interrupt must be modeled in the process by a corresponding transition condition indicating that something has happened in the outside world that forces the process to terminate.

This process design is only one part of the solution. The other part of the solution concerns the implementation of the activity or activities leading to process interrupts: They must be designed in such a way that they handle events that finally result in process interrupts.

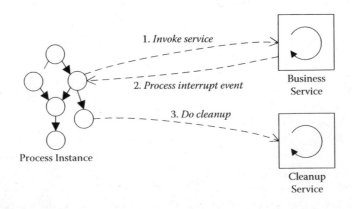

FIGURE 9.12
A process interrupt transition.

Activities are controlled by the outside world from the viewpoint of the process engine. That means the application that implements an activity is where business logic is executed. The business logic has the task to decide whether an event has happened that forces a process to stop or not. Hence, if an interrupting event occurs, the activity implementation must handle it and signal it to the process.

Both parts are strongly interdependent as the events handled by the activity implementations must be interpreted by the process design. We generally recommend realizing this interdependency using a reusable generic attribute in the GENERIC PROCESS CONTROL STRUCTURE to handle the process interrupt. It can thus be easily tracked when a process has been interrupted according to the logged value of this attribute.

The PROCESS INTERRUPT TRANSITION pattern implies an additional development effort for implementing the event handling in activity implementations and to implement the cleanup activity. The cleanup activity is optional. It might be possible that it is not necessary to free any resources because none has been allocated. In that case, a cleanup is not required.

The process models containing a PROCESS INTERRUPT TRANSITION are becoming a little bit more complex because the conditions of process interrupt and no process interrupt must be modeled in addition to the normal transition conditions. Thus, the logic of the transition conditions is becoming more complex.

If a transition condition already exists from one activity to the next, the logical AND operator must be applied to add the transition condition. The transition condition would then look as follows: "no-process-interrupt AND existing transition condition." That is, the process only has to make the transition to the next activity if there is no process interrupt and the normal transition condition is true.

Example: UML-Based Design of a PROCESS INTERRUPT TRANSITION

Figure 9.13 shows a simple process model in UML containing a PROCESS INTERRUPT TRANSITION. The process interrupt is caused by the activity rendered in gray. An ordinary gateway is used to evaluate the transition condition. If the process got interrupted, a *do cleanup* activity is invoked.

If the activity causing the interrupt is implemented as a service, many options exist for how the service can obtain knowledge about the business event that is the root cause of the interrupt. Consider if the activity causing the interrupt is realized as a subprocess. Such a subprocess could be designed following the model in Figure 9.14.

This subprocess mainly passes the interrupt on to the process model shown in Figure 9.13. In the subprocess, the *activity implementation* has to determine whether something has happened that causes a process interrupt, and if that is the case, the activity implementation informs the process instance by setting the corresponding attribute of the GENERIC PROCESS CONTROL STRUCTURE. This informs the invoking process instance about the interrupt and allows the process instance to react accordingly.

Example: PROCESS INTERRUPT TRANSITION in WebSphere MQ Workflow

Figure 9.15 illustrates a sample process model that has been implemented with WebSphere MQ Workflow, which applies the PROCESS INTERRUPT TRANSITION pattern. The model shows the transition from one activity to a next activity only if the interrupt condition is false. If the condition is true, a cleanup activity is executed, and the process terminates.

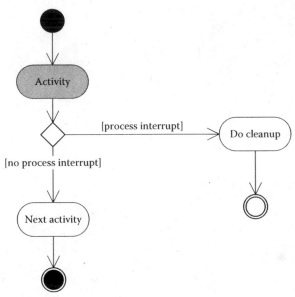

FIGURE 9.13
UML example of a process interrupt transition.

The activity-processing application (i.e., the *activity implementation*) sets the *processInterrupt* attribute if an event has occurred that causes the process instance to terminate abnormally. Some projects have implemented this behavior in a programming framework in terms of an event listener that automatically sets the attribute if a process interrupt event is fired.

Example: Process Interrupt Transition in BPEL

In BPEL, the pattern can be implemented in two different ways. The first variant uses a *choice* node in the BPEL process that is based on a corresponding data attribute in the process control data structure. The second variant uses a BPEL event handler (explained in the last paragraph of this example).

Let us first consider the choice node variant. The choice node implements the PROCESS INTERRUPT TRANSITION if a process interrupt occurs as indicated by the corresponding attribute. Figure 9.16 shows such a dedicated attribute for a process interrupt in a GENERIC PROCESS CONTROL STRUCTURE implementation.

The BPEL process contains a choice node navigating to a *cleanup* activity if the process interrupt occurs. The attribute needs to be set by the actual activity where the process interrupt may occur. This can happen during a service invocation, for instance. Figure 9.17 shows the corresponding BPEL fragment modeled in WebSphere Integration Developer.

The second variant is to use an event handler. If a process interrupt may potentially occur at any time in a process, it can be modeled as an occurring event with a corresponding event handler that does the cleanup. This might be more suitable than modeling an explicit transition for every activity. We have already seen this variation in Chapter 4 in the context of the claims management example. It is highlighted in Figure 9.18.

ACTIVITY INTERRUPT

A number of situations require stopping process activities while they are processed. Consider the example of human interactions: Humans often start working on a task but

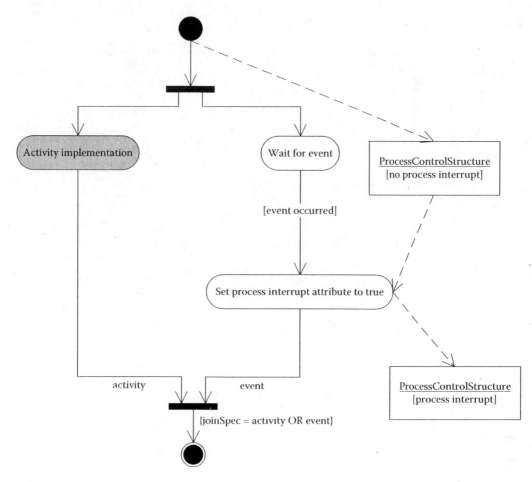

FIGURE 9.14
An activity implementation subprocess.

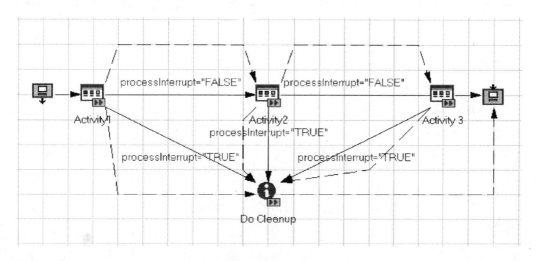

FIGURE 9.15
A process interrupt transition in WebSphere MQ Workflow.

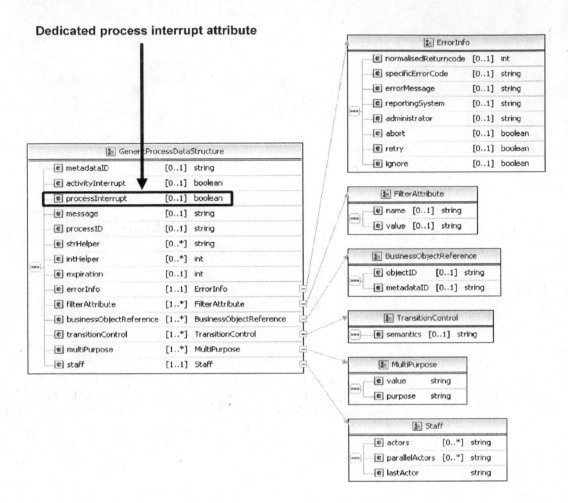

FIGURE 9.16
A process interrupt transition in a generic process control structure.

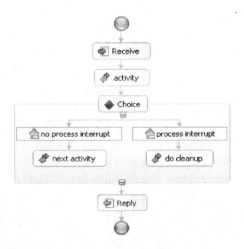

FIGURE 9.17
BPEL fragment with a process interrupt followed by a cleanup.

Handling of a Process Interrupt Event

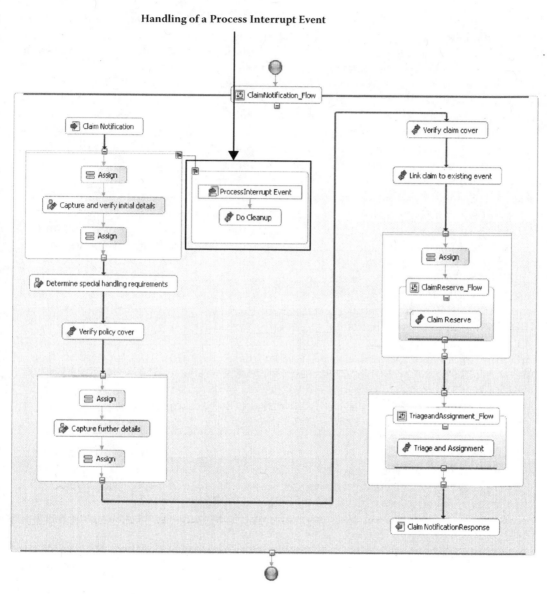

FIGURE 9.18
Process interrupt event example.

will not finish the whole task in one session. Rather, they want to store what they have done, keeping the changes they have made, and leave their work for a while (e.g., until the next day or after the lunch break) and finish their work later.

Often, such situations require the process control data to be updated while an activity runs. The process instance must not move on to the next process activity but should rather stay at the current position. As a next process step, the process engine should restart the current activity with the updated process control data.

How can an activity "in process" be interrupted without losing any data?

To "interrupt" an activity mainly means to store the changes for later use and to finish the activity later. The domain view of a process model usually does not consider these technical details, but a technical view of the business process apparently has to consider situations in which activities can be interrupted.

The problem in this context is that a process instance usually moves on to the next process activity in case the current process activity has been finished. Activities are atomic units in a technical view of a business process when they are executed on a process engine. Usually, if an activity is finished, the output data of the activity will be transferred to the process instance and will be passed further as input data to the next activity in the transition (i.e., the process instance makes a transition into the next state represented by the following activity). However, in case of an activity interrupt, an activity will actually not be completely finished yet but will only be interrupted to finish its work later.

To process an activity, a process engine provides check-out and check-in mechanisms. A check-in of a checked-out activity means that the activity has been finished, and the process control data can be updated during check-in. Usually, this implies that the process instance will move on according to the process model. A check-in of an activity usually implies a change in the process state of the process instance. In case of an activity interrupt, it is not desired that the process instance moves on, but rather the check-in means that the current activity should be restarted with updated process control data. Thus, it is necessary to provide a mechanism that distinguishes these two types of check-in.

Model an exit condition for the activity to be interrupted. If the exit condition is false, the process engine performs an ACTIVITY INTERRUPT. That is, the activity passes the updated data to the process instance, and the process engine does not move on the next process activity but restarts the current activity. It then applies the updated control data as input data to the restarted activity (see Figure 9.19).

The main goal of the ACTIVITY INTERRUPT pattern is that activities can be interrupted without losing any relevant data. The state of the outside world (business object states) is kept consistent with the state in the process instance. Using this mechanism, scenarios like the following can be implemented: People can stop working on a task related to an activity and can go on working on the task later, starting from the last change made (imagine a coffee or lunch break).

Applying the ACTIVITY INTERRUPT pattern can also have additional benefits, such as supporting recovery from failures. For example, if the process engine crashes, the system can set up on a consistent state after restart.

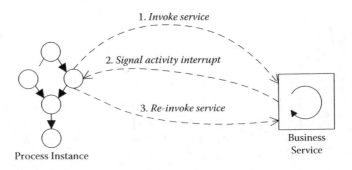

FIGURE 9.19
An activity interrupt.

The process control data structure must contain an attribute to report the activity interrupt to the process instance. To implement the ACTIVITY INTERRUPT pattern, some process engines make use of looping activities with backward data mapping. For instance, IBM WebSphere MQ Workflow [WFBT03] supports implementing this concept. However, in this case the process models become a little more complex because an additional exit condition must be modeled, together with the backward data mapping.

A main question about applying the ACTIVITY INTERRUPT pattern is: Which kinds of process data changes require an ACTIVITY INTERRUPT? The concept of separation of business logic from process logic implies that actual changes to business data will be made in a business object that is managed outside the process engine. The business objects are accessed using BUSINESS OBJECT REFERENCES. That is, the process model will not be concerned with changes to business data but with changes to process control data only. It might happen that a new business object is created somewhere in the outside world around the process engine, and the process instance must store the reference to that business object.

For this reason, theoretically, the only event that might happen that implies manipulation of process data is creation of new business objects, which need to be referenced in the further process flow. If a changed business object is already known by the process instance, it is only necessary to stay in the same process activity and not to move on to the next activity. No further changes to process data are necessary. If new business objects are created, it is also necessary to store the references to them. Ultimately, storing these new references will be necessary in any case, whether the activity is interrupted or not.

Unfortunately, this is the theory but not the reality. The process data structure may also include attributes that have helper and support functions. Those attributes might be affected by those changes to business data. The application will then store the modified control information that is in fact related to some business data changes. For instance, this can be necessary to reflect an application-specific state of the referenced business objects in the process instance. For this reason, the practical answer to the question is the following: New business object creations and modification of process-related helper and support attributes concerning business object changes will imply changes to process control data in the context of an ACTIVITY INTERRUPT.

To support these considerations, usually the BUSINESS OBJECT REFERENCE pattern is applied to separate business data and control data. Hence, this pattern can be seen as a conceptual basis for the ACTIVITY INTERRUPT pattern. Moreover, application of the ACTIVITY INTERRUPT pattern influences the design of a process control data structure as an attribute is often required to handle the restart of an activity. Consequently, using the ACTIVITY INTERRUPT pattern will influence the design of a GENERIC PROCESS CONTROL STRUCTURE.

Example: UML-Based Design of an ACTIVITY INTERRUPT

Figure 9.20 shows an Activity Interrupt in UML. It illustrates that the reference to a newly created business object *objA* will be stored in the process control data structure, but a change to an already referenced business object *objB* has no effect on the process control data structure because the object reference is already there. Changing a business object is simply a change in the internal state of the object and for this reason has no impact on the process control data.

The example of deleting a business object offers two choices: On the one hand, one can argue that if the business object is deleted, the reference in the process control data structure should be deleted as well. On the other hand, this depends on application-specific issues; there might also be reasons to keep the reference.

The recommended design decision in the context of dealing with BUSINESS OBJECT REFERENCES is to define a reusable generic attribute in the process control data structure that handles the ACTIVITY INTERRUPT.

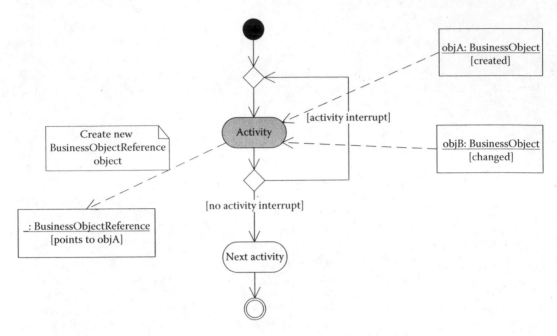

FIGURE 9.20
UML example for activity interrupt.

Example: ACTIVITY INTERRUPT in WebSphere MQ Workflow

This example illustrates an application of the ACTIVITY INTERRUPT pattern with WebSphere MQ Workflow. To implement an activity restart, an exit condition has been assigned to an activity. FDL (the process definition language of WebSphere MQ Workflow) directly supports the definition of exit conditions for activities. To implement the concept of reusing the output data of an activity as input data for the restarted activity, data mapping from the output of an activity to its input container has been defined (data loop connector). The defined generic control structure contains a special reusable attribute called *activityInterrupt* to implement the exit condition.

The following FDL fragment illustrates the implementation using the exit condition and the data loop connector. The FDL contains a simple process with one activity that implements the ACTIVITY INTERRUPT pattern. This fragment is actually representative for any activity implementation as this fragment specification can be applied to any activity in any process to implement an ACTIVITY INTERRUPT.

```
PROCESS 'ActivityInterruptSample' (
'GenericProcessControlStructure',
'GenericProcessControlStructure' )
  DO NOT PROMPT_AT_PROCESS_START
  PROGRAM_ACTIVITY 'Activity' (
'GenericProcessControlStructure',
'GenericProcessControlStructure' )
    START MANUAL WHEN AT_LEAST_ONE CONNECTOR TRUE
    EXIT AUTOMATIC WHEN "activityInterrupt=""FALSE"""
    PRIORITY DEFINED_IN INPUT_CONTAINER
    PROGRAM 'Foo'
    SYNCHRONIZATION NESTED
  END 'Activity'
  DATA
```

```
    FROM SOURCE 1 TO 'Activity'
    MAP '_STRUCT' TO '_STRUCT'
  DATA
    FROM 'Activity' TO SINK 1
    MAP '_STRUCT' TO '_STRUCT'
  DATA
    LOOP 'Activity'
    MAP '_STRUCT' TO '_STRUCT'
END 'ActivityInterruptSample'
```

Example: ACTIVITY INTERRUPT in BPEL with WebSphere Process Server

With WebSphere Process Server, the ACTIVITY INTERRUPT pattern can be implemented using an API plus modeling an exit condition for an activity. An exit condition is defined for the BPEL activity based on a process control data attribute. If the exit condition is false, the activity does not move on to the next step. Moreover, the WebSphere Process Server API provides dedicated functions to communicate with the process engine. In this context, the API provides separate functions to set the input and output message of an activity. These functions can be used for updating the data. With the API of WebSphere Process Server, it is actually possible to update the input and output messages of an activity without checking in the activity. For this reason, setting the process control data attribute representing the exit condition has an additional support function to document the interrupt and to have a clear way of modeling it. Technically, it is actually not mandatory to set the exit condition as the API separates the check-in function from setting the input and output messages. This technically allows updating the data without implicitly initiating the process instance to move to the next step.

When applying the GENERIC PROCESS CONTROL STRUCTURE pattern, a general dedicated attribute can be specified in the data structure for the exit condition to model the ACTIVITY INTERRUPT. An example of a data structure implementation with a dedicated attribute in WebSphere Integration Developer is presented in Figure 9.21.

A possible implementation of the pattern with WebSphere Process is to set the input and output message from a use case within a user interface interaction. In addition, the attribute that is referenced by the exit condition is set to false so the activity does not terminate. The Web Service API or Enterprise Java Beans (EJB) API can be used for this purpose. The use case can thus be completed, saving its data, without actually completing the BPEL activity. Completing an activity is a separate API call in WebSphere Process Server. When the task is opened again from the task list, the input data will be available. Usually, this functionality is implemented in a user interaction framework to achieve this kind of behavior as a general functionality for all user interactions. When the task is completed, the attribute controlling the exit condition is set to true, and the process moves on.

PROCESS-BASED ERROR MANAGEMENT

In process-driven architectures, errors occur in many external systems that are connected to a process engine. In most cases, these errors must be handled and managed. This can prove to be difficult due to the heterogeneous nature of the external systems reporting errors that are connected to the business processes.

How can errors that are reported by external systems, integrated using activities in a process flow, be handled and managed?

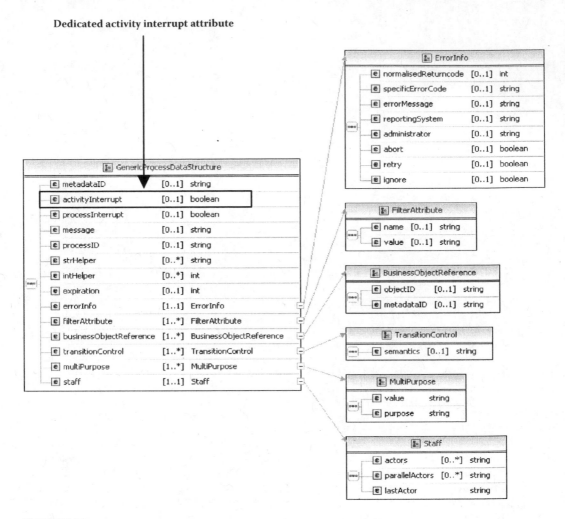

FIGURE 9.21
Activity interrupt in a generic process control structure.

During the execution of activities, it is possible that errors occur that must be reported to the process engine to manage the error. One must keep in mind that we are dealing with a highly distributed environment, and the business process is the central control mechanism. Thus, all different kinds of systems and applications can be integrated in the business process. As a result, there can be many experts and teams involved in resolving system errors—each of these people or teams could be responsible for a certain application.

Usually, error management cannot be delegated to a single person or even a single team due to the potentially large amount of integrated applications and the high distribution of all systems. If one keeps in mind that a business process might cross national and organizational boundaries, it becomes clear that managing occurring errors is a significant and difficult issue.

The process-driven architecture approach is actually an attempt to provide some standardized layer to which anything can connect that is relevant to doing business. Consequently, a standardized way of managing errors also is required. It must be clear that

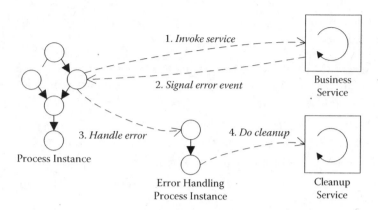

FIGURE 9.22
Process-based error management.

we are not dealing with errors that occur inside the process engine as the process engine is one system in a (usually distributed) architecture that has its own error-handling mechanisms (log files, exceptions, error queues, etc.), but we are dealing with errors from various integrated external systems. Management of errors that occur inside the process engine can be delegated to one team that is responsible for the process engine as a component. However, as the business process is the central point at which everything is connected, one can conclude that also a process-oriented approach will be necessary for managing errors of integrated external systems.

Define special attributes for error handling in the process data structure and embed any activity that integrates external systems in an error-handling control flow. The integrated external system can thus report errors to the process instance, and the process instance can react to those errors. This means a process-oriented approach is applied to handle errors as management of errors is captured by the process model itself (see Figure 9.22).

Process-based error management means that if an error occurs, it will be treated as an event that must be handled by the process model. The process must then move into an exception-handling mechanism to provide the right team or person with the necessary information to manage the error. Conclusively, there must be an error-handling process activity defined in the process model. Output of this activity will be information, whether the activity where the error occurred must be repeated, the error can be ignored, or the whole process instance must be aborted. The process model is again only interested in the result of the error management activity. Consequently, the process model just has to delegate the issue to someone who handles the error and who provides information on how to proceed in the process.

The process engine is responsible for assigning the error-handling activity to the right person or team as it is responsible for distributing any activity. Information on whom to assign the error-handling activity must be provided by the external system that reports the error because we can assume that each external system has the knowledge about who is responsible for error messages that occur in that external system. For this reason, if an external system reports an error to the process engine, it also has to provide information regarding who is responsible for managing the error.

An external system that reports an error to the process engine must provide the following information, which must be kept in the process data structure:

- A standardized error code that indicates the general type or class of error. This error code can be used by the process model to react to an error in a standard way as this error code represents agreed and unified error code semantics.
- The external system-specific error code.
- The external system-specific error message or error description.
- The name or identifier of the external system that reports the error.
- The actor (person, team, organizational unit) responsible for managing the error (i.e., the administrator of the error).

It has been mentioned that the output of an error-handling activity can generally be three different decisions: retry, ignore, and abort. As a result, attributes are necessary in the process data structure to report that decision to the process instance.

To realize the pattern, it is helpful if the process engine provides mechanisms of dynamic staff resolution because the administrator of the "manage error" activity will be dynamically defined by the external system reporting the error. For instance, IBM WebSphere MQ Workflow allows dynamic staff resolution.

A drawback of the pattern is that for each occurring error, a manage error activity instance will be generated. This may result in many such activity instances because errors are reported to every process instance. Thus, one error source might report the same error to many process instances repeatedly.

Plus, additional development effort is necessary to implement the manage error activity. It might be necessary to provide some sort of bulk operations on the manage error activity instances, for example, to set the retry, ignore, or abort option for a whole set of manage error activity instances. This is useful if the same errors are reported repeatedly.

Application of this pattern principally influences the design of a process control data structure as special attributes are required to report and manage errors. Consequently, it will influence the design of a GENERIC PROCESS CONTROL STRUCTURE.

Example: UML-Based Design of PROCESS-BASED ERROR MANAGEMENT

Figure 9.23 shows an overall process design that can be used for managing errors in the process flow. Basically, the PROCESS-BASED ERROR MANAGEMENT pattern is about embedding an activity that integrates external systems in an error-handling control flow. In practice, the error-handling activity is often embedded in a reusable subprocess. This subprocess can then be modeled in the process flow whenever required.

Example: PROCESS-BASED ERROR MANAGEMENT in WebSphere MQ Workflow

Let us illustrate Process-Based Error Management with WebSphere MQ Workflow. It offers a mechanism for integrating applications via XML-based message adapters. The whole mechanism is encapsulated in a concept called the user-defined program execution server (UPES). The basis of the UPES concept is the MQ Workflow XML messaging interface. MQ Workflow does not communicate with applications directly but uses WebSphere MQ (MQ Series) [WFPG03].

The UPES concept is all about communicating with external applications via asynchronous XML messages to execute external business logic of an activity in a process

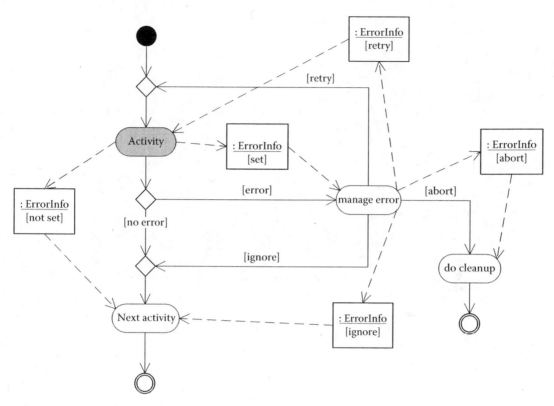

FIGURE 9.23
Process-based error management example in UML.

automatically. Consequently, the UPES concept is literally about "informing" an application that a process activity requires execution of business logic (which is actually implemented by the application), "receiving" the result after the execution has been completed by the application, and further relating the asynchronously incoming result back to the activity instance that originally requested execution of the business logic (as there may be hundreds or thousands of instances of the same process activity). Thus, a UPES is an XML adapter that represents an interface to one or many applications related to integrated business logic in process activities.

If an activity instance sends out an XML request to a UPES implementation, that message will have a defined format. The request is automatically generated by MQ Workflow. It contains the data structures and their contents associated to the activity. Furthermore, it is important to mention that the request contains an activity implementation CORRELATION IDENTIFIER. Via this CORRELATION IDENTIFIER, the request is associated to an activity instance in the process engine. The reply message must contain this CORRELATION IDENTIFIER to relate the response back to the corresponding activity instance.

As far as an implementation of the PROCESS-BASED ERROR MANAGEMENT pattern is concerned, the concrete UPES implementation ensures that the result message delivered to MQ Workflow does contain the necessary error information, such that the process model can react to the error information as defined by the pattern. The actual error information will be accessible in the process control data as MQ Workflow automatically picks up result messages, associates them with an activity instance, and transfers the message data to the process control data of the process instance (the data structures of the result message and the process model must match).

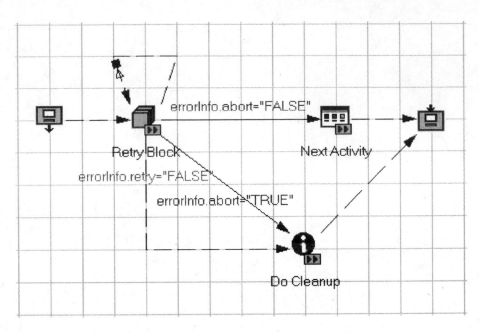

FIGURE 9.24
Process-based error management example in WebSphere MQ Workflow.

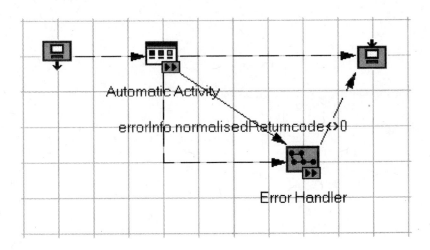

FIGURE 9.25
Block activity details for process-based error management.

The basic process fragment that handles a reported error is depicted in Figure 9.24, which shows a block activity that contains the actual error reporting activity. The block activity is necessary to implement the loop if the *retry* flag has been set. For this reason, the block activity implements an exit condition that the *retry* flag must not be set (*retry="FALSE"*).

The detailed diagram of this block activity is shown in Figure 9.25. This figure shows the transition to the subsequent activity in case the process should not be aborted and the transition to the cleanup activity if the process instance must be terminated.

Figure 9.25 shows the automatic activity that implements the XML message-based communication with an external application via the UPES mechanism. If the result of this activity indicates an error, a transition to an error handler is made. If no error is reported, the block activity is terminated normally. One has to consider that the *retry*, *abort*, and *ignore* flags must be reset for every single loop. The *Error Handler* process is a small process model with only one activity that represents the error management by an administrator.

The error administrator is dynamically associated to a concrete actor (e.g., a person or role) by the value of the attribute *errorInfo.administrator* in the process control data. Within the error-managing activity, the error administrator can view all the error information and thus try to fix the problem. The result of the error management activity will be the decision whether to *retry* the activity, *abort* the process, or *ignore* the error. The decision is reported in the corresponding attributes in the process control data structure. The following FDL fragment demonstrates the definition of the *Error Handler* process and highlights the dynamic association of the error administrator according to the value of the corresponding attribute in the process control data structure.

```
PROCESS 'Error Handler' (
'GenericProcessControlStructure',
'GenericProcessControlStructure' )
  DO NOT PROMPT_AT_PROCESS_START
  PROGRAM_ACTIVITY 'Manage Error' (
'GenericProcessControlStructure',
'GenericProcessControlStructure' )
    START MANUAL WHEN AT_LEAST_ONE CONNECTOR TRUE
    EXIT AUTOMATIC
    PRIORITY DEFINED_IN INPUT_CONTAINER
    DONE_BY PERSON TAKEN_FROM 'errorInfo.administrator'
    PROGRAM 'Foo'
    SYNCHRONIZATION NESTED
  END 'Manage Error'
  DATA
    FROM SOURCE 1 TO 'Manage Error'
  DATA
    FROM 'Manage Error' TO SINK 1
END 'Error Handler'
```

Example: Process-Based Error Management in BPEL

In a BPEL implementation with WebSphere Integration Developer being executed on WebSphere Process Server, the PROCESS-BASED ERROR MANAGEMENT pattern can be implemented in a straightforward manner. Figure 9.26 shows an activity that invokes a service. The result message of this service may contain error information. The process control flow reacts on this error information that is reported in the process control data. The three possible options for managing the error (i.e., retry, abort, and ignore) are modeled in the BPEL process flow.

Another possible option for modeling the pattern in BPEL is with an exception handler. In this case, exceptions can be caught, and corresponding actions may be taken according to the type of exception. However, one has to mention that the retry loop implies some limitations in this case. The exception handler might remodel the service invocation, but this implies only one possible repetition of the service invocation. In case the service invocation should be repeated more than once, this needs to be modeled explicitly. Some services may also rather report their error information in dedicated response data rather than throwing exceptions. For this reason, the appropriate variant needs to be decided in conjunction to the specific situation. In Figure 9.27, a timeout exception is handled with such an event handler. A TIMEOUT HANDLER also represents a specific pattern explained further in this chapter.

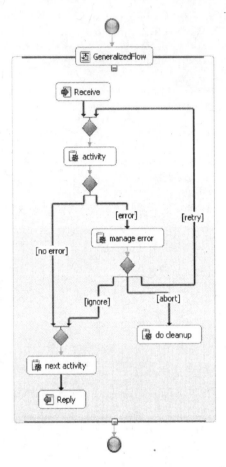

FIGURE 9.26
Example for process-based error management in the BPEL process flow.

Timeout Handler

During the execution of a process instance, activities are scheduled according to the definition of the process model. Once an activity is instantiated and started by the process
engine, the execution of the process flow suspends until the activity is finished. If an activity implementation contains a rather time-consuming logic or if it waits for an event to
occur, we must deal with situations in which the activity implementations never reply or
the event never occurs. Usually, a timeout mechanism is used in such situations.

How can a timeout be handled in a process model in a generic and reusable fashion?

If the process model contains activities that may raise a timeout event, you must alter
the process model to handle the timeout correctly according to the business requirements.
As this situation occurs frequently, it is not useful to let the process designers model and
implement the timeout mechanisms repeatedly for each design situation that requires

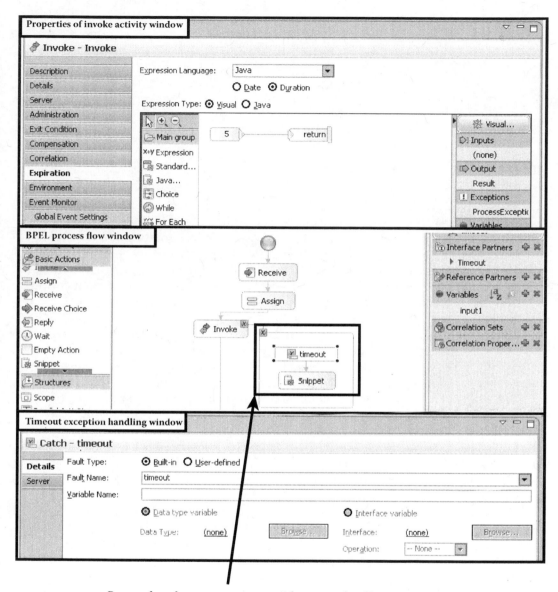

Process-based error management with an event handler

FIGURE 9.27
Process-based error management realized using an event handler.

dealing with a timeout. Instead, generic and reusable timeout mechanisms should be designed for each design situation in which a timeout can occur. These timeout mechanisms should then be reused in each design situation requiring timeout handling.

The process model that contains an activity that may raise a timeout event has to handle this situation in a defined way to continue the process execution. Often, the process flow shall not continue as if the activity were finished regularly, but not every timeout situation should be handled this way. In other words, the timeout mechanism must allow the process designer to define how the timeout should be handled.

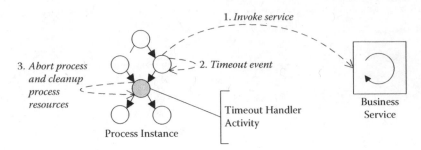

FIGURE 9.28
A timeout handler.

Define a special activity type for timeout handling that provides a TIMEOUT HANDLER as
its activity implementation. Place the TIMEOUT HANDLER in the process flow after activities
that may raise a timeout event. Let the process flow branch to the timeout handler when
a timeout event occurs. The process flow branch to the timeout handler when
a timeout event occurs. The process designer can model how the process flow should
proceed after the TIMEOUT HANDLER has been reached by choosing one of the following
options: retry the activity, abort the process, or ignore the timeout (see Figure 9.28).

A TIMEOUT HANDLER is realized as an activity type that is responsible for handling timeout situations in a process model. Wherever an activity that may raise a timeout event is
defined in a process, model a decision point that checks whether a timeout has taken place.
In case of a timeout, it branches to the TIMEOUT HANDLER.

When the TIMEOUT HANDLER is instantiated, it evaluates the given situation, processes
this input according to its configuration, and terminates with the resulting decision how
to handle the situation. This result is to

- *retry* the execution of the activity that caused the timeout,
- *ignore* the timeout and proceed in the process flow, or
- *abort* the process execution and *clean up* any process resources.

To determine an appropriate action (retry, ignore, or abort), the timeout handler depends
on information about the timeout situation. Hence, an appropriate process control structure (e.g., designed following the GENERIC PROCESS CONTROL STRUCTURE pattern) needs to
be passed to and from the timeout handler. This structure must at least contain the following information to make a decision:

- The name or unique identifier of the process causing the timeout.
- The name or unique identifier of the activity that caused the timeout.
- A retry count that is initially zero and will be incremented with each retry by the
  timeout handler.
- The context in which the timeout occurred. This can, for example, be a BUSINESS
  OBJECT REFERENCE, the ID of an event source to which the activity was registered, or
  the ID of an external system that was not accessible.

Provided with this information, the TIMEOUT HANDLER is able to decide for one of the
possible actions. The decision can be made by human interaction or fully automatically.
To achieve a high degree of reuse, it makes sense to externalize some handling logic in

configurations of the timeout handler. For instance, this may include a configuration for each activity that states the maximum retry count before aborting the process or a configuration that ignores timeouts of certain event sources.

Using the TIMEOUT HANDLER pattern, timeouts reported by activities during process execution can be handled generically within the process model according to defined rules. Activities that may finish with a timeout are not responsible for handling the timeout themselves. Furthermore, the process designer does not need to evaluate each single timeout situation and model the process respectively. Rather, the timeout handler component will be configured to direct the process flow accordingly. This means separation of concerns can be reached here.

Activities that finish with a timeout might have to supply additional information to the timeout handler such that decisions can be made. Handling timeouts might be necessary in many cases but also leads to higher complexity of the process models. Thus, higher development and testing effort is involved. For this reason, it should be considered case by case whether handling timeouts is necessary to avoid unnecessary effort. A TIMEOUT HANDLER is a specialization of the PROCESS-BASED ERROR MANAGEMENT pattern, with handling timeouts as a special type of error.

Example: UML-Based Design of a TIMEOUT HANDLER

Figure 9.29 shows a process model in UML in which a TIMEOUT HANDLER is used after processing an activity that may raise a timeout. This TIMEOUT HANDLER retries the activity a number of times (defined before by the process designer using a "maximum retry" field in the process control data structure). Otherwise, it aborts or ignores the timeout. To manage the number of retries, we must pass a timeout information data structure to the TIMEOUT HANDLER and increment the number of retries each time we retry. Usually, the timeout information data structure should be modeled as part of a GENERIC PROCESS CONTROL STRUCTURE. The process model in Figure 9.30 shows how the timeout information can be passed to and from the timeout handler.

Example: TIMEOUT HANDLING in WebSphere Process Server

BPEL engines like Oracle BPM Suite or IBM WebSphere Process Server allow handling exceptions. Handling timeouts is realized as just one case of an exception in the context of these BPEL engines. That is, the exception-handling mechanisms of those BPEL engines can be used for timeout handling. In IBM WebSphere Process Server, a timeout is actually a built-in fault, and a corresponding off-the-shelf fault handler can be used (i.e., a TIMEOUT HANDLER). Figure 9.31 shows an example of modeling a timeout exception with WebSphere Process Server.

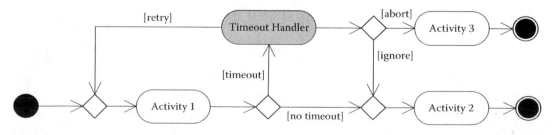

FIGURE 9.29
Timeout handler example in UML. (From C. Hentrich. Synchronization patterns for process-driven and service-oriented architectures. *Springer LNCS Transactions on Pattern Languages of Programs*, 103–135, 2009.)

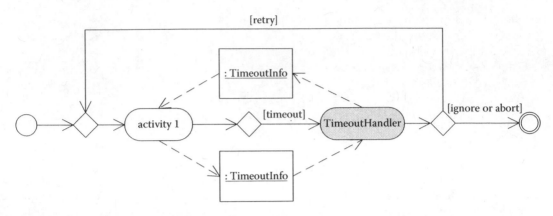

FIGURE 9.30
Retries in a timeout handler. (From C. Hentrich. Synchronization patterns for process-driven and service-oriented architectures. *Springer LNCS Transactions on Pattern Languages of Programs,* 103–135, 2009.)

Examples: Support for TIMEOUT HANDLER in Process Engines and Enterprise Service Buses

- Leading BPEL engines like BEA Agualogic Fuego, IBM WebSphere Process Server, and Oracle BPM Suite provide exception-handling mechanisms that provide timeout handling.
- The TIMEOUT HANDLER pattern has also been implemented with older workflow engines such as IBM WebSphere MQ Workflow or Staffware.
- Also, message buses support this kind of timeout handling. Examples are WebSphere Advanced enterprise service bus (ESB) or the former version WebSphere Business Integration Message Broker.

WAITING ACTIVITY

Processes are modeled to be executed on a process engine. When modeling business processes, it is often required to suspend the process for a defined period of time.

How is a waiting position modeled in a process that can be configured either at process design time or during process execution?

Consider a process for order entry and order processing. Regulatory constraints might force the order processing not to start before the defined period of legal order revocation has passed. The execution of the process instance has to wait for a defined period of time before the next activities can be scheduled.

This scenario deals with a fixed or static time frame that does not change depending on other data processed in the system. The period is known during process design time, and it can be supplied within the process model or in an external configuration. Yet, the time to wait may not always be known during process design (e.g., because it depends on a user input during process execution). In that case, the process execution has to wait for a time that has to be evaluated during runtime.

As this situation is recurring, it should be supported in a generic and reusable fashion to avoid realizing implementations of waiting positions in executable processes over and over again.

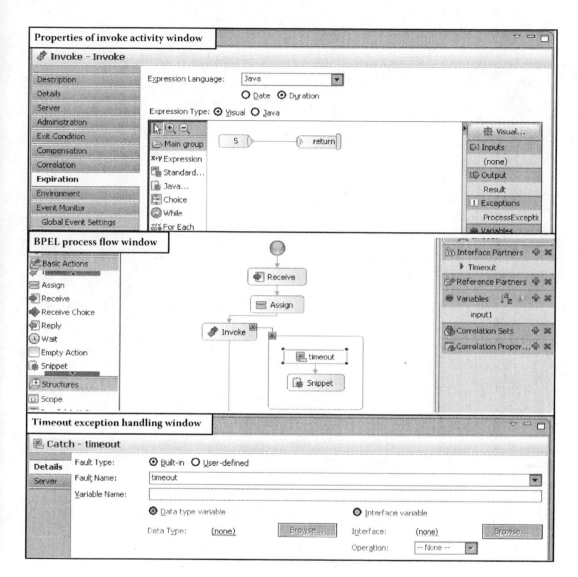

FIGURE 9.31
Timeout handler in WebSphere Process Server.

Define a special activity type for modeling waiting positions in the process. Such a WAITING ACTIVITY uses an internal timer and waits for a defined time frame to elapse until it terminates. The time frame can be configured either during design time or at runtime of the process. The termination of the WAITING ACTIVITY causes the process execution to continue (see Figure 9.32).

A WAITING ACTIVITY implements a statically or dynamically configured timer. The WAITING ACTIVITY is responsible for starting the timer when the activity is instantiated and automatically terminates when the timer reaches the configured value. Thus, the process flow will be suspended for the desired time at that process step if the process engine schedules this activity.

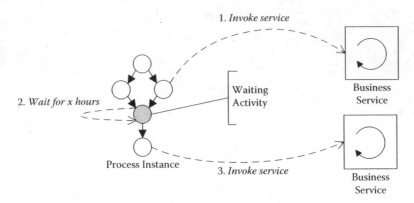

FIGURE 9.32
A waiting activity.

The value specifying the time frame to wait for is either

- statically supplied to the activity, for example, as metadata within the process model,
- supplied from an external configuration source, or
- dynamically calculated during runtime and supplied from within the process instance via the input data of the activity.

Hence, we distinguish static and dynamic timers:

- A *static timer* is configured during design time. Use a static timer if the time to elapse is not influenced by any measure within the system environment.
- A *dynamic timer* is configured during runtime (e.g., by a previously executed activity). Use a dynamic timer if the value of the timer can only be evaluated during runtime or will undergo changes initiated through other system components.

When modeling a WAITING ACTIVITY, the process flow can be actively suspended for a defined period of time at a defined process step. When using a dynamic timer, it must be ensured that the evaluated time frame is reasonable. A wrong evaluation could result in an unexpected long suspension of the process execution. Waiting activities delay the flow of activities, which can sometimes be seen as a negative consequence. Choosing the right waiting interval might be crucial to avoid unnecessary delay. For this reason, the business requirements need to be clear to avoid such unnecessary delay. Defining the wait logic might be a considerable effort that needs to planned and developed. The WAITING ACTIVITY pattern should for this reason only be applied when the business requirements and wait logic are clear. The additional development effort introduced by this added complexity needs to be considered.

Example: UML-Based Design of a TIMEOUT HANDLER

Let us illustrate a Timeout Handler design in UML. To model a WAITING ACTIVITY is trivial. We just need to define one activity as the WAITING ACTIVITY and pass the necessary waiting time frame information. This passing of information should usually follow the GENERIC PROCESS CONTROL STRUCTURE pattern. Figure 9.33 shows a WAITING ACTIVITY with a static timer.

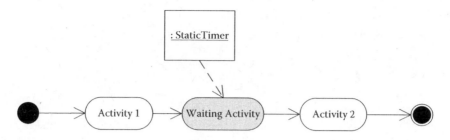

FIGURE 9.33
UML example of a waiting activity using a static timer.

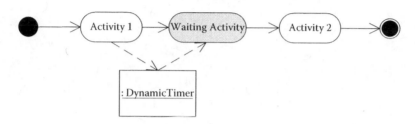

FIGURE 9.34
UML example of a waiting activity using a dynamic timer.

FIGURE 9.35
Waiting activity example in WebSphere MQ Workflow. (From C. Hentrich. Synchronization patterns for process-driven and service-oriented architectures. *Springer LNCS Transactions on Pattern Languages of Programs,* 103–135, 2009.)

Modeling passing information for a dynamic timer is almost identical. We just need to write the timer information during process execution time (e.g., in previously executed activity) (see Figure 9.34).

Example: Waiting Activity in WebSphere MQ Workflow

Many process engines offer integrated support for implementing the WAITING ACTIVITY pattern with static or dynamic timers. The example illustrated in Figure 9.35 is an implementation using the expiration mechanism of IBM WebSphere MQ Workflow. The model and configuration shown in the figure are defined with MQ Workflow Buildtime. Figure 9.36 shows the configuration dialog for the expiration mechanism that offers support for both static and dynamic implementations. The input value for a dynamic configuration can be obtained from the input data of the activity. To implement a dynamic waiting activity using the expiration mechanism, you need to model a sequence of two activities. The first is responsible for acquiring the value for the timer and passing it to the second one, which uses this value in its input data for the expiration configuration.

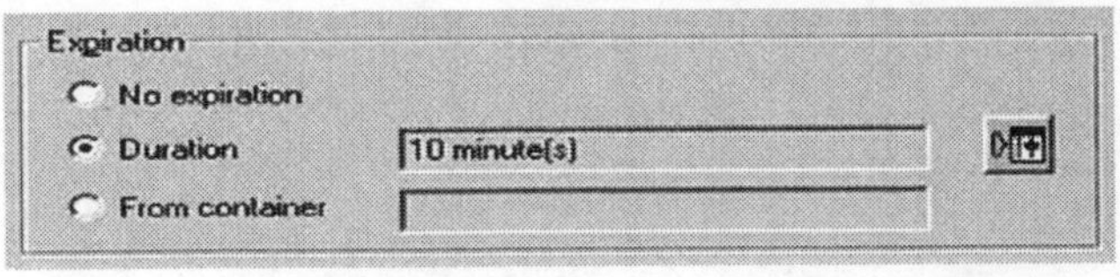

Expiration

- ○ No expiration
- ◉ Duration | 10 minute(s) |
- ○ From container | |

FIGURE 9.36
Configuration dialog for the expiration mechanism. (From C. Hentrich. Synchronization patterns for process-driven and service-oriented architectures. *Springer LNCS Transactions on Pattern Languages of Programs*, 103–135, 2009.)

FIGURE 9.37
Waiting activity example in BPEL.

Example: WAITING ACTIVITY in BPEL with WebSphere Process Server

WebSphere Process Server provides a special activity type for modeling in BPEL a WAITING ACTIVITY. The duration can be specified in the properties of the activity as a fixed value or can be dynamically set by an attribute in the process data. Figure 9.37 shows how such a WAITING ACTIVITY can be modeled in the development tool WebSphere Integration Developer.

Examples: Support for WAITING ACTIVITY in Process Engines and ESBs

- Leading BPEL engines like BEA Agualogic Fuego, Tibco WebMethods, IBM WebSphere Process Server, and Oracle BPM Suite provide support for modeling of WAITING ACTIVITIES.
- The WAITING ACTIVITY pattern has also been implemented with older workflow engines such as IBM WebSphere MQ Workflow or Staffware. Those engines also provide modeling wait states according to defined rules (e.g., to wait for a certain period of time). This can be done with a static value from a prior set variable.
- Some message buses also support this kind of waiting states. Examples are WebSphere Advanced ESB or the former version WebSphere Business Integration Message Broker.

10

Integrating Events into Process-Driven SOAs

Introduction

Chapter 3 introduced the basics about the combination of process-driven service-oriented architectures (SOAs) and *event-driven architecture* (EDA). In this context, it is important to note that a process instance runs in its own *data and event space* (In this chapter this is called the *process space*). If events outside the context of a process instance occur that need to be considered by the process instance, problems may arise in how to capture those events by the process instance. In this chapter, we call the external space where external events are raised the *event space*.

The patterns introduced in this chapter provide solutions to capture events that occur in the event space and consider them in the process space of a process instance.

Please note that there also are events raised within the event space of the process engine. We have seen a number of examples in Chapter 9, such as process-internal error events or exception events in the context of the PROCESS-BASED ERROR MANAGEMENT pattern or timeout events in the context of the TIMEOUT HANDLER pattern. In this chapter, we concentrate on the external events from the event space.

In terms of the event space design, we assume a basic model similar to the one shown in Figure 10.1. Events are produced by event sources. Event listeners consume these events. They are notified about the events by the event sources to which they have registered as listeners previously.

The basic pattern for linking the process space to the event space is the EVENT-BASED ACTIVITY pattern. It describes how to design activities that actively wait for specific external events to happen. Only if the events happen does the EVENT-BASED ACTIVITY terminate and allow the process instance to proceed. An EVENT-BASED ACTIVITY implementation acts as an event listener that resides in the event space and informs the process instance about external events once they have happened. Figure 10.2 illustrates the design of an EVENT-BASED ACTIVITY.

Applying the EVENT-BASED ACTIVITY pattern requires considering timeout and error handling since a controllable process execution highly depends on deterministic behavior of such EVENT-BASED ACTIVITIES. The process designer is responsible for handling these situations within the process model. For this purpose, the related TIMEOUT HANDLER pattern can be applied. The TIMEOUT HANDLER pattern describes a solution for handling timeouts that are reported by components integrated in the process flow. EVENT-BASED ACTIVITIES are typically considered as such components as listening for an event should include a defined timeout value. The PROCESS-BASED ERROR MANAGEMENT pattern provides a solution for dealing with reported errors.

The WAITING ACTIVITY pattern describes a solution for controlling process execution based on a dynamic or static timer. In the context of EVENT-BASED ACTIVITIES, the timer can

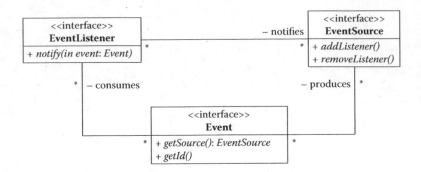

FIGURE 10.1
Event space design: basic model. (From C. Hentrich. Synchronization patterns for process-driven and service-oriented architectures. *Springer LNCS Transactions on Pattern Languages of Programs*, 103–135, 2009.)

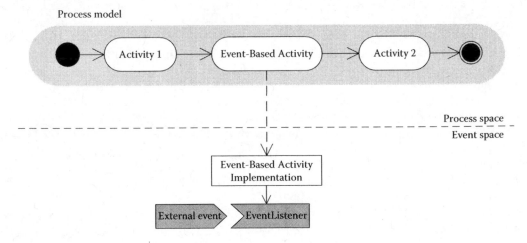

FIGURE 10.2
Linking process space and event space using event-based activities. (From C. Hentrich. Synchronization patterns for process-driven and service-oriented architectures. *Springer LNCS Transactions on Pattern Languages of Programs*, 103–135, 2009.)

be perceived as an event source and the waiting activity as a special type of EVENT-BASED ACTIVITY.

Some process modeling languages and the corresponding process engines support (asynchronous) event handlers that can be used as a mechanism to react to events. Consider, for example, BPEL (Business Process Execution Language) event handlers. These *event handler* mechanisms are an alternative to applying the EVENT-BASED ACTIVITY pattern. Event handlers handle events within the process space. In contrast, the EVENT-BASED ACTIVITY pattern advocates separation of concerns: It requires an event activity implementation in the event space. Event handlers are often defined globally for the process or a subscope of the process, whereas an EVENT-BASED ACTIVITY can be placed at a specific point in the process flow. The pattern relationships of the EVENT-BASED ACTIVITY pattern are illustrated in Figure 10.3.

The second pattern in this chapter is EVENT-BASED PROCESS INSTANCE. It deals with the problem of how to instantiate a process on the occurrence of a defined external event. The EVENT-BASED PROCESS INSTANCE pattern solves this problem by providing an event-based process instantiator component that resides in the event space. It can also be offered as a

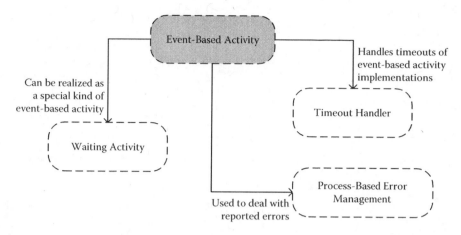

FIGURE 10.3
Event-based activity pattern relationships.

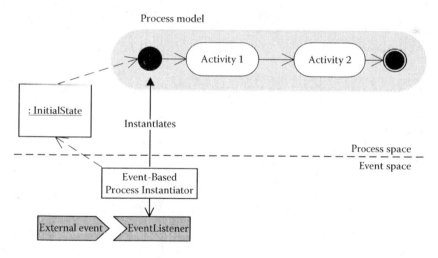

FIGURE 10.4
Linking process space and event space using an event-based process instance. (From C. Hentrich. Synchronization patterns for process-driven and service-oriented architectures. *Springer LNCS Transactions on Pattern Languages of Programs,* 103–135, 2009.)

service by the process engine. The event-based process instantiator is responsible for providing the initial state of the process instance and starting the process. It acts as an event listener for specific external events. Figure 10.4 illustrates the solution of the EVENT-BASED PROCESS INSTANCE pattern.

Please note that the EVENT-BASED ACTIVITY pattern employs the same event listener and event source mechanism as the EVENT-BASED PROCESS INSTANCE pattern. That is, there is a potential of reuse in implementations if both patterns are realized (which often makes sense if the application requires event-based process behavior).

A special variant of EVENT-BASED PROCESS INSTANCE is the EVENT-BASED PROCESS SPLIT pattern. It offers a solution for the problem of processes that are suspended for a long time because of an EVENT-BASED ACTIVITY waiting for an external event. In principle, we could just let the running process instance wait until the event arrives. But, many waiting process

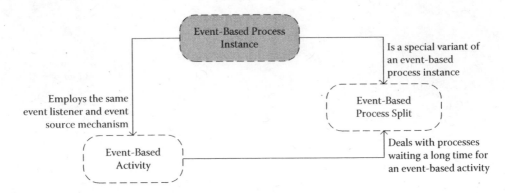

FIGURE 10.5
Event-based process instance pattern relationships.

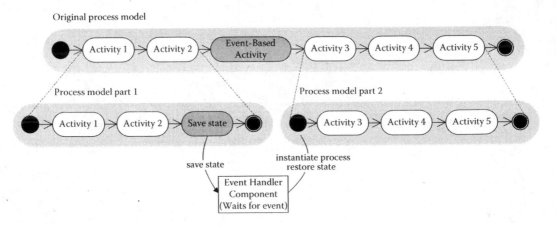

FIGURE 10.6
Splitting process models using event-based process split.

instances could have negative impacts on qualities such as performance of the process engine or the manageability of running instances. To optimize such qualities, the EVENT-BASED PROCESS SPLIT pattern describes how to externalize the event-based activity to an external event handler component and split the original business process into several parts at the points where the event-based activity is located. Figure 10.5 illustrates the pattern relationships of the EVENT-BASED PROCESS INSTANCE pattern.

The special usage of EVENT-BASED PROCESS INSTANCES in the EVENT-BASED PROCESS SPLIT pattern requires the state of the first process to be stored and used as the initial state for the instantiated process.

Figure 10.6 illustrates splitting the process models. The new process is split into two parts. The first part contains all activities of the original process model before the event-based activity. The last activity of the first part saves the state of the process instance in the event handler component. Then, the event handler component waits for the incoming event. Finally, the second part of the process restores the state and continues with the remaining activities of the original process.

The EVENT-BASED PROCESS SPLIT pattern can potentially be used in all situations in which processes must wait for external events. The EVENT-BASED ACTIVITY pattern is an example for such situations, as illustrated in Figure 10.7.

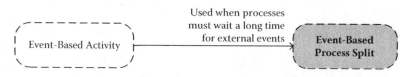

FIGURE 10.7
Event-based process split pattern relationships.

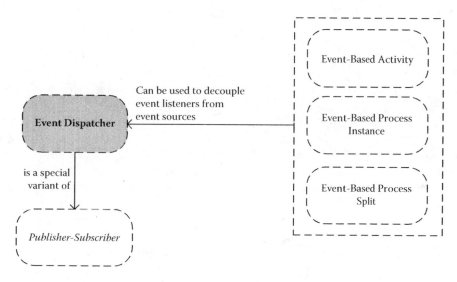

FIGURE 10.8
Event dispatcher pattern relationships.

The last pattern in this chapter is the EVENT DISPATCHER pattern. It is applied when event sources must be flexibly linked to event listeners. To achieve a decoupling of event sources and listeners, a central EVENT DISPATCHER is used to manage the occurring events. Event sources signal events to the EVENT DISPATCHER, and the EVENT DISPATCHER forwards events to event listeners.

In the context of the EVENT-BASED ACTIVITY, EVENT-BASED PROCESS INSTANCE, and EVENT-BASED PROCESS SPLIT patterns, the EVENT DISPATCHER pattern can be used to decouple event listeners from event sources, adding a higher degree of abstraction from concrete implementations. You should use the EVENT DISPATCHER pattern in this context if the system has to deal with many event sources, and frequent changes are expected. This use of the EVENT DISPATCHER pattern also offers the chance to exchange event sources without any major impacts.

The EVENT DISPATCHER pattern is a special variant of the PUBLISHER/SUBSCRIBER [BMR+96, BHS07a] pattern. The EVENT DISPATCHER specialty is that it focuses in events and not components. That means different components may fire the same events. The dispatcher is registering events and not components. Moreover, subscribing for events is selective (i.e., event listeners only listen to a subset of all registered events, which represents the dispatching rule). The pattern relationships of the EVENT DISPATCHER pattern are shown in Figure 10.8.

In general, all patterns introduced in this chapter require you to combine your process-driven SOA with concepts from EDA. All the patterns introduce some additional complexity to your architecture and require additional development effort. Hence, the patterns introduced in this chapter should only be applied if the business requirements point to using the EDA style.

EVENT-BASED ACTIVITY

Consider a business process design that is becoming too complex, for example, because it involves interactions with other business applications or external data sources. Many of these interactions can be understood in terms of events that happen in the business applications or external data sources, such as state changes in the applications or changes of the data. Hence, handling of external events needs to be considered in the process design.

How are events in a process flow handled that occur external to a process instance?

During the execution of a process instance, the evaluation of defined conditions shapes the decision logic of the process and thus influences the execution path of the process. Such conditions are based on variables known in the process instance. Process design in a more complex business scenario may also have to consider handling of events triggered by external systems, such as business object status changes or events produced by another process instance executed in parallel.

In this context, the *process space* (i.e., the process execution environment) is separate from the *event space* (i.e., the environment in which the external event occurs and in which it can be perceived). That means that there is no direct relation between a process instance and an occurring external event. A condition in a process can only evaluate process variables: It is not sufficient for retrieving a notification of an event.

Consider an asynchronous print job that is sent to an output system when a user finishes an activity. If a subsequent activity of the process instance depends on the document created during the print job, it shall not be scheduled as long as the document is not available. Since the state of the document creation is not known in the scope of the process engine, it cannot be evaluated by the process using a condition in the process. In addition, such a condition could not simply be evaluated once but would have to be continuously checked until it is satisfied as the process does not know when the event occurs. The problem in this scenario is that the creation of the document is an event that occurs outside the process space. Therefore, the scheduling of the activity cannot be easily influenced by this external event.

This scenario illustrates a recurring issue: A process instance shall wait at a defined process activity for an external event to occur before continuing with the process execution. This issue also brings up two closely related aspects that need to be considered:

- How are errors handled while waiting for an event?
- What happens if the event never occurs?

Hence, a strategy for error and timeout handling has to be considered in this context as well.

Model an EVENT-BASED ACTIVITY that actively waits for external events to occur and that terminates if they do occur. The EVENT-BASED ACTIVITY implementation acts as an event listener and reports occurring events to the process instance (see Figure 10.9).

An EVENT-BASED ACTIVITY acts as an event listener and registers to event sources from which it would like to retrieve notifications about occurring events. If it is notified of the events that the activity is waiting for, the activity terminates, and the process execution continues.

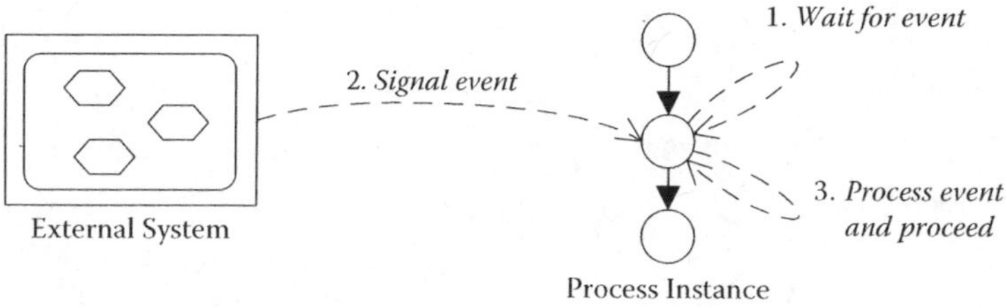

FIGURE 10.9
An event-based activity.

The activity implementation of an EVENT-BASED ACTIVITY (i.e., the event listener implementation) is typically realized by registering as an OBSERVER [GHJV94, BHS07a] to the event source. The event source simply notifies all registered observers if an event (e.g., a change of its state) occurs. The subjects to observe (i.e., the event sources) must be known to the activity implementation of an EVENT-BASED ACTIVITY.

EVENT-BASED ACTIVITIES solve the problem of handling external events outside the data and event space of the process engine. The activity implementation has the task to connect the event space of the process instance with an external event space. An EVENT-BASED ACTIVITY modeled in a process is linked to its activity implementation when it is instantiated by the process engine. As an event listener, the activity implementation receives notifications of the occurring events. If it is notified about the events it has been waiting for, the activity implementation will terminate the activity in the process and proceed to the next activity.

A coupling between the process and the event space of the activity implementation is only present in terms of a reference from the activity to its implementation. This has the advantage that the process engine and the process designer are independent of concrete events and event sources. However, all logic concerning which events the process has to wait for is then contained in the event-based activity implementation outside the data and event space of the process. If shared knowledge about events and event sources is needed, corresponding identifiers can be supplied in the data container of the activity during design time and be evaluated in the implementation during runtime.

A consequence of applying the EVENT-BASED ACTIVITY pattern is that the process flow is interrupted, and its further execution depends on the occurrence of one or more defined external events. This way, the business process design can integrate a broad range of enterprise system resources (external business applications, data sources, other business processes, and so on) as the process flow may be synchronized with external systems via the EVENT-BASED ACTIVITY.

Additional efforts are needed for realizing timeout and error handling in order not to block the process execution for an undefined amount of time. As a negative consequence, the handling of events and modeling of EVENT-BASED ACTIVITIES make the processes more complex. For this reason, the EVENT-BASED ACTIVITY pattern should only be applied in business scenarios that actually require external events to be handled in the process.

Example: UML-Based Design for Implementing the EVENT-BASED ACTIVITY Pattern

Figure 10.10 shows a sample class structure for EVENT-BASED ACTIVITIES in the Unified Modelling Language. In this design, an EVENT-BASED ACTIVITY in the process space delegates to an event-based activity implementation in the event space. The event-based activity implementation is an event listener that can subscribe to events produced by event sources.

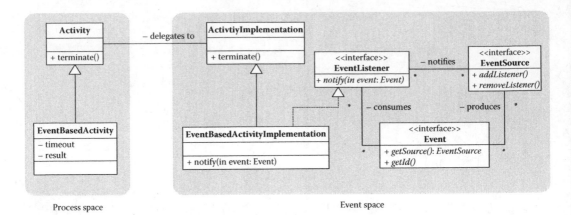

FIGURE 10.10
UML example for the event-based activity pattern.

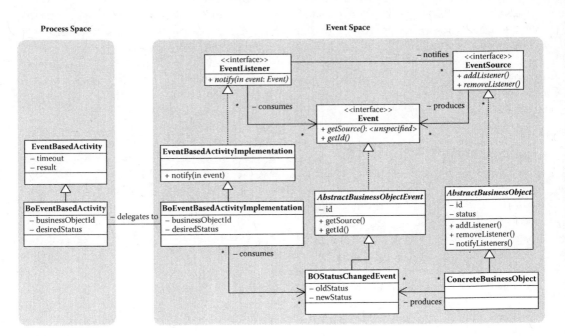

FIGURE 10.11
UML example for waiting for a status change in a business object. (From C. Hentrich. Synchronization patterns for process-driven and service-oriented architectures. *Springer LNCS Transactions on Pattern Languages of Programs*, 103–135, 2009.)

Example: Waiting for a Status Change in a Business Object

Consider implementing a scenario in which the process flow often has to wait for a specific status change of business objects managed outside the process engine. In this scenario, using a generic EVENT-BASED ACTIVITY implementation is applicable. The generic EVENT-BASED ACTIVITY implementation for business object status change events used in this example is shown in Figure 10.11.

This example assumes a process engine according to the WfMC (Workflow Management Coalition) standards [Wfm95, Wfm96] is used to realize the process space. In addition, we assume any object-oriented application execution environment (e.g., a

Java Platform Enterprise Edition (JEE) application server) is used for realizing the activity implementations in the event space. Both process and event space components are highlighted in Figure 10.11.

This specific design registers as a listener for a business object. The business object is referenced by the EVENT-BASED ACTIVITY using a unique ID (following the BUSINESS OBJECT REFERENCE pattern).

Once notified of a *BoStatusChangedEvent*, the EVENT-BASED ACTIVITY implementation compares the new status to the one specified in the input data of the activity. If the new status is equal to the desired status, the activity implementation terminates the activity, and the process execution continues. The following code fragment provides the details of the EVENT-BASED ACTIVITY implementation used in this example:

```
public abstract class EventBasedActivityDelegate implements
    EventListener {
  // field initialized from activity's input data
  // container
  private int timeout;

  // Initialization
  public EventBasedActivityDelegate() {
    // Create a timeout event source
    EventSource source = new TimeOutEventSource(timeout);
    // Register as listener
    source.addListener(this);
  }

  public synchronized void notify(Event event) {
    if (event.gctId() == TIMEOUT_EVENT) {
      // Terminate the activity
      terminate(TIMEOUT);
    }
  }
  ...
}

public class BoEventBasedActivityDelegate extends
    EventBasedActivityDelegate{
  // fields initialized from activity's input
  // container
  private String businessObjectId;
  private int desiredStatus;

  // Initialization
  public BoEventBasedActivityDelegate() {
    // Initialize timeout counter
    super();
    // Get the business object to register to
    EventSource source =
      BoManager.getBusinessObject(
        businessObjectId());
    // Register as listener
    source.addListener(this);
  }

  public synchronized void notify(Event event) {
    if (event.getId() == BO_STATUS_CHANGED_EVENT) {
      BoStatusChangedEvent statusEvent =
        (BoStatusChangedEvent) event;
      // Compare new status to desired status
```

```
        if (statusEvent.getNewStatus() == desiredStatus) {
          // Terminate the activity
          terminate(SUCCESS);
        }
      } else {
        // handle the event in the super class
        super.notify(event);
      }
    }
    ...
}
```

Example: EVENT-BASED ACTIVITY in BPEL with WebSphere Process Server

BPEL engines such as WebSphere Process Server usually provide an Application Programming Interface (API) to communicate with the engine. For this reason, the example provided in the previous section also works for WebSphere Process Server or other BPEL engines that provide an API. The only difference would be the implementation of the *terminate* method. In a WebSphere Process Server implementation, this method would invoke the corresponding API functions to set the output message of the activity and to complete the activity. Another example is the Open Database Conectivity (ODBC)/Java Database Connectivity (JDBC) bindings in WebSphere Process Server. With these bindings, it is possible to define inbound interfaces that react on changes in a database. Those changes represent triggers or events that can be captured in business process models. In this example, a status field of a business object would be such a database trigger that is captured by WebSphere Process Server as an event. The following code fragment highlights the process engine API-specific implementation of the *terminate* method from the example in the previous section for WebSphere Process Server:

```
public class BoEventBasedActivityDelegateWSProcessServer extends
    BoEventBasedActivityDelegate {

  // IBM WebSphere Process Server API specific implementation
  // of the terminate method
  public terminate(Status status) {
    // Generate wrapper object for API implementation
    ProcessEngineAPI api = new WebSphereProcessServerAPI();
    // termine the activitiy in WebSphere Process Server
    api.terminate(status);
  }
}
```

Examples: Support for EVENT-BASED ACTIVITIES in Process Engines and Enterprise Service Buses

The EVENT-BASED ACTIVITY pattern is supported out of the box in a number of different technologies, including some process engines and enterprise service buses (ESBs).

Many BPEL engines, such as BEA Agualogic Fuego, Tibco WebMethods, IBM WebSphere Process Server, and Oracle Fusion, provide various mechanisms that can be used to realize EVENT-BASED ACTIVITIES. An example of a mechanism implemented in some process engines is inbound interfaces.

The pattern has also been implemented with older workflow engines such as IBM WebSphere MQ Workflow or Staffware. In this case, the event-handling implementation was delegated to an external program and not directly integrated into the features of the engine. As a result, an implementation from scratch was necessary.

Also, message buses support this kind of event handling. Examples are WebSphere Advanced ESB or the former version, WebSphere Business Integration Message Broker.

EVENT-BASED PROCESS INSTANCE

Processes are executed on a process engine and need to be modeled in complex business scenarios. Sometimes, a process instance must be started on a certain event that happens in an external system, such as a business application or an external data source.

How can process instances be dynamically created by a process engine on the basis of occurring external events?

In a typical process-driven environment, process instances are instantiated and started by the process engine due to user interactions. For example, a user triggers the creation of a process instance from within an application. Process instances are also created during execution of the process model if it involves subprocesses, which will be instantiated dynamically by the process engine once the execution has reached the corresponding process activity to start a subprocess.

These types of process creation either involve human interactions or require the processes to be statically modeled as subprocesses that will be called from within another process model.

In some situations, neither human interactions nor other processes are the cause of a process instantiation, but an external system, such as a business application or an external data source, is the cause.

In addition, sometimes processes are instantiated as subprocesses but it is not possible to statically define the processes instantiation in a process model. For example, this might be the case if the amount of instances, or the type of processes to be instantiated, depends on dynamic parameters that are only available at runtime. Furthermore, it may not always be desirable to start processes from other process instances as this requires the invoking process instances to run during the execution time of the subprocess.

If the creation of process instances shall neither be triggered directly by a user interaction nor be due to a static process model, it is necessary to instantiate a process automatically if an external event takes place within the system environment.

The basic problem to achieve this goal is that the event to occur will not always be visible in the scope of the process engine, and the engine may not support dynamic process instantiation. How is it possible to create instances of defined process models when an event occurs outside the scope of the process engine? How can the instantiated process be supplied with correct input data?

Provide EVENT-BASED PROCESS INSTANCES that are created based on external events using an event-based process instantiator. The event-based process instantiator can be provided either as a service by the process engine or as a component external to the process engine. It acts as an event listener to specific external events and instantiates a process or a set of processes once the defined events occur (see Figure 10.12).

The event-based process instantiator is responsible for instantiating one or more processes and starting them with a defined initial state on the occurrence of an external event. It acts as an event listener (i.e., it waits to be notified about occurring events from defined event sources to which it registers).

Since external events will occur outside the scope of the process engine, the event-based process instantiator usually resides within the external event space (i.e., the space in which the events occur or where the events can be perceived). An event-based process instantiator

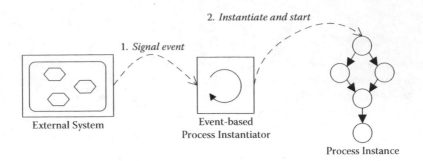

FIGURE 10.12
An event-based process instance.

can also be offered by the process engine as a service. If the EVENT-BASED PROCESS INSTANCE to be started requires a predefined set of information, the event-based process instantiator is responsible for supplying this initial state to the newly created process instance. This is possible either by the means of an external configuration or by using any other data storage.

A number of process modeling languages and corresponding engines support an API for process instantiation or even event-based process instantiation mechanisms. An EVENT-BASED PROCESS INSTANCE implementation should make use of these mechanisms.

A consequence of using the EVENT-BASED PROCESS INSTANCE pattern is that process instances can be dynamically instantiated and started depending on external events. If the process to start requires an initial state to be supplied, the event-based process instantiator is responsible for supplying it; therefore, the corresponding information has to be stored outside the process engine. This may result in additional effort for ensuring data consistency.

It also needs to be considered that the business requirements should be the driver to implement this pattern. The EVENT-BASED PROCESS INSTANCE pattern increases the complexity of the architecture. This added complexity is a negative consequence if the business scenario does not require event-based process instantiation. Realizing an EVENT-BASED PROCESS INSTANCE requires an additional development effort if no suitable implementation is offered by the process engine.

Example: UML-Based Design for Implementing the EVENT-BASED PROCESS INSTANCE Pattern

Figure 10.13 shows a sample class structure for EVENT-BASED PROCESS INSTANCES. This design uses a process adapter that offers a programming interface to the process engine to start a process instance. The EVENT-BASED PROCESS INSTANCE implementation distinguishes between event listeners and event sources. An event source is a component that fires events and notifies all listeners that have registered to this source about the events. When notified, the event listener determines whether the event is of interest using its unique ID or checking the event source that emitted it. An event-based process instantiator component is responsible for instantiating processes using the *instantiateProcess* method of the *Process Adapter*.

Examples: EVENT-BASED PROCESS INSTANCES Using WebSphere MQ Workflow in Supply Chain Management, Document Management, and B2B/B2C Applications

EVENT-BASED PROCESS INSTANCES can be used in many situations. To illustrate this, let us briefly introduce scenarios from a few projects in which we have applied the pattern in WebSpere MQ Workflow from the domain of supply change management, document

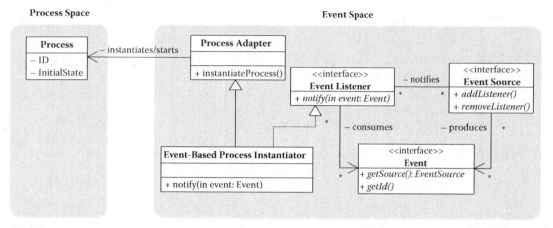

FIGURE 10.13

UML example for event-based process instance. (From C. Hentrich. Synchronization patterns for process-driven and service-oriented architectures. *Springer LNCS Transactions on Pattern Languages of Programs,* 103–135, 2009.)

management, business-2-business (B2B) applications, and business-2-consumers (B2C) applications.

In a supply chain management system, the EVENT-BASED PROCESS INSTANCE pattern has been applied for automatic process instantiation when an event-based interface to several other legacy applications needed to be implemented. These applications are creating events via WebSphere MQ messages. The messages are picked up by an event handler as an incoming message represents an event that needs to be processed. A special input queue has been defined for the event handler.

This event handler transforms this application-specific input message into an XML (Extensible Markup Language) message that suits the format of the *WebSphere MQ Workflow* XML interface and sends the XML message to this messaging interface. Depending on the data in the input message, which basically identifies the application firing the event, different processes are automatically instantiated. The event handler has been implemented in Java and runs on the WebSphere Application Server. In this application, the event handler manages the relationship to the internal business, whereas those legacy applications are viewed as external components that are only indirectly integrated into the process flow by an event-processing mechanism.

Other implementations of this pattern can be found in document management applications, where a process is automatically instantiated after a document has been scanned. The type of process to be instantiated depends on the type of document that has been scanned. Usually, special scanning software with *object character recognition* (OCR) features is used, such that the software recognizes the document type automatically and instantiates the corresponding business process to process the document.

Events that happen in this context are newly scanned documents posted to the event handler, hence the scanning software plays the role of the event originator. The event handler queues the documents that have been scanned and creates the process instances. The process instances usually carry references to scanned documents that are stored in a content management system (following the BUSINESS OBJECT REFERENCE pattern). Applications of this kind are common in the banking and insurance industries.

We have also applied the pattern in a number of B2B or B2C constellations, where service interfaces are offered to create certain process instances. Actually, the offered service is a business process. The type of business process to be instantiated depends on the service request. Some implementations already use *Web services* as the service interface implementation. For instance, one project has been conducted in the German railway industry; business customers may request certain railway routes from point A to point B via several stations at a certain date and time. The request is made via a

Web-based user interface, and a corresponding business process is instantiated to construct the route and to report the finished route back to the customer. Thus, in this case placing a service request is an event to automatically instantiate a process.

Example: EVENT-BASED PROCESS INSTANCE in BPEL with WebSphere Process Server

In Chapter 4, we presented an example from the insurance industry. This example models claims management processes. For instance, in the context of this claims management example, it is possible that a fraud is detected during the execution of the *claims reserve* process. This is modeled as an EVENT-BASED INSTANCE as the fraud-handling business process is triggered by an event. To achieve this, a corresponding event handler is modeled in the BPEL process. The fraud event initiates an activity with a service invocation to instantiate the fraud-handling business process. Figure 10.14 shows the BPEL model as defined in the development tool WebSphere Integration Developer.

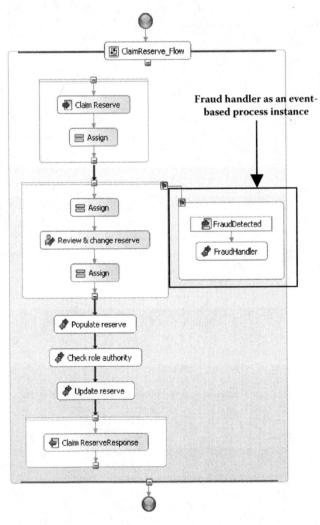

FIGURE 10.14
BPEL example for event-based process instance.

Examples: Support for EVENT-BASED PROCESS INSTANCE in Process Engines and ESBs

- Leading BPEL engines like BEA Agualogic Fuego, Tibco WebMethods, or IBM WebSphere Process Server, and Oracle BPM Suite provide process instantiation features based on events. The engines implement the pattern as a feature of the engine.
- The pattern has also been implemented with older workflow engines, such as IBM WebSphere MQ Workflow or Staffware. In this case, an external program has been implemented that has used the API of the engine to create processes based on events.
- Also, message buses support this kind of message flow instantiation based on events. Examples are WebSphere Advanced ESB or the former version, WebSphere Business Integration Message Broker.

EVENT-BASED PROCESS SPLIT

A domain view of a business process is mapped to a technical view of the process. The technical view of the business process implies waiting for events, such as a customer placing an order. Such events can be initial events (i.e., a process instance is created and started on a process engine with a defined initial state after the event occurred). Or, they can be in-between events (i.e., a running process instance contains an activity waiting for an event).

How are event-based activities modeled and implemented in processes with minimal performance impact on the process engine?

Consider the following typical example: Sometimes, there are EVENT-BASED ACTIVITIES modeled in business processes that have a long duration. For instance, consider an activity that waits for something to happen (i.e., an event) and then initiates the next process activity. Often, it takes weeks and even months until that event occurs. Principally, there is nothing wrong about modeling those EVENT-BASED ACTIVITIES—it is actually the preferred way of modeling.

However, this design may cause serious performance problems because all those process instances exist in the process engine but nothing really happens with them as they are all in a waiting position. This may result in many unnecessary data in the process engine (increasing waiting process instances are in the queue) and may thus make the response time of the process engine increasingly slower.

We have to keep in mind that a process engine manages all kinds of processes. It is better not to generate any unnecessary workload in the process engine to keep the performance of the engine adequate. Moreover, one has to remember that in some projects several thousand process instances are created every day. It would thus be useful if those "temporarily useless" process instances could be removed from the process engine and restored later, after the desired event has occurred.

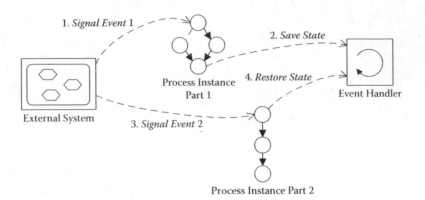

FIGURE 10.15
An event-based process split.

Externalize EVENT-BASED ACTIVITIES to an external event handler component and split the original business process into several parts at the points where event-based activities appear. The event handler stores the relationships between events and processes to be created on a process engine, as well as the initial state of these processes. If an event is fired, the event handler automatically looks up which processes are associated to that event and creates an instance of the processes on a process engine with the defined initial state (see Figure 10.15).

An EVENT-BASED PROCESS SPLIT means externalization of the "problematic" EVENT-BASED ACTIVITIES to an external event handler component and to split the process model into several parts. That is, an EVENT-BASED ACTIVITY is transformed into an activity that externalizes the state of the process instance to that external event handler component (actually, this is an application of the MEMENTO design pattern [GHJV94, BHS07a]), and the process model is divided at the point where such an EVENT-BASED ACTIVITY occurs.

The event handler component observes whether the event occurs and activates the next part of the process if the desired event occurs. The state of the previous part of the process is restored when the next part of the process is created. Thus, an original process model including one EVENT-BASED ACTIVITY will be split into two (or more) process models. The first part is instantiated normally and terminates after having registered its state at the event handler. The second part is automatically instantiated by the event-handling component right after the event has occurred.

Principally, those two process instances are independent from the point of view of the process engine. The dependency must be managed by that external event handler component. To achieve this, it is useful to provide an artificial process ID to link the different instances. That artificial process ID will be part of the externalized state and will thus be restored in the following part of the process. The process data structure must contain a process ID attribute for these purposes. Often, this will be realized as part of a GENERIC PROCESS CONTROL STRUCTURE.

A client might register at an event handler to listen to certain events to instantiate a business process with a defined starting state. The event handler observes events and instantiates the defined business process with the defined starting state if an event occurs that someone registered listens to. As a result, the event handler is connected to several event originators that fire events. Thus, a client could be any application and any system and not

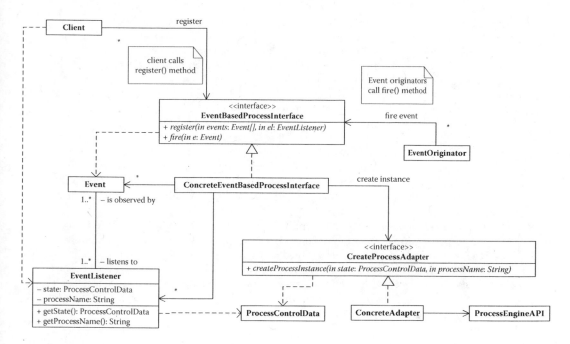

FIGURE 10.16
UML example for event-based process split.

only a process-activity implementation. That means it is advisable to provide an event-based interface to the *process engine*. The mentioned *starting state* of the business process can be defined as the current contents of the process control data structure because they will define the internal process data of the business process (i.e., its state).

The EVENT-BASED PROCESS SPLIT pattern provides automated event-based process instantiation in a generic fashion. The pattern solves the performance problem related to EVENT-BASED ACTIVITIES activities with very long duration.

The pattern also supports flexible event-based networking of processes, as a process instance might fire events that cause other processes to be instantiated dynamically on a different process engine in a B2B constellation, for instance.

Example: UML-Based Design of an EVENT-BASED PROCESS SPLIT

Figure 10.16 shows an example design in UML that has been used for realizing the EVENT-BASED PROCESS SPLIT pattern. The example basically implements an EVENT-BASED PROCESS INSTANCE variant that applies asynchronous event processing and messaging in the context of process instantiation. In addition, it is possible to obtain the process control data to save the process state. A callback is used because the control is temporarily transferred to an event handler, and the specified object to be called is the *CreateProcessAdapter* if an event occurs.

Example: EVENT-BASED PROCESS SPLIT in BPEL for Supply Chain Management

The pattern is often used when the overall business process leaves the organizational boundaries of control, for instance, if parts of the overall business process run inside another company (i.e., a supplier that produces and delivers products). Let us consider an example from the domain of supply chain management. The business process leaves the organizational boundaries and will proceed when the supplier has delivered its products to the requestor. This may take quite some time, depending on the products to be delivered by the supplier, perhaps days to weeks or even months. Imagine a manufacturing process of cars, motorbikes, or even airplanes. As the technical architecture outside its own organizational boundaries may not be influenced, the organization usually communicates with the supplier via dedicated interfaces. In the automotive industry or any other production-oriented business dependent on suppliers, this is a common scenario. When the organization uses a BPEL engine that communicates with a supplier via Web services interfaces or file-based interfaces, the EVENT-BASED PROCESS SPLIT is a suitable way of implementation. The state of the internal business process is stored when the business process leaves the organizational boundaries and an order is sent to the supplier. Often, several orders are sent to suppliers in parallel, depending on the specific business scenario. Imagine different suppliers for tires, seats, engines, or other technical parts of a car. An event listener is implemented that instantiates the following part of the internal business process on the BPEL engine if the products have been delivered.

In addition, the pattern is suitable if the business process leaves the internal boundaries of the SOA implementation, for instance, if parts of a business process run inside an Enterprise Resource Planning (ERP) system that communicates with BPEL processes. In the scenario, imagine the payment processes for the delivered products being managed by an SAP system that is hosted by another department within the organization, for instance, in a different location or even a different country. In this case, the actual payment process is not captured as a BPEL process but runs inside the SAP implementation. The BPEL processes thus represent the glue between all involved parties to integrate them via EVENT-BASED PROCESS SPLITS.

Examples: Support for EVENT-BASED PROCESS SPLITS in Process Engines and ESBs

- Leading BPEL engines like BEA Agualogic Fuego, Tibco WebMethods, or IBM WebSphere Process Server, and Oracle Fusion provide dedicated interfaces for triggering a business process with a given state via standard APIs such as Web Services or messaging interfaces. These APIs can be used to initiate an Event-Based Process Split.
- Also, message buses support this kind of process split by providing process-triggering adapters for different technologies and systems such as BAAN and SAP, for instance. Examples are WebSphere Advanced ESB or the former version, WebSphere Business Integration Message Broker.

EVENT DISPATCHER

External events occur outside the scope of the process engine. Often, events are fired from various event sources. These event sources have different life cycles and may change over time. Registering to concrete event sources thus implies an issue of inflexibility.

How are event listeners and event sources decoupled while flexibly linking them together?

If each event-based component has to register at event sources directly to obtain notifications from events of this source, this implies the component needs knowledge not only about the events it is waiting for but also about the sources that fire these events. Problems arise when there are several sources for the same event. The event observer has to know these concrete sources and register to all of them. If event sources change, this will consequently have an impact on the components observing the events. As a result, this solution might not be flexible enough.

Another problem arises if one takes the runtime aspect into account. For instance, if an event-based component (such as an EVENT-BASED ACTIVITY implementation or the instantiator of an EVENT-BASED PROCESS INSTANCE) is instantiated, it may register immediately to the event source so it does not miss an occurring event during its lifetime. This may be a problem if the concrete event source is not always present. If an event source is implemented by a component that has a limited lifetime (i.e., an instance of the component will be created and destructed several times during the runtime of the application), an event listener might not always have the chance to register.

Consider a scenario in which a process shall wait for a business object state to change. If the process designer employs an EVENT-BASED ACTIVITY to realize this requirement, this component will have to register with an event source that fires such a business object event. If the business object is defined as the event source itself, listeners would have to register directly with it. This will be a problem if the business objects are only instantiated on demand.

This scenario can be generalized as follows: Event listeners not only need knowledge of the concrete event source to register to but also depend on runtime aspects that may not always suit the flexibility requirements.

Use a central EVENT DISPATCHER that manages occurring events and offers a central access point for event-based components. Event sources signal events to the EVENT DISPATCHER, and the EVENT DISPATCHER forwards events to event listeners who are registered for these events (it notifies the event listeners) (see Figure 10.17).

An EVENT DISPATCHER is a central component that is responsible for gathering, managing, and delegating events from event sources to event listeners. It offers a common interface for event listeners and sources to register to and to remove from the EVENT DISPATCHER.

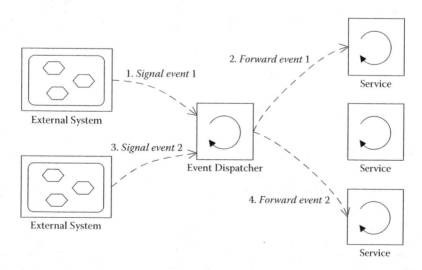

FIGURE 10.17
An event dispatcher.

The EVENT DISPATCHER implementation follows the classical PUBLISHER/SUBSCRIBER architecture [BMR+96, BHS07a]: To be able to act as such a central component, all event sources of the considered application or system must register at the EVENT DISPATCHER, thereby offering their service of event notification in the system. When an event source registers, the EVENT DISPATCHER itself registers as a listener at that source. Consequently, the EVENT DISPATCHER does not initially have to know about all concrete event sources, yet it is informed about each event that will occur in the system. If the event source no longer fires events, or if it will be destructed, it removes itself from the EVENT DISPATCHER.

All event listeners (i.e., event-based components waiting for defined events to occur) simply have to register at the EVENT DISPATCHER. The EVENT DISPATCHER is responsible for delegating the events to event listeners having registered for them. For this to work, the listeners must provide a systemwide unique identifier of the events in which they are interested. If the event source is known, the listener may also state to be notified about all events of that specific source. Information regarding which events to route to which listener must be provided by the listeners or may be centrally configured.

Introduction of an EVENT DISPATCHER allows SOAs to support centralized common handling for all events. This includes aspects such as centrally configured logging, verification, or filtering.

By introducing an EVENT DISPATCHER, event listeners and event sources of the application or system can be decoupled. This also decouples process components from other application resources. Concrete implementations of event sources may be changed without any impact on defined listeners (i.e., event-based components) because these listeners do not directly register with these components anymore. Event listeners no longer depend on runtime aspects of the event sources from which they request notification. The introduction of systemwide unique event identifiers and event source identifiers is essential for central event management.

This added complexity introduced by an EVENT DISPATCHER is actually a negative consequence. For this reason, the pattern should only be applied if the business requirements point to using the pattern. If flexible dispatching of events is not required from the business point of view, then applying the pattern involves unnecessary development and maintenance effort.

The EVENT DISPATCHER also has the disadvantage to introduce a single point of failure: When the EVENT DISPATCHER fails, all dependent components do not receive events any longer.

Example: EVENT DISPATCHER Design in UML

Figure 10.18 is a sample design of an event dispatcher in UML. It offers means to add and remove event listeners and event sources. Event listeners can be notified about events managed by the EVENT DISPATCHER.

Example: Dispatching Business Object State Change Events

The example introduced in the EVENT-BASED ACTIVITY pattern includes business objects as event sources and an EVENT-BASED ACTIVITY registering at such an event source to react on a state change event of a certain business object. The example is applicable in the context of any object-oriented application scenario (e.g., a JEE environment). As mentioned, it might be the case that the business objects are instantiated and destructed by the application on demand. An EVENT-BASED ACTIVITY might fail registering at the business object directly.

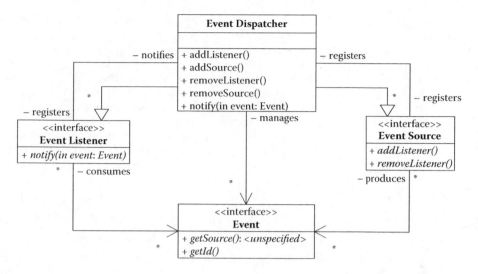

FIGURE 10.18

UML example for an event dispatcher. (From C. Hentrich. Synchronization patterns for process-driven and service-oriented architectures. *Springer LNCS Transactions on Pattern Languages of Programs*, 103–135, 2009.)

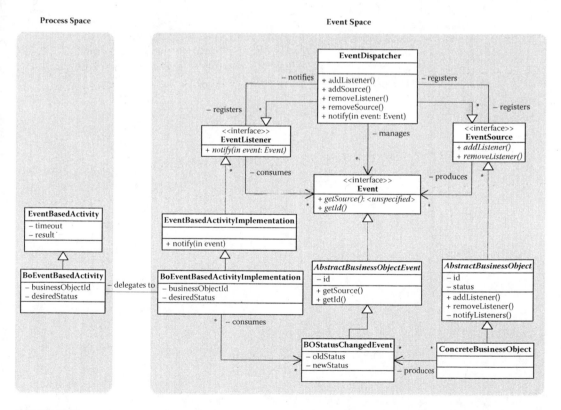

FIGURE 10.19

UML example for dispatching business object state change events. (From C. Hentrich. Synchronization patterns for process-driven and service-oriented architectures. *Springer LNCS Transactions on Pattern Languages of Programs*, 103–135, 2009.)

The example shown in Figure 10.19 introduces an EVENT DISPATCHER in this context. The EVENT-BASED ACTIVITY registers at the EVENT DISPATCHER and supplies an identifier for the event source in which it is interested. The example uses a business object ID that serves as an event source ID in this case.

Once other application components access business objects, the business objects will be instantiated and register at the EVENT DISPATCHER during initialization. If the application component commits a modification that results in a change of the state of the business object, then the event source (i.e., the business object) will fire an according event and will notify its listeners (the EVENT DISPATCHER). The EVENT DISPATCHER checks the event source and compares all registered listeners. It forwards the event to the EVENT-BASED ACTIVITY, which then checks for the desired state for which it is waiting.

Examples: Support for EVENT DISPATCHER in Process Engines and ESBs

- Leading BPEL engines like BEA Agualogic Fuego, Tibco WebMethods or IBM WebSphere Process Server, and Oracle Fusion provide event-dispatching mechanisms.
- The pattern has also been implemented with older workflow engines, such as IBM WebSphere MQ Workflow or Staffware. In this case, the event-dispatching implementation was delegated to an external program and not directly integrated into the features of the engine. As a result, an implementation from scratch has been necessary.
- Also, message buses support this kind of event dispatching. Examples are WebSphere Advanced ESB or the former version, WebSphere Business Integration Message Broker. Special routing flows are usually designed to implement the dispatching rules and to instantiate further reusable flows based on the rules.

11

Invoking Services from Processes

Introduction

In the previous chapters, we presented central architectural patterns needed for designing a process-driven service-oriented architecture (SOA). We identified two kinds of process engines: MACROFLOW ENGINES and MICROFLOW ENGINES. Usually, graphical modeling tools for process modeling languages are used to design the macroflows, and in some cases, microflows are designed in a similar way. In a process-driven SOA, the basic idea to connect the process and services worlds is that activities in the processes invoke services. While this seems easy from a high-level perspective, the details of the service invocations from a process are often not trivial.

All patterns in this chapter address the problem that we want to separate the process view of a service invocation and the technical details of that invocation (as illustrated in Figure 11.1). One reason is simply to support *separation of concerns* as well as *reuse* of recurring service invocation activity types in the process models and engine implementations. Another reason is to best *support the stakeholders* who need to work with the process models. For instance, the business analyst who models the business process is usually not familiar with programming language abstractions necessary to invoke services. In a similar way, the implementer of a microflow (who might be a programmer) also benefits if recurring service invocation schemes are supported in a reusable fashion.

In addition, each pattern in this chapter addresses specific requirements for the link between process instance and service, such as the following:

- Does the activity require a result from the service invocation?
- Is the result required immediately after it is available?
- Is it tolerable to wait in the process flow for the result?
- Does the activity require an acknowledgment of the receipt of the service invocation?
- Are multiple results required?
- Is the service actually another process that runs asynchronously (a subprocess)?
- Is the recipient of the service invocation known to the process?
- Is a deadline or other time constraints associated to fulfilling the invocation?

As there are many alternatives how to invoke a service from a process, different patterns are needed, and the design and implementations of these patterns are pretty different. Also, the considerations when and why the patterns should be selected in a process-driven SOA are not the same. The patterns in this chapter propose one of two basic solutions to this problem:

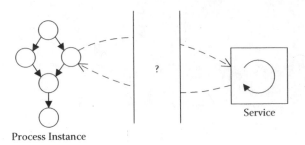

Process Instance

FIGURE 11.1
Process view of a service invocation versus technical details of that invocation.

- Provide the necessary abstractions in the process modeling language as one or more predefined and reusable *activity types*. In addition, often other support needs to be provided by the engine and modeling tools, such as management of data dependencies between processes and services, as well as data-mapping facilities.

- Provide a *kind of service* that realizes the required invocation semantics. This solution is useful if custom behavior on the service implementation side is required. This solution is also useful if the process engine cannot easily be extended with the required invocation semantics.

To distinguish the two kinds of patterns in the remainder of this chapter, we use *activity* as the last word in a pattern name if the pattern primarily advises to introduce an activity type and *service* if the pattern advises to design a particular kind of service.

The patterns and the main drivers to select them for realizing service invocation semantics are the following:

- The SYNCHRONOUS SERVICE ACTIVITY describes how to model a synchronous service invocation in a business process activity. The SYNCHRONOUS SERVICE ACTIVITY provides a solution if an acknowledgment of the service request is necessary and it is tolerable to wait (block) for the result.

- The FIRE-AND-FORGET SERVICE ACTIVITY shows how to model a service invocation without any expected output of the service. Hence, FIRE-AND-FORGET SERVICE ACTIVITY is inherently asynchronous, and the process flow can directly continue. FIRE-AND-FORGET SERVICE ACTIVITY has two variants: one that provides an acknowledgment of the receipt of the invocation and one that spares the acknowledgment.

- The ASYNCHRONOUS RESULT SERVICE and the MULTIPLE ASYNCHRONOUS RESULTS SERVICE patterns address how to model service invocations with asynchronous replies in a business process—with one or multiple results.

  - If the result of a service request must be determined asynchronously later in the process (callback), then ASYNCHRONOUS RESULT SERVICE is applied.

  - If there is more than one reply from a service request, then the MULTIPLE ASYNCHRONOUS RESULTS SERVICE pattern must be used.

- The ASYNCHRONOUS SUBPROCESS SERVICE pattern illustrates how to design a service that only instantiates a subprocess—without waiting in the calling process for the termination of the subprocess. This is often not supported by process engines and must hence be depicted as a service invocation.

- The FIRE EVENT ACTIVITY pattern describes how to model activities that fire certain events to be processed by external systems. This pattern provides invocation semantics that are more loosely coupled to the process design than a service invocation because the recipient of the service invocation need not be known to the process.

- The CONDITION DEADLINE SERVICE pattern addresses how to model time-bound dependencies of business processes on required states of business objects. This way deadlines on the receipt of a business object, or a state of it can be realized.

The pattern relationships of the asynchronous patterns as alternatives to a SYNCHRONOUS SERVICE ACTIVITY are depicted in Figure 11.2.

All the service patterns can be realized in a reusable fashion if they are implemented as INTEGRATION ADAPTERS. In the context of a PROCESS INTEGRATION ARCHITECTURE, it makes sense to foster their reuse by providing them in an INTEGRATION ADAPTER REPOSITORY. This is shown in Figure 11.3.

Depending on the technology used, some of the aspects of service and process integration that are the focus of this chapter are handled in the implementation of a process engine (i.e., the MACROFLOW ENGINE or MICROFLOW ENGINE) or a service framework. Hence, engine and service framework designers and developers are a primary target audience of the patterns in this chapter. However, developers and designers using these engines and frameworks must also be aware of the design trade-offs, when selecting a service invocation scheme. Hence, the contents of these patterns should also be considered by process-driven SOA designers and

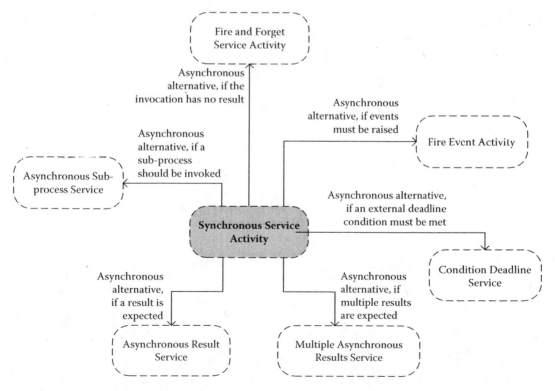

FIGURE 11.2
Synchronous service activity pattern relationships.

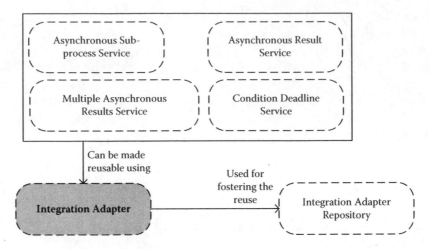

FIGURE 11.3
Integration adapter pattern relationships.

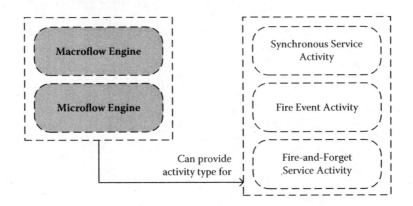

FIGURE 11.4
Macroflow and microflow engine pattern relationships.

developers who merely use the facilities provided by engines and service frameworks. Finally, some of the patterns are not yet supported by many technologies. In such cases, the patterns must be implemented using the extension mechanisms of the engine and service framework.

How service framework designers can support the service patterns is depicted in Figure 11.3: using INTEGRATION ADAPTERS. In Figure 11.4, we see the typical support for the activity patterns: using a special activity type in the MACROFLOW ENGINE or MICROFLOW ENGINE.

All patterns in this chapter except for SYNCHRONOUS SERVICE ACTIVITY use asynchronous communication. That means the replies associated to a particular request are arriving concurrently, and the network connection cannot be used to correlate the request and the reply. Hence, the CORRELATION IDENTIFIER pattern [HW03] must be used to let the requester that has received a response know to which original request the response is referring. This pattern advises that each response message should contain a correlation ID, a unique identifier that indicates which request message this response is for. The correlation ID is sent

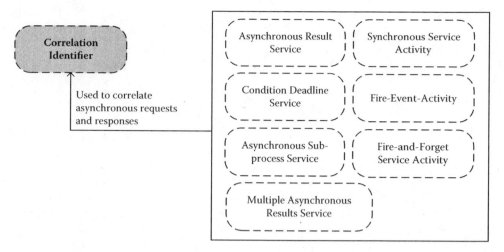

FIGURE 11.5
Correlation identifier pattern relationships.

back with the reply so the requester can perform the proper correlation. This is visualized in Figure 11.5.

Synchronous Service Activity

Services must be invoked from a process flow, and the business scenario requires a synchronous communication between the process and the service. That is, the process depends on the functional interface of the service and needs to react on the possible results of the service. It does not make sense for the process activity to proceed as long as the result has not been received.

> How are the data dependencies and the service results mapped to a process so that a service can be invoked synchronously?

In a process-driven SOA, a service represents a business function related to a corresponding business process activity. However, a service has a functional interface, and to invoke a service synchronously from the process flow, the business process designer has to consider the functional input and output parameters of the service. That is, there are data dependencies between the process activity and the associated service. Such data dependencies can be observed on both the macroflow and microflow levels. In addition, if a service is invoked synchronously and the possible results of the service have an impact on the control flow of the process, the results of the service need to be considered as well.

The data dependencies mean that the process model must be designed in such a way that the other activities of the process deliver and receive the correct data items, which is often nontrivial because this is not the major concern of business analysts designing processes. As these are rather general issues, it is desirable to resolve them using a general concept for modeling synchronous service invocations in process flows, which can be offered as a reusable abstraction to the process modelers.

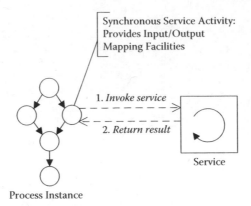

FIGURE 11.6
A synchronous service activity.

Provide a reusable activity type for modeling a service invocation as a SYNCHRONOUS
SERVICE ACTIVITY that maps the functional input parameters of the associated service to
its input data objects and the functional output parameters of the service to its output
data objects. The service is fed with the input parameters from the input objects of the
activity, and the output parameters of the service are given back and stored in the output objects of the activity. The process flow, which follows the invoking activity, implements the decision logic to react on the results of the service based on the attributes of
the output objects (see Figure 11.6).

The control data object structures of the process engine need to be designed to depict the
requirements of the processes. Hence, these requirements must be gathered during the
design of the processes themselves.

How the actual invocation is performed depends on the techniques provided by the
process engine. For example, the process engine might allow the developers to directly
invoke a Web service or provide some kinds of messaging mechanisms. During the invocation, the in- and output parameters of the service are mapped to the control data objects
used as input and output of the associated process activity. This is usually done via a data-
mapping tool or in programmatic fashion.

A service invocation in a process needs to be viewed in context with preceding and succeeding process activities. At the level of data integration, often modeling gaps occur that
need to be addressed in the preceding or succeeding process activities (activities might
need to be added if they are missing). For this reason, the level of data integration must be
considered right when designing a process flow containing service invocations.

A SYNCHRONOUS SERVICE ACTIVITY blocks on results. Results of the service invocation will
usually be captured by decision logic in the process. Consider, for instance, the case that
the service reports an error—this error needs to be captured by the decision logic in the
process, and the process needs to react on the error somehow. The possible cases that influence the path during the process represented by the results of the service invocation must
be captured by decision logic of the process right after the invocation. This is achieved by
modeling decision nodes based on the attributes of the output data objects that carry the
service results.

The pattern can be applied at both the macroflow and microflow levels. In both cases, the services that are invoked are often INTEGRATION ADAPTERS.

For designing the control data objects, the GENERIC PROCESS CONTROL STRUCTURE pattern can be applied to solve some key versioning issues concerning the data structures. Generic attributes for handling input and output parameters of services can be defined in the process control data objects that can be reused for various service invocations.

Often, it is useful to keep the processes only concerned with the control aspects of the process but not with the business data. In this case, the control data only contains BUSINESS OBJECT REFERENCES. That is, the actual service being invoked by the process activity only takes a BUSINESS OBJECT REFERENCE as an input parameter. The service itself gathers the concrete data from the business object via the reference. Especially, INTEGRATION ADAPTERS for macroflows are often designed that way as this type of service represents a facade that hides the microflow and the corresponding logic for data gathering and transformation for invoking the actual business application services in the back end.

Example: Simple Example Structure of a SYNCHRONOUS SERVICE ACTIVITY

Figure 11.7 illustrates an example structure of a SYNCHRONOUS SERVICE ACTIVITY. Input data is taken from the process control data (written by the previous activity). The service is invoked by the activity of the type SYNCHRONOUS SERVICE ACTIVITY. Finally, the output is mapped to the process control data and consumed by subsequent activities. Data mapping is in both cases handled automatically using data-mapping rules.

Example: SYNCHRONOUS SERVICE ACTIVITY in IBM WebSphere MQ Workflow

This example demonstrates how the SYNCHRONOUS SERVICE ACTIVITY pattern can be implemented. To show that the pattern is broadly applicable and not restricted to rather modern SOA technology specifics, such as Web services, the example illustrates a more traditional message-based service invocation with IBM WebSphere MQ Workflow.

MQ Workflow offers a mechanism for invoking services via message adapters based on XML (Extensible Markup Language). The whole mechanism is encapsulated in a concept called the user-defined program execution server (UPES). The basis of the UPES concept is the MQ Workflow XML messaging interface. The UPES concept is all about communicating with external services via asynchronous XML messages. Consequently, the UPES concept is literally about invoking a service that a process activity requires, receiving the result after the service execution has been completed, and further relating the asynchronously incoming result to the process activity instance that originally requested execution of the service (as there may be hundreds or thousands of instances of the same process activity).

Thus, a UPES is an XML adapter that represents an interface to one or many services. Figure 11.8 illustrates the process of communication between MQ Workflow and a service via a UPES. The figure gives an overview of the UPES mechanisms.

1. First, the UPES must be defined and must be related to process activities of process models. Thus, a UPES definition is part of the modeling stage and is included in the final process definition. Basically, from the viewpoint of MQ Workflow, a UPES definition consists of nothing more than a message queue definition. An activity related to the UPES thus knows in which queue to put the XML request.
2. If the execution of a process instance comes to the point at which an activity instance is related to a UPES (as defined by the process template), then an XML request will automatically be put in the queue that has been defined for the UPES.

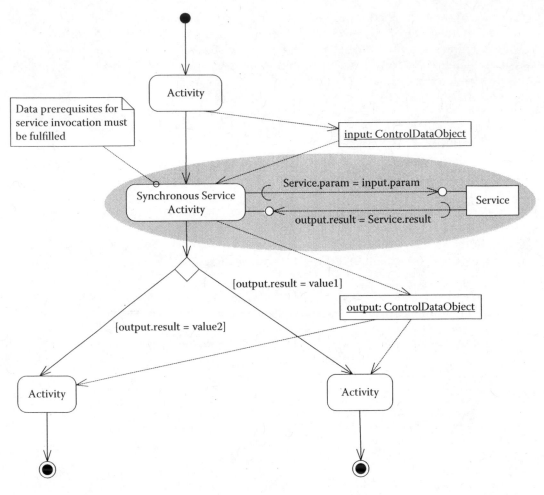

FIGURE 11.7
Example structure of a synchronous service activity.

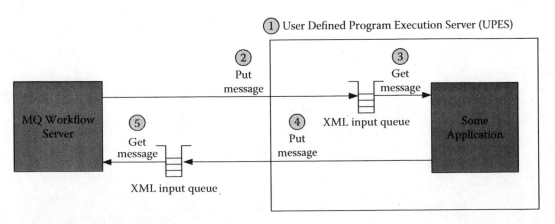

FIGURE 11.8
Process of communication between MQ Workflow and a service via a UPES.

3. The actual UPES implementation is an adapter that listens to the specific UPES queue. It takes the XML message out of the queue, transforms it into a format that can be understood by the service, and initiates execution of the service. The UPES implementation represents an INTEGRATION ADAPTER.

4. If the service has finished execution, the UPES implementation will take the result, transform it into the XML format that can be understood by MQ Workflow, and will send the result back to MQ Workflow. MQ Workflow has one specific XML input queue for communicating with UPESs.

5. MQ Workflow takes the return message out of the input queue, relates the result back to the activity instance, and changes the state of the activity instance accordingly.

Modeling the process for this service invocation with WebSphere MQ Workflow is quite straightforward. A control data object is defined to capture the input and output parameters of the service. This control data object is assigned as input and as output of the process activity that invokes the service. The process activity is defined as a UPES activity that puts an XML request message in a queue. The result is sent back by the UPES as a result of the XML message. The request and the return messages are correlated via a CORRELATION IDENTIFIER [HW03].

The following XML fragments show the structure of the request and response messages—the CORRELATION IDENTIFIER named *ActImpCorrelID* is highlighted in the XML. The XML example also highlights that the request message contains the control data object with a customer ID, a currency, and a credit amount; these are used as the input parameter for the service. The service being invoked is a credit check, which delivers, based on a customer ID, a currency, and a credit amount, whether a customer is creditworthy for the requested credit amount.

```
<WfMessage>
     <WfMessageHeader>
          <ResponseRequired>Yes</ResponseRequired>
     </WfMessageHeader>
     <ActivityImplInvoke>
          <ActImplCorrelID>FFABCEDF0123456789FF</ActImplCorrelID>
          <Starter>user1</Starter>
          <ProgramID>
               <ProcTemplID>84848484FEFEFEFE</ProcTemplID>
               <ProgramName>FMCINTERNALNOOP</ProgramName>
          </ProgramID>
          <ProgramInputData>
               <_ACTIVITY>Invoke Credit Check Service</_ACTIVITY>
               <_PROCESS>CreditRequest#123</_PROCESS>
               <_PROCESS_MODEL>CreditRequest</_PROCESS_MODEL>
               <ControlDataObject>
                    <CustomerID>4711</CustomerID>
                    <CreditAmount>10000</CreditAmount>
                    <Currency>Euro</Currency>
               </ControlDataObject>
          </ProgramInputData>
     </ActivityImplInvoke>
<WfMessage>
```

The response XML provides the result of the credit check service. The result is contained in the output parameter *Risk* and may have the values low, medium, or high. The example XML shows that the credit check result is low.

```
<WfMessage>
    <WfMessageHeader>
        <ResponseRequired>No</ResponseRequired>
    </WfMessageHeader>
    <ActivityImplInvokeResponse>
        <ActImplCorrelID>FFABCEDF0123456789FF</ActImplCorrelID>
        <ProgramRC>0</ProgramRC>
        <ProgramOutputData>
            <ControlDataObject>
                <Risk>Low</Risk>
            </ControlDataObject>
        </ProgramOutputData>
    </ActivityImplInvokeResponse>
</WfMessage>
```

The process model for invoking the credit check service is shown in Figure 11.9. The process model illustrates that the execution path differentiates whether a low, medium, or high risk has been reported by the credit check service. Note that the notation used in the figure is the WebSphere MQ Workflow visual modeling language. The figure shows a screenshot taken from the modeling tool, thus illustrating the actual implementation. The actual language used by MQ Workflow is Flowmark Definition Language (FDL), and the graphical models are translated automatically in this language.

Figure 11.10 shows how the control data object carrying the necessary attributes for invoking the service is assigned as input and as output of the activity. The request message is generated automatically by MQ Workflow. The response message of the service contains the risk assessed by the service in the output object. The figure shows the configuration that needs to be done in the modeling component of MQ Workflow.

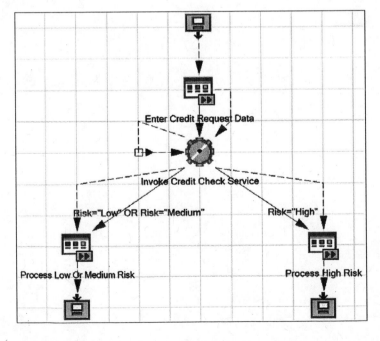

FIGURE 11.9
Process model for invoking a credit check service using a synchronous service activity.

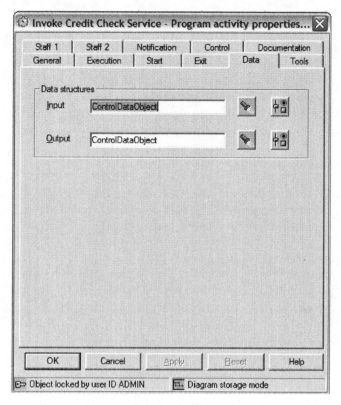

FIGURE 11.10
Dialog for control data object assignment

Example: SYNCHRONOUS **S**ERVICE **A**CTIVITY **in Process Engines**

- IBM WebSphere Process server has synchronous Web services invocation mechanisms based on a architectural model called Service Component
  Architecture (SCA), which makes use of this pattern. Also, implementations
  based on MQ or JMS (Java Messaging Service) are possible as SCA abstracts
  from the actual protocol binding of services. BPEL (Business Process Execution
  Language) is used as the flow-modeling language.
- IBM WebSphere MQ Workflow applies the pattern in its UPES concept to
  invoke functions from external systems. The proprietary flow notation FDL is
  used for modeling the flows and the service invocations from a flow model. It
  is the preceding product of WebSphere Process Server.
- BEA Fuego also applies the pattern in conjunction with synchronous service
  invocations, based on Web services. BEA uses a proprietary notation and language for modeling the flows and service invocations.
- The FileNet P8 Business Process Manager implements the pattern for invoking
  Web services from a workflow. At this time, FileNet still uses a proprietary
  modeling language, XPDL (Workflow Process Definition Language) for modeling the flow models.

FIRE-AND-FORGET SERVICE ACTIVITY

Services must be invoked from a process flow, and in the business scenario, the result of the service does not need to be considered by the process. A communication between a service and a process flow needs to be modeled that is not a synchronous communication but rather just places the service request without waiting for any result to be returned from the service.

How is a service from a process activity invoked without considering its result in later stages of the process flow?

Depending on the functionality of a service, it sometimes makes sense not to wait for the service result. The service request is placed at some point in time, and the process flow continues without considering the result of the service. Often, this design is useful if the service execution takes longer. For instance, consider a batch-oriented function encapsulated in a service, and the batch job only runs once a day.

Similar to the SYNCHRONOUS SERVICE ACTIVITY pattern, the data dependencies need to be mapped to provide the right input data for the service by the process activity. For this reason, all the issues identified in the SYNCHRONOUS SERVICE ACTIVITY pattern on providing the right input data for the service by the process activity are the same in this special case.

Provide a reusable activity type for modeling a service invocation as a FIRE-AND-FORGET SERVICE ACTIVITY that decouples the request for execution of a service from the actual execution of the service. Depict the functional input parameters of the associated service request in the input data objects of the invoking process activity. Thus, invoking the service, from the point of view of the process activity, only means placing a request for service execution (see Figure 11.11).

The FIRE-AND-FORGET SERVICE ACTIVITY solution separates the request from the execution of the service. This must be realized both at the process design level and at the remote invocation level. At the remote invocation level, there are two main variants that have both been described as remote invocation strategy patterns:

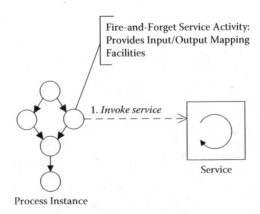

FIGURE 11.11
A fire-and-forget service activity.

- An asynchronous execution of the service is performed that fires a request for service execution but forgets about the actual execution. The respective remote invocation strategy that needs to be used is described in the FIRE-AND-FORGET pattern [VKZ04].

- Alternatively, placing the request may also be understood as a service—a service that does not execute actual business logic but only takes the request for executing business logic. Possibly, this request should be acknowledged. In this case, the solution will be a SYNCHRONOUS SERVICE ACTIVITY in which the service only receives a request for execution and returns an acknowledgment of the receipt of the request. The respective remote invocation strategy that needs to be used is described in the SYNC WITH SERVER pattern [VKZ04].

In the SYNC WITH SERVER variant, the result might also contain different options (e.g., request acknowledged or not acknowledged). For instance, if the input values of the request are invalid, the request might not be acknowledged but rather an error message is returned. In the pure FIRE-AND-FORGET variant, in contrast, the request is only sent, and no acknowledgment or error is returned. As the sender is notified about the successful delivery of the service invocation, the SYNC WITH SERVER variant can be considered to be more reliable than pure FIRE AND FORGET.

From the perspective of the invoking process activity, the request of a service is decoupled from its execution. However, the result of the service invocation cannot be determined by the invoking process, and possible errors of the execution are not reported. The FIRE-AND-FORGET SERVICE ACTIVITY pattern should only be applied if the result of the execution is not relevant for further process steps.

The process engine used must technically support the FIRE-AND-FORGET variant. The SYNC WITH SERVER variant does not need to be supported. Instead, a SYNCHRONOUS SERVICE ACTIVITY can be used, and only the invoked service knows that it must only send an acknowledgment that the request has been placed.

In comparison to SYNCHRONOUS SERVICE ACTIVITY, both variants have the benefit that the process flow can be directly continued without having to wait (block) for a result. In case of the FIRE-AND-FORGET variant, not even an acknowledgment must be awaited, but for this reason, this variant is less reliable than the SYNC WITH SERVER variant and should only be used if best-effort semantics are tolerable.

Example: Simple Example Structure of a FIRE-AND-FORGET SERVICE ACTIVITY

Figure 11.12 illustrates the structure of the SYNC WITH SERVER variant of the FIRE-AND-FORGET SERVICE ACTIVITY pattern. A service request is placed by invoking a service synchronously. This service accepts a request for actual service execution and immediately returns only an acknowledgment as its output.

The FIRE-AND-FORGET variant of the FIRE-AND-FORGET SERVICE ACTIVITY pattern is illustrated in Figure 11.13. This variant does not send an acknowledgment of the request and simply places the request, neglecting any possible return values. In this case, the process engine used needs to support this mechanism as the process activity needs to be able to place the request for service execution, and the process needs to proceed to the next step automatically. If the engine only supports synchronous invocations, then the service must be designed accordingly, as explained. In all cases, the right input data must be provided, as already addressed by the SYNCHRONOUS SERVICE ACTIVITY pattern.

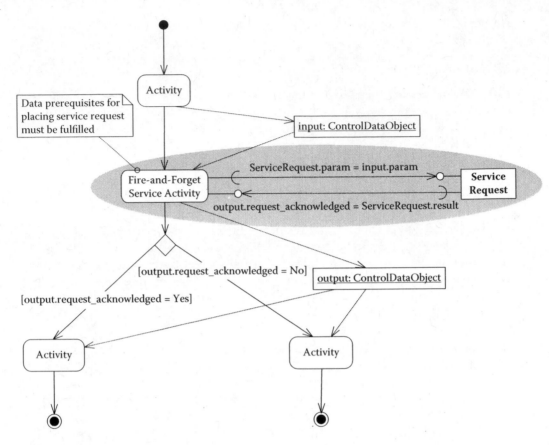

FIGURE 11.12
Example for the sync with server variant of a fire-and-forget service activity.

Example: FIRE-AND-FORGET SERVICE ACTIVITY in IBM WebSphere MQ Workflow

Let us illustrate an example of a Fire-and-Forget Activity in WebSphere MQ Workflow. The SYNC WITH SERVER variant that places the service request synchronously is basically a service design issue of decoupling the service request from its actual function and a variation of the SYNCHRONOUS SERVICE ACTIVITY pattern—we again take the example of the credit check service presented in the SYNCHRONOUS SERVICE ACTIVITY pattern. The example shows how sending the service request can be implemented with WebSphere MQ Workflow and the UPES communication mechanism.

The only difference compared to the example in the SYNCHRONOUS SERVICE ACTIVITY pattern is that the return value will not be the actual calculated risk but only an acknowledgment of the service request, as shown in the following XML structure:

```
<WfMessage>
      <WfMessageHeader>
            <ResponseRequired>No</ResponseRequired>
      </WfMessageHeader>
      <ActivityImplInvokeResponse>
            <ActImplCorrelID>FFABCEDF0123456789FF</ActImplCorrelID>
            <ProgramRC>0</ProgramRC>
            <ProgramOutputData>
                  <ControlDataObject>
```

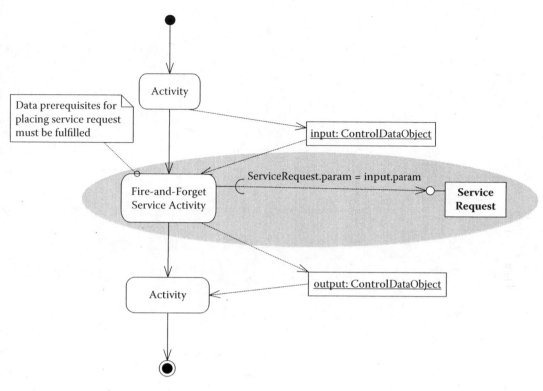

FIGURE 11.13
Example for the fire-and-forget variant of a fire-and-forget service activity.

```
                       <RequestAcknowledged>Yes</RequestAcknowledged>
                  </ControlDataObject>
              </ProgramOutputData>
          </ActivityImplInvokeResponse>
     </WfMessage>
```

Figure 11.14 shows a process model that is analogous to the model in the example from the SYNCHRONOUS SERVICE ACTIVITY pattern description. The control data object will be assigned as input and output of the process activity invoking the service, and the control data object needs to have an attribute defined to report whether the request has been acknowledged. The process may then decide on the basis of the value of this attribute which path to take (i.e., whether the request has been acknowledged).

The FIRE-AND-FORGET variant of this pattern is about firing a request without considering any return value from the service. To apply this variant, the process engine used must also support this unidirectional communication mechanism. MQ Workflow supports the unidirectional communication directly by setting configuration parameters in the process model. First, the process model looks even simpler as there is no decision logic necessary after sending the service request. This is shown in Figure 11.15.

The activity invoking the service must be defined as to expect no reply. This is done in MQ Workflow by setting an asynchronous mode for the UPES communication in the process activity. This is simply done by setting an attribute of the process activity, as shown in Figure 11.16.

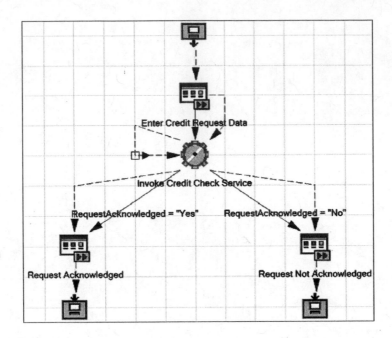

FIGURE 11.14
Process model for invoking a credit check service using a fire-and-forget service activity: sync with server variant.

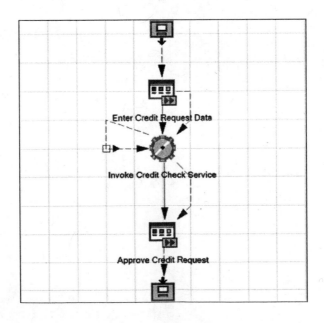

FIGURE 11.15
Process model for invoking a credit check service using a fire-and-forget service activity: fire-and-forget variant.

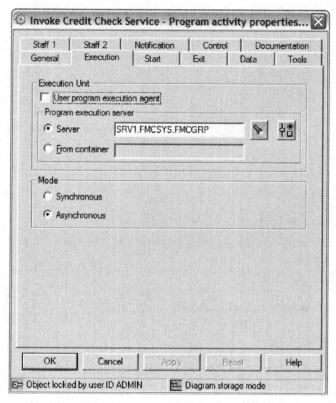

FIGURE 11.16
Dialog for setting the asynchronous mode for the UPES communication in the process activity.

Examples: Known Uses of Fire-and-Forget Service Activity

- The known uses given for the synchronous service activity also apply for the fire-and-forget service activity as this is in principle also a basic pattern related to service invocation from processes.
- In an SOA project for a telecommunications customer, the pattern has been, based on IBM's WebSphere Business Integration Message Broker, used to define a modeling template for asynchronous service invocations.
- In a large project on architectural standards in a bank in Germany, the pattern has been used to fire off services that result in Customer Information Control System (CICS) transactions where the process did not need to wait until the actual transaction was finished. Many projects in this bank have been based on this architectural standard.

Asynchronous Result Service

Services must be invoked from a process flow, and the business scenario requires picking up the service result later. However, because other process steps need to be executed in the meantime, blocking on the result as in the synchronous service activity pattern is not tolerable. The communication between the service and the process flow should be modeled analogous to the well-known callback invocation style; the process just places the service request and picks up the service result later in the process flow.

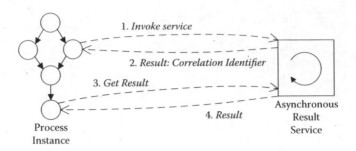

FIGURE 11.17
An asynchronous result service.

How is a service from a process activity invoked and the service result picked up at a later stage in the process flow?

Sometimes, using the FIRE-AND-FORGET SERVICE ACTIVITY pattern is not sufficient as there will be some reply that must be picked up at a later point in time. The process should place a service request, do some other activities in the meantime, and then pick up the result of the previously initiated request. The problem is how to pick up the result later in the process flow and how to relate a result to a request that has been previously made.

In addition, the process (or the process engine) must deal with the situation that many invocations of the same service can be placed in parallel. For instance, different process instances of the same process that are running in parallel likely invoke the same service. Also, one and the same process could invoke a service twice. If asynchronous invocations are chosen, the results will arrive concurrently. If a specific process instance wants to pick up a specific result of one of those invocations, the result must be somehow related to the right request. This relationship is necessary in order not to pick up a result that has been made by another process instance. How can this relationship be realized?

Split the request for service execution and the request for the corresponding result into two SYNCHRONOUS SERVICE ACTIVITIES and relate the two activities by a CORRELATION IDENTIFIER that is kept in a control data object. This CORRELATION IDENTIFIER is the output of the first service request, is temporarily saved in a request repository, and is then—later in time—used as an input for the second request that picks up the result (see Figure 11.17).

Designing two separate SYNCHRONOUS SERVICE ACTIVITIES enables the separation of the actual service request from picking up the result. The first SYNCHRONOUS SERVICE ACTIVITY represents the actual service request, and the second one represents a service invocation that picks up the result. However, to relate a service request and a result, it is necessary to provide a CORRELATION IDENTIFIER generated by the first service. That means the first service, representing the request, must create a CORRELATION IDENTIFIER that is provided as the output of the service. The identifier is then stored in a control data object of the process and is thus carried along the process activities that may follow.

When invoking the second service to pick up the result, the CORRELATION IDENTIFIER is given as input to the service. The service is thus able to identify the result to the request and to give the right result back to the invoker.

Applying the ASYNCHRONOUS RESULT SERVICE pattern affects not only the process modeling level, but also has further architectural consequences that imply that additional effort is needed. In particular, a suitable remote invocation strategy must be selected. This is necessary for dealing with situations in which the result service does not deliver a result, for instance, because the function associated to the service is not yet completed. There are two main options:

- The process can be actively triggered by a RESULT CALLBACK [VKZ04] service invocation that "actively" informs the process about the availability of the result. That is, a real callback is sent as a service invocation to the process.
- The process design follows the POLL OBJECT pattern [VKZ04]: The process loops the activity invoking the result service (it "polls" it) until the result is available.

In both cases, it might be necessary to implement a timeout (e.g., to deal with network failures or other remoting errors).

Example: Simple Example Structure of an ASYNCHRONOUS RESULT SERVICE with a REPOSITORY

If a service generates multiple results or is frequently used in an asynchronous fashion, it makes sense to buffer the results in a REPOSITORY [Eva04]. For instance, consider a legacy system that is accessed asynchronously but operates itself in batch mode. A service accessing this legacy system would queue the requests and execute them one after another, and once a result arrives, it would put it into the results REPOSITORY.

Consider the desire to access such a repository-based service using an ASYNCHRONOUS RESULT SERVICE. The first service registers the requests, which are stored in a REPOSITORY with their CORRELATION IDENTIFIER generated by the service and passed back to the invoker. Then, the actual function associated to the service will be executed, and the result will also be stored in the REPOSITORY related to the request identified by the CORRELATION IDENTIFIER.

The second service used to pick up the result looks into the REPOSITORY to determine the right result based on the CORRELATION IDENTIFIER given as input to the service. If a result is stored in the REPOSITORY for the specific CORRELATION IDENTIFIER, then this result is passed back to the invoker. If there is no result stored, then a corresponding error message will be returned. Two possible cases must be distinguished: The CORRELATION IDENTIFIER provided by the service is invalid (i.e., it does not exist in the REPOSITORY), or there is no result yet but the CORRELATION IDENTIFIER is valid. Depending on which case applies, a corresponding result message will be returned.

Once the result is received, the request entry in the request repository should be deleted. The repository possibly needs to implement some cleanup activity (e.g., if results are not retrieved). Some additional logic might be necessary to identify such dead entries in the repository and delete them or possibly indicate errors.

Figure 11.18 shows how the two services are invoked in sequence with other activities between them. It also illustrates the functional architecture that is used to maintain the relationship between a request service and a result service via a CORRELATION IDENTIFIER.

Sequence diagrams illustrate in more detail the behavior that happens when a process instance invokes the two services. The first sequence diagram (Figure 11.19) shows how the service request is placed. The sequence diagram depicts how the actual function associated to the service request is invoked asynchronously while the activity placing the request terminates, and the process moves on to the next activity. This is indicated by destroying the process activity object placing the request after the service request has been sent.

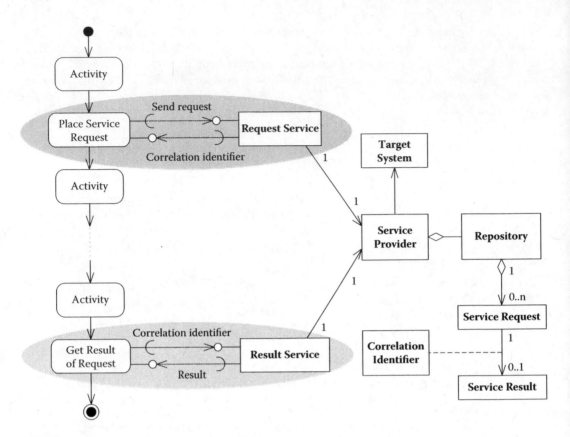

FIGURE 11.18
Example structure for an asynchronous result service.

The second sequence diagram (Figure 11.20) shows how the result is determined for a request that has been placed previously. The diagram illustrates how the result of the service is retrieved from the repository and sent back to the process activity. The right result is determined by providing the correlation ID that has been stored in the control data object.

Example: ASYNCHRONOUS RESULT SERVICE in IBM WebSphere MQ Workflow

We illustrate an implementation of ASYNCHRONOUS RESULT SERVICE with WebSphere MQ Workflow and extend the example from the FIRE-AND-FORGET SERVICE ACTIVITY pattern description toward an asynchronous reply. Consider that the credit check service is provided by an external organization, and it takes about 24 hours to obtain a result. In this case, it actually makes sense to apply the ASYNCHRONOUS RESULT SERVICE pattern and do some other activities in between so time is not wasted. Undoubtedly, this only makes sense if there are sensible business activities possible in the meantime. In this example, it is sufficient that the actual result of the service is available at a later point in the process and that it is possible to do further activities without having the result.

First, the process model needs to have two service invocation activities. The first service is placing the request, and the second service is picking up the result. The process model will look as shown in Figure 11.21.

The first service placing the request gives back the correlation ID that is used as an input parameter in the second service invocation. The request XML of the first service is as straightforward as shown in the SYNCHRONOUS SERVICE ACTIVITY pattern, but the

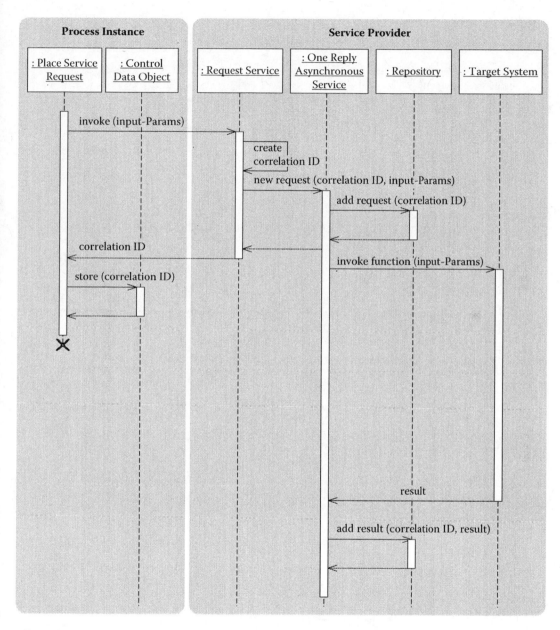

FIGURE 11.19
Behavior of an asynchronous service invocation.

response XML of the first service will be different as it contains not only the acknowledgment of the request but also the correlation ID.

```
<WfMessage>
    <WfMessageHeader>
        <ResponseRequired>No</ResponseRequired>
    </WfMessageHeader>
    <ActivityImplInvokeResponse>
        <ActImplCorrelID>FFABCEDF0123456789FF</ActImplCorrelID>
        <ProgramRC>0</ProgramRC>
```

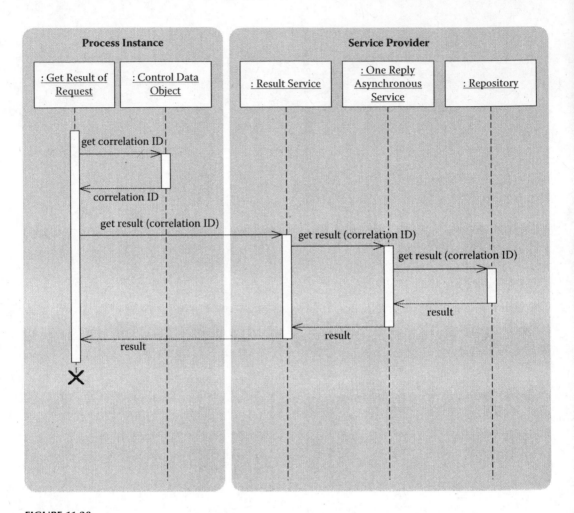

FIGURE 11.20
Behavior of an asynchronous result retrieval.

```
<ProgramOutputData>
        <ControlDataObject>
                <RequestAcknowledged>Yes</RequestAcknowledged>
                <CorrelationID>XYAZ4711</CorrelationID>
        </ControlDataObject>
</ProgramOutputData>
    </ActivityImplInvokeResponse>
</WfMessage>
```

The second service invocation requires the correlation ID as its input parameter. For this reason, the request XML of the second service will look as shown next. The response XML of the second service will be the same as shown in the SYNCHRONOUS SERVICE ACTIVITY pattern. It becomes clear how the single service from the SYNCHRONOUS SERVICE ACTIVITY pattern is split into two services that are asynchronously linked by a correlation ID.

```
<WfMessage>
        <WfMessageHeader>
                <ResponseRequired>Yes</ResponseRequired>
        </WfMessageHeader>
```

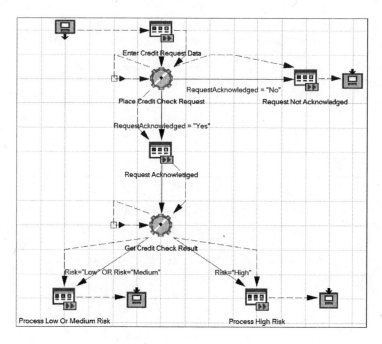

FIGURE 11.21
Credit check service using an asynchronous result service.

```
<ActivityImplInvoke>
        <ActImplCorrelID>FFABCEDF0123456789FF</ActImplCorrelID>
        <Starter>user1</Starter>
        <ProgramID>
                <ProcTemplID>84848484FEFEFEFE</ProcTemplID>
                <ProgramName>FMCINTERNALNOOP</ProgramName>
        </ProgramID>
        <ProgramInputData>
                        <_ACTIVITY>Get Credit Check
                                Result</_ACTIVITY>
                        <_PROCESS>CreditRequest#123</_PROCESS>
                        <_PROCESS_MODEL>CreditRequest</_PROCESS_MODEL>
                        <ControlDataObject>
                                <CorrelationID>XYAZ4711</CorrelationID>
                        </ControlDataObject>
        </ProgramInputData>
        </ActivityImplInvoke>
<WfMessage>
```

Examples: Known Uses of ASYNCHRONOUS RESULT SERVICE

- In principle, the ASYNCHRONOUS RESULT SERVICE pattern is supported by the process technologies given as known uses in the SYNCHRONOUS SERVICE ACTIVITY pattern as basic support for synchronous services is required. Provided this support is given, the pattern can be implemented.
- In a project in the automobile industry, the pattern has been applied to kick off batch processes from business processes. The batch job runs overnight; in the meantime, other process steps have been executed. The result of the batch job is picked up by the process the following day, assuming that the job must be completed overnight.

- In projects related to transaction banking, the pattern applies to a similar scenario, with larger or complex transactions initiated from a business process. The pattern has been defined as a modeling template in an architectural standard of a bank in Germany for those types of services related to larger transactions. The technologies used have been an OS/390-based WebSphere MQ Workflow installation in conjunction with a CICS-based transaction server.

Multiple Asynchronous Results Service

Services must be invoked from a process flow, and the business scenario requires picking up multiple service results while other process steps need to be executed in the meantime. A communication between a service and a process flow needs to be modeled that is not a simple asynchronous communication, but that rather places the service request and picks up multiple replies from the service later in the process flow.

How are a service from a process activity invoked and multiple service replies picked up at a later stage in the process flow?

Sometimes, the ASYNCHRONOUS RESULT SERVICE pattern is not sufficient because there is not only one response from the service but multiple possible responses that must be considered. For instance, some services deliver some kind of intermediate results that represent the progressing status of the function or task of the service. In such cases, the process might only move on until a certain stage after the original service request has been placed, and it will only proceed if the previous service invocation has reached a certain intermediate stage that is reported as a status response from the service to the process instance.

The service thus sends several replies that influence the process flow as each response may have certain results that imply decision nodes in the process. For example, the service may itself be a business process; intermediate responses report certain states or results of activities in this process. Depending on a state or completed activity of the service, the business process needs to react correspondingly. For example, this design makes sense if the service is a facade for a whole business process running in an external organization (business process outsourcing), and the service reports several intermediate states of this external business process. The internal business process logic needs to react on the states or completed activities of the external business process.

Extend the ASYNCHRONOUS RESULT SERVICE toward allowing multiple results associated to events representing completed intermediate actions or states of the service. Thus, the result service delivers results based on expected events that are given as input to the result service (see Figure 11.22).

The ASYNCHRONOUS RESULT SERVICE pattern also offers nearly all functionality required to realize multiple results from one service. The only issue is that it is restricted to only one reply being returned asynchronously by the service. For this reason, the pattern is extended to allow multiple results by introducing the concept of an *event*. The result service allows requesting a result that is associated to a defined event representing a completed intermediate activity or state of the service.

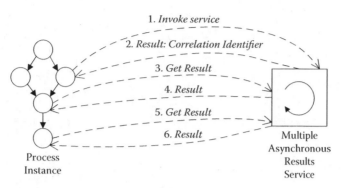

FIGURE 11.22
A multiple asynchronous results service.

The service stores multiple results to the same correlation ID, for which each result is related to an event. Events are unique within the space of the correlation ID, that is, an event may occur only once for a correlation ID. When invoking the result service, the correlation ID and the desired event will be given as input parameters to the service. That way, a result can be uniquely identified and is related to an intermediate state of the service. Alternatively, a dedicated result service can be offered for each possible event.

The consequences of the MULTIPLE ASYNCHRONOUS RESULTS SERVICE pattern are basically the same as in ASYNCHRONOUS RESULT SERVICE as the MULTIPLE ASYNCHRONOUS RESULTS SERVICE pattern is an extension of it. The only slight difference is that this pattern provides a solution to multiple replies instead of only one reply. The additional notion of events makes the solution more flexible. This has the drawback, however, that the design is more complex than an ordinary ASYNCHRONOUS RESULT SERVICE.

Example: Simple Example Structure of a MULTIPLE ASYNCHRONOUS RESULTS SERVICE

Figure 11.23 shows an example design following the MULTIPLE ASYNCHRONOUS RESULTS SERVICE pattern. It is almost identical to the previous example of a ASYNCHRONOUS RESULT SERVICE except for additional parameters for identifying service results via events.

The sequence diagram for placing the service request is presented in Figure 11.24. Here also, the only difference in this sequence diagram, compared to the corresponding sequence diagram of the ASYNCHRONOUS RESULT SERVICE, is that the event is considered as an input parameter. To provide the event information as an input parameter, there must be an attribute that carries the event information in the control data object of the process.

Example: MULTIPLE ASYNCHRONOUS RESULTS SERVICE in IBM WebSphere MQ Workflow

In this example, we extend the credit check example from the ASYNCHRONOUS RESULT SERVICE pattern to MULTIPLE ASYNCHRONOUS RESULTS SERVICE in IBM WebSphere MQ Workflow. We assume that the credit check service is still provided by an external organization, and that it takes about 24 hours to complete. However, this time we assume that there is one intermediate completion of an activity reported. This intermediate state provides information whether the requester is on a blacklist. Thus, we will not know the final risk factor, but we will receive information whether the candidate is on a blacklist. Depending on this information, the business process may take some other steps that can be done before the final result is delivered by the service.

The process model now shows three service invocations. The first invocation represents the original service request. The second invocation checks whether the requester

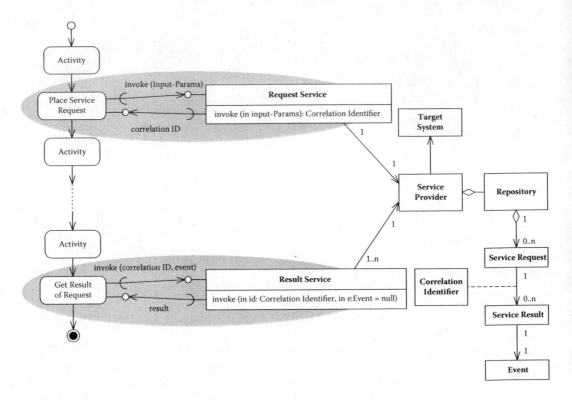

FIGURE 11.23

Example structure of a multiple asynchronous results service.

is on the blacklist, and the third invocation retrieves the final risk factor. The process model implemented with WebSphere MQ Workflow is shown in Figure 11.25.

From the point of view of this process model, it looks at first sight as if there are three independent service invocations. However, the invocations are all linked at a deeper conceptual level by the correlation ID and, moreover, by the functional architecture of the services. The XML structures of the service placing the request are not different from the structures illustrated in the example of the ASYNCHRONOUS RESULT SERVICE pattern. The two result services need to consider the event information. For this reason, the input XML of the blacklist check service looks like this:

```
<WfMessage>
    <WfMessageHeader>
        <ResponseRequired>Yes</ResponseRequired>
    </WfMessageHeader>
    <ActivityImplInvoke>
        <ActImplCorrelID>FFABCEDF0123456789FF</ActImplCorrelID>
        <Starter>user1</Starter>
        <ProgramID>
            <ProcTemplID>84848484FEFEFEFE</ProcTemplID>
            <ProgramName>FMCINTERNALNOOP</ProgramName>
        </ProgramID>
        <ProgramInputData>
            <_ACTIVITY>Check Blacklist</_ACTIVITY>
            <_PROCESS>CreditRequest#123</_PROCESS>
            <_PROCESS_MODEL>CreditRequest</_PROCESS_MODEL>
            <ControlDataObject>
                <CorrelationID>XYAZ4711</CorrelationID>
```

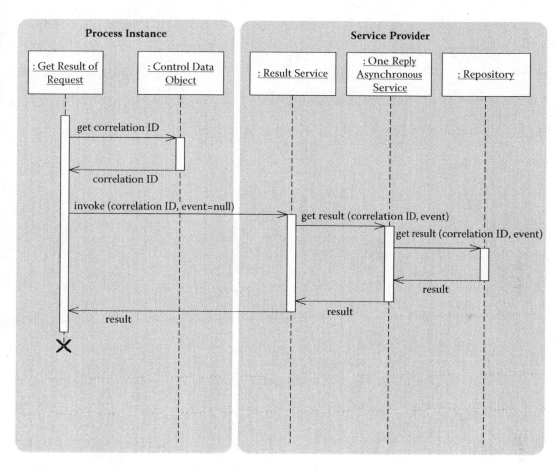

FIGURE 11.24
Behavior of a service invocation using a multiple asynchronous results service.

```
                    <Event>Blacklist</Event>
                </ControlDataObject>
            </ProgramInputData>
        </ActivityImplInvoke>
<WfMessage>
```

The output XML delivers the result of the blacklist check. To report this result to the process instance, the control data object needs an attribute to carry that information. That way, the decision logic can be defined according to the result of the blacklist check. The resulting XML from the service sent to MQ Workflow is as follows:

```
<WfMessage>
    <WfMessageHeader>
        <ResponseRequired>No</ResponseRequired>
    </WfMessageHeader>
    <ActivityImplInvokeResponse>
        <ActImplCorrelID>FFABCEDF0123456789FF</ActImplCorrelID>
        <ProgramRC>0</ProgramRC>
        <ProgramOutputData>
            <ControlDataObject>
                <Blacklist>Yes</Blacklist>
            </ControlDataObject>
```

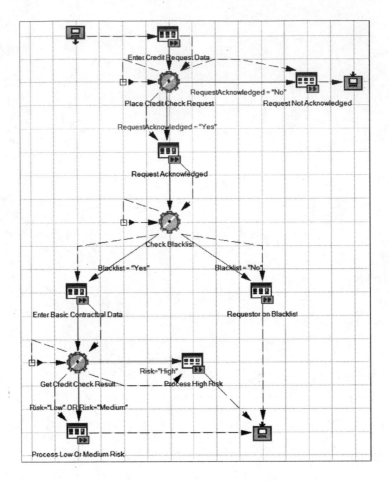

FIGURE 11.25
Multiple asynchronous results service in WebSphere MQ Workflow.

```
                </ProgramOutputData>
            </ActivityImplInvokeResponse>
    </WfMessage>
```

The second service result invocation finally queries for the final event that reports the risk factor. For this reason, the input XML needs to specify that the questioned event is the calculated risk value. It shows the same correlation ID as the blacklist service.

```
<WfMessage>
        <WfMessageHeader>
                <ResponseRequired>Yes</ResponseRequired>
        </WfMessageHeader>
        <ActivityImplInvoke>
                <ActImplCorrelID>FFABCEDF0123456789FF</ActImplCorrelID>
                <Starter>user1</Starter>
                <ProgramID>
                        <ProcTemplID>84848484FEFEFEFE</ProcTemplID>
                        <ProgramName>FMCINTERNALNOOP</ProgramName>
                </ProgramID>
                <ProgramInputData>
```

```
                    <_ACTIVITY>Get Credit Check
                        Result</_ACTIVITY>
                    <_PROCESS>CreditRequest#123</_PROCESS>
                    <_PROCESS_MODEL>CreditRequest</_PROCESS_MODEL>
                    <ControlDataObject>
                        <CorrelationID>XYAZ4711</CorrelationID>
                        <Event>RiskFactor</Event>
                    </ControlDataObject>
                </ProgramInputData>
            </ActivityImplInvoke>
    <WfMessage>
```

Examples: Known Uses of MULTIPLE ASYNCHRONOUS RESULTS SERVICE

- In principle, the MULTIPLE ASYNCHRONOUS RESULTS SERVICE pattern is supported by the process technologies given as known uses in the SYNCHRONOUS SERVICE ACTIVITY pattern as basic support for synchronous services is required. Provided that this support is given, the pattern can be implemented.
- The pattern has been used in projects in various industries, such as telecommunications and automotive, to implement loosely coupled coordination of different independent departments and even external organizations. The progress of the processes in the different units has been coordinated by exchanging intermediate states according to the pattern. For instance, in a telecommunications project in Spain, the pattern has been used to communicate with an external cable provider to report on progress of an installation process.
- IBM's order management and invoicing solution Webshop is designed to offer a service interface based on Web services that allows querying intermediate states of an order. These services can be invoked from any workflow tool that integrates Webshop according to the pattern.

FIRE EVENT ACTIVITY

Business processes are executed on a process engine, and the business scenarios of the processes require communicating process states to other partners. Specific states of business processes must be communicated to some unknown target systems, or functions of systems unknown to the business process need to be initiated by a process activity.

How are a state of the process communicated or functions of unknown target systems initiated by a process activity?

Each business process instance has its own data space. The process has logical relations to systems outside the process engine or to other process instances. During the execution of business processes, sometimes states are generated that need to be communicated to the space outside a process instance (e.g., to inform other systems about the completion of certain business activities). Sometimes, the execution of functions needs to be initiated by a process but the process has no knowledge which system will execute that function.

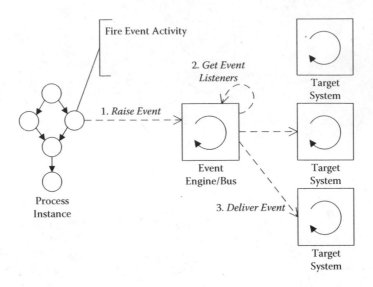

FIGURE 11.26
A fire event activity.

The process does not know how the function is going to be fulfilled and by which system. For instance, if the process needs to communicate a state, it might even be the case that the state is relevant to many other systems and not only one system.

Consider, for instance, situations in which the constellation of target systems is subject to regular change or the systems are outside the influence of the organization hosting the process instance. This can happen if the external systems are placed in a restricted security area or are hosted by external organizations. In such cases, the process might have no knowledge about the target systems.

This situation cannot simply be solved by invoking a service of a target system as the target system that offers the service is not known at process design time. Instead, the business process design should not be dependent on details of the target systems.

Interpret the states to be communicated and the initiation of external functions as events generated by process activities. In the process models, model FIRE EVENT ACTIVITIES raise events. These activities fire appropriate events when they are reached in the process flow. The events are sent to an eventing infrastructure, such as an event engine or an event bus. Target systems subscribe to the events as event listeners. The eventing infrastructure delivers the events to the target systems, and they are responsible for processing the events (see Figure 11.26).

Each process activity must have an implementation, that is, some component that realizes the function of the activity. In the case of a FIRE EVENT ACTIVITY, the activity implementation represents an event source. Like any other process activity, the FIRE EVENT ACTIVITY delegates the execution of the function associated to it implementation. The function associated to a FIRE EVENT ACTIVITY is to create events. More precisely, its function is to create the specific events associated to a specific FIRE EVENT ACTIVITY in a business process. For this reason, different FIRE EVENT ACTIVITIES in a business process may create different events as they potentially represent different event sources.

An event source notifies event listeners that have registered themselves to the event source about occurring events. The event listeners process the events for which they receive notification. An event listener is thus an OBSERVER [GHJV94, BHS07a] of an event source. Any possible target system may implement an event listener. That way, the target systems are responsible to process the events, but the business process does not need to know them explicitly or have knowledge about what they do with the events. From a business point of view, logically some contract might be associated to an event (i.e., there may be specific requirements associated to the event on how to process it). If such requirements exist, the observer of the event is also responsible for considering them. However, whether such requirements exist depends on the specific business context.

How the FIRE EVENT ACTIVITY delegates the execution of its function to its implementation may vary. Generally, any technology offered to invoke a function by a process activity can be used.

Usually, even listeners do not directly subscribe to the business process, but an intermediate eventing infrastructure is used, such as an event engine (or a complex event-processing engine) or an event bus. Often, eventing functionality is provided by an enterprise services bus or message bus software.

A business process is able to communicate with unknown target systems by applying this pattern. The target systems may change without affecting the business process design or implementation. Another business process may also be a target system. In that way, the pattern can be used to allow basically independent business process instances to communicate with each other. The pattern implies a functional architecture that represents additional implementation effort.

The invocation of the function realized by the implementation of the process activity that fires the event can be designed as a SYNCHRONOUS SERVICE ACTIVITY or a FIRE-AND-FORGET SERVICE ACTIVITY. If the events fired by a process activity have implications for other business processes that wait for these events to occur, then the EVENT-BASED ACTIVITY pattern applies. The EVENT DISPATCHER pattern can be used to decouple the FIRE EVENT ACTIVITIES from the target systems.

Example: Simple Example Structure of a FIRE EVENT ACTIVITY

Figure 11.27 illustrates a simple FIRE EVENT ACTIVITY design. This design omits the eventing infrastructure and only shows the direct links of the classes involved on the process engine and target systems sides. Usually, the eventing infrastructure can be reused off the shelf and would be used to realize some of the associations in the figure.

Example: FIRE EVENT ACTIVITY for Cancelling Complex Orders

A typical example of using a FIRE EVENT ACTIVITY is a process that cancels a complex order (e.g., in a telecommunications company). Consider that an order may contain various products, especially if it is a business customer that places the order. Each product might have its own ordering business process and fulfillment process that is further orchestrated by some umbrella business process that coordinates the overall order. What happens if the customer cancels the whole order while the order is still in fulfillment? In this case, it does not make sense to go on with the order fulfillment. But, how do the order fulfillment processes of each single requested product recognize that the whole order has been cancelled?

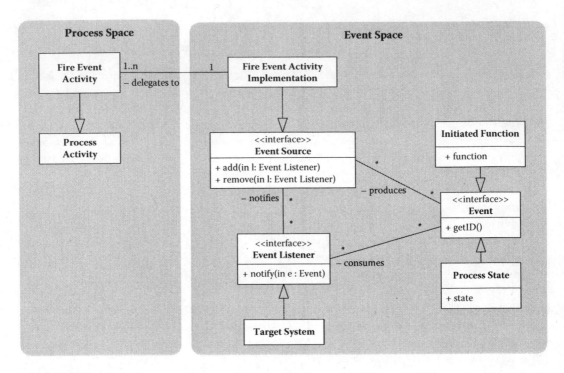

FIGURE 11.27
Example structure of a fire event activity.

The cancellation is a separate business process independent from the ongoing order processes. In this case, the cancellation process also does not know whether there are ongoing ordering processes. It might be the case that the fulfillment processes have also already executed business activities in external organizations (e.g., a cable provider, by invoking services of these external partners). Thus, the cancellation of the order should result in rolling back these business activities and stop all ongoing order fulfillment business processes. As the business processes do basically develop independently and should be loosely coupled, the FIRE EVENT ACTIVITY pattern is used to publish the cancellation event. Any partner system or business process interested in this event can capture it and react correspondingly.

The order fulfillment business processes contain EVENT-BASED ACTIVITIES that implement event listeners, react on this event, and stop the fulfillment processes in a controlled way. Another event listener informs external business partners about the cancellation. This way, the cancellation process is loosely coupled with the external world. However, the business logic, caused by the raised event, can still be executed without the cancellation process knowing about any system involved in this event. Each system that listens to the event is responsible for processing the event (separation of concerns). The cancellation process is not responsible for it as it is not able to decide on all the consequences that may result from the cancellation event. As a result, the complexity generated by this parallelism becomes manageable by applying the FIRE EVENT ACTIVITY pattern.

Examples: Known Uses of a FIRE EVENT ACTIVITY

- In principle, the FIRE EVENT ACTIVITY pattern is supported by the process technologies given as known uses in the SYNCHRONOUS SERVICE ACTIVITY pattern as basic support for synchronous services is required. Provided that this support is given, the pattern can be implemented.

- In real project situations, it often appears that processes are interrelated. For instance, in order management processes, as we find them in the telecommunications industry, there are usually parts of larger orders being processed in separate business processes. At a certain time, these partial orders need to be consolidated. To achieve this, each partial order process implements FIRE EVENT ACTIVITIES to communicate that a partial order has passed a certain state (e.g., the partial order is fulfilled). A coordinating process collects all the events and coordinates the progress of the overall order.
- In the insurance business, we find similar scenarios in claims handling. Larger claims contain subclaims, and the processing of some complex claims takes up to several years. Each subclaim thus runs as a single process, and the overall claim also needs to be coordinated. This is also achieved by implementing FIRE EVENT ACTIVITIES in the subclaims processes to achieve loose coupling of the interrelated claims processes.
- IBM's WebSphere Process Server offers direct technology support of the pattern by offering event generation and even event-handling features in its tooling.
- BEA Fuego also offers such event generation and event-handling features.

ASYNCHRONOUS SUBPROCESS SERVICE

Business processes are modeled with subprocesses and are executed on a process engine. From a logical business perspective, one can observe two types of subprocess relationships. The first is basically like a functional decomposition, and the second is more like an asynchronous invocation by which the calling process does not wait until the subprocess has finished execution. Unfortunately, this second variant is usually not directly supported by process engines.

How are subprocesses that must be asynchronously invoked realized, even though usually process engines provide no direct support for this type of subprocess?

A subprocess is just an encapsulation of business activities that have some value in terms of reusability or that represent a coherent complex logical unit of work. When invoking a subprocess in another process, the normal behavior of a process engine is defined as follows: Step into the subprocess, step through all activities of the subprocess, and then return to the invoking process and continue with the remaining activities after the subprocess invocation. Hence, subprocesses are basically a functional decomposition. In some cases, this behavior is not wanted. It is required that the calling process should not wait until the subprocess has finished its execution, but instead it should directly continue with its own activities after subprocess invocation.

When business modelers create business process models, they often implicitly assume that kind of asynchronous subprocess relationship. It is rather like initiating another process than having it fully enclosed in the calling process. As a result, when realizing these business processes on a process engine and more formal models of the processes need to be created, it is actually an issue how to model this asynchronous subprocess relationship if the process modeling constructs of the process engine do not support it.

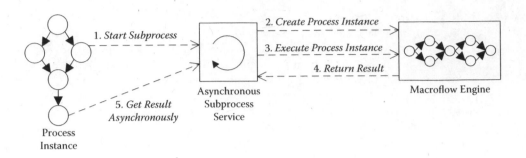

FIGURE 11.28
An asynchronous subprocess service.

In the process models, model an activity that invokes an ASYNCHRONOUS SUBPROCESS SERVICE. This service only functionally encapsulates the instantiation of the subprocess on the process engine but not the whole execution of the subprocess. It creates a new process instance on the process engine and executes it asynchronously (see Figure 11.28).

Instead of modeling a subprocess via the process modeling language of the process engine, a SYNCHRONOUS SERVICE ACTIVITY or a FIRE-AND-FORGET SERVICE ACTIVITY is modeled that invokes a service that just instantiates the desired business process. The name/identifier of the process to be instantiated and the input parameters are provided as inputs to the ASYNCHRONOUS SUBPROCESS SERVICE by the activity. For this reason, the control data object that is provided as input to the SYNCHRONOUS SERVICE ACTIVITY or the FIRE-AND-FORGET SERVICE ACTIVITY must contain attributes to represent these parameters.

The only result that the ASYNCHRONOUS SUBPROCESS SERVICE might provide is an acknowledgment to the invoking process that indicates whether the creation was successful. The service wraps the (maybe service-based) API of the process engine and creates the process instance via the Application Progamming Interface (API).

Asynchronous instantiation of subprocesses is possible without direct support of the process modeling language of the process engine. The process engine must have an API that allows creation of a process instance of a defined process with defined input parameters.

To provide a more loosely coupled relationship between the service and the API of the process engine or to provide more flexible ways of instantiating processes, the pattern can also be realized using the FIRE EVENT ACTIVITY and the EVENT-BASED PROCESS INSTANCE patterns. The FIRE EVENT ACTIVITY is used to fire an event that represents the request for instantiation of a process. The realization of the EVENT-BASED PROCESS INSTANCE pattern contains an event listener that picks up the event and creates the requested process instance. This way, another level of functional flexibility is provided as the service request and the process instantiation are more loosely coupled.

Example: Simple Example Structure of an ASYNCHRONOUS SUBPROCESS SERVICE

Figure 11.29 shows a simple example design of an ASYNCHRONOUS SUBPROCESS SERVICE. An activity of the process instance initiates the service, and then the process instance resumes its work without waiting for a result. The service uses the API of the process engine the process should run on to create the subprocess instance. The API of the process engine can be a local interface or a remote interface (for instance, service based).

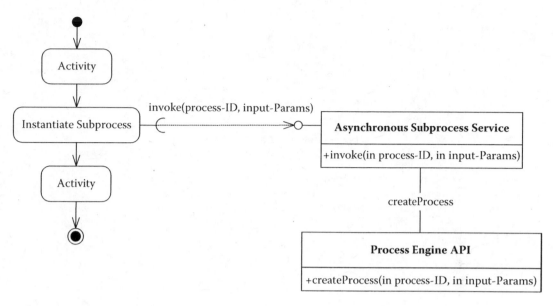

FIGURE 11.29
Example structure of an asynchronous subprocess service.

Example: ASYNCHRONOUS SUBPROCESS SERVICE in IBM WebSphere MQ Workflow

WebSphere MQ Workflow provides a Java API that can be used to instantiate a process via an ASYNCHRONOUS SUBPROCESS SERVICE. The service can be invoked with WebSphere MQ Workflow just according to the example in the SYNCHRONOUS SERVICE ACTIVITY pattern. Thus, the process ID and the input parameters are provided in an XML message. The service itself can be realized as a Java program that listens to the queue, picks up the XML message, instantiates the process via the Java API of MQ Workflow, and sends a return message based on the result of the instantiation. The Java implementation to create the process instance is simple:

```
import com.ibm.workflow.api.ExecutionService;
import com.ibm.workflow.api.FmcException;
import com.ibm.workflow.api.ProcessTemplate;

import java.util.Vector;

private ExecutionService service;

...

final class WorkflowSessionMQWF
{

    ...

    public void createProcess(String processName,
                          ProcessInputDataMQWF inputData)
                          throws WorkflowExceptionMQWF
    {
        ProcessTemplate[] template = null;
```

```
try {
      String temp = "NAME='"+processName+"'";
      template = this.service.queryProcessTemplates(temp, "NAME",
                     new Integer(1));
      if(template.length == 0){
            throw new WorkflowExceptionMQWF(
               WorkflowExceptionMQWF.NO_TEMPLATE_EXCEPTION);
      }
      if(inputData == null){
            throw new WorkflowExceptionMQWF(
               WorkflowExceptionMQWF.NO_INPUTDATA_EXCEPTION);
      }
      template[0].createAndStartInstance2(processName, "", "",
                     inputData.getContainer(), false);
} catch (FmcException e) {
      throw new WorkflowExceptionMQWF(e);
}
}

...


}
```

The implementation shows basically an application of the API of MQ Workflow to instantiate a process. The Java code shows that the process is identified by a unique name, representing the process ID as defined in the pattern. The process name is given to the *createProcess* method as an input parameter. Other input parameters are passed in an object of type *ProcessInputData*. This data represents the actual input parameters of the process.

First, the appropriate process definition is queried as identified by the process name. This is done invoking the *queryProcessTemplates* method of the *ExecutionService* class, which is part of the API. If there is no process definition (process template) found for this name, then an exception is thrown. After that, an instance of the process definition is created by calling the *createAndStartInstance2* method of the *ProcessTemplate* class.

Examples: Known Uses of Asynchronous Subprocess Service

- In a large program in an insurance company in the United Kingdom, the ASYNCHRONOUS SUBPROCESS SERVICE pattern has been applied to offer a service provided on a service bus to instantiate asynchronous processes. This service can be called flexibly by business processes to instantiate various processes asynchronously. FileNet P8 Business Process Manager has been used as a process engine. That way, it has been possible to invoke another FileNet workflow from a FileNet workflow asynchronously. As a result, the pattern has become an essential part of the architectural standard of the program. WebSphere Business Integration Message Broker has been used for implementation of the service bus, and service has been offered as a Web service.
- In a larger project in the automobile business, the pattern has been used to offer asynchronous instantiation of processes based on WebSphere MQ Workflow. The service has been offered as an MQ Series-based messaging interface. The pattern has been applied based on the same technology and principles in other projects, such as in telecommunications and banking. Actually, these MQ-based implementations could be found even before SOA became a more well-known term. There are other implementations that use the same principles in other industries, such as banking and telecommunications. The same pattern applies when modern Web services technology is used.

CONDITION DEADLINE SERVICE

Business processes are executed on a process engine, and the business scenarios require time-bound actions. Often, the flow logic of a business process depends on a certain business object or a specific state of a business object to be delivered in time. For instance, an e-mail approval for an order on the Web might be needed in a certain time frame; otherwise, the order is cancelled. That is, the business process expects certain conditions related to business objects to be present by some defined deadline—these conditions reflect the state of the business objects. The process logic thus needs to distinguish whether the related conditions of the business objects are met in time.

How is a process instance that is dependent on some business object state to be delivered at a specific point in time modeled?

Business objects are manipulated via business processes. The business objects are created, updated, or deleted. Often, business objects, or rather certain states of business objects, influence the control flow of business processes. That means the business processes are dependent on certain conditions related to the business objects. For this reason, business objects are used for synchronizing the execution of business processes.

Consider a business process that creates a customer business object and another business process that is executed in parallel and may only proceed beyond a certain activity if the customer business object has been created. That way, the activities of different business processes are coordinated by the common customer business object. Usually, the coordination is also time bound (i.e., the conditions associated to those business objects have deadlines, representing the latest point in time when the condition must be true for the dependent process to proceed normally).

In the process models, model a CONDITION DEADLINE SERVICE that is invoked by a SYNCHRONOUS SERVICE ACTIVITY. The service checks a specific condition with a given deadline of a defined business object. It delivers a result that indicates whether the condition is true or false and whether the deadline is reached or not. If the condition is false and the deadline is not yet reached, then invoke the service again by modeling a loop in the business process (see Figure 11.30).

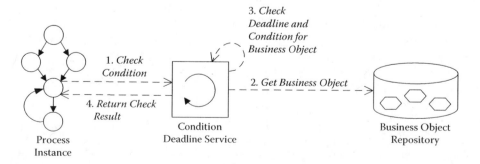

FIGURE 11.30
A condition deadline service.

The CONDITION DEADLINE SERVICE takes a business object ID, a condition that specifies the desired state of the business object, and deadline for the delivery of the state as input parameters. The output of the service provides information whether the condition is true or false for the required business object and whether the deadline is past or not. The business objects should be available, for instance, in a central BUSINESS OBJECT POOL. The service retrieves the business object identified by its ID from the BUSINESS OBJECT POOL and checks whether the condition is true for the business object and whether the deadline is reached. The service reports both results of the checks back to the invoking activity.

The process model distinguishes three business events:

- First, the condition is true, and the deadline is not reached.
- Second, the condition is false, and the deadline is past.
- Third, the condition is false, but the deadline is not reached, which leads to another invocation of the service after some time has elapsed to recheck.

Logically, a fourth case is also possible: that the deadline is past, and the condition is true. However, the time intervals should be designed that way they avoid this fourth case as it is actually not a valid business event.

It might be hard to design one generic service that checks all possible conditions for all types of business objects. In reality, often multiple dedicated services need to be designed that check for fixed conditions on a certain type of business object associated to the service. The drawback of this design is that effort for designing and implementing each CONDITION DEADLINE SERVICE is required. But, this is also a benefit of the pattern: Arbitrary conditions on business objects can be flexibly encoded in the service and integrated into processes using the same architectural scheme.

Example: Simple Example Structure of a CONDITION DEADLINE SERVICE

Figure 11.31 shows a simple CONDITION DEADLINE SERVICE that has the task to check the simple condition whether a business object has been delivered in time. Depending on the outcome of the check, the business process terminates in three different branches.

Example: CONDITION DEADLINE SERVICE for Order Fulfillment

An example of a business requirement for the CONDITION DEADLINE SERVICE pattern is the expected arrival of documents. One can imagine a business process that processes a customer order. At a certain stage during the order fulfillment process, the signed contract of the customer is necessary. The signature of a contract is usually time bound. The customer is asked to send the signed contract back within 14 days, for instance. If the signed contract does not arrive within this time interval, then the order fulfillment process must not proceed normally. Thus, the decision logic of the business process depends on the event of the document arrival in conjunction with a certain deadline. The document not only must arrive but also must be properly signed by the customer.

If the signed contract arrives, the corresponding business object state is changed to reflect the arrival of the documents. The documents might be stored as associated objects to the customer object. The service will thus check for the appropriate state, which might simply be indicated by a corresponding status attribute of the customer object or rather some aggregated business objects as the customer might have several open orders. The object ID provided to the service references the open order, and the service checks for the status. If the status indicates that the contract associated to the order has been signed, the service will report this information accordingly to the process.

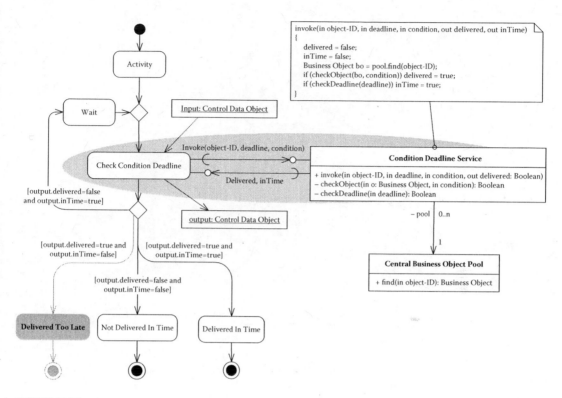

FIGURE 11.31
Example structure of a condition deadline service.

Examples: Known Uses of CONDITION DEADLINE SERVICE

- IBM WebSphere Process Server offers off-the-shelf features to query for certain states in a database that can be used to implement a Condition Deadline Service. The Information Aggregator BPEL currently allows doing inline SQL queries from a process. This way it is possible to query for a certain state and to react in the process accordingly. BPEL offers looping functions to rerun the query if the deadline is not exceeded.
- The BEA tool Fuego, which is based on BEA Aqualogic, offers similar database features to easily implement the Condition Deadline Service pattern. This is another example of a broader technology support of the pattern.
- In enterprise content management processes in the insurance and telecommunications businesses, the pattern has been used to implement waiting positions in processes for documents that have been requested. The previous example illustrated this in more detail. Similar implementations can also be found in banking, for instance. Many of the document-based processes show implementations of the Condition Deadline Service pattern.

12

Synchronization of Processes Running in Parallel

Introduction

In this chapter, we describe three patterns that address synchronization issues of parallel business processes. In this context, *synchronization* means that execution in terms of the progression through the different activities of a process needs to be synchronized with other business processes running in parallel. The synchronization issues reflect requirements of complex business scenarios, and the synchronization dependencies cannot be modeled directly in the business processes via static control flow dependencies. As a result, conflicting forces arise due to the need for loosely coupling the synchronization concerns with the business process models. Besides technical forces, such as the problems of concurrent data access, supporting business agility is central. Business processes are subject to constant change. Hence, any suitable synchronization mechanism must be loosely coupled to support changes in the connected business processes.

The patterns describe *architectural* synchronization solutions as opposed to synchronization within a business process design. That is, other architectural components than the process engine or external systems play a role in the solutions of the patterns.

The three patterns presented are as follows:

- The REGISTER FOR ACTION pattern describes how to synchronize the execution of functionality of a target system with business processes running in parallel.
- The BUNDLE PROCESS AGENT pattern describes how business objects being generated by different parallel processes can be processed in a consolidated way.
- The PROCESS CONDUCTOR pattern addresses how to enable designers to model dependencies between parallel business processes by flexible orchestration rules.

Consider a simple example to illustrate the use of the patterns: Various business processes of a company require contacting the customer via phone, but the company wants to avoid contacting the customer too often in a specific period of time. Hence, the phone calls should be consolidated. In such business scenarios that require synchronization of multiple process instances, the patterns described in this chapter can be applied.

If only a specific *action*, like "put phone call into a task list" needs to be performed after synchronization has taken place, the REGISTER FOR ACTION pattern should be applied. However, the phone call might also require a business process preparing the phone call, and this business process then usually needs access to the private business objects of the synchronized processes. In this more complex scenario, the BUNDLE PROCESS AGENT pattern

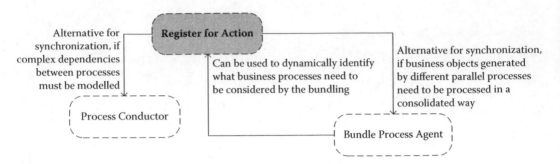

FIGURE 12.1
Register for action pattern relationships.

can be applied. Finally, if the need for synchronizing occurs within the processes and requires each of the processes to be stopped until the synchronizing action (which might be yet another business process) has happened, then PROCESS CONDUCTOR is applicable.

This simple scenario should illustrate one important design issue: Which of the patterns is chosen depends on the design of the business processes that need to be synchronized. In some scenarios, the patterns are mutual alternatives; in others, combining them makes sense. For example, the BUNDLE PROCESS AGENT pattern can be combined with the REGISTER FOR ACTION pattern to dynamically identify which business processes need to be considered by the bundling.

Figure 12.1 shows the main pattern relationships of the three patterns from the perspective of the REGISTER FOR ACTION pattern.

REGISTER FOR ACTION

Business processes are executed on process engines. Sometimes, the execution of an action depends on the states of multiple business process instances running in parallel. When this is the case, the action can only be executed if those parallel business process instances have reached a certain state represented by a specific process activity.

As business processes are created and changed while the system is running, it is not advisable to define synchronization dependencies statically in the models. Instead, it should be possible to define and evaluate the synchronization dependencies at runtime while still allowing business processes to change independently.

How can multiple, dynamically created process instances be synchronized with minimal communication overhead and still be kept independently changeable?

Business processes are dynamically instantiated on process engines at different points in time. For this reason, there are usually several instances of one or more business processes running in parallel. Each of them has a different state of progression in terms of the process activity they have reached so far during execution.

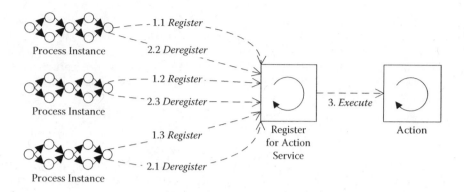

FIGURE 12.2
A register for action service.

When a specific *action*, such as a business function, service, or another business process, has a logical dependency to multiple business process instances, synchronization with all the process instances can be difficult. First, the action might not know which business process instances of the many possible parallel instances it is dependent on. But, even if it knows the instances that it is dependent on, polling them for synchronization would incur a communication overhead. The same problem of a communication overhead for synchronization would also occur if the process instances would run a synchronization protocol, for instance, before triggering a callback that executes the action.

In addition, before the action can synchronize with the process instances, it needs to know that it must wait for one or more instances. That is, a mechanism is required to communicate that there is a new dependent process instance to wait for.

Business processes can change over time, and new processes are constantly created while the overall system is running. This includes that a state at which an action must be executed might change, be added to a process, or be removed from the process. The actions that depend on business processes must be able to cope with such process changes. The effects of these changes should be minimized and should not have an impact on other components to be manageable. A consequence is that the synchronization dependencies of the actions cannot be statically modeled in the models of the business processes or the actions but must be defined and evaluated at runtime. In other words, a loose coupling between the action and the business processes it is dependent on is required.

Use a REGISTER FOR ACTION component that offers registration and deregistration services to be invoked from business processes. The registration informs the REGISTER FOR ACTION component to wait with the desired action to be initiated until a specific process instance has deregistered itself. When all registered processes have deregistered themselves, the action will be executed (see Figure 12.2).

The REGISTER FOR ACTION component offers two services:

- A registration service, by which a process instance can register itself with its instance ID

- A deregistration service that allows a process instance to deregister itself via its instance ID

Invocation of the deregistration service means that the process has reached the state that is relevant for the action. The two services are invoked by process activities. Each registration invocation must have one corresponding deregistration invocation in a business process. This design has the consequence that the place of invocations can change as the business processes change over time. In other words, the REGISTER FOR ACTION component and the business processes are loosely coupled.

The REGISTER FOR ACTION component waits until all registered business processes have deregistered themselves. After the last deregistration, the action is executed by the REGISTER FOR ACTION component.

An important detail of a REGISTER FOR ACTION design is to determine the point in time when registration ends. As most scenarios of the pattern concern long-running business processes, a registration delay is a practical solution that works in many cases. The registration delay runs a certain amount of time from the point in time when the first registration to the REGISTER FOR ACTION instance happens. For instance, if a registration delay of one day is chosen, then all registrations that accumulate throughout that day will be included. Of course, the length of the delay can be adjusted based on either previous experiences or experimentation. An alternative to a registration delay is introducing a specific registration type that ends the registration process for one REGISTER FOR ACTION instance.

Modeling the deregistration service invocation might be an issue for some business processes: Deregistration should often be invoked as early as possible so unnecessary delays for the action to be executed are not produced. If the business process contains complex decision logic, there may be various paths that may lead to a deregistration service invocation at many different positions in the process. As the process execution may follow only one case-specific path, deregistration must be found on all possible paths if a registration has been previously performed.

To place the deregistration service invocations at the right positions and to avoid multiple invocations of the deregistration service in case of loops in the process is sometimes not trivial if the business process is of higher complexity. The easiest way might be to put deregistration simply at the end of the business process and thus avoid the possible complex logic that is initiated by the different possible paths or loops. However, this is not always possible or optimal if deregistration as early as possible is required.

In the REGISTER FOR ACTION pattern, the service invocations from the business processes might be realized as SYNCHRONOUS SERVICE ACTIVITIES or FIRE-AND-FORGET SERVICE ACTIVITIES. The realization using SYNCHRONOUS SERVICE ACTIVITIES is usually better suited as it is important for the business processes to be informed whether the registration and deregistration were successful. If the target action is related to a more complex business process, then this consolidation can be achieved by using a BUNDLE PROCESS AGENT.

The ACTIVATOR pattern [SSRB00, BHS07a] has a similar structure as REGISTER FOR ACTION. It, however, solves a different problem: the on-demand activation and deactivation of service execution contexts to run services accessed by many clients without consuming resources unnecessarily. The patterns can be used together with REGISTER FOR ACTION using a shared structure. That is, the registration and deregistration services could be used for on-demand activation and deactivation.

Also, PUBLISHER/SUBSCRIBER [BMR+96, BHS07a] can be combined with REGISTER FOR ACTION using a shared structure. That is, the registration and deregistration services could be used to subscribe and unsubscribe to events for the time of registration. This way, the REGISTER FOR ACTION component can communicate with its currently registered processes.

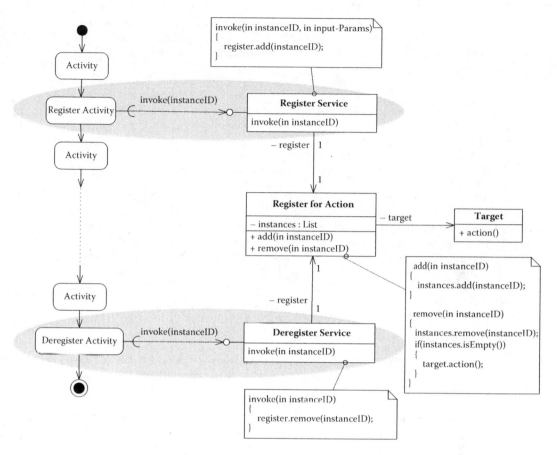

FIGURE 12.3
Register for action example configuration.

Example: REGISTER FOR ACTION Example Configuration

Figure 12.3 shows on the left-hand side a business process that invokes a register service. At the end of the business process, an activity invokes a deregister service. Both services are interfaces to a REGISTER FOR ACTION component, which maintains an instance list. When all instances are removed from this list, the action is invoked.

Example: Saving Costs of Sending Postal Mail

In the context of business processes that create information that must be sent by mail to recipients, the pattern provides significant potential to save postal costs. If each business process produces its own letters to be sent to recipients, high postal costs will be created. It would be better to gather all the information created from the business processes and to include them in one letter. Sending fewer letters will save significant postal costs. However, the problem is how to gather all the information and when is the point in time to pack all the gathered information in one letter and send it to a recipient.

By applying the REGISTER FOR ACTION pattern, it is possible to control and coordinate sending out letters to various recipients. The action associated in this context is sending a letter out to a recipient. This can be coordinated by registering all business processes that will create information to be packed in one letter for a specific recipient. Thus, the registration service can be designed to capture an additional parameter to specify the recipient. That way, it is possible to pack all the information created for one recipient on one letter as the letter will be sent when all registered business processes have deregistered themselves for a recipient.

The logic associated to the registration service and the REGISTER FOR ACTION component might be even more complex (e.g., to distinguish different priorities for the information to be sent out quickly or to send it out later). As a result, there may be more complex rules to control and synchronize the business processes. However, the basic pattern represented by REGISTER FOR ACTION will always be the same.

Especially in a customer order or service management context, the pattern is useful for these kinds of purposes to control communication to recipients. It is suitable not only for postal communication but also for various communication channels (e.g. fax, e-mail, or even telephone). The general purpose of gathering relevant information first, before initiating the communication, generally applies to all these channels.

Even as far as the telephone communication is concerned, it becomes clear that calling the recipients only once to discuss many open questions that stem from different parallel clearing business processes, for instance, will be better for customer satisfaction than contacting the customer several times to clarify a single issue at a time, perhaps an issue of minor importance. The pattern provides flexible means to capture all these business scenarios and to automate significant parts of the business logic.

Examples: Known Uses of REGISTER FOR ACTION

- The REGISTER FOR ACTION pattern has been used in projects to control batch processing of larger transactions. Each business process generates transactions to be made, but actually performing all gathered transactions needs to be done when all related transactions to be made are identified. That way, transaction costs can be saved by putting related transactions, addressed to the same account, in one larger transaction.
- The REGISTER FOR ACTION pattern has also been used to control the point in time when consolidated outbound communication to one concrete party needs to be performed in an order management context.
- The previous purposes for the REGISTER FOR ACTION pattern have been used in projects in the telecommunications industry in the context of order management and in the insurance industry in the context of claims handling. The pattern has also been used in banking as far as the mentioned transaction-processing issues are concerned.

BUNDLE PROCESS AGENT

Business processes are executed on a process engine, and during their execution business objects are created and manipulated by the business process instances. Each business process instance creates and manages its own set of business objects to avoid data inconsistencies, locking overheads, deadlocks, and other problems created by concurrent data access. Business scenarios, such as consolidated sending of postal mail in batches, require consolidating the business objects being generated by many different process instances and then processing them using a central but parallel-running business process. Hence, the usual mechanisms of a process engine, in which each process instance keeps its business objects in a private data space, are not sufficient to support such scenarios.

How are business objects from various business process instances gathered and processed in a consolidated way without causing unwanted effects of concurrent data access?

Business process instances running on a process engine have their own data space and are thus disjoint entities. When business objects are created during the execution of a business process, only the business process instances creating the objects know about their existence. That is, the business objects created by a business process instance are per default private to the business process instance. This helps to avoid unwanted effects, such as data inconsistencies, locking overheads, or deadlocks, when business process instances are running in parallel because the actions of the business process instances control all accesses to these business objects.

This technical concept can be applied to implement most business scenarios. However, there is a special case for which this technical solution does not work well alone: Consider that the business objects created by many different parallel business process instances are input objects to be processed by a central business process that logically gathers all these business objects and then processes the consolidated set of business objects. A typical example is that the business requires these business objects to be handled in a consolidated way, such as sending one letter per postal mail for a number of parallel transactions with a customer instead of sending multiple letters. In this case, the parallel-running consolidation process instance must gather the objects and process them. Unfortunately, usually process engines do not directly support such scenarios.

It is necessary only to centrally process those business objects that actually should be processed in a consolidated way. It might be that this is only a subset of business objects owned by a process instance. A process instance should still have control over what business objects should be processed in a consolidated way and should thus be able to publish only those objects that it considers relevant.

Each of the involved business processes can potentially change over time. Hence, the consolidation architecture should not impose restrictions on the business process design that would hinder rapid changeability.

Send the business objects to be processed centrally to a BUNDLE PROCESS AGENT via a dedicated service, specified in the model of the business process. The BUNDLE PROCESS AGENT creates an instance of a bundle (consolidation) process, if no instance exists yet, and for each bundle it makes sure that only one instance of the consolidation process is running at a time. The business object bundle is gathered from different business processes invoking that dedicated service for sending the business objects. When a specified end criterion is reached, such as a deadline or a specified number of business objects in the bundle, then the bundle is centrally processed by the bundle process (see Figure 12.4).

Design an architectural component that serves as a BUNDLE PROCESS AGENT, which offers a service to be invoked by business processes to send business objects that need to be processed centrally. The BUNDLE PROCESS AGENT stores the business objects being sent to it in a container that serves as a temporary repository. The container is not intended as the actual persistence mechanism of the business objects—it is rather intended to capture only which objects need to be processed centrally.

For this reason, this container might only keep BUSINESS OBJECT REFERENCES rather than the business objects themselves. However, it is also possible to send copies of actual

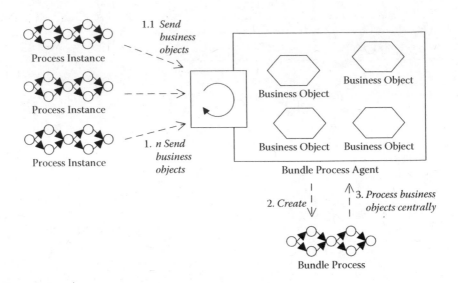

FIGURE 12.4
A bundle process agent.

business objects and not just references. Often, these objects then only contain a subset of the business data of the original business objects (i.e., the subset of data relevant for processing the business objects centrally). In this case, it is advisable to introduce special types of business objects designed for these purposes.

The BUNDLE PROCESS AGENT waits until a specified end criterion is reached. For instance, this can be a deadline or specified maximum amount of business objects that can be bundled in one bundle. When the end of bundling is reached, the BUNDLE PROCESS AGENT instantiates a *bundle process* that processes the business objects centrally. The container with the business objects is cleared after the processing has been initiated to be ready to store new objects for the next iteration. Only one instance of the bundle process is running at a time for each bundle; that is, the processing of a set of business objects must be finished before the next instance of a bundle process can be started. Of course, different bundles can be assembled in parallel. For instance, business objects for postal mail communication with customers are bundled to send them together; then, there is one bundle per customer.

During the execution of the bundle process, new business objects are sent to the BUNDLE PROCESS AGENT by business processes running in parallel for the next iteration. These objects are again stored in the container. This way, only business objects relevant for the next iteration are kept in the container as the container is emptied when a new iteration (i.e., a new instance of the bundle process) has been started. The BUNDLE PROCESS AGENT repeats this process in a loop.

The BUNDLE PROCESS AGENT is implemented as a COMPONENT CONFIGURATOR [SSRB00] to allow controlled configuration of the agent at runtime. When it is initialized, it performs the following functions:

1. It checks whether there are new business objects in the container to be processed by a bundle process.
2. If there are new objects, it checks whether an instance of the bundle process is still running. Only if there is no instance running is a new instance created that processes the new objects in the container. The container is cleared to be empty

for new objects after the process instance has been started. If an existing instance is still running, then no action is performed (i.e., no new bundle process is created and the business object container is not emptied).

3. The agent loops back to step 1 until the loop is aborted by some event to finalize the execution or to suspend the execution.

There is one concurrency issue involved in this algorithm. The service that allows business processes to send new business objects to the container might conflict with the clearing action of the container that is initiated by the algorithm described. That means a new instance of the bundle process might be created with the given objects in the container at that point in time. After the instance is created, the algorithm prescribes to clear the container. If there are new objects added to the container while the creation of the new instance is still in progress, then these objects will be deleted from the container with the clearing action without being processed by the bundle process. To avoid such a situation, the container must provide locking and unlocking functions that are used for the time a new instance of a bundle process is created.

The BUNDLE PROCESS AGENT pattern thus resolves issues according to complex bundling of business objects that need to be centrally processed and offers a general architectural solution that is both flexible and extensible. Different bundle processes can be used for different purposes, although this will increase the complexity of the architecture. However, there might be a larger effort involved to design a BUNDLE PROCESS AGENT component. For this reason, the pattern may only be suitable in projects and programs that have a larger strategic perspective.

The BUNDLE PROCESS AGENT pattern can be combined with the REGISTER FOR ACTION pattern to dynamically identify which business processes need to be considered by the bundling. As far as the service invocation from business processes is concerned, the SYNCHRONOUS SERVICE ACTIVITY pattern or the variation of the FIRE-AND-FORGET SERVICE ACTIVITY, including acknowledgment, is usually recommended to achieve some level of security that the business objects being sent have arrived at the initiated target. According to the MACRO-/MICROFLOW pattern, the bundle process can be implemented as a macroflow or microflow.

Example: BUNDLE PROCESS AGENT Example Configuration

Figure 12.5 provides an overview of the conceptual structure of how the BUNDLE PROCESS AGENT might look like when including the service that provides the functionality to add business objects to the container. The structure also resolves the described concurrency issues by providing locking functionality to the container.

Figure 12.5 shows business processes that invoke a special *Send Bundle Object Service* to send business objects. The processes may run in parallel, and the services might be invoked at different points in time in the processes (i.e., the service invocation might be modeled several times in one process and might be used in various process models). The service simply adds the objects to the container. To resolve the concurrency issue, explained previously, it uses locking and unlocking mechanisms. The class *Bundle Process Agent* implements the COMPONENT CONFIGURATOR [SSRB00] and invokes the *run()* method of class *Bundle Process* in a loop. The *run()* method of class *Bundle Process* retrieves the business objects from the container and creates a new bundle process if no instance is running and the container is not empty. It also uses the locking and unlocking mechanisms to prevent the concurrency issue.

The class *Process Engine* provides an interface to the Application Programming Interface (API) of the process engine being used to implement the business processes—in

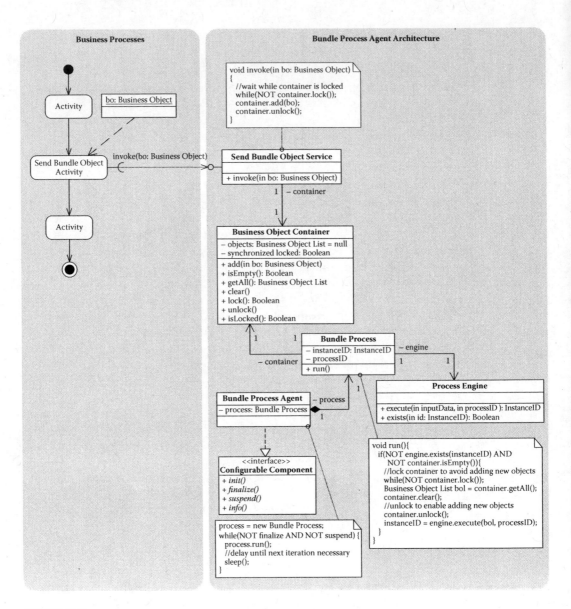

FIGURE 12.5
Bundle process agent example structure.

this case, especially the bundle process. The *execute()* method instantiates a bundle process with the given input data, which are the business objects from the container in this case. The *exists()* method allows checking whether an instance of the bundle process, identified by a unique ID, is still running in the engine.

Example: Handling Complex Orders

This example shows how two distinct strategic goals (mentioned in the known uses) have been realized using the BUNDLE PROCESS AGENT pattern. In one larger project in the telecommunications industry, two important issues occurred in the context of processing complex orders from larger customers. Complex orders consisted of a number of suborders processed in parallel business processes by different organizational units in the telecommunications company. These suborders are independent to a certain degree from an internal perspective of the company. For this reason, the business processes for these suborders run in parallel to speed up the completion of the overall order. However, to improve customer satisfaction and to reduce costs, issues that occur during the processing of suborders need to be clarified with the customer, whose perspective is on the overall order.

If each business process is implemented with its own issue resolution process, the customer needs to be contacted for each single issue that might occur in a suborder, or issue resolution might only be structured according to suborders. As a result, each process needs to implement its own issue resolution procedure in some way. To reduce the number of customer interactions and to save communication costs, the issue clarification process needs to be consolidated and treated as its own concern. That way, different processes can use the same clarification procedure, and changes to these business processes associated to processing of suborders can remain independent.

Moreover, each customer has its own communication preferences; that is, some want to be contacted by letter, others prefer e-mail or fax, and other customers prefer direct telephone communication. In addition, some serious issues require written communication. Consequently, it is required to treat issue resolution as its own concern and to centralize the rules around the communication preferences. A concept for classification of occurring issues and a central processing of those occurring issues is required. The actual issue clarification process needs to be implemented as a rather complex business process itself that gathers all the occurring issues from those various parallel-running suborder processes. The rather complex rules for communication need to be implemented by the issue clarification process.

The BUNDLE PROCESS AGENT pattern has been applied to deal with these requirements. A classification scheme for possible occurring issues has been designed in a business object model. The parallel running suborder processes have just sent a type of issue that occurred during the process to the BUNDLE PROCESS AGENT. The bundle agent creates an issue clarification process that processes the issues centrally according to communication preferences. For instance, a list of issues that result from various suborders can thus be clarified in a single telephone call with the customer or can be communicated in a single letter. Direct communication via telephone of a consolidated list of issues has thus sped up the clarification process or has saved mailing costs as a number of relevant issues have been gathered in a single letter.

The overall clarification process can be implemented in a controlled way considering the customer view and preferences of the overall order, while still having the ability to process the suborders according to different specialized internal departments. A special team to improve the clarification process as a separate concern can thus be implemented without affecting actual order processes. In that way, it has been possible to design the business process models according to different levels of expertise and to assign dedicated resources with expertise on issue resolution.

The issue classification scheme via the special business object model and the service for sending occurring issues via a service provides a clear interface that allows new or improved suborder processes to use it in a flexible way. The service has provided a defined interface for handling issues for clarification in a universal way. Customer satisfaction has been improved by classification of the issues and reducing the number of necessary interactions with the customers.

Examples: Known Uses of BUNDLE PROCESS AGENT

- The BUNDLE PROCESS AGENT pattern has been used in several projects to consolidate outbound communication to the same party to save costs by putting the communication content resulting from various business processes running in parallel in one bundled communication. The bundle process controls the actual generation of the communication, including format and media (i.e., letter, e-mail, fax, or even telephone) and the procedure to control the outcome of the communication. The purpose in this context was also to improve customer satisfaction via the consolidation of the communication and by reducing the number of interactions and applying preferred communication mechanisms.

- The pattern has also been used to gather issues to be clarified with customers that resulted from various business processes running in parallel associated to a complex order. The issues are collected first and are then clarified with the customer rather than discussing each issue separately with the customer. That way, issues can be clarified in relation to each other. The bundle process controls the clarification procedure in terms of a dedicated business process.
- The first two purposes of the pattern have been used in the context of order management in the telecommunications industry and of claims handling in the insurance industry. The pattern has served in this context as an architectural solution to the consolidation issues mentioned in larger strategic architecture projects.

Process Conductor

Interdependent processes are in execution on a process engine. The interdependency implies that execution of the processes needs to be synchronized at runtime. When business processes are executed on a process engine, there are often points in these processes at which dependencies to other processes need to be considered. That means a process may only move to a certain state but can only move on if other parallel processes have also reached a certain state. Further execution of these parallel-running processes need to be orchestrated at runtime as it cannot be decided at modeling time when these states are reached or what these states are. This is due to the separate execution of the processes and the fact that each process is a component that may change individually over time. In most cases, the rules for the orchestration need to be flexibly adaptable.

How can the interdependencies between processes be flexibly captured without tightly coupling the processes?

At some point in a process, it might be necessary that the process is only allowed to move on if other processes have also reached a certain state. However, each individual process does not know what these states of other processes are and when they are actually reached as each process runs at its own speed within its own data space. Moreover, each business process needs to be treated as a separate component and may change individually over time. Thus, processes need to be loosely coupled as far as this aspect is concerned.

The reason for this is that it is hard to specify in a single process model what states of other processes are relevant from the point of view of an individual process and when these states are reached or what the relevant dependent processes are. If this is statically modeled in a process, somehow the implementation will be inflexible, and changes to orchestration rules usually have an impact on all involved processes. That means the actual orchestration appears to be a complex concern of its own, and the rules for orchestration cannot be defined attached to an individual process model. Consequently, the orchestration rules should not be captured as some types of static relationships of a process to other processes. The dependencies that will be generated if each process should know the rules for orchestration will be hard to manage. If the rules change, then each individual process needs to be changed as well. For this reason, a tight coupling of the rules to each individual process is an inappropriate approach.

As a result, each process needs to be treated as an encapsulated component that does not know anything about the orchestration rules or the processes to which it has dependencies. Each process must only know its own points in the process at which the dependency occurs but not what this dependency is about. New processes might be created over time, which create new dependencies, and this must not affect existing process models to make the changes manageable. Each process model itself may also change (e.g., new steps are added without affecting the actual rules for orchestration as they need to be treated as a separate concern). The very problem is thus that the processes are standing in dependency but must actually not know very much about each other as the dependency needs to be separated from the process to treat it as a separate concern and to make the processes and the complexity generated by these dependencies manageable.

Introduce a PROCESS CONDUCTOR component that offers configurable orchestration rules to conduct a number of business process instances. The PROCESS CONDUCTOR offers a service that is only invoked synchronously by the business process instances. Each process instance provides its current state in terms of the activity it currently performs as an input parameter to this service. The service returns a result to a specific process instance only when the orchestration rules allow the process to move to the next step. This way, the order of the process instances to proceed is determined via the orchestration rules of the PROCESS CONDUCTOR (see Figure 12.6).

A central aspect of the PROCESS CONDUCTOR pattern is that the central conductor is only invoked synchronously. That is, when a business process reaches a critical state at which it may only move on if certain other dependent processes have also reached a certain state, then a SYNCHRONOUS SERVICE ACTIVITY is modeled at this point in the process that invokes a service. At this point, the process to be conducted blocks on the synchronous invocation until the conductor returns a result. The PROCESS CONDUCTOR service reports the state of a process instance and the ID of the instance to the PROCESS CONDUCTOR component. The

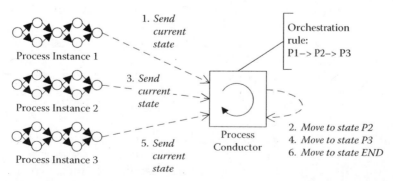

FIGURE 12.6
A process conductor.

states and corresponding process IDs are stored in a container. The PROCESS CONDUCTOR component applies orchestration rules that are configurable to determine the order of events that need to be fired to initiate dedicated process instances to move on.

The PROCESS CONDUCTOR applies its orchestration rules to the states and corresponding process IDs in the container. The orchestration rules simply define an order of the process states, that is, an order of terminating the corresponding process activities. The conductor then fires events to the process instances identified by their IDs in the order that is determined by the orchestration rules. Hence, the service implementation to report the state and the process ID can be implemented as an EVENT-BASED ACTIVITY. The process engine receives the events and terminates the activities in the order directed by the conductor. As a consequence, the processes move on to the next step in the right order. The conductor repeats this process in a loop as new processes may have registered for the next iteration.

The triggers to start one iteration of this procedure to apply the orchestration rules and to fire events to the processes can be twofold. It can happen repeatedly in defined time intervals, or it can be initiated by other dedicated event triggers (e.g., a master process has invoked the service of the PROCESS CONDUCTOR to register an initiation state that triggers the orchestration rules).

The registration of the state and process ID and the waiting position for the actual termination event to occur can also be designed as an ASYNCHRONOUS RESULT SERVICE. In this case, the business process needs to model two activities: one that places the request and a second one that gets the result (i.e., waits for the termination event).

The EVENT-BASED PROCESS SPLIT pattern can also be used in conjunction with a PROCESS CONDUCTOR in case it might take a long time until the termination event occurs, and it makes sense to split the process into two parts. That means if the termination event occurs, the second part of the process will be instantiated rather than modeling a waiting position.

One must note that the pattern generally assumes that the process engine processes the terminate events in the sequence that they are fired. This implies that the activities will terminate in the intended order (i.e., the order the terminate events have been fired), and the processes will correspondingly move on in the right order. If this cannot be assumed, then it might be that the activities of the processes do not terminate in the right order, and consequently the processes do not move on in the right order as well. To resolve this issue, the implementation can be extended by an additional service that is invoked from a business process. This additional service confirms that the activity has terminated. This is modeled as a second SYNCHRONOUS SERVICE ACTIVITY right after the first one. The next process, according to the rules, is only notified after the confirmation from the preceding business process has been received.

This may only be necessary if the order of termination is important within one iteration of notification. In many cases, this is not important as it is rather the whole iteration that represents the order (i.e., all processes of one iteration may literally move on at the same time, and slight differences do not matter). This also depends on the underlying rules and what these rules are further based on. According to the MACRO-/MICROFLOW pattern, this may also depend on whether we are at microflow or macroflow level. Transactional microflows usually run in much shorter time (sometimes milliseconds), and even slight time differences might matter, while these slight time differences might not matter at all at the macroflow level.

The pattern provides a flexible solution to determine the order of process steps that need to be synchronized by configurable rules. New processes and rules can be added without changing the architecture. Existing rules can also be modified without changing the implementation of running business processes. However, this flexible concept requires additional design and implementation effort. The design might be quite complex depending on the requirements regarding the complexity of the synchronization. For this reason, the pattern is most suitable in larger projects in which architecture evolution and business agility are required.

The PROCESS CONDUCTOR pattern is a central bottleneck, and it also incurs the risk of deadlocks in case the orchestration rules of the PROCESS CONDUCTOR are misconfigured or a business process fails to signal its state. In such cases, usually manual intervention is required. It makes sense to monitor the PROCESS CONDUCTOR component for such events.

Example: PROCESS CONDUCTOR Example Configuration

Figure 12.7 shows an example of the general architectural concept of the solution using the OBSERVER pattern [GHJV94, BHS07a] to notify the EVENT-BASED ACTIVITY of a process that waits for a terminate event to occur. The very order of sending these terminate events (i.e., the order of invoking the *notify()* method of the observer class) is defined by the orchestration rules of the conductor. The orchestration rules just order a list of states associated to process instances and deliver those process instances that need to be informed in the next iteration. In the example in Figure 12.7, this logic is hidden in the *runOrchestrationRules()* method. That method takes a list of states associated to process instance IDs, runs the rules over them, and delivers the list of process instances that apply to the rules for the next iteration. Those process instances are removed from the list given as an input parameter. The *Process Conductor* class itself is implemented using the COMPONENT CONFIGURATOR [SSRB00] pattern. In Figure 12.7, the class *Process Conductor* is the observable that is observed by a *Report State Service*. This service is invoked by activities from business processes as a SYNCHRONOUS SERVICE ACTIVITY. The service notifies the process engine about terminating an activity when it receives a corresponding *TerminateEvent* from the conductor. Read and write operations on the container are synchronized using locking and unlocking mechanisms.

A variation of the pattern is that the registration of the state and process ID and the waiting position for the actual termination event to occur can also be designed as an ASYNCHRONOUS RESULT SERVICE. To model this variant, the *Report State Service* offers two methods: one that places the request and one that gets the result. The combination of state and ID may serve as a CORRELATION IDENTIFIER [HW03] for the second method invocation. The architectural concept then needs to change slightly according to the description of the ASYNCHRONOUS RESULT SERVICE pattern. Using this design principle, the terminate event is rather captured by a pull mechanism from the perspective of the process conductor. The pull mechanism is represented by the second service invocation from the business process that actively asks for a result, and the termination event thus might not be immediately reported to the process engine (i.e., if the second method is invoked after the event has actually occurred).

On the contrary, the original solution in Figure 12.7 seems rather to use a push mechanism while following the EVENT-BASED ACTIVITY pattern as the event is fired and reported to the process engine as soon as it occurs. However, from the viewpoint of the business process, both scenarios follow a pull mechanism as all services are actively invoked and represent blocking calls. In the second scenario, it is two method invocations instead of just one. The second method to obtain the result represents the EVENT-BASED ACTIVITY in this second scenario.

The second variation of the solution can be used when sending the request needs to be decoupled from capturing the termination event, for instance, if other process steps can be undertaken in the meantime but the conductor needs to be informed early. Doing it that way creates more time for the conductor to calculate the order of the terminate events (e.g., if complex, time-consuming rules need to be applied or it is not necessary to report the termination event to the process engine as soon as possible). Figure 12.8 illustrates the variation of the pattern using an ASYNCHRONOUS REPLY SERVICE.

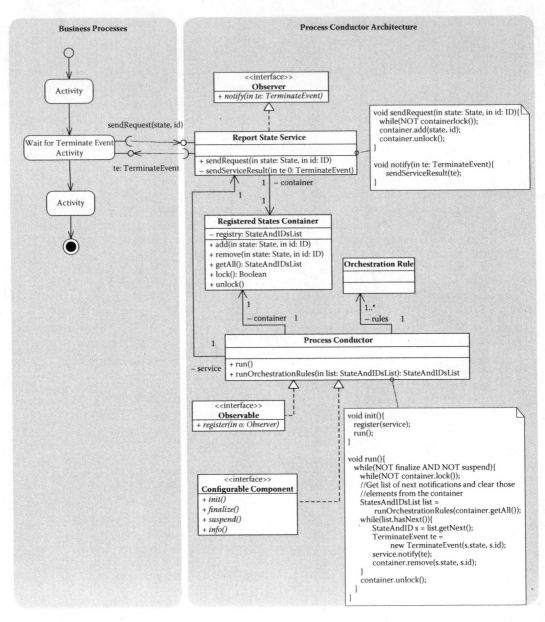

FIGURE 12.7
Process conductor example structure.

Example: Just-in-Time Production Optimization

In a just-in-time (JIT) production scenario in the automotive industry, the order of a car needs to be processed. The order arrives with given ordering details of the car model that needs to be manufactured in a JIT process. The parts for the car are delivered by different suppliers, and the order details related to the parts delivered by a certain supplier are forwarded to each of the suppliers via a service interface. The manufacturing process in terms of the internal ordering, delivery, and assembly of the parts from those different suppliers needs to be coordinated. To coordinate the processes, a MACROFLOW

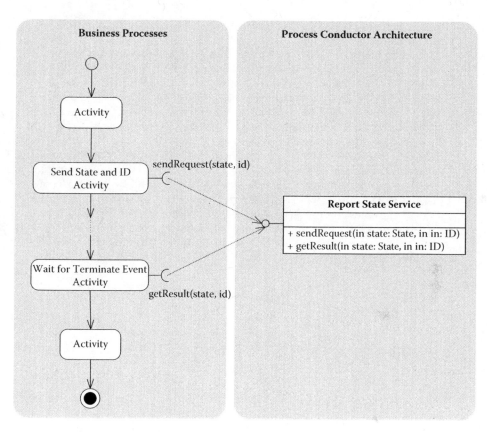

FIGURE 12.8
Process conductor example structure: variation using an asynchronous reply service.

ENGINE is used. The selected tool to implement the MACROFLOW ENGINE is WebSphere MQ Workflow.

The processes for ordering, delivering, and assembling the parts need to be coordinated as a parallel process instance is created for each supplier. Appropriate coordination of the process is crucial to optimize the manufacturing costs (e.g., reducing stock costs by agreeing on service levels with suppliers in terms of delivery times and placing the order to the suppliers at the right point in time). To allow coordination of the processes and to allow optimization, the PROCESS CONDUCTOR pattern has been applied. The timely coordination of orders to suppliers, parts delivery, and assembly can thus be implemented using flexible orchestration rules. The rules can be modified according to improved service-level agreements and to optimize the overall manufacturing process over time. The rules have been implemented and flexibly configured using the ILOG JRules rules engine [Ilo09]. The rules have been accessed by the PROCESS CONDUCTOR via a Java interface.

Example: Known Uses of PROCESS CONDUCTOR

- The PROCESS CONDUCTOR pattern has been used in projects in the telecommunications industry to control technical activation of dependent products in larger orders. Each product can be processed in parallel to improve efficiency up to a certain point. Further technical activation of the products is then controlled by product rules as certain products are dependent on each other (e.g., an Internet account can only be activated if the physical DSL (digital subscriber line) connection has been established).

- The pattern has been used to design synchronization points in parallel claims-handling processes in the insurance industry. That is, a set of parallel subclaims processes that belong to an overall claim is triggered and can only move to a certain point. At this point, the parallel processes need to be synchronized; that is, the first process that reaches the point must wait until all others also have reached their synchronization point. Which processes need to be synchronized is defined by configurable rules.
- In logistic processes in the transportation industry, the pattern has been used to flexibly coordinate the transportation of goods delivered by different suppliers and parties. Orchestration rules have been used to allow flexible packaging and to coordinate between different types of transportation (e.g., trucks, planes, ships, and trains). That way, it is possible to rather easily configure modified types of packaging and transportation due to changed conditions or different transportation criteria (e.g., security, delivery speed, and costs) that apply to different types of goods.

Appendix: Related and Referenced Patterns

Overview of Related Patterns

In this section, we give a brief overview of some related pattern material that could be interesting for further reading on specific topics.

Much related work taking process perspectives in conjunction with patterns can be found in the workflow and process domains. Many languages have been proposed for the design and specification of workflow processes. Similarly, languages and tools have been proposed for business process modeling (e.g., extended event-driven process chains [EPCs] in ARIS and various Unified Modelling Language (UML) profiles). Also, in other domains such as Enterprise Resource Planning (ERP), Customer Relationship Management (CRM), Product Data Management (PDM), and Web services, languages have been proposed to model processes and other perspectives such as the organization and data perspective. Some of these languages are based on well-known modeling techniques such as Petri Nets and UML. Other languages are system specific.

The work on workflow patterns conducted by van der Aalst et al. was the first attempt to collect a structured set of patterns at the level of process-aware information systems (summarized in [Wor08, AHKB03]). Several authors have used these workflow patterns to evaluate existing workflow management systems or newly designed workflow languages. The work has also been augmented with other pattern collections, such as service interaction patterns [BDH05]. These works on patterns strongly focus on the workflow perspective and do not take an overall architectural perspective. The workflow patterns rather address finer-grained structural elements of workflows than software patterns as emergent design solutions.

Other authors have used the term *workflow patterns* or similar terms also, but they addressed different issues. In [WMH00], a set of workflow patterns inspired by language/action theory and specifically aiming at virtual communities was introduced. Patterns at the level of workflow architectures rather than control flows were given in [MB97]. Collaboration patterns involving the use of data and resources were described in [Lon98]. Patterns for exception handling in process execution languages were introduced in [RAH06]. Schümmer and Lukosch provided patterns for human-computer interaction [SL07], and some of them include process or service perspectives.

Buschmann, Henney, and Schmidt described many software architecture patterns for distributed systems [BHS07a] and integrated patterns from different sources in a consistent manner to provide a comprehensive summary on architecture patterns. However, these distributed systems architecture patterns do not address SOAs specifically.

The *Pattern-Oriented Software Architecture* book introduced a number of general architectural patterns [BMR+96]. These are implicitly used in our pattern language. For instance, it is assumed in a service-oriented architecture (SOA) that a BROKER architecture is used.

The enterprise integration patterns [HW03] are also related to this work as they mainly describe asynchronous messaging solutions. This communication paradigm is often used in process-driven SOAs. We have referenced these patterns in many cases in this book.

In a similar way, remoting patterns [VKZ04] that describe designs and architectures for distributed object middleware are related. We have provided details on these patterns in Chapter 3.

Specific architectural guidance for SOA construction is given in [Jos07]. However, this book focuses on neither process-driven SOAs nor patterns specifically and hence can be seen as complementary to our pattern language.

In his work on microworkflows [Man00, Man02], Manolescu provided a workflow approach that is used to realize mainly microflow-type workflows for object-oriented composition. The work is also based on patterns.

The typical tooling around process engines has been described in pattern form by Manolescu (see [Man04]). These patterns can be used to link our rather architectural patterns on process engines, MACROFLOW ENGINE and MICROFLOW ENGINE, to the tooling provided by concrete technologies.

Evans identified that it is not only design patterns but also many different types of patterns that are influential when developing systems in a certain domain [Eva04]. This work does not yet combine aspects of organizational flexibility with an SOA and pattern-based approach, however.

Erl proposed a number of SOA patterns [Erl09]. Most of Erl's patterns mainly focused on either generic Web service infrastructure or abstract principles. They can be seen as complementary to this book as they do not cover the process-driven perspective.

Rob Daigenau is currently writing a book on SOA patterns. This work focuses on patterns situated at the same layer as discussed in Erl's book, but it is more technically detailed.

Thumbnails of Referenced Patterns

Some patterns are directly related to and referenced in the patterns and other parts of this book. These patterns and their sources are summarized in the following table:

Pattern	Problem	Solution
ABSOLUTE OBJECT REFERENCE [VKZ04]	The OBJECT ID of a remote object allows the INVOKER to dispatch the remote invocation to the correct target object. However, the REQUESTOR, in combination with the CLIENT REQUEST HANDLER, first has to deliver the invocation containing the target remote object's OBJECT ID to the SERVER REQUEST HANDLER and INVOKER.	Provide ABSOLUTE OBJECT REFERENCES that uniquely identify the INVOKER and the remote object. Let the ABSOLUTE OBJECT REFERENCE include endpoint information, for example, the host and port number of the network peer, the ID of the INVOKER, as well as the OBJECT ID of the target remote object. Clients exchange references to remote objects by exchanging the respective ABSOLUTE OBJECT REFERENCES.
ACTIVATOR [SSRB00, BHS07a]	Some types of services in a distributed system should only consume resources when they are accessed actively by clients. Clients should be shielded as much as possible from where services are located, how they are deployed on hosts in a network, and how their life cycle is managed.	Minimize resource consumption by activating services on demand and deactivating services when they are no longer accessed by clients. Use proxies to decouple client access transparently from service behavior and life-cycle management.

Pattern	Problem	Solution
(OBJECT) ADAPTER [GHJV94, BHS07a]	Applications can benefit from reusing existing code. An existing class, however, does not always provide the interface that its clients expect but instead might provide too much, too little, or the wrong style.	Introduce a separate ADAPTER between the component and its clients that converts the provided interface of the component into the interface that the client expects and vice versa.
AGGREGATOR [HW03]	How do we combine the results of individual, but related messages so that they can be processed as a whole?	Use a stateful filter, an AGGREGATOR, to collect and store individual messages until a complete set of related messages has been received. Then, the aggregator publishes a single message distilled from the individual messages.
BROKER [BMR+96, VKZ04]	Distributed software system developers face many challenges that do not arise in single-process software. One is the communication across unreliable networks. Others are the integration of heterogeneous components into coherent applications, as well as the efficient use of networking resources. If developers of distributed systems must overcome all these challenges within their application code, they may lose their primary focus: to develop applications that resolve their domain-specific responsibilities well.	Separate the communication functionality of a distributed system from its application functionality by isolating all communication-related concerns in a BROKER. The BROKER hides and mediates all communication between the objects or components of a system.
CANONICAL DATA MODEL [HW03]	How are dependencies minimized when integrating applications that use different data formats?	Design a CANONICAL DATA MODEL that is independent from any specific application. Require each application to produce and consume messages in this common format.
CLIENT-DEPENDENT INSTANCES [VKZ04]	In situations in which the application logic of the remote object extends the logic of the client, it becomes important to think about where to put the common state of both. Keeping the common state solely in the client requires the client to transmit its state with every invocation. Keeping the common state solely in the server, for example, in a STATIC INSTANCE, requires complex mechanisms to keep the states of individual clients separate inside the remote object.	Provide remote objects whose lifetime is controlled by clients. Clients create CLIENT-DEPENDENT INSTANCES on request and destroy them when no longer needed. As an instance is owned by a client, the client can consider the state of the instance to be private. Clients typically use a factory remote object to request the creation of new instances.

Pattern	Problem	Solution
CLIENT PROXY [VKZ04]	One of the primary goals of using remote objects is to support a programming model for accessing objects in distributed applications that is similar to that for accessing local objects. A REQUESTOR solves part of this problem by hiding many network details. However, using the REQUESTOR is cumbersome since the methods to be invoked on the remote object, their arguments, as well as location and identification information for the remote object have to be passed by the client in a format defined by the REQUESTOR for each invocation. The REQUESTOR also does not provide static-type checking, which further complicates client development.	Provide a CLIENT PROXY to the client developer that supports the same interface as the remote object. For remote invocations, clients only interact with the local CLIENT PROXY. The CLIENT PROXY translates the local invocation into parameters for the REQUESTOR and triggers the invocation. The CLIENT PROXY receives the result from the REQUESTOR and hands it over to the client using an ordinary return value.
CLIENT REQUEST HANDLER [VKZ04]	To send requests from the client to the server application, several tasks have to be performed: connection establishment and configuration, result handling, timeout handling, and error detection. In the case of timeouts or errors, the REQUESTOR and subsequently the CLIENT PROXY have to be informed. Client-side connection management, threading, and result dispatching need to be managed in a coordinated and optimized fashion.	Provide a common CLIENT REQUEST HANDLER for all REQUESTORS within a client. The CLIENT REQUEST HANDLER is responsible for opening and closing the network connections to server applications, sending requests, receiving replies, and dispatching them back to the appropriate REQUESTOR. In addition, the CLIENT REQUEST HANDLER copes with timeouts, threading issues, and invocation errors.
COMPONENT CONFIGURATOR [SSRB00]	How is an application allowed to link and unlink its component implementations at runtime without having to modify, recompile, or relink the application statically?	Use COMPONENT CONFIGURATORS as central components for reifying the runtime dependencies of configurable components. These configurable components offer an interface to change their configuration at runtime.
CONTENT-BASED ROUTER [HW03]	How do we handle a situation in which the implementation of a single logical function (e.g., inventory check) is spread across multiple physical systems?	Use a CONTENT-BASED ROUTER to route each message to the correct recipient based on message content.
CONTENT ENRICHER [HW03]	How do we communicate with another system if the message originator does not have all the required data items available?	Use a specialized transformer, a CONTENT ENRICHER, to access an external data source to augment a message with missing information.
CORRELATION IDENTIFIER [HW03]	How does a requestor that has received a response know to which original request the response is referring?	Each response message should contain a CORRELATION IDENTIFIER, a unique identifier that indicates which request message this response is for.

Pattern	Problem	Solution
DOMAIN MODEL [Fow02, BHS07a]	Requirements and constraints inform the functionality, quality of service, and deployment aspects of a software system but do not themselves suggest a concrete structure to guide development. Without precise and reasoned insight into the scope and application domain of a system, however, its realization is likely to be a "big ball of mud" that is hard to understand and convey to customers and a poor architectural basis on which to build.	Create a model that defines and scopes the business responsibilities and variations of a system: Model elements are abstractions meaningful in the application domain, while their roles and interactions reflect the domain workflow.
DYNAMIC ROUTER [HW03]	How can you avoid the dependency of the router on all possible destinations while maintaining its efficiency?	Use a DYNAMIC ROUTER, a router that can self-configure based on special configuration messages from participating destinations.
ENTERPRISE SERVICE BUS [Erl09]	How is it possible in a large business architecture to integrate various applications and back ends in a comprehensive, flexible, and consistent way?	Unify the access to applications and back ends using services and service adapters and use message-oriented, event-driven communication between these services to enable flexible integration.
ENVELOPE WRAPPER [HW03]	How can existing systems participate in a messaging exchange that places specific requirements, such as message header fields or encryption, on that message format?	Use an ENVELOPE WRAPPER to wrap application data inside an envelope that is compliant with the messaging infrastructure. Unwrap the message when it arrives at the messaging target.
FIRE AND FORGET [VKZ04]	In many situations, a client application needs to invoke an operation on a target system simply to notify the target system of an event. The client does not expect any return value. Reliability of the invocation is not critical as it is just a notification on which both client and server do not rely.	Provide FIRE-AND-FORGET operations. The client does not get any acknowledgment from the target system receiving the invocation.
INTERFACE DESCRIPTION [VKZ04]	The interfaces of a CLIENT PROXY and remote object need to be aligned to ensure that an INVOKER can properly dispatch invocations. To ensure that messages arrive properly at the INVOKER, marshaling and demarshaling need to be aligned. Client developers need to be able to access the interfaces of the remote objects the client application may use.	Provide an INTERFACE DESCRIPTION in which you describe the interface of remote objects. The INTERFACE DESCRIPTION serves as the contract between CLIENT PROXY and INVOKER. CLIENT PROXY and INVOKER use either code generation or runtime configuration techniques to adhere to that contract.

Pattern	Problem	Solution
INVOCATION CONTEXT [VKZ04]	Remote invocations typically only contain necessary information, such as operation name, OBJECT ID, and parameters. But, INVOCATION INTERCEPTORS often need additional information to provide add-on services. A straightforward solution would be to add this information to the operation signature of remote objects. But, this would prevent the transparent integration of add-on services, which is the goal in the first place, as signatures would change depending on the requirements of the add-on services. Changing operation signatures for reasons other than business logic is tedious and error prone.	Bundle contextual information in an extensible INVOCATION CONTEXT data structure that is transferred between client and remote object with every remote invocation. For transparent integration, INVOCATION INTERCEPTORS can be used to add and consume this information. The format and data types used for the contextual information in the INVOCATION CONTEXT depend on the use case.
INVOCATION INTERCEPTOR [VKZ04]	In addition to hosting remote objects, the server application often has to provide a number of add-on services, such as transactions, logging, or security. The clients and remote objects themselves should be independent of those services.	Provide hooks in the invocation path, for example, in the INVOKER and REQUESTOR, to plug in INVOCATION INTERCEPTORS. INVOCATION INTERCEPTORS are invoked before and after request and reply messages pass the hook. Provide the interceptor with all the necessary information to allow it to provide meaningful add-on services.
INVOKER [VKZ04]	When a client sends invocation data across the machine boundary to the server side, the targeted remote object has to be reached somehow. The simplest solution is to let every remote object be addressed over the network directly. But, this solution does not work for large numbers of remote objects as there may not be enough network endpoints for all the remote objects. Also, the remote object would have to deal with handling network connections, receiving and demarshaling messages, and so on. This is cumbersome and overcomplex.	Provide an INVOKER that accepts client invocations from REQUESTORS. REQUESTORS send requests across the network; these requests contain the ID of the remote object, operation name, operation parameters, as well as additional contextual information. The INVOKER reads the request and demarshals it to obtain the OBJECT ID and the name of the operation. It then dispatches the invocation with demarshaled invocation parameters to the targeted remote object. That is, it looks up the correct local object and its operation implementation, as described by the remote invocation, and invokes it.
LAYERS [BMR+96, BHS07a]	Regardless of the interactions and coupling between different parts of a software system, there is a need to develop and evolve them independently, for example, due to system size and time-to-market requirements. However, without a clear and reasoned separation of concerns in the software architecture of the system, neither the interactions between the parts nor their independent development can be supported appropriately.	Define one or more layers for the software under development, with each layer having a distinct and specific responsibility.

Pattern	Problem	Solution
LAZY ACQUISITION [KJ04, VKZ04]	Creating servants for all the remote objects that might possibly be accessed by clients during server application startup can result in a waste of resources. The total resources needed for all servants might even exceed the physically available resources in the server process. In addition, instantiating all servants during server application startup leads to long startup times.	Instantiate servants only when their respective remote objects are actually invoked by clients. However, let clients assume that remote objects are always available. The INVOKER triggers the LIFE-CYCLE MANAGER to lazily instantiate the servant when it is accessed by a client.
LEASING [KJ04, VKZ04]	Remote objects and their servants that are no longer needed should be released in time to free unused system resources. However, the LIFE-CYCLE MANAGER cannot determine when a particular remote object is no longer used so that it can release it safely. In most scenarios, neither the LIFE-CYCLE MANAGER nor the remote object itself have knowledge of the clients and so do not know whether they intend to access the remote objects in the future.	Associate each client's use of a remote object with a time-based lease. When the lease for a particular client expires, the server application may assume that the client no longer needs the remote object. As soon as all leases for a remote object have expired, the servant is destroyed by the LIFE-CYCLE MANAGER, and the remote object can be unregistered from the distributed object middleware. It is the responsibility of the client to renew the lease for as long as it requires the remote object to be available.
LIFE-CYCLE MANAGER [VKZ04]	The life cycle of remote objects needs to be managed by server applications. Based on configuration, usage scenarios, and available resources, servants have to be instantiated, initialized, or destroyed. Most important, all this has to be coordinated.	Use a LIFE-CYCLE MANAGER to manage the life cycle of remote objects and their servants. Let the LIFE-CYCLE MANAGER trigger life-cycle operations for servants of remote objects according to their configured life-cycle strategy. For servants that have to be aware of life-cycle events, provide life-cycle callback operations. The LIFE-CYCLE MANAGER will use these operations to notify the servant of upcoming life-cycle events. This allows servants to prepare for the events accordingly.
LOOKUP [KJ04, VKZ04]	To use a service provided by a remote object, a client has to obtain an ABSOLUTE OBJECT REFERENCE to the respective object. Further, the remote object providing the service might change over time, either because another instance takes over the role or because the server application has been restarted, so that the transient reference changes. Despite such changes, clients need a valid initial reference to access the service.	Implement a lookup service as part of the distributed object middleware. Let server applications register references to remote objects and associate them with properties. Clients then use the lookup service to query for the ABSOLUTE OBJECT REFERENCES of remote objects based on these properties. The most common case is to use unique names for each reference of a remote object.

Pattern	Problem	Solution
MARSHALLER [VKZ04]	For remote invocations to work, invocation information has to be transported over the network. The data required to describe invocations consists of the OBJECT ID of the target remote object, the operation name, the parameters, the return value, and possibly other INVOCATION CONTEXT information. Only byte streams are suitable as a data format for transporting this information over the network.	Require each nonprimitive type used within remote object invocations to be serializable into a transport format that can be transported over a network as a byte stream. Use compatible MARSHALLERS on the client and server sides that serialize invocation information. Depending on the environment, the serialization may be provided by the data types themselves. References to remote objects are serialized as ABSOLUTE OBJECT REFERENCES.
MEMENTO [GHJV94, BHS07a]	It is often necessary to record the internal state of an object. Allowing other objects to access the state of an object directly breaks encapsulation and introduces unnecessary complexity in dependent objects.	Snapshot and encapsulate the relevant state of the originating object within a separate MEMENTO object and pass this MEMENTO to the clients of the object instead of letting them access the internal state of the object directly.
MESSAGE BROKER [HW03]	How can you decouple the destination of a message from the sender and maintain central control over the flow of messages?	Use a central MESSAGE BROKER that can receive messages from multiple destinations, determine the correct destination, and route the message to the correct channel. Implement the internals of the message broker using the design patterns presented in this appendix.
MESSAGE BUS [HW03]	What is an architecture that enables separate applications to work together, but in a decoupled fashion such that applications can be easily added or removed without affecting the others?	Structure the connecting middleware between these applications as a MESSAGE BUS that enables them to work together using messaging.
MESSAGE FILTER [HW03]	How can a component avoid receiving uninteresting messages?	Use a special kind of MESSAGE ROUTER, a MESSAGE FILTER, to eliminate undesired messages from a channel based on a set of criteria.
MESSAGING MAPPER [HW03]	How do you move data between domain objects and the messaging infrastructure while keeping the two independent of each other?	Create a separate MESSAGING MAPPER that contains the mapping logic between the infrastructure and the domain objects.
MESSAGE TRANSLATOR [HW03]	How can systems using different data formats communicate with each other using messaging?	Use a special filter, a MESSAGE TRANSLATOR, between other filters or applications to translate one data format into another.
MODEL VIEW CONTROLLER (MVC) [BMR+96, BHS07a]	User interfaces are prone to change requests: Some must support multiple look-and-feel skins; others must address specific customer preferences. However, changes to a user interface must not affect the core functionality of an application, which is generally independent of its presentation and also changes less frequently.	Divide the interactive application into three decoupled parts: processing, input, and output. Ensure consistency of the three parts with the help of a change propagation mechanism.

Pattern	Problem	Solution
NORMALIZER [HW03]	How do you process messages that are semantically equivalent but arrive in a different format?	Use a NORMALIZER to route each message type through a custom MESSAGE TRANSLATOR so that the resulting messages match a common format.
OBJECT ID [VKZ04]	The INVOKER is responsible for dispatching invocations received from the SERVER REQUEST HANDLER. It invokes the operation of a remote object on behalf of a client. However, the INVOKER handles invocations for several remote objects and has to determine the remote object corresponding to a particular invocation.	Associate each remote object instance with an OBJECT ID that is unique in the context of the INVOKER with which the remote object is registered. The client, or the CLIENT PROXY, respectively, has to provide the OBJECT ID so that the REQUESTOR can include it in the invocation request, and the INVOKER can dispatch the request to the correct remote object.
OBSERVER [GHJV94, BHS07a]	Consumer objects sometimes depend on the state of, or data maintained by, another provider object. If the state of the provider object changes without notice, however, the state of the dependent consumer objects can become inconsistent.	Define a change propagation mechanism in which the provider (known as the *subject*) notifies the consumers (known as the *observers*) whenever its state changes so that the notified OBSERVERS can perform whatever actions they deem necessary.
PER-REQUEST INSTANCE [VKZ04]	A server application serves remote objects that are accessed by a large number of clients, and access to the remote objects needs to be highly scalable with respect to the number of clients. When many clients access the same remote object concurrently, the performance of the server application decreases dramatically due to synchronization overhead.	Let the distributed object middleware activate a new servant for each invocation. This servant handles the request, returns the results, and is then deactivated. While the client expects to get a new instance from request to request, the activation and deactivation can be optimized internally, for example, by using POOLING of servants.
POLL OBJECT [VKZ04]	There are situations for which an application needs to invoke an operation asynchronously but still requires knowing the results of the invocation. The client does not necessarily need the results immediately to continue its execution, and it can decide for itself when to use the returned results.	As part of the distributed object framework, provide POLL OBJECTS, which receive the result of remote invocations on behalf of the client. The client subsequently uses the POLL OBJECT to query the result.
POOLING [KJ04, VKZ04]	Instantiating and destroying servants regularly, as in the case of PER-REQUEST INSTANCES, causes a lot of overhead in terms of additional load for the server. Among other issues, memory needs to be allocated, initialization code for the servants needs to be executed, and the servants have to be registered with the distributed object middleware.	Introduce a pool of servants for each remote object type hosted by the server application. When an invocation arrives for a remote object, take a servant from the pool, handle the request, and put it back into the pool. Subsequent invocations will follow the same procedure when reusing the instance. The state of the remote object is removed from the servant before it is put into the pool; servants taken from the pool are initialized with the state of the remote object they should represent.

Pattern	Problem	Solution
PROTOCOL PLUG-IN [VKZ04]	Developers of client and server applications often need to control the communication protocol used by the CLIENT REQUEST HANDLER and SERVER REQUEST HANDLER. In some cases, differences in network technologies require the use of specialized protocols; in other cases, existing protocols need to be optimized to meet real-time constraints. Sometimes, it might even be necessary to support multiple protocols at the same time. Communication protocols should be configurable by developers, who might have only a limited knowledge of low-level protocol details.	Provide PROTOCOL PLUG-INS to extend CLIENT REQUEST HANDLERS and SERVER REQUEST HANDLERS. Let the PROTOCOL PLUG-INS provide a common interface to allow them to be configured from higher layers of the distributed object middleware.
PUBLISHER/ SUBSCRIBER [BMR+96, BHS07a]	Components in some distributed applications are loosely coupled and operate largely independently. If such applications need to propagate information to some or all of their components, however, a notification mechanism is needed to inform the components about state changes or other interesting events that affect or coordinate their own computation.	Define a change propagation infrastructure that allows publishers in a distributed application to disseminate events that convey information that may be of interest to others. Notify subscribers interested in those events whenever such information is published.
QOS OBSERVER [VKZ04]	Distributed object middleware constituents, such as REQUEST HANDLERS, MARSHALLERS, and PROTOCOL PLUG-INS, provide hooks to implement a wide variety of quality-of-service characteristics. Applications might want to react to changes in the quality of service currently provided. The application-specific code to react to such changes should be decoupled from the middleware itself.	Provide hooks in the distributed object middleware constituents where application developers can register QOS OBSERVERS. The observers are informed about relevant quality-of-service parameters, such as message sizes, invocation counts, or execution times. Since the QOS OBSERVERS are application specific, they can contain code to react appropriately if service quality worsens.
REPOSITORY [Eva04]	How is the exposure of technical infrastructure and database access mechanisms that complicates the client in distributed and concurrent data accesses minimized?	Delegate all object storage and access to a REPOSITORY.

Pattern	Problem	Solution
REQUESTOR [VKZ04]	Invocation of remote objects requires that operation parameters are collected and marshaled into a byte stream since networks only allow byte streams to be sent. A connection also needs to be established and the request information sent to the target remote object. These tasks have to be performed for every remote object accessed by the client and can therefore become tedious for client developers.	In the client application, use a REQUESTOR for accessing the remote object. The REQUESTOR is supplied with the ABSOLUTE OBJECT REFERENCE of the remote object, the operation name, and its arguments. It constructs a remote invocation from these parameters and sends the invocation to the remote object. The REQUESTOR hides the details of the client side distributed object communication from clients.
RESULT CALLBACK [VKZ04]	The client needs to be actively informed about results of asynchronously invoked operations on a target system.	Provide a callback-based interface for remote invocations on the client. The invocation returns immediately after sending the invocation to the server.
SERVER REQUEST HANDLER [VKZ04]	Before a request can be dispatched by an INVOKER, the server application has to receive the request message from the network. Managing communication channels efficiently and effectively is essential since typically many requests may have to be handled, possibly even concurrently. Network communication needs to be managed in a coordinated and optimized way.	Provide a SERVER REQUEST HANDLER that deals with all the communication issues of a server application. Let the SERVER REQUEST HANDLER receive messages from the network, combine the message fragments to complete messages, and dispatch the messages to the correct INVOKER for further processing. The SERVER REQUEST HANDLER will manage all the required resources, such as connections and threads.
SERVICE [Eva04]	How is it possible to avoid that some domain concepts are hard to model as objects because they have no state?	Define one or more related operations as a stand-alone interface declared as a SERVICE and make the SERVICE stateless.
SERVICE ABSTRACTION LAYER [Vog01]	How do you develop a system that can fulfill requests from different clients communicating over different channels without having to modify your business logic each time a new channel has to be supported or a new service is added?	Provide a SERVICE ABSTRACTION LAYER as an extra layer to the business tier containing all the necessary logic to receive and delegate requests. Incoming requests are forwarded to service providers, which are able to satisfy requests.
STATIC INSTANCE [VKZ04]	The server application has to provide a number of previously known remote object instances—the number may even be fixed over the lifetime of the server application. The remote objects must be available for a long period without any predetermined expiration timeout. The state of the remote object must not be lost between individual invocations and must be available to all clients.	Provide STATIC INSTANCES of remote objects that are independent of the client's state and life cycle. These static instances are activated before any client's use, typically as early as during application startup, and deactivated when the application shuts down. For easy accessibility by clients, the instances are registered in LOOKUP after their activation.

Pattern	Problem	Solution
SYNC WITH SERVER [VKZ04]	FIRE AND FORGET is a useful but extreme solution in the sense that it can only be used if the client can really afford to take the risk of not noticing when a remote invocation does not reach the targeted system. The other extreme is a synchronous call by which a client is blocked until the remote method has executed successfully and the result arrives back. Sometimes, the middle of both extremes is needed.	Provide SYNC WITH SERVER semantics for remote invocations. The client sends the invocation, as in FIRE AND FORGET, but waits for a reply informing it about the successful reception, and only the reception, of the invocation.

References

[AH02]   W. M. P. van der Aalst and K. M. van Hee. *Workflow Management: Models, Methods, and Systems.* MIT Press, Cambridge, MA, 2002.

[AHKB03] Wil M. P. van der Aalst, A. H. M. ter Hofstede, B. Kiepuszewski, and A. P. Barros. Workflow patterns. *Distributed and Parallel Databases* 14(1): 5–51, 2003.

[Act07]   Active Endpoints. ActiveBPEL Open Source Engine. http://www.active-endpoints.com/active-bpel-engine-overview.htm, 2007.

[Ale77]   C. Alexander. *A Pattern Language—Towns, Buildings, Construction.* Oxford University Press, New York, 1977.

[Ale79]   C. Alexander. *The Timeless Way of Building.* Oxford University Press, New York, 1979.

[Apa07]   Apache ServiceMix Project. Apache ServiceMix. http://www.servicemix.org/, 2007.

[BDH05] A. P. Barros, M. Dumas, and A. H. M. ter Hofstede. Service interaction patterns. Business Process Management, 3rd International Conference, BPM 2005, Nancy, France, September 5–8, 2005.

[Bar03]   D. K. Barry. *Web Services and Service-oriented Architectures.* Morgan Kaufmann, New York, 2003.

[BCM+96] K. Beck, R. Crocker, G. Meszaros, J. Vlissides, J. O. Coplien, L. Dominick, and F. Paulisch. Industrial experience with design patterns. In *ICSE '96: Proceedings of the 18th International Conference on Software Engineering,* pp. 103–114. IEEE Computer Society, Washington, DC, 1996.

[BHS07a] F. Buschmann, K. Henney, and D. C. Schmidt. *Pattern-Oriented Software Architecture Volume 4 – A Pattern Language for Distributed Computing.* J. Wiley and Sons Ltd., 2007.

[BHS07b] F. Buschmann, K. Henney, and D. C. Schmidt. *Pattern-Oriented Software Architecture Volume 5—On Patterns and Pattern Languages.* Wiley, New York, 2007.

[BMR+96] F. Buschmann, R. Meunier, H. Rohnert, P. Sommerlad, and M. Stal. *Pattern-Oriented Software Architecture—A System of Patterns.* Wiley, New York, 1996.

[Bpm08]   Bpmn2Bpel. A tool for translating BPMN models into BPEL processes. http://code.google.com/p/bpmn2bpel/, 2008.

[CHT03]   K. Channabasavaiah, K. Holley, and E. M. Tuggle. Migrating to service-oriented architecture—part 1. IBM Developer Works. http://www-106.ibm.com/developerworks/webservices/library/ws-migratesoa/, 2003.

[Cha04]   D. A. Chappell. *Enterprise Service Bus.* O'Reilly, Sebastopol, CA, 2004.

[CGH+05] L. Cherbakov, G. Galambos, R. Harishankar, S. Kalyana, and G. Rackham. Impact of service-orientation at the business level. *IBM Systems Journal,* 44(4): 653–668, 2005.

[Com09]   COMPAS Consortium. COMPAS—compliance-driven models, languages, and architectures for services. http://www.compas-ict.eu/, 2009.

[Cop96]   J. Coplien. *Software Patterns, SIGS Management Briefings.* SIGS Books and Multimedia, New York, 1996.

[Dik08]   L. Dikmans. Transforming BPMN into BPEL: Why and how. http://www.oracle.com/technology/pub/articles/dikmans-bpm.html, 2008.

[DAH05]   M. Dumas, W. M. P. van der Aalst, and A. M. ter Hofstede. *Process-Aware Information Systems: Bridging People and Software through Process Technology.* Wiley, Hoboken, NJ, 2005.

[Ecl09]   Eclipse. Eclipse Modeling Framework Project (EMF), http://www.eclipse.org/modeling/emf/, 2009.

[Emm00]   W. Emmerich. *Engineering Distributed Objects.* Wiley, New York, 2000.

[Erl09]   T. Erl. *SOA Design Patterns.* Prentice Hall/Pearson, Upper Saddle River, NJ, 2009.

[Eva04]   E. Evans. *Domain-Driven Design: Tackling Complexity in the Heart of Software.* Addison-Wesley, Boston, 2004.

[FBP03]   A. N. Fletcher, M. Brahm, and H. Pargmann. *Workflow Management with SAP WebFlow: A Practical Manual.* Springer, New York, 2003.

[For08]   Fornax Project. Sculptor. http://www.fornax-platform.org/cp/display/fornax/Sculptor+(CSC), 2008.

[Fow96]   M. Fowler. *Analysis Patterns: Reusable Object Models.* Addison-Wesley, Boston, 1996.

[Fow02]   M. Fowler. *Patterns of Enterprise Application Architecture.* Addison-Wesley, Boston, 2002.

[GHJV94]   E. Gamma, R. Helm, R. Johnson, and J. Vlissides. *Design Patterns: Elements of Reusable Object-Oriented Software.* Addison-Wesley, Boston, 1994.

[Gft07]   GFT. GFT Inspire business process management. http://www.gft.com/gft_international/en/gft_international/Leistungen_Produkte/Software/Business_Process_Managementsoftware.html, 2007.

[Hay95]   D. C. Hay. *Data Model Patterns: Conventions of Thought.* Dorset House, New York, 1995.

[Hen06]   C. Hentrich. A language of analytical patterns for the agile enterprise. *International Journal of Agile Systems and Management (IJASM),* 1(2): 146–165, 2006.

[HW03]   G. Hohpe and B. Woolf. *Enterprise Integration Patterns.* Addison-Wesley, Boston, 2003.

[Ibm08]   IBM, WebSphere software. http://www-01.ibm.com/software/websphere/, 2008.

[Ilo09]   ILOG. WebSphere ILOG JRules. http://www.ilog.com/products/jrules/, 2009.

[iWa07a]   iWay Software. iWay adapter technologies. http://www.iwaysoftware.jp/products/integrationsolution/adapter_manager.html, 2007.

[iWa07b]   iWay Software. iWay Adapter Manager technology brief. http://www.iwaysoftware.jp/products/integrationsolution/adapter_manager.html, 2007.

[JB96]   S. Jablonski and C. Bussler. *Workflow Management: Modeling Concepts, Architecture, and Implementation.* International Thomson Computer Press, London, 1996.

[JBo08]   JBoss. jBPM documentation. http://www.jboss.org/jbossjbpm/jbpm_documentation/, 2008.

[Jos07]   N. M. Josuttis. *SOA in Practice—The Art of Distributed System Design.* O'Reilly, Sebastopol, CA, 2007.

[Kel09]   W. Keller. Patterns for object/relational mapping and access layers. http://www.object-architects.de/ObjectArchitects/orpatterns/, 2009.

[KJ04]   M. Kircher and P. Jain. *Pattern-Oriented Software Architecture, Volume 3: Patterns for Resource Management.* Wiley, New York, 2004.

[LR00]   F. Leymann and D. Roller. *Production Workflow, Concepts and Techniques.* Prentice Hall, Upper Saddle River, NJ, 2000.

[Lon98]   J. Lonchamp. Process model patterns for collaborative work. In Proceedings of the 15th IFIP World Computer Congress. Telecooperation Conference. Telecoop. Vienna, Austria, 1998.

[Man00]   D. A. Manolescu. Micro-workflow: A workflow architecture supporting compositional object-oriented software development. Ph. D. thesis and computer science technical report UIUCDCS-R-2000–2186, University of Illinois at Urbana-Champaign, October 2000, Urbana, IL.

[Man02]   D. A. Manolescu. Workflow enactment with continuation and future objects. ACM SIGPLAN Notices, v.37 n.11, November 2002.

[Man04]   D. A. Manolescu. Patterns for orchestration environments. The 11th Conference on Pattern Languages of Programs (PLoP2004), September 8–12, 2004, Allterton Park, Monticello, IL, 2004.

[McH95]   P. McHugh. *Beyond Business Process Reengineering—Towards the Holonic Enterprise.* Wiley, New York, 1995.

[MB97]   G. Meszaros and K. Brown. A pattern language for workflow systems. In Proceedings of the 4th Pattern Languages of Programming Conference. Washington University Technical Report 97-34 (WUCS-97-34), 1997.

[Mey97]   B. Meyer. *Object-Oriented Software Construction.* 2nd ed. Prentice Hall, Upper Saddle River, NJ, 1997.

[Mic09]   Microsoft. SQL Server Integration Services. SQL Server 2008 Books Online, http://msdn.
           microsoft.com/en-us/library/ms141026.aspx, February 2009.

[MIS09]   MISMO. Mortgage Industry Standards Maintenance Organization. http://www.mismo.
           org, 2009.

[MK08]   K. Mittal and S. Kanchanavally. Introducing Java Page Flow Architecture. http://www.
           developer.com/open/article.php/10930_3531246_1, 2008.

[Mul07]   Mule Project. Mule open source ESB (enterprise service bus) and integration platform.
           http://mule.mulesource.org/, 2007.

[NT97]   D. A. Nadler and M. L. Tushman. *Competing by Design—The Power of Organisational
           Architecture*. Oxford University Press, New York, 1997.

[Net08]   NetBeans 6.1. Developer guide to BPEL Designer. http://www.netbeans.org/kb/61/
           soa/bpel-guide.html, April 2008.

[Nov08]   Novell. Novell exteNd Director 5.2. http://www.novell.com/documentation/extend52/
           Docs/Start_Director_Help.html, 2008.

[OFX09]   OFX Consortium. Open financial exchange. http://www.ofx.net, 2009.

[Ora09]   Oracle. Oracle Warehouse Builder user's guide 11g release 1 (11.1): Data transforma-
           tion.   http://download.oracle.com/docs/cd/B28359_01/owb.111/b31278/concept_
           transformdata_intro.htm, 2009.

[Pal02]   P. Athena. *Case Handling with FLOWer: Beyond Workflow*. Pallas Athena, Apeldoorn,
           Netherlands, 2002.

[Pri03]   C. Prior. *Workflow and Process Management*. Maestro BPE P & Y Limited, Australia, 2003.

[Rei07]   J. P. Reilly. *Getting Started with the SID: A SID Modeler's Guide*. TeleManagement Forum,
           ISBN 0-9794281-0-6, 2007.

[RAH06]   N. Russell W. M. P. van der Aalst, and ter A. H. M. Hofstede. Exception handling patterns
           in process-aware information systems. BPM Center Report BPM-06-04. http://www.
           BPMcenter.org, 2006.

[SW03]   C. Sauer and L. Wilcocks. Establishing the business of the future: the role of organisa-
           tional architecture and information technologies. *European Management Journal*, 21, 2003.

[SB03]   D. C. Schmidt and F. Buschmann. Patterns, frameworks, and middleware: Their synergis-
           tic relationships. In 25th International Conference on Software Engineering, pp. 694–704,
           Chichester, UK, May 2003.

[SL07]   Schümmer, T. and S. Lukosch, Patterns for computer-mediated interaction. Wiley & Sons.,
           2007.

[SKJ07]   A. W. Scheer, H. Kruppke, and W. Jost. *Agility by ARIS Business Process Management*.
           Yearbook Business Process Excellence 2006/2007. Springer, Berlin, 2007.

[SSRB00]   D. C. Schmidt, M. Stal, H. Rohnert, and F. Buschmann. *Patterns for Concurrent and
           Distributed Objects. Pattern-Oriented Software Architecture*. Wiley, New York, 2000.

[Sun09]   Sun. NetBeans 6.1. SOA Documentation: developer guide to the BPEL Designer. http://
           www.netbeans.org/kb/61/soa/bpel-guide-navigation.html, 2009.

[Tib09]   TIBCO. Spotfire. Spotfire Technology Network: creating a transformation, http://stn.
           spotfire.com/stn/Tasks/CreatingTransformation.aspx, 2009.

[Tmf09]   TM Forum. Solution Frameworks (NGOSS). http://www.tmforum.org/Solution
           Frameworks/1911/home.html, 2009.

[TZD07]   H. Tran, U. Zdun, and S. Dustdar. View-based and model-driven approach for reducing the
           development complexity in process-driven SOA. In Proceedings of International Conference
           on Business Processes and Services Computing, Leipzig, Germany, September 2007.

[Vog01]   O. Vogel. Service abstraction layer. In Proceedings of EuroPlop 2001, Irsee, Germany, July
           2001.

[VKZ04]   M. Völter, M. Kircher, and U. Zdun. *Remoting Patterns. Pattern Series*. Wiley, New York,
           2004.

[VSW02]   M. Völter, A. Schmid, and E. Wolff. *Server Component Patterns Component Infrastructures
           Illustrated with EJB*. Wiley, New York, 2002.

[W3C04]   W3C. Web Services Architecture, W3C Working Group Note 11 February 2004: Web services architecture definition from W3C. http://www.w3.org/TR/ws-arch/wsa.pdf, 2004.

[Web07]   webMethods. webMethods Fabric 7. http://www.webmethods.com/products/fabric, 2007.

[WMH00] H. Weigand, A. de Moor, and W. J. van den Heuvel. Supporting the evolution of workflow patterns for virtual communities. *Electronic Markets,* 10(4): 264, 2000.

[Wfm95]   WFMC. *The Workflow Reference Model (WFMC-TC-1003).* Workflow Management Coalition, 1995.

[Wfm96]   WFMC. *Terminology and Glossary (WFMC-TC-1011).* Technical report. Workflow Management Coalition, 1996.

[Wor08]   Workflow Patterns home page. http://www.workflowpatterns.com/, 2008.

[ZHD07]   U. Zdun, C. Hentrich, and S. Dustdar. Modeling process-driven and service-oriented architectures using patterns and pattern primitives. *ACM Transactions on the Web (TWEB),* 1(3), 14:1–14:44, 2007.

Index